CAPITAL PUNISHMENT IN BRITAIN

CAPITAL PUNISHMENT IN BRITAIN

Foreword by Rt. Hon. Ann Widdecombe MP

RICHARD CLARK

First published 2009

ISBN 978 0 7110 3413 6

Published by Ian Allan Publishing

an imprint of Ian Allan Publishing Ltd, Hersham, Surrey, KT12 4RG
Printed in England by Ian Allan Printing Ltd, Hersham, Surrey, KT12 4RG

Code: 0909/B2

Visit the Ian Allan Publishing website at www.ianallanpublishing.com

Contents

Foreword by

the Rt. Hon. Ann Widdecombe MP

The Romans gave the world civilisation, fine literature, brave architecture, central heating and crucifixion. The Tudors gave us Shakespeare and hanging, drawing and quartering. Charles II gave us the Royal Society, St Paul's Cathedral and the display of a head cut off the exhumed body of his enemy, Oliver Cromwell. It is only in the last couple of centuries that supposedly civilised societies, which produced art, poetry, fine music and exquisite manners, could bring themselves to be repulsed by legal cruelty and far more recent still is the debate about the very validity of the State's taking life. Long periods of peace, growing life expectancy and the erosion of class barriers encourage focus on the value of individual lives and it is largely in countries where these conditions prevail that capital punishment has disappeared or where its continuance is fiercely debated.

The history of execution, of its place in law rather than in the whim of the powerful, of its gradual restriction to offences against life itself and of the battle against it, is one which reflects the true extent of the civilisation of the human race. In its long and often inglorious history the death penalty has not merely despatched some of the greatest villains but has also produced some of the world's greatest icons and martyrs: St Thomas More and Edith Cavell spring to mind. It has also ensured that the name of an obscure Roman governor of a far flung province two thousand years ago, Pontius Pilate, has attained immortality by being mentioned daily across the globe whenever billions of Christians say the Creed.

Is State execution on the agenda of history or is it destined to play a role in human justice for centuries to come? What will determine the answer to that question?

For a small minority human life is so sacrosanct that if one man in an aeroplane is about to bomb five million the moral prohibition against killing him is absolute. For such thinkers the value of human life cannot accumulate and the one is as valuable as the five million. They are the extreme pacifists. At the other end of the scale are those who believe that there is nothing at all special about human life: that it is not different in moral quantity from that of the life of any other animal and that it can be taken, without qualms, in a fairly wide range of circumstances.

The overwhelming majority reject both pieces of reasoning and believe that, while human life must in all normal circumstances be preserved, there is a limited number of situations in which it is right to take it. Self defence, whether on the part of an individual or nation, is an obvious example.

I have always cleaved to the proposition that the guiding principle in taking human life must be whether it is done to save life. Hence the only exception I would make to my objection to abortion is when the mother's life is genuinely in danger and there is, effectively, a choice of two lives. I apply the same test to capital punishment, having no interest in it as a retribution, but being ready to countenance it if it can be shown to save life.

Let us therefore look at the results of the abolition of capital punishment in Britain. In 1965, the death penalty was abolished as an experiment for five years and therefore, during the period 1965 to 1970, statistics were still collected on the basis of capital and non capital murder instead of, as we do today, lumping all murder together. In those five years the figures for capital murder went up 125% and there was a concomitant rise in the number of incidents where firearms were taken on armed robberies.

That figure should have given even the most ardent abolitionist pause for thought, but, instead, the removal of capital punishment was confirmed. There is, of course, one compelling argument against the death penalty: that human justice can never be infallible so it should also never be irreversible. However, the huge advances in modern science, particularly with DNA, make the possibility of error exceedingly small. Indeed mistakes in the latter days of capital punishment, when its use was much more discriminating, are difficult to find.

For years James Hanratty was held up by abolitionists as an example of an innocent man executed, but with the advent of DNA it was shown he was guilty after all. The grievously sad case of Timothy Evans is almost the only mistake still considered to be one and, in today's science, he would almost certainly never have been convicted. Derek Bentley was posthumously pardoned after more than forty years, but the issues in that case, relating to his mental age, were different and would not have arisen today when the law recognises the concept of diminished responsibility.

Certainly it was right to see if Britain could dispense with capital punishment and, had Parliament decided in 1970 to restore it, it would have been right to try again at a later stage. No society which claims to be civilised can *want* execution any more than it can *want* war. Nevertheless, sometimes the moral necessity is compelling.

Society's natural wish to do away with the death penalty was manifest in a series of changes over the years which ended up in a hotchpotch of law in 1957 when liability to hang seemed to depend on the method used and on who was killed. In a worthy endeavour to identify premeditation, you could be hanged for poisoning your wife but not for killing her by battering her head with a heavy saucepan. All therefore a deliberate murderer had to do was to choose a method of despatch outwith those which led to the eight o'clock walk. Meanwhile if you killed a police or prison officer you hanged regardless of method used.

It is perhaps unsurprising that the use of the death penalty became more sparing. Its existence rather than regular use became the deterrent, a more acceptable state of affairs in the second half of the twentieth century.

The impact of abolition on armed robbery was significant. Until then if a firearm was used upon a robbery with fatal results all those involved were liable to a capital charge (Bentley was hanged under this provision even though it was his accomplice who used the gun), so criminals regularly frisked each other to make sure none of them was armed before they went forth upon their shady purposes. In the five-year period following 'experimental' abolition, there was a fourfold increase in murder by shooting, and murder committed in the course of theft rose threefold. Both of these categories were deemed capital under the 1957 Act.

Given the weight of evidence for the deterrent effect of execution, it is probable that most people who oppose the death penalty do so instinctively. There comes a line which one is not prepared to cross. I believe there is a moral case for capital punishment because it saves life, but if it could be conclusively shown that even more life would be saved if one preceded the execution with torture I would not be prepared to countenance the introduction of the rack and I can imagine that few would. Most of us could not put our feet over that particular line in the sand.

Capital punishment will never return to Britain and when I was shadow Home Secretary I did not waste time calling for it, preferring instead to concentrate on remedies which were available. Meanwhile the murder rate rises inexorably…

1

Introduction

– the origins of capital punishment in Britain. Peine forte et dure

Britain has used many forms of capital punishment for civilian criminals over the centuries. These include beheading; boiling alive; burning at the stake; drowning; hanging; hanging, drawing and quartering; and decapitation by machine. The use of each of these methods will be examined in detail in later chapters.

Hanging was by far the most common form of execution and is thought to have been introduced in the 6th century, having been brought to Britain by the Saxons. It became the normal method because it was convenient, not excessively cruel and could be carried out anywhere upon either individual prisoners or groups by unskilled executioners. It also served as a highly visible deterrent. The term Gala Day comes from the Anglo Saxon, literally translating as 'gallows day'. Obviously public hangings were popular then too. The Anglo Saxons used hanging to punish traitors, particularly heinous murderers and arsonists. However, most murderers were subject to wergild, which translates as 'person price' and is similar to the payment of 'blood money' recognised in Islamic Sharia law to this day. Each person had a value put on them and also on their body parts. A person who killed or injured them had to pay the set level of compensation. Corporal punishment and mutilation were the typical punishments for less serious crimes as prisons did not exist. Although death by hanging was specified for theft in Anglo Saxon times, a fine was normally substituted up to the reign of Henry I (1100–1135).

It is noteworthy that in the first written laws, the Dooms of Aethelberht (King of Kent 560–616), there is no mention of capital punishment at all. Each of his laws required the payment of compensation. King Alfred (871–899) did include the death penalty in his written laws. What we would now call high treason, and drawing a weapon or fighting in the King's presence, were to be punished thus. However, the manner of execution was not specified. Later, about the year AD930, King Athelstan raised the age of criminal responsibility from 12 to 16 because he felt that the execution of children was too cruel and was concerned at the number of juveniles being put to death.

There are, of course, no statistics for executions in the Anglo Saxon period, but one gets the impression that the numbers were small as the local kings were reluctant to kill potential fighting men and saw criminals as a useful form of constantly needed income.

The death penalty ceased altogether under William the Conqueror and was little used by his son William Rufus. His successor Henry I was rather more in favour of capital punishment and abolished the practice of substituting a fine for hanging in thefts of over 12d (5p) in 1109. All crimes classified as felonies attracted the death penalty unless specifically stated otherwise in the written law. Capital felonies were the crimes of murder, manslaughter, arson, highway robbery and larceny. Mayhem and petty larceny (stealing to the value of less than 12d) were the only non capital felonies. Hanging was the normal punishment, although beheading and drowning – typically in a drowning pit – particularly for murder, were also used.

Richard I (Richard the Lion Heart) specified drowning for shipboard murders by soldiers going to the Crusades. They were to be bound to their victim's body and thrown overboard. It is not known if this ever occurred in practice.

It was not just the King's courts that could inflict the death penalty in early times. Grants of jurisdiction to Lords of Manors, abbeys and towns usually carried the right of *cum fossa et furca*, i.e. pit and gallows, for drowning and hanging criminals. It is recorded that the owner of Castle Baynard in London which had been constructed by William the Conqueror had the right to drown traitors apprehended in his jurisdiction in the River Thames. Similarly during the time of Edward I the Abbot of Peterborough had a man hanged for theft at Collingham in Nottinghamshire.

From the early 13th century these rights of execution began to be replaced by the formal court system, described below.

Henry II (1154–1189) introduced several important reforms of the criminal justice system at the Assize of Clarendon in 1166, which returned power over criminal trials to the Crown. One was the concept of a Grand Jury to be made up of 24 free men whose function was to determine whether any murders, robberies or thefts had been committed in their area since Henry became king and, if so, to bring charges against those responsible and against any persons harbouring these criminals. These charges were then heard by a travelling judge, known as Justice in Eyre who was the forerunner of the later Circuit Judge. Trial by ordeal was still used, however, and if the accused failed the ordeal they were typically executed. If they passed the ordeal, they were banished so it was not the fairest of systems.

These changes wrested a great deal of power over judicial matters from the Church and were very unpopular with it. The Roman Catholic Church had previously largely ignored the common law and operated its own legal system which was ultimately answerable to the Pope. The ongoing tussle between Church and State led to the murder of the Archbishop of Canterbury, Thomas Becket, in 1170 at the behest of Henry II. As a result, in 1172, Henry did penance at the cathedral of Avranches in France, thus reconciling himself with the Catholic Church in what became known as the Compromise of Avranches. This permitted the Church to continue with its own legal system for clergy unless they were accused of high treason, highway robbery or arson and also introduced the Benefit of Clergy provision into English law. Initially to get the benefit the accused had to appear in court wearing ecclesiastical regalia, but over time this provision was removed and they had to read a passage from the Bible instead. Obviously this extended the benefit to anyone who was literate, not just priests. In fact it could extend to the illiterate as in most cases the passage to be read was from the 51st Psalm and could be memorised. It became known as 'the neck verse' as it saved many a neck from the noose. The authorities did come to recognise this and would sometimes require a different verse to be read when the prisoner was accused of a particularly serious offence. Although we will return to this subject later and record its development, it is worth noting here that this bizarre 'benefit' was to last until 1827.

Certainly by 1189, before which anything that happened is judged to be 'time immemorial', what we see as the beginnings of the Assize Court system was in operation. Cases were heard in each county by the

King's judges sent out from London on circuits. The courts were known as Eyres and the records of some of them still exist. These judges tried the more serious felony cases with a twelve man jury and could pass death sentences. Lesser offenders were dealt with at Quarter Sessions and it is thought that these did not have the power to order death. Hanging became the normal method of execution, with either a tree or a gallows being used. However, death was not the only possible penalty. Outlawing, i.e. banishing the criminal, was also used, even for crimes such as murder. The person outlawed forfeited their possessions to the King and had no legal rights. This meant that he or she could be killed without the protection of the law. A surviving set of Assize Rolls from 1221 show that only two men were sentenced to hang, both for murder. Ordeal trials by water or red hot iron could still be ordered by these courts in the early 13th century. It would appear that mutilation in lieu of death was also an option. One case has a woman sentenced to have her eyes gouged out instead of being hanged.

The Assize system dealt not only with criminals but also acted as an early form of Coroner's Court which determined whether a death was homicide or accident. These same rolls record the investigation into the death of a man who fell from his horse whilst drunk and determined a verdict of misadventure.

By the year 1177 Tyburn had become the place of execution for London. The first execution for which we have the name of the prisoner was in this year when one John Senex was hanged for housebreaking. In 1196, William Fitz Osbert (or Osbern) was hanged at Tyburn with nine of his supporters. Osbert was known as the 'Bearded' on account of his long beard and had championed London's poor against the depredations of the local government, leading a revolt against them. The Archbishop of Canterbury, Hubert Walter, who was also a London Justiciar, was given the task of stopping this revolt and sent men to arrest or kill Osbert, who was finally surrounded in the church of St Mary le Bow. As Osbert refused to surrender, Walter had the church set on fire, forcing Osbert out. He was arrested and after a quick trial was dragged to Tyburn behind a horse and hanged. At this time Tyburn was also known as 'the Elms' due to the number of elm trees that grew along the banks of the River Tyburn (or Tybourne). It is not clear whether these trees were used for hangings or whether a permanent gallows had been erected by this time. In 1220, Henry III ordered the construction of two gibbets (or gallows) at the Elms in the place where hangings had previously been carried out. These were presumably used for the hangings in 1221 of a former sheriff of London, Constantine Fitz-Athulf, his nephew and one Geoffrey, who were executed without trial on the orders of Justiciar Hubert de Burgh for sedition.

In 1212, King John is reputed to have ordered the hanging of 28 young men and boys at Nottingham Castle. They were the sons of rebel Welsh chieftains whom he had taken hostage. John was three years later forced to put his seal to the Magna Carta at Runnymede which for the first time guaranteed rights and standardised the judicial system. It set up the Court of Common Pleas and laid down rules for the proper conduct of criminal trials. These required evidence to be heard from credible witnesses and forbade conviction on the basis of rumour or suspicion. A particularly important passage of the Charter reads: 'No freeman shall be taken and imprisoned or disseised (dispossessed) or exiled or in any way destroyed, nor shall we go upon him nor send upon him, except by the lawful judgement of his peers and by the law of the land.'

Peine forte et dure

There was a special sentence, although not strictly capital punishment, for those prisoners who refused to plead or stood mute through their trial for a capital felony which could result in their death. It was called 'peine forte et dure' or pressing to death and is thought to have been introduced in the reign of Edward 1 (1272–1307). Initially the pressing was not part of the sentence, which required a very rigorous form of imprisonment, probably as described below, but without the addition of the weights. The use of weights is thought to have been added either during Edward III or Henry IV's time.

Before the punishment was imposed, the judge spelt out to the accused what was to happen to them and usually allowed them a little time to consider whether they wished to remain mute. The procedure was documented as follows: 'That the person be sent to the prison from whence he came and put into a dark lower room and there to be laid naked upon the bare ground upon his back without any clothes or rushes under him or to cover him except for his privy members, his legs and arms drawn and extended with cords to the four corners of the room and upon his body laid as great a weight of iron as he can bear and more. On the first day he shall have three morsels of barley bread without drink, the second day he shall have three draughts of water, of standing water next the door of the prison, and this shall be his diet until he die.'

This particularly horrible procedure crushed the rib cage of the person and ultimately suffocated them as they became unable to breathe due to the weight of iron (or stone) bearing down on them. However, the prisoner was allowed to change his mind at any time and offer a plea to the court. The reason people refused to plead was that if convicted they would not only be executed but also forfeit all of their land, leaving their family in penury.

Writing in 1583 in *De Republica Anglorum* Sir Thomas Smith said of this practice: 'he [that] is judged mute, that is dumme by contumacie, his condemnation is to be pressed to death, which is one of the cruellest deathes that may be: he is layd upon a table, and an other uppon him, and so much weight of stones or lead laide uppon that table, while as his bodie be crushed, and his life by that violence taken from him. This death some strong and stout hearted man doth choose, for being not condemned of felonie, his bloud is not corrupted, his lands nor goods confiscate to the Prince'.

One documented case of peine forte et dure occurred as late as 1721 after the arrest of two highwaymen. Thomas Phillips alias Cross and William Spigget or Spiggot came to trial at the January 1721 Sessions of the Old Bailey, charged with highway robbery. Both initially refused to plead until the various items, including money and horses, taken from them at the time of their arrest were returned to them. This was refused and the judge spent some time explaining to them the consequences of their refusal, reading out the sentence above. They both persisted and were therefore taken back to Newgate to be pressed. When taken to the Press Room, Phillips decided to change his mind before the procedure commenced. Spigget endured pressing for about 30 minutes with some 300 lbs weight upon him before submitting to his trial. One early newspaper reported the pressing, saying: 'It is observable that the like Instance hath not been for a great many Years past, and perhaps not in the

Memory of any Man living.' Spigget and Phillips were both convicted and hanged at Tyburn on Wednesday 8 February 1721.

Peine fort et dure was abolished in Britain in 1772 during the reign of George III. From that time, when a person refused to plead they were to be judged guilty and suffer the normal punishment. There are at least two instances where this law was put into practice: at the Old Bailey in 1778 and at Wells in 1792. By an Act of George IV (1820–1830) the law was modified to record an automatic plea of not guilty if the prisoner refused to answer the charges against them.

2
The Tudor period

It is claimed that Henry VIII authorised 72,000 executions during his 38-year reign (1509–1547). When he came to the throne the population of Britain was estimated at 2.7 million. It is possible that he executed so many, but impossible to verify exact numbers; in any case, he did seem rather keen on capital punishment.

One will have probably heard the expression 'getting into hot water'. It originates from Statute 22 passed by Henry in 1531, which made boiling to death a legal form of capital punishment and reclassified murder by poisoning as high treason, removing Benefit of Clergy from it. Apparently poisonings were rare at this time and it was decided to make an example in the case of one Richard Roose, who was the cook for the Bishop of Rochester. Roose poisoned a number of people, resulting in two deaths, and was executed at Smithfield on 15 April 1531. A large metal cauldron full of water was suspended from a tripod over a fire, and into this the unfortunate Roose was lowered.

This method of execution was again used in 1531 when a maidservant was boiled to death in the market place of (King's) Lynn in Norfolk for poisoning her mistress. It was employed again on 17 March 1542 for another maidservant named Margaret Davy who had poisoned three households for whom she worked. This Act was finally repealed by Edward VI in 1547.

It is not clear whether these three prisoners were lowered into already boiling water or whether they were placed into cold water and then the fire lit afterwards. In either case it was a particularly horrific form of execution and thus attracted even larger crowds than normal. A further instance was reported in the Chronicles of the Grey Friars when a man was boiled to death in 1522 for the high treason offence of coining; if so this makes a total of four recorded boilings.

By 1540, there were eleven capital crimes defined: high treason, including counterfeiting and clipping coin, and murder by poison; petty treason; murder; rape; piracy; arson of a dwelling house or barn with corn in it; highway robbery; embezzling one's master's goods; horse theft; stealing from churches (sacrilege); and robbery in a dwelling house. Witchcraft was added to the list of felonies in 1542 (see Chapter 6).

Another unusual case from Henry VIII's time was that of 28-year-old Elizabeth Barton, the Maid of Kent, who was hanged at Tyburn with five of her followers on 20 April 1534. They were Edward Bocking, John Dering, Henry Gold, Hugh Rich and Richard Risby. Afterwards their heads were impaled on pikes and displayed on London Bridge. Elizabeth had been born in 1506 in the village of Aldington in the parish of Ashford, Kent. She suffered from epilepsy and as a result of a teenage illness had become subject to bouts of hysteria and religious fervour. She took to going into trances and making prophesies and it was this that was to be her downfall. She claimed that were Henry to divorce Catherine of Aragon he could no longer remain king and would die an ignominious death. In 1532, Henry passed through Canterbury on his way back to London from France and Elizabeth managed to get an audience with him, telling him her prophesy. Henry divorced Catherine and married Anne Boleyn in January 1533. Elizabeth continued to denounce her king which was, of course, a treasonable act and so she was arrested in November 1533. She and her followers were examined by the Star Chamber and ordered to be exposed at St Paul's Cross and read a confession. The following January a Bill of Attainder was issued against her and five of her co-defendants which condemned them to the gallows. (A Bill of Attainder is a legislative Act that declares a person guilty of a serious crime without a formal trial, and was permitted and used between 1321 and 1798.) It is unclear why Elizabeth was hanged rather than burned at the stake as her crime was treason. However, it should be noted that Henry was still able to order a particular form of execution at this time. In the case of Anne Boleyn he chose beheading rather than burning.

The infamous 'Triple Tree' gallows was erected at Tyburn on 1 June 1571 as a permanent gallows for the City of London and County of Middlesex. It was first used for the execution of Dr John Storey who, having refused to recognise the legitimacy of Elizabeth I as Queen, was hanged, drawn and quartered for treason. Executions at Tyburn post-1571 are described in Chapter 8.

Surviving the noose

Hanging when carried out with little or no drop does not cause instant death. Neither does it cause severe physical damage to the neck, but rather squeezes the life out of the person over a period of time due to constriction of the neck causing pressure on the carotid artery and vagal nerve and pressure on the trachea (windpipe). Respiration does not stop either automatically or totally but rather reduces over time. Pressure on the carotid artery typically causes a reflex which slows and eventually stops the heart. The vertebrae protect the vertebral and spinal arteries which also supply blood to the brain and thus the brain, in what is a virtually comatose state, does not necessarily become totally starved of oxygen. It is notable that in none of the cases examined below did the person exhibit signs of obvious brain damage after their recovery.

In some cases a person would be seen to struggle for up to three minutes before dangling limp and unconscious on the rope; in other cases they became still almost immediately they were suspended. However, in either case whole body death could take up to 30 minutes to ensue. In early times the practice of leaving the person on the rope for one hour had not been instituted and they were taken down when the sheriff or City marshal thought they were dead.

There are at least five reliable cases where a person was revived after a normal execution.

On 14 December 1650, 22-year-old Anne Green was led into the Castle Yard at Oxford Castle to be hanged for concealing a birth. Anne was a servant in the household of Sir Thomas Read and had become pregnant. She did her best to hide her condition to avoid losing her job and after she had given birth concealed the baby which was later found dead. Anne was made to climb a ladder set against the gallows beam and the hangman put the noose around her neck. When she had finished her devotions the ladder was turned over, leaving her suspended. People in the crowd, her friends perhaps, hung on her legs to shorten her sufferings, a not unusual occurrence. This was stopped by the authorities as it was feared that the rope would break under the strain. So after about half an hour Anne's apparently lifeless body was taken down and placed in a coffin to be anatomised at the university.

Although Anne's execution occurred before 1752, the law required the bodies of those executed at Oxford to be given to the University for dissection. There were three doctors – William Petty, Thomas Willis and Ralph Bathurst – who were to carry out the dissection and upon opening the coffin they noticed that Anne appeared to be breathing. They thus set to work on reviving her, sitting her up and administering hot drinks to her which reportedly made her cough. They also massaged her limbs to restore circulation in them. After a while they were able to produce a reflex in the eyes. She was kept warm and put to bed and within twelve hours had recovered sufficiently to speak a few words. Her recovery continued and she was able to eat proper food after four days and was completely well within a month.

Asked about her feelings, Anne told the doctors she had no memory of the actual hanging, although she had a recollection of a man in a grey cloak, perhaps her hangman. The doctors had made careful observation of their patient and had noted that on receipt of the body her face was swollen and had taken on a dark red hue, typical of lack of oxygen. Once she was fully recovered Anne was reprieved and set free, it being decided that she had suffered sufficiently, although theoretically she could have been hanged again. She moved to the countryside where she later married and bore three children. It is thought that she died aged 37 although the cause of her 'second' death is not known.

Another woman to survive was Margaret Dickson, who like Anne had concealed the death of her baby and was convicted of murder. After trial at the High Court of Justiciary in Edinburgh, Margaret was condemned and ordered to be executed on Wednesday 2 September 1724. She was taken to the gallows set up in the Grassmarket and dealt with in the usual way, with the executioner hanging on her legs to hasten unconsciousness. She remained suspended for the 'usual time' (unspecified) and was placed in her coffin at the foot of the gallows, the lid being nailed down. Her relatives claimed her body and took the coffin for burial in the churchyard of Inveresk, the town of her birth, near Musselburgh, some six miles away.

As was not unusual at the time there was an altercation between Margaret's relatives and some young men who were thought to be apprentice surgeons and wanted the body for dissection. In the course of this the coffin became damaged and thus much less airtight. A while later her family stopped for refreshment in the village of Peffermill, leaving the coffin outside the inn. Two passers-by were no doubt horrified to hear noises coming from the coffin and alerted the family who immediately opened it to find a very much less than dead Margaret. A local doctor bled her at the scene and she started to recover. She was taken on to Musselburgh to stay with her brother and was reported in a contemporary broadsheet to have been delirious for the next two days, but well enough to attend church on the following Sunday.

Unlike the situation in England, Scottish law did not require Margaret to undergo her punishment for a second time and as she had been hanged once she was now free. She remarried her husband and earned a living selling salt in Edinburgh, where as 'Half Hanged Maggie Dickson' she was something of a celebrity. She was recorded as giving birth to several children and still being alive in 1753, although there is no record of her eventual death.

John Smith was hanged at Tyburn on Wednesday 24 December 1705 for the crime of housebreaking. He had been suspended for some 15 minutes when there was agitation in the crowd and shouts of 'reprieve'. He was immediately cut down and taken to a nearby house by his friends where he was kept warm and bled and made a full recovery. Unlike Anne Green he was able to describe the sensations of his execution. Initially he felt considerable pain and great pressure inside his head, but after a while the pain subsided and he began to see bright lights as he passed into unconsciousness. His recovery he reported as being intensely painful and was quoted as saying that he could have 'wished those hanged who had cut him down'.

On Monday 24 November 1740, two carts left Newgate prison for the journey to Tyburn. In one were three men – William Meers, William Duell and Thomas Clark – and in the other cart two women – Eleanor Mumpman and Margery Stanton.

William Duell was a boy of sixteen or seventeen and had been convicted of the vicious rape of Sarah Griffin at Acton. Sarah later died from the injuries inflicted by Duell and his accomplices, one of whom died in Newgate before he could be tried, the others not being captured. For this crime Duell was sentenced to be hanged and then anatomised. The multiple hangings were carried out by John Thrift in the normal manner and Duell's body was conveyed to Surgeons' Hall for dissection as required.

James Guthrie, the Ordinary of Newgate who officiated at the executions, recorded the events of later in the day. When the body reached Surgeons' Hall it was left in a passage where a member of staff who was to clean it heard a groan and immediately informed the surgeons. They bled Duell and when he seemed to have recovered somewhat ordered a coach to take him back to Newgate. Here he was put in a warm cell and given warm wine and water to drink. He soon recovered fully. Duell was reprieved and transported to America, but no more is known of his fate.

Our last case is perhaps less surprising. Inetta de Balsham was hanged on 16 August 1264 for harbouring thieves, but having been suspended for only a minute or so a reprieve arrived and she was immediately cut down. She was going a little blue in the face after just this short time on the rope, but made a full recovery. Some versions of this story claim that she had been hanging for a whole day or even two days, but this is not remotely likely. Inetta was subsequently pardoned by Henry III.

Execution by drowning

Drowning seems to have been more common in Scotland than in England and was used instead of hanging mainly for women convicted of theft. It was occasionally used for male criminals as a mercy. The last recorded drownings took place in 1685 when 18-year-old Margaret Wilson and 63-year-old Margaret (Mc)Lachlan were sentenced to be 'ty'd to palisados fixed in the sand, within the flood mark, and there to stand till the flood overflowed them and drowned them' at Wigtown on 11 May 1685. The execution would have meant the women being tied to the stakes for anything up to six hours before the rising water overwhelmed them. These two unfortunate women became known as the Solway or Wigtown Martyrs. Their 'crime': refusing to accept the established Church of Scotland.

3

Treason and its punishment

Perhaps nowadays people think of murder as the most heinous crime, but certainly in earlier times high treason was the worst offence that one could commit because it was a direct assault on the State and the authority of the monarch. Thus the punishment for treason has always tended to be far more severe than that for murder. Treason was never a 'Clerygeable' offence, i.e. those convicted of it could not claim Benefit of Clergy.

In Chapter 1 we saw mention of treason in Anglo Saxon times. Prior to 1351 what precisely constituted treason tended to be a matter of the King and his judges' opinion, which was hardly satisfactory. In 1348, the Commons petitioned King Edward III for a proper definition of treason and this led to the passing of the Treason Act of 1351 from which modern law on the subject stems. The original was written in Norman French and was entitled 'A Declaration what Offences shall be adjudged Treason'. Edward declared as follows: 'When a man doth compass or imagine the death of our lord the King, or of our lady his Queen or of their eldest son and heir; or if a man do violate the King's companion, or the King's eldest daughter unmarried, or the wife the King's eldest son and heir; or if a man do levy war against our lord the King in his realm, or be adherent to the King's enemies in his realm, giving to them aid and comfort in the realm, or elsewhere, and thereof be probably attainted of open deed by the people of their condition. If a man slea (kills) the chancellor, treasurer, or the King's justices of the one bench or the other, justices in Eyre, or justices of Assize, and all other justices assigned to hear and determine, being in their places, doing their offices: and it is to be understood, that in the cases above rehearsed, that ought to be judged treason which extends to our lord the King, and his royal majesty.'

The same Act also defined petty treason (originally petit treason), described later in this chapter.

Over time the law developed and additional Acts were passed.

The Treason Act of 1495, entitled 'An Acte that noe person going with the Kinge to the Warres shalbe attaynt of treason' was designed to protect those who had fought for the rightful king against a pretender to the throne. Henry VII had succeeded to the throne as a result of winning the Battle of Bosworth in 1485 and had decided to try and execute those who had fought for Richard III by backdating his ascension to the throne to 21 August 1485, the day before the battle.

As we saw in the previous chapter, Henry VIII made murder by poisoning high treason in 1531, although this law lasted only until 1547.

The Treason Act of 1695 was a rather fairer Act which introduced the concept of a defence and allowed the accused to have the benefit of counsel at their trial. It also required that there be at least two witnesses to the alleged treason. A time limit of three years was introduced whereby an accused had to have been indicted by a Grand Jury within that time. The subsequent prosecution could use only the evidence put before the Grand Jury and the defendant was allowed to have a copy of this.

The Treason Act of 1702 added a fifth category of treason: 'if any person or persons shall endeavour to deprive or hinder any person who shall be the next in succession to the crown from succeeding after the decease of her Majesty to the imperial crown of this realm and the dominions and territories thereunto belonging'.

The Treason Act of 1708 which came into force the following year extended the English treason laws to Scotland which was now part of the United Kingdom. This Act also made it treasonable to counterfeit the Great Seal of Scotland and to murder Scottish judges who were known as Lords of Session or Lords of Justiciary. This was the same as the English law but adapted to use the Scottish names. Petty treason was not introduced as an offence in Scotland, however.

So how was treason to be punished? It seems that the reigning monarch was able to decide the punishment or at least, in later times, select one of two options.

For male traitors the normal form of execution was hanging, drawing and quartering, whilst for women it was to be burning at the stake, unless the monarch decided otherwise. Hanging, drawing and quartering was specially introduced for the execution of William Maurice in 1241, who had been convicted of piracy. Burning is dealt with in Chapter 5.

The sentence for men convicted of high treason was 'That you be drawn on a hurdle to the place of execution where you shall be hanged by the neck and being alive cut down, your privy members shall be cut off and your bowels taken out and burned before you, your head severed from your body and your body divided into four quarters to be disposed of at the King's pleasure.' As you will see from the sentence, it should properly be called drawing, hanging and quartering as the condemned was drawn to the place of execution tied to the hurdle or sledge which was dragged by a horse. This is confirmed by contemporary law books. Drawing does not refer to the removal of the intestines in this context and remained part of the sentence for high treason long after the disembowelling and dismemberment had ceased. The hurdle was similar to a piece of fencing made from thin branches interwoven to form a panel to which the prisoner was tied. Once at the gallows, the prisoner was hanged in the normal way, i.e. without a drop, to ensure that the neck was not broken and then cut down whilst still conscious. The penis and testicles were cut off and the stomach was slit open. The intestines and heart were removed and burned before the victim. The other organs were torn out and finally the head was cut off and the body divided into four quarters. The head and quarters were parboiled to prevent them rotting too quickly and then displayed upon the city gates as a grim warning to all. At some point in this excruciating process, the prisoner inevitably died of strangulation and/or haemorrhage and/or shock and damage to vital organs. It has to be one of the most sadistic forms of execution ever devised.

In 1283, David, the last Welsh Prince of Wales, was tried for treason at Shrewsbury in Shropshire and was sentenced 'to be drawn to the gallows as a traitor to the King who made him a Knight, to be hanged as the murderer of the gentleman taken in the Castle of Hawarden, to have his limbs burnt because he had profaned by assassination the solemnity of Christ's passion and to have his quarters dispersed through the country because he had in different places compassed the death of his lord the king'.

Sir William Wallace is a Scottish hero on whose exploits the film *Braveheart* is based. He led a resistance movement against the English in Scotland and was bought to trial at Westminster Hall in 1305. In his defence he stated: 'I could not be a traitor to Edward, for I was never his subject.' On 23 August 1305, he was dragged to Smithfield behind two horses and made to suffer the full punishment in excruciating detail. After death his head was put on display on London Bridge and his quarters sent to Berwick, Newcastle, Perth and Stirling. The King, Edward I, decided where the body parts should be displayed.

There were a significant number of treason trials during the reign of Henry VIII. Most were for refusing to recognise Henry as the head of the Church of England. Between 1535 and 1580, a total of 105 Catholic martyrs were hanged, drawn and quartered at Tyburn in London. Others suffered normal hanging or beheading at the king's pleasure.

Guy (Guido) Fawkes and his fellow 'Gunpowder Plot' conspirators are possibly the most famous and best remembered traitors. The aim of their plot was to restore the Catholic religion to Britain by killing the King, James I, and his Protestant government by blowing up the Houses of Parliament on the occasion of the State Opening on 5 November 1605. Fawkes was captured and tortured on the rack to get him to reveal the names of the others who were then arrested. They were tried at Westminster Hall in January 1606 and all seven were sentenced to be hanged, drawn and quartered. The executions took place on 30 and 31 January of that year. The first three – Sir Everard Digby, Thomas Bates and Robert Winter – were put to death near St Paul's Church, whilst Guy Fawkes, Ambrose Rookwood, Thomas Winter and Robert Keyes died the following day in Old Palace Yard in front of the Houses of Parliament. Their heads were placed upon spikes on London Bridge. Strangely, by tradition, we burn the 'guy' on the bonfire on Fireworks Night in commemoration of the Gunpowder Plot, although Fawkes was not burned.

King Charles I was beheaded on 30 January 1649 and Oliver Cromwell assumed power, running the country with his son until the Restoration in 1660, when Charles II regained the throne. In August of that year, Charles passed the Act of Indemnity and Oblivion which gave a free pardon to anyone who had supported Cromwell's government. He retained the right to try for treason those who had taken part in the trial and execution of his father. To this end a special court was set up in October 1660 to try the remaining Regicides as they were known. Ten were sentenced to be hanged, drawn and quartered. They were Thomas Harrison, John Jones, John Carew, Hugh Peters, Adrian Scroope,

Thomas Scot, Gregory Clement, Francis Hacker, Daniel Axtell and John Cooke. Harrison was the first to die, being executed at Charing Cross on Saturday 13 October and was subjected to the full gruesome rigours of his sentence. Two days later John Carew suffered the same fate, although his quartered body was allowed to be buried rather than put on display. The following day, John Cooke and Hugh Peters were executed. Cooke's head was displayed on a pole at Westminster Hall with Harrison's, whilst Peters' was displayed on London Bridge. Wednesday the 17th saw the executions of Scot, Clement, Scroope and Jones. Finally on Friday 19 October it was Hacker and Axtell's turn. Oliver Cromwell, Henry Ireton, Thomas Pride and John Bradshaw were all dead by this time, but were posthumously tried for high treason. They were found guilty and in January 1661 their corpses were exhumed and hung in chains at Tyburn.

An unusual execution for treason occurred on 24 September 1652 when 34-year-old Captain James Hind was hanged, drawn and quartered at Worcester. Hind was a committed Royalist and highway robber. He sought revenge on the Regicides and could claim Oliver Cromwell, Hugh Peters and Sergeant John Bradshaw amongst his victims. Hind and his friend Thomas Allen happened across Cromwell soon after the execution of Charles I and a fight ensued. Allen was captured and later executed but Hind escaped. Eventually he was caught after his landlord gave him away. His quartered body parts were displayed around Worcester and his head placed upon a spike on the Bridge Gate over the River Severn.

Oliver Plunkett, the Catholic bishop of Armagh and Primate of All Ireland, became the last Catholic martyr when he was drawn to Tyburn and executed on trumped up treason charges on 11 July 1681. He was made a saint by Pope Paul VI. In all, 264 Catholics suffered at Tyburn for their faith. The men were typically subjected to the full punishment and the women just to hanging. A permanent memorial to them is being planned in 2009.

The Monmouth Rebellion led to the 'Bloody Assize' presided over by the Lord Chief Justice, Judge Jeffreys, assisted by four other senior judges. The first hearing was held at Winchester on 25 August 1685, the court then proceeding through the Western Circuit, finishing at Wells in Somerset on 23 September and dealing with some 1400 rebels. Of these, around 300 were condemned to be hanged, drawn and quartered, 144 at Wells alone.

There were also hanging, drawing and quartering executions as a result of the 1715 Rebellion. Three men were convicted of high treason by the Court of King's Bench on 22 November 1715 and were drawn to Tyburn for execution on 7 December of that year. They were John Dorrell, Captain John Gordon and Captain William Kerr.

The 1745 Jacobite Rebellion led to a considerable number of trials for high treason which resulted in 91 sentences of hanging, drawing and quartering being passed by a Special Commission at Carlisle, of which 33 were carried out during October and November 1746: twenty at Carlisle, six at Brampton and seven at Penrith. A further 22 executions took place at York during November 1746 after trials by a Special Commission. Seventeen more were carried out at Kennington Common, the place of execution for the County of Surrey, between July and November. These included Sir John Wedderburn, John Hamilton, Andrew Wood, Alexander Leith and Captain James Dawson. (Kennington Common is now known as Kennington Park, near Camberwell in London.)

The execution of 37-year-old Francis Townley at Kennington Common on 30 July 1746 is described thus: 'After he had hung for six minutes, he was cut down, and, having life in him, as he lay on the block to be quartered, the executioner gave him several blows on the breast, which not having the effect designed, he immediately cut his throat, after which he took his head off then ripped him open, and took out his bowels and threw them into the fire which consumed them, then he slashed his four quarters, put them with the head into a coffin, and they were deposited till Saturday, 2 August, when his head was put on Temple Bar, and his body and limbs suffered to be buried.' The head was stolen by agents of his family from Temple Bar and held, in secret, by the Townley family until 1945 when it was interred in the Townley vault in Burnley. Francis Townley had commanded the Jacobite Manchester Regiment which surrendered to the Duke of Cumberland after briefly holding Carlisle in late 1745.

Thereafter, there were only a further four hanging, drawing and quartering executions in the 18th century. Dr Archibald Cameron was convicted under an Act of Attainder in 1746 for his part in the '45 rebellion and was executed at Tyburn on Thursday 7 June 1753. He was allowed to hang for 20 minutes before being cut down. His head was removed, but it is unclear whether the rest of the sentence was carried out. His remains were buried in the Savoy Chapel. His was to be the last Jacobite Rebellion execution.

François Henri de la Motte was put to death at Tyburn on Friday 27 July 1781 for conspiring against the life of the King. He was hanged for nearly half an hour before his head was cut off and shown to the crowd, and his heart cut out and burned. His body was then scored with a knife as a symbolic form of quartering. A year later David Tyrie was executed at Portsmouth on Saturday 24 August 1782 (possibly on the shoreline), having been tried by a Special Commission at Winchester and convicted of giving information to an enemy (France) in time of war. His sentence was carried out in full and he is probably the last so to suffer.

The last 18th century occurrence was at Maidstone on 7 July 1798 when James O'Coigley was executed for 'compassing and imagining the death of the King and adhering to the King's enemies' – the French. In the 19th century, there were four recorded sets of executions for high treason in all of which the prisoners were hanged until dead and then beheaded, the rest of their sentence being remitted.

The first was the execution of the seven Despard Conspirators, which took place at Horsemonger Lane gaol in Surrey on Monday 21 February 1803. Colonel Edward Despard had planned to seize the Tower of London and the Bank of England and assassinate the king, George III. Despard, John Francis, John Wood, James Broughton, James Sedgewick, Arthur Wrutton and John McNamara were put to death by William Brunskill, having been symbolically drawn around the prison yard first.

The Treason Act of 1814 which came into force on 27 July of that year formally removed the disembowelling part of the punishment and substituted normal hanging followed by post mortem decapitation. However, the monarch could still substitute death by beheading instead, up to 1870, although nobody was ever beheaded under this Act. After 1870, normal hanging in private became the only penalty. There were very few executions for treason, the last taking place in 1946 (see Chapter 19).

The next executions for treason took place outside Friar Gate gaol in Derby on Friday 7 November 1817 when Jeremiah Brandreth, William Turner and Isaac Ludlam, known as The 'Pentrich Martyrs', were to suffer for attempting to lead a revolution. They were hanged for half an hour (until dead) before being taken down, whereupon the executioner cut off their heads with an axe and held Brandreth's up to the crowd, exclaiming: 'Behold the head of the traitor, Jeremiah Brandreth.' This was the last use of an axe for decapitation in Britain.

The five Cato Street conspirators became the last to suffer this fate in England when they were executed in front of Newgate prison on Monday 1 May 1820 for conspiring to murder several members of the Cabinet. The case became known as the Cato Street Conspiracy as the plot was hatched in a house in this street off the Edgware Road. They were a group of five middle-aged men: Arthur Thistlewood, James Ings, John Brunt, Richard Tidd and William Davidson. Their security had been breached by a government agent and all were arrested and tried at the Old Bailey. Having been found guilty, they were sentenced by the Lord Chief Justice as follows: 'That you, each of you, be taken hence to the gaol from whence you came, and from thence that you be drawn on a hurdle to a place of execution, and be there hanged by the neck until dead; and that afterwards your heads shall be severed from your bodies, and your bodies divided into four quarters, to be disposed of as his Majesty shall think fit. And may God of His infinite goodness have mercy upon your souls.'

The sheriff for the City of London, Mr Rothwell, was in charge of the actual arrangements for carrying out the sentence and decided, it would seem, principally to avoid traffic congestion, to do away with the drawing to the place of execution on a hurdle. Barricades were erected to keep the expected large crowds of spectators back and an additional platform added at the back of Newgate's normal gallows. Work went on with these arrangements all weekend. Soldiers were drafted in to provide security. The new platform was covered in sawdust to absorb the blood, and the men's coffins placed on it in readiness. Jeremy Botting, the executioner, prepared his charges in the normal way on the front section of the gallows. They were attended on the gallows by the Rev Cotton, the Ordinary. At 8 o'clock the drop fell and the traitors were suspended. It took about five minutes for all visible signs of life to be extinguished, but they were left on the ropes for half an hour to ensure total death. The bodies were then drawn back up onto the platform and placed on their coffins with the neck of each over a small block set at the end of their coffin. The rope was removed and each head severed by a masked man using a surgical knife. The executioner showed each of the heads to the crowd, proclaiming: 'This is the head of a traitor.' It is thought that a medical man or a butcher actually performed the decapitation.

The last recorded instance of hanging and decapitation took place a few months later in Scotland. Twenty-two men were tried at Stirling on 13/14 July for high treason for their parts in the '1820 Rising'. They were a group of radicals campaigning for universal male suffrage, better working conditions and a Scottish Parliament, who had attempted to seize the Carron Ironworks near Falkirk, but were captured by the British army at Bonnymuirtried. Andrew Hardie and John Baird, the two leaders, pleaded guilty at trial and all 22 received the death sentence on 4 August. Hardie and Baird were executed at Stirling on Friday 8 September. After hanging for half an hour, their bodies were cut down and placed in their coffins, with their necks over one edge. Their heads were then cut off and shown to the crowd. On the gallows, Hardie told the spectators: 'I die a martyr to the cause of truth and injustice.' The remaining 20 conspirators were reprieved.

High treason coining offences

The term 'coining' comprised a number of offences, including counterfeiting, colouring and clipping coin or possessing the equipment to do so, eg coin moulds and crucibles for melting the metal. Clipping or filing the edges of coins reduced their value and produced the raw material for forging new coins. It was also a very simple process that could be done by anyone without special equipment. Colouring coins was done in an attempt to give them greater value, eg a silver coin could be coloured gold. All of these activities debased the currency and public confidence in it, which is why such crimes were treated so seriously. Uttering forgeries, i.e. passing them into circulation, was also a capital offence. It is interesting to note that men convicted of the high treason offences of coining were not normally subjected to disembowelling, decapitation and quartering, just being drawn to the place of execution and hanged in the normal way, yet women convicted of these offences were burned at the stake until 1789 (see Chapter 5).

At the Sessions of the Old Bailey on 15 October 1690, Thomas Castle was sentenced to be hanged, drawn and quartered for forging shillings. It is noteworthy that in the Ordinary's Account he describes the sentence as 'Drawn, Hanged and Quartered', confirming that drawing referred to the drawing to the place of execution on a hurdle or sledge and not to disembowelling. Castle was spared the full punishment and was drawn on a sledge to Tyburn and hanged on Friday 24 October. Thomas Rogers and his wife Ann were also convicted of clipping 40 pieces of silver at the same Sessions. Thomas Rogers was sentenced to be hanged, drawn and quartered and Ann to be burned, but both were reprieved. Coining was a common crime at the time and court records contain many instances of trials for it.

In 1662, the Royal Mint introduced a mechanised process to manufacture a new coinage which had milled edges in an attempt to reduce the incidence of clipping and filing the edges of the previously handmade coins which were referred to as 'hammered'. The famous scientist Sir Isaac Newton became Warden of the Royal Mint and oversaw the Great Recoinage of 1696–1699 which replaced all the old hammered coins in circulation. Newton did a great deal to try and stamp out the practice of coining and to catch the coiners. His largest 'fish' was William Chaloner who was thought to have made as many as 30,000 counterfeit guinea coins. Chaloner was executed at Tyburn on 22 March 1699. It is not known whether his sentence was carried out in full, in view of the scale of the offence. Coining continued to be classed as high treason until 1832 when it was reclassified as a felony.

Petty treason

The Treason Act of 1351 also defined petit (petty) treason as the killing of one's superior, and covered the murder of a husband by his wife, a master or mistress by a servant, or a superior ranking member of the clergy by a lower ranking one. The same Act removed three other crimes that had formerly been treasonable, viz. attempted murder of a husband by his wife, forgery of his master's seal by a servant, or committing adultery with his master's wife.

Why were these forms of killing treasonable rather than merely murders? The reason was that they involved disloyalty to or betrayal of the victim to whom the perpetrator owed loyalty. Petty treason remained a distinct crime until 1828 when it was reclassified as ordinary murder by the Offences Against the Person Act of that year. The male punishment for petty treason was to be drawn to the place of execution on a hurdle or sledge and there be hanged in the normal way (without disembowelling and quartering), whereas the female punishment was burning at the stake. Normally the condemned woman was strangled first (see Chapter 5).

Unlike high treason, petty treason was a Clerygeable offence up to 1532. The provisions of the 1695 Act did not apply to petty treason, but the defence of provocation was permitted, and if successful reduced the crime to manslaughter.

Executions in the 18th century for this crime were not common. From 1735 to 1783, just four executions are recorded at Tyburn for petty treason. Ann Mudd was burned on 26 June 1737 for killing her husband, and James Hall hanged on 14 September 1741 for murdering his master. In the decades 1755–1764 and 1765–1774, there were two more. Richard Greenstreet was hanged on 14 December 1761 for the murder of his master, and Elizabeth Herring burned on 13 September 1773 for the murder of her husband.

4

Beheading

Beheading goes back a very long way in history because, like hanging, it was a cheap and practical method of execution in early times when a sword or an axe was always readily available. The Greeks and the Romans considered beheading a less dishonourable form of execution than other methods in use at the time. The Roman Empire used beheading for its own citizens whilst crucifying others. In Roman Britain there is evidence of its use for the execution of Alban at Verulamium for refusing to renounce Christianity circa AD304. Verulamium was later renamed St Albans in his honour and it is thought that the execution site is where its abbey was built. There is evidence from skeletal remains of beheadings in Saxon times in Britain, although we have no details as to the implement used.

Beheading is probably as humane as any modern method of execution if carried out correctly and the prisoner is decapitated by a single blow. Consciousness is thought to be lost within two or three seconds, due to a rapid fall in the blood supply to the brain. The person dies from shock and anoxia due to haemorrhage within less than 60 seconds. However, because the muscles and vertebrae of the neck are tough, severance may require more than one blow. It has often been reported that the eyes and mouths of the decapitated have shown signs of movement, and has been calculated that the human brain has enough oxygen stored for metabolism to persist for about seven seconds after the head is cut off.

There were two distinct forms of beheading: by the sword and by the axe. The axe was the usual method in Britain, although Waltheof, Earl of Northumberland, and Anne Boleyn were executed with a sword, as possibly was Archbishop Scrope. Where a person was to be decapitated with a sword, a block was not used; instead they were generally made to kneel down on the scaffold. A typical European execution sword was 36-48" (900-1200 mm) long and 2-2½" (50-65 mm) wide, with the handle being long enough for the executioner to use both hands to give maximum leverage. It weighed around 4 lbs (2 kg).

Where an axe was the chosen implement, a wooden block, often shaped to accept the neck, was required. Two patterns of block were used: the high block, 18-24" (450-600 mm) high, where the prisoner knelt behind it and lent forward so that their neck rested on the top; or the low block where the person lay on the scaffold or a low bench with their neck over the block. The neck on a high block presented an easier target due to the head pointing slightly downwards, thus bringing the neck into prominence. It also meant that the axe was at a better angle at that point in the arc of the stroke to meet the neck full on. The high block was favoured in later times in Britain. British hangmen normally got the job of beheading those condemned, but were generally very poor at it due to the rarity of such sentences.

In the last chapter we looked at the punishment of ordinary people for treason. From the time of William the Conqueror, those of noble birth who were convicted of treason were typically permitted to be executed by beheading. The first recorded instance of this took place on 31 May 1076 when Waltheof, Earl of Northumberland, was executed on St Giles Hill, near Winchester. Waltheof had been convicted of treason for taking part in the Revolt of the Earls against the King and was executed with a sword. This was the first recorded beheading under William.

Over the centuries several members of Royalty were beheaded, including Charles I, Anne Boleyn, Mary Queen of Scots and Lady Jane Grey (see below). Many earls, lords and knights and at least two bishops were executed by this method. The Archbishop of York, Richard Scrope, was beheaded on 8 June 1405 for treason on the orders of Henry IV who had attended his trial at Bishop Scrope's Palace. The execution took place in a field near the Palace. It is said that he was beheaded with a sword and specifically asked his executioner to strike him five times with it, in celebration of the five blows to Christ. The fifth blow removed his head. He was subsequently buried in York Minster and came to be regarded as a martyr.

The majority of English beheadings took place at the Tower of London. Seven were carried out in private within the grounds, of which five were of women. The spot indicated as 'The site of the scaffold' on Tower Green which visitors can see today was not used for all executions, although the plaque implies that it was. Those beheaded in private on

Tower Green were Lord Hastings on 13 June 1483; Anne Boleyn on 19 May 1536; Margaret Pole, Countess of Salisbury on 28 May 1541; Catherine Howard and her lady-in-waiting, Jane, Viscountess Rochford, on 13 February 1542; Lady Jane Grey on 15 February 1554; and Robert Devereux, Earl of Essex, on 25 February 1601.

Public beheading on Tower Hill outside the walls of the Tower of London was used when the government of the day wished to make an example of a traitor (or traitors) of noble birth. It is thought that around 120 men were beheaded there between 1388 and 1747, and there was a permanent scaffold from 1485. Only a very small number of beheadings were carried out elsewhere in the country.

Anne Boleyn, Henry VIII's second wife, was convicted on trumped up charges of adultery and treason and was sentenced to death by burning at the stake or beheading at the King's pleasure. Fortunately for Anne, he chose the latter and perhaps through a pang of conscience imported a skilled headsman from Calais in France to ensure the execution was performed as humanely as possible.

On 19 May 1536, 29-year-old Anne was led to the Parade Ground within the Tower with an escort of Yeoman of the Guard (Beefeaters). She was wearing a loose ermine-trimmed grey damask robe over a red underskirt. Her hair was 'up', covered with a white coif and a small black cap, and she wore a cross on a gold chain at her waist and carried a white handkerchief and a prayer book. She had to climb 4 feet up the steps to the scaffold to meet her headsman who was wearing a black suit and half mask covering the upper part of his face. The long two-handed execution sword was concealed under the straw on the scaffold.

Anne made a short speech to the assembled witnesses and then removed her cape and her hair coif and cap, which was now replaced by a white cap. She knelt on the platform and prayed with her chaplain. When she had finished, one of her ladies-in-waiting blindfolded her with a large handkerchief. All was now ready and the headsman took up the sword and beheaded her with a single blow. Her ladies-in-waiting recovered her head and, as there was no coffin provided, the body was placed in an old arrow box and duly buried in the Chapel Royal of St Peter ad Vincula within the Tower.

Henry VIII finally got a son and heir in Edward VI in October 1537.

When his father died ten years later, Edward became king but was still a child, so was guided in his duties by his uncle Edward Seymour, Duke of Somerset, as Lord Protector. He led the Regency Council from 1547 to 1549, being replaced by John Dudley, Earl of Warwick, from 1550. Dudley trumped up a charge of treason against his predecessor, who was beheaded on Tower Hill at 8 o'clock on the morning of 22 January 1552. According to a contemporary account of the scene recorded by one Henry Machyn, 'there was a sudden rumbling a little before he died, as if it had been guns shooting and great horses coming, so that a thousand fell to the ground for fear, for they who were at one side thought no other but that one was killing another, so that they fell down to the ground, one upon another with their halberds, some fell into the ditch of the Tower and other places, and a hundred into the Tower ditch, and some ran away for fear'. Dudley's supremacy was to be short-lived, however. He too was beheaded under the rule of Mary I at Tower Hill on 22 August 1553.

Lady Jane Grey, the daughter of the Duke of Suffolk, was born in October 1537 and was only 16 years old when she was proclaimed Queen on 10 July 1553 by Protestant nobles, including her father, after the premature death of Edward VI. She reigned, uncrowned, for just nine days, being unable to win public acceptance because of her religion in what was at heart still a predominantly Catholic country. Catholic Queen Mary took over the throne and thus Jane was deposed and imprisoned in the Tower for six months before being condemned for treason and executed on 13 February 1554. She was led to a scaffold erected on Tower Green in front of the White Tower. She made a speech and recited a psalm before using a large white handkerchief to blindfold herself and kneeling on a cushion in front of the high block. Having blindfolded herself she couldn't see the block and fumbling for it said: 'What shall I do? Where is it? Where is it?' One of the people on the scaffold guided her down and before the fatal blow she said: 'Lord, into Thy hands I commend my spirit.' Earlier on the same day her husband, Lord Guildford Dudley, whom she had married on 21 May 1553, was beheaded on Tower Hill, and her father suffered the same fate eleven days later for his part in the alleged conspiracy to seize the throne for his daughter.

Sir Thomas Wyatt was beheaded on 11 April 1554 at the age of 23 for leading a rebellion against Mary I that began in Rochester in Kent and proceeded to London. Wyatt had some 3,000 men with him, but they deserted in the face of strong military opposition and he was captured.

Elizabeth I, who was the daughter of Henry VIII and Anne Boleyn, ascended to the throne on 17 November 1558 on the death of her half sister Mary I. Elizabeth was a Protestant and worked to establish a Protestant Church which would become the Church of England. One of the problems Elizabeth faced was Mary Queen of Scots who was endeavouring to restore the Catholic faith in Scotland. Mary was forced to abdicate the Scottish throne and was held prisoner in England for 19 years from 1568 to 1587, when Elizabeth finally sanctioned her execution at Fotheringhay Castle near Oundle in Northamptonshire on 8 February 1587.

Mary was born at Linlithgow in Scotland in December 1542, the daughter of James V of Scotland. James died just six days later and thus the baby Mary became Queen. She was the cause of plots and conspiracies against Elizabeth, who signed Mary's death warrant only with great reluctance, on the advice of her ministers. This warrant was delivered to Fotheringhay on the afternoon of 7 February and it seems that Mary almost welcomed the release that death would bring her. She asked for a little more time to prepare herself, but was told that the execution would proceed as planned the following day between 7 and 8am. The scaffold was stated to be some 12 feet square and 2 feet high and had been erected within a hall in the castle. She was duly brought into the room and asked one of her attendants: 'Please help me mount this. This is the last request I shall make of you.' Once on the scaffold she made a speech, in which she begged Elizabeth to spare her ladies-in-waiting from sharing her fate. With their help she prepared herself and knelt down at the block. It took three strokes of the axe to decapitate Mary and afterwards the executioner held up the severed head to the witnesses, proclaiming: 'God save Queen Elizabeth! May all the enemies of the true Evangel thus perish!' Mary was buried eventually in Peterborough Cathedral and later reburied in Westminster Abbey, close to Elizabeth's own grave.

A replica of the scaffold used for the 1601 execution of Robert Devereux, Earl of Essex, has been constructed for exhibition in the

Tower. The original was set up in the middle of the Parade Ground and was made of oak, some 4 feet high and having a 9 feet square platform (1.2 m high x 2.75 m square) with a waist-high rail round it. The prisoner reached it by a short flight of stairs and was not restrained throughout the execution as it was expected that people of noble birth would know how to behave at their executions. Devereux lay at full length on the platform and placed his neck on the low block with his arms outstretched. It is recorded that three strokes of the axe were required to decapitate him. This was to be the last beheading within the Tower of London.

Sir Walter Raleigh (or Ralegh as he spelled it) was a famous adventurer, author and favourite of Elizabeth I. He was executed in Old Palace Yard at Westminster on the bitterly cold morning of 29 October 1618. He had originally been condemned for treason against James I in 1603, and although reprieved was imprisoned in the Tower of London until 1616 when he persuaded James to let him lead an expedition to the New World to discover gold. The expedition was a signal failure and led to his death sentence being restored. On the scaffold he made a speech and when he had finished asked to see the headsman's axe. He ran his thumb along the blade and remarked: 'This is sharp medicine, but it will cure all diseases.' With that, he laid himself on the block and gave the signal to the executioner, who took two blows to sever the head. This was placed into a leather bag, embalmed and given to his wife. His body was buried in the chancel of St Margaret's Church, Westminster.

Charles I was the only king of England to be executed, having been convicted of high treason and 'other crimes' for his activities during the Civil War against the Parliamentarians led by Oliver Cromwell. A special Act of Parliament had to be passed to create a means to try him before a court composed of Commissioners. The trial began on 20 January 1649, but the king refused to recognise the court or to enter a plea. He was beheaded on Tuesday 30 January 1649 on a raised scaffold in front of the Palace of Whitehall. In Charles' case the executioner managed to sever the head with a single blow. His head was sewn back onto the body and after the family had paid their last respects, he was buried in St George's Chapel at Windsor Castle.

Archbishop William Laud, the 71-year-old Archbishop of Canterbury, fell to the headman's axe on Tower Hill on 10 January 1645. Laud was condemned for treason by a Bill of Attainder in November 1644.

Lord William Russell was beheaded at Lincoln's Inn Fields on 21 July 1683 for his part in the Rye House Plot against Charles II. The executioner, Jack Ketch, struck Russell four blows with the axe before finally decapitating him.

James Scott, Duke of Monmouth, the illegitimate son of Charles II, led the Monmouth Rebellion and was defeated at the Battle of Sedgemoor on 6 July 1685. The 36-year-old was captured three days later and taken to London. An Act of Attainder was passed and he was sentenced to be beheaded on Tower Hill on 15 July of that year. Again Ketch got the job and Monmouth is reported to have referred to the execution of William Russell as he handed Ketch a purse of money on the scaffold. However, the bribe did him no good and it took repeated blows of the axe to kill him. In the end a knife was used to sever Monmouth's head completely.

The last female execution by beheading was that of 71-year-old Lady Alice Lisle who was to die for treason at Winchester on 2 September 1685, having been convicted of sheltering two traitors, John Hickes and Richard Nelthorpe, who had escaped the Battle of Sedgemoor. Lady Alice was tried at Winchester before the Lord Chief Justice, Judge Jeffreys, as part of the 'Bloody Assize' and was initially sentenced to be burned at the stake. This was reduced to beheading by James II and her sentence was carried out in the market place.

Following trial at Westminster Hall on Monday 28 July 1746, William, Earl of Kilmarnock, and Arthur, Lord Balmerino, were convicted of treason for their parts in the 1745 Rebellion. Kilmarnock pleaded guilty and Balmerino innocent. Their executions were carried out by John Thrift, London's then hangman, on 18 August 1746 in order of precedence with Kilmarnock going first as he was an earl. The block used for these executions was described as being of elm, 2' long, 1' 3" thick and 1' 8" high, with the top shaped to accept the chin. The axes (one for each prisoner) were described as having long wooden handles and sharp semicircular blades.

This was a huge show for the general public who flocked to see it. Thrift was given a new white suit for each execution and the scaffold was draped with black cloth and covered in fresh straw which was replaced after the first execution. The condemned were allowed to walk to their execution accompanied by friends from a nearby house where they were being held. There was no hurry once the scaffold was reached and it is said that Kilmarnock examined the axe and showed Thrift where to strike. Both men were permitted to give the signal when they were ready to die. It was the custom for the prisoner to forgive the executioner and to give him a purse of money in the hope of having the job done efficiently. Thrift succeeded in severing the head of Kilmarnock with a single blow, but Balmerino was not so lucky and required three strokes of the axe to decapitate him completely.

Octogenarian Simon Fraser, Lord Lovat, was another Jacobite and became the last person to be beheaded in Britain. His trial commenced on 9 March 1747 at Westminster Hall and lasted five days, resulting in conviction for his part in the '45 Rebellion. He was executed on Tower Hill on 9 April. In view of his advanced age and considerable girth he had to be assisted onto the scaffold and is said to have remarked: 'Why should there be such a bustle about taking off an old grey head that cannot get up three steps without three bodies to support it?' His execution went quite smoothly, Lovat being decapitated by a single blow when he dropped his handkerchief as a signal. However, a spectator stand collapsed killing some twenty people.

The block used for this execution, together with the axe, was on display in the Tower. As we have seen, it was normal for the executioner to pick up the severed head and display it to the crowd, proclaiming: 'Behold the head of a traitor!', although at the request of the prisoners this was not done in the cases of these last three noblemen.

5

Burning at the stake

Burning at the stake was used in England and Wales for both sexes to punish heresy and for women convicted of both high and petty treason. The male punishment of hanging, drawing and quartering was not deemed acceptable for women as it would have involved nudity. Very few ordinary women were convicted of high treason in the normal sense, but a substantial number were to suffer at the stake for the various coining offences mentioned in Chapter 3. The other form of treason for which women were burned was the petty treason murder of their husband or employer.

Although many people might associate burning at the stake with witchcraft, it was not used for this in England, only in Scotland where it was inflicted on both sexes (see Chapter 6). It is claimed that some 200,000 people were burned for witchcraft in Europe during the 16th and 17th centuries. Burning was particularly favoured by the Spanish Inquisition as it did not involve shedding of the victim's blood, which was disallowed under the prevailing Roman Catholic doctrine, and because it ensured that the condemned had no body to take into the next life, which was believed to be a very severe punishment in itself. It was also thought at that time that burning cleansed the soul, which was considered important for those convicted of witchcraft and heresy.

It is not known when burning was first used in Britain, but there is a recorded burning in 1222 when a deacon of the church was burned at Oxford for embracing the Jewish faith so he could marry a Jew. He was tried by an ecclesiastical council under Archbishop Stephen Langton and convicted of bestiality for having sex with a Jewish woman.

When Henry IV came to the throne in September 1399 he owed a debt to the Church for its assistance in getting him there. At this time the Church was worried by the Lollard movement which it viewed as heretical because it questioned the power and authority of the Catholic Church and had also translated the Bible into English, enabling ordinary, educated people to read it in their own language, thus undermining the power of priests as the sole interpreters of it. The Archbishop of Canterbury, Thomas Arundel, persuaded Henry to pass into law an Act named *de haeretico comburendo*, loosely translated as 'regarding the burning of heretics', that gave the clergy power to arrest and try those it suspected of heresy. When a person was condemned by these church courts a writ of *de haeretico comburendo* was issued to the civil authorities for their execution. This Act became law in 1401 and the first to suffer under it was one William Sautre, a priest. It is thought that he was burned at Smithfield in London in March 1401 for denying the doctrine of transubstantiation. A tailor named John Badby was similarly executed at Smithfield in 1409 or 1410 for the same offence.

In 1413, the law was extended to include the following: 'Whoever read the scriptures in the mother tongue (instead of Latin) should be condemned as traitors and heretics, and should forfeit land, cattle, body, life and goods from his heirs for ever.'

An unusual execution occurred on 14 December 1417 when Lollard leader Sir John Oldcastle was hanged and then burned together with his gallows at St Giles' Fields in London. He was apparently hanged for treason and burned for heresy. Mere suspicion of nonconformist religious views could be enough to warrant death. Foxe's *Book of Martyrs* records that Thomas Norris was burned at Norwich in 1507 because his parish priest suspected he was a Lollard.

In 1534, Henry VIII became Supreme Head of the Church and issued two proclamations against heresy. He particularly disliked the Anabaptist movement and his new laws led to the burning of a number of its followers, including a group of Dutch Anabaptists who had fled from persecution in Holland in 1535. Anabaptists held radical religious views that were tolerated by neither the Catholic nor Protestant religions. These views included adult baptism, pacifism, refusal to recognise secular laws and polygamy. Anabaptists continued to be persecuted under Mary I and Elizabeth I.

Anne Askew, aged 24, was burned as a heretic with three others at Smithfield on 16 July 1546 for preaching sermons in London and distributing banned Protestant literature. She had been tortured on the rack whilst imprisoned in the Tower of London to try and get her to implicate her friend Catherine Parr, Henry VIII's sixth wife. As a result of this torture she had to be carried to the stake in a chair. In the normal way she was offered a pardon if she recanted her religious views, but she refused to.

Mary I reigned for five years from 1553 to 1558 and was a devout Catholic. She quickly repealed Acts that had made Protestantism the official religion, and at first this may well have been welcomed by many ordinary people. Initially she was tolerant of Protestants, but by 1555 had turned upon them and persecuted heretics with typical religious zeal. In the ensuing three years it is estimated that some 282 persons were burned at the stake for heresy because they refused to renounce their Protestant religion. The Queen became known as 'Bloody Mary' and, to the relief of many, died in 1558, the country returning to Protestantism under Elizabeth I.

The first to die was John Rogers, the vicar of St Sepulchre's Church in London, who was burned on 14 February 1555. Included in this huge number of executions were three Protestant bishops whom Mary and the Catholic Church regarded as heretics. They were Hugh Latimer, the Bishop of Worcester, and Nicholas Ridley, the erstwhile Bishop of Rochester, who were burned at Oxford on 16 October 1555, and the Archbishop of Canterbury, Thomas Cranmer, who was put to death there on 21 March 1556. Ironically these same bishops had been active in the persecution of Anabaptists and Catholics a few years earlier, little knowing that they would soon share the same fate. Latimer's reported last words as he was chained to the stake were: 'Be of good cheer, Master Ridley, and play the man, for we shall this day light such a candle in England as I trust by God's grace shall never be put out.' Cranmer had written a letter to the Pope recanting his faith, but finally decided against sending it. At the stake he told the audience: 'I have sinned, in that I signed with my hand what I did not believe with my heart. When the flames are lit, this hand shall be the first to burn.' He then purposely thrust the offending hand into the flames.

The usual place for burnings in London was at West Smithfield (now called just Smithfield). A permanent memorial stands close to the spot where they took place and a number of early woodcut pictures of them survive, showing groups of sufferers chained to stakes with bundles of rushes and faggots (bundles of dry brushwood) heaped round them.

One shows seven people – five men and two women – being burned together on 27 January 1556. Another shows three men and two women. Burnings also took place in Essex, Kent, Sussex, Suffolk and a few elsewhere such as Carmarthen, Chester, Coventry, Gloucester and Oxford. John Foxe recorded these executions in his famous *Book of Martyrs* published in 1563. Reading passages from it, one is struck by the amazing courage of so many of those who were about to suffer a horrible death for what they believed in. It seems that many welcomed their execution, perhaps as a way of proving their faith. It was not the practice to strangle heretics before they were burned, so they suffered the full agonies of being burned alive.

Bartholomew Legate was burned at Smithfield on 18 March 1612 after trial by a full Consistory Court in February 1612 that found him guilty of heresy. His brother, Thomas, died awaiting trial in Newgate. The last recorded burning for heresy was carried out in the market place of Lichfield in Staffordshire on 11 April 1612, when Edward Whightman from nearby Burton upon Trent was executed. A plaque marking the spot can still be seen.

Two slightly different methods of burning were used in Britain. The first consisted of using bundles of rushes and faggots piled around the base of a wooden stake to which the prisoner was attached by chains or iron hoops. In some illustrations one can see the prisoner standing on a platform, for instance an upturned barrel, with the faggots piled at its base. This form of burning typically subjected the prisoner to a far more agonising death as it took some time before the flames reached head level, burning the lower parts of the body first and taking a considerable amount of time to kill.

The second method was to tie the condemned to the stake and heap faggots all round them, effectively hiding their sufferings from sight so that they died inside a wall of flames. It is said that Joan of Arc died by this method. It is thought that this caused a much quicker death because the victim was forced to breathe the flame and hot gasses surrounding their face. The heat of the air caused the lining of the trachea to swell up, thus blocking the airway and leading to suffocation within a few minutes. In most executions for treason the prisoner was strangled with a rope before the fire was lit. This was normal practice in England in the 17th and 18th centuries. Later the condemned woman was hanged first before being burned.

Elizabeth Gaunt became the last woman to be burned at the stake for high treason, in the sense that we would understand it, at Tyburn on 23 October 1685. She was convicted of helping to conceal James Burton, one of those involved in the Rye House Plot of 1683 against Charles II. In an effort to save his own skin, Burton testified against at Elizabeth at her trial at the Old Bailey on October 19. She was drawn to Tyburn on a sledge and once there fastened to the stake by an iron chain around her body under her arms. She made a speech and held up the Bible, claiming it commanded her to shelter Burton. She was denied strangulation, apparently at the King's insistence, and was thus burned alive.

Catherine Hayes was burned at Tyburn on Monday 9 May 1726 for the petty treason murder of her husband, John. She had persuaded her two lovers to kill her husband with an axe, a crime for which the two men were to hang. She was dragged to Tyburn on a hurdle and when she had finished praying, was fastened to the stake by an iron chain round her body. A rope halter was put round her neck, running through a hole in the stake and the faggots piled round her. When Richard Arnet, the hangman, lit the fire he found the flames too fierce to allow him to pull the strangling rope, so the poor woman was burned alive. She was reduced to ashes within an hour.

According to Blackstone's Commentaries, every woman convicted of counterfeiting gold or silver coin of the realm was sentenced to be drawn to the place of execution and there 'to be burned with fire till she was dead'.

Cecelia Labree was burned at West Smithfield for coining on Wednesday 2 May 1705, having been convicted at the April Sessions. She had been convicted of this offence before at the May 1697 Sessions and been sentenced to be burned but had been reprieved. Sadly she didn't learn her lesson. During 1705–1714 only one other woman was burned in London. She was Joyce Hodgkis who was executed on Wednesday 22 September 1714 for the petty treason murder of her husband. It is not clear where this execution was carried out.

Barbara Spencer was burned at Tyburn on Wednesday 5 July 1721 for counterfeiting shillings. She was a rebellious young woman of about 23 years of age who wanted easy money and coining seemed to offer this. When arrested she had 28 shilling coins and a pair of moulds with a further counterfeit shilling in them. She was drawn to Tyburn and strangled at the stake prior to the faggots being lit. This may well have been the first time a woman was burned at Tyburn, rather than at Smithfield, for this crime.

Elizabeth Wright, aged around 50, was burned on 19 December 1733 for possessing a pair of moulds to make sixpenny pieces. Her 26-year-old daughter and a male accomplice were reprieved. She was drawn to Tyburn on a sledge and once there was lifted into one of the carts to pray with twelve men who were to hang that day. After prayers she was taken to the stake set up nearby and strangled before the fire was lit. It is not known if she was executed before the men or made to witness their execution.

Wednesday 2 October 1734 saw a triple burning at Tyburn. The three prisoners were Mary Haycock, Elizabeth Tracey and her sister Catharine Tracey (or Bougle) for counterfeiting and possession of coining equipment. The 37-year-old Mary Haycock was convicted of having and concealing two counterfeiting flask moulds. Elizabeth Tracey, who was 27, had been found guilty of making three sixpenny pieces and 20 shilling coins (£1.07 in today's money). Catharine had made 40 sixpenny pieces and 12 shillings. Hardly massive crimes! They were taken in one cart to Tyburn whilst three men who were to hang were taken in another. The Ordinary of Newgate, James Guthrie, recorded that the three women met their deaths with great courage. This was London's only recorded multiple burning in the 18th century.

Although burning at the stake was a less common punishment by this time, at least 32 women suffered this fate between 1735 and 1789. They were:

Name	Date	Place	Crime
Margaret Onion	08/08/1735	Chelmsford	Murdered husband
Mary Fawson	08/08/1735	Northampton	Murdered husband
Ann Mudd	25/06/1737	Tyburn	Murdered husband
Mary Bird	01/07/1737	Ely	Murdered husband
Mary Groke (age 16)	18/03/1738	Winchester	Murdered mistress
Ann Goodson	12/04/1738	Guildford	Murdered husband
Susannah Broom (age 67)	21/12/1739	Tyburn	Murdered husband

Elizabeth Moreton (or Owen)	10/08/1744	Evesham	Murdered husband
Mary Johnson	?/04/1747	Lincoln	Murdered husband
Amy Hutchinson	07/11/1749	Ely	Murdered husband
Elizabeth Packard	?/?/1750	Exeter	Murdered husband
Ann Whale (age 21)	08/08/1752	Horsham	Murdered husband
Ann Williams	13/04/1753	Over, near Gloucester*	Murdered husband
Susannah Bruford (age 19)	03/09/1753	Wells (Somerset)	Murdered husband
Mary Ellah	28/03/1757	York	Murdered husband
Margaret Bedingfield	08/04/1763	Ipswich	Murdered husband
Mary Heald	23/04/1763	Chester	Murdered husband
Mary Saunders	21/03/1764	Monmouth	Murdered mistress
Mary Norwood (age 33)	08/05/1765	Ilchester (Somerset)	Murdered husband
Ann Sowerby	10/08/1767	York	Murdered husband
Susannah Lott	21/07/1769	Maidstone	Murdered husband
Mary Hilton (or Hulton)	06/04/1772	Lancaster	Murdered husband
Elizabeth Herring	13/09/1773	Tyburn	Murdered husband
Margaret Ryan	18/03/1776	Maidstone	Murdered husband
Elizabeth Bordingham	30/03/1776	York	Murdered husband
Ann Cruttenden (age 80)	08/08/1776	Horsham	Murdered husband
Isabella Condon	27/10/1779	Tyburn	Coining
Rebecca Downing	29/06/1782	Exeter	Murdered mistress
Mary Bailey	08/03/1784	Winchester	Murdered husband
Phoebe Harris	21/06/1786	Newgate	Coining
Margaret Sullivan	25/06/1788	Newgate	Coining
Catherine Murphy	18/03/1789	Newgate	Coining

*Over is a village about a mile from Gloucester, where the county gallows stood at that time.

Elizabeth Webber (or Webster) was probably burned at York in December 1739 for the murder of her husband but her execution cannot be confirmed. Alice Davis was most probably burned on 31 March 1758 for filing a golden guinea coin. Unfortunately there is no Ordinary's Account to confirm this.

In the 18th century reprieves for petty treason were rare or non-existent. It was reported in *The Sherborne Mercury* that 16-year-old Mary Groke was burned at the stake on Saturday 18 March 1738 at Gallows Hill on the outskirts of Winchester in Hampshire for the petty treason murder by poisoning of her mistress Justin(e) Turner. She was executed alongside two men, John Boyd and James Warwick, who were being hanged for highway robbery and horse theft. She was made to witness the men's execution before suffering her own. Mary was the youngest woman to be burned in the 18th century.

Margaret (Ann) Bedingfield was a 21-year-old Suffolk farmer's wife who fell for one of her husband's farmhands, 19-year-old Richard Ringe. As her husband John was an impediment to the affair they decided to kill him. The murder was amateurish and they were both convicted of petty treason. On Friday 8 April 1763, each prisoner was tied to a sledge in Ipswich prison and drawn to Rushmore, then a village just north of Ipswich, where the county gallows stood and a stake had been set up for Ann. Ringe addressed the huge crowd who had come to watch, warning them to avoid the snares of wicked women and to consider chastity as a virtue. Ann was meanwhile tied to the stake with an iron chain and a rope halter was placed around her neck, with the free rope passing through a hole bored in the stake. When all was ready, Ringe was turned off from the gallows and Ann was strangled by the hangman. When she ceased to show signs of life, bundles of faggots were piled round her and lit, the fire reducing her body to ashes.

Susannah Lott and Benjamin Bush were found guilty of the poisoning murder of her husband John on 17 July 1769. They were executed together on Friday 21 July, he by hanging and she by burning. The scene was described thus: 'A post, about seven feet high, was fixed in the ground; it had a peg near the top, to which Mrs Lott, standing on a stool, was fastened by the neck; when the stool was taken away, she hung about a quarter of an hour, till she was quite dead: a chain was then turned around her body, and properly fastened to the post, when a large quantity of faggots being placed round her, and set on fire, the body was consumed to ashes.' This is the first confirmed occasion where a woman was hanged first, rather than being strangled at the stake, before burning.

At the September 1773 Sessions of the Old Bailey, Elizabeth Herring was indicted for 'feloniously, traitorously, and of her malice aforethought, making an assault upon Robert Herring, her husband, and with a certain case knife giving him a mortal wound on the right side of the throat, of the length of one inch, and the depth of two inches, of which wound he instantly died, on August the 5th of that year'. She was convicted of petty treason (note the word 'traitorously' in the indictment) and the Recorder passed the following sentence upon her: 'You Elizabeth Herring are to be led from hence to the gaol from whence you came; and on Monday next you are to be drawn on a hurdle to the place of execution; where you are to be burnt with fire until you are dead.' The sentence was carried out at Tyburn in front of some 20,000 spectators on Monday 13 September 1773.

Isabella Condon became the last woman to be burned at Tyburn. Her indictment read as follows: 'For that, one piece of false, feigned, and counterfeit money, to the likeness and similitude of the current coin of this realm called a shilling, she did feloniously, traitorously, and against the duty of her allegiance, falsely make, forge, and coin.' She was put to death on 27 October 1779.

The last woman to be burned for petty treason murder of her husband was Mary Bailey at Winchester, on Monday 8 March 1784. Her co-accused, John Quinn, was hanged first. The last three burnings in England were all for coining offences and took place at Newgate prison, these being Phoebe Harris on Wednesday 21 June 1786, Margaret Sullivan on Wednesday 25 June 1788 and Catherine Murphy (also known as Christian Bowman) who died on Wednesday 18 March 1789.

Phoebe Harris was to be the first woman burned at Newgate, as distinct from Tyburn or Smithfield, and her execution was carried out just after 8am on Wednesday 21 June 1786. A huge crowd, estimated at some 20,000 people, had turned out to watch.At 7.30am six men – Edward Griffiths, George Woodward, William Watts, Daniel Keefe, Jonathan Harwood and William Smith – were brought out through Newgate's

Debtors' Door and led up onto the gallows. They were prepared in the usual way and the drop reportedly fell around 8am. After they were suspended, Phoebe was led from the Debtors' Door by two sheriff's officers to a stake that had been erected halfway between the gallows and Newgate Street. This was some 11 feet high and had a metal bracket at the top from which a noose dangled. Phoebe was described as 'a well made little woman of something more than thirty years of age, with a pale complexion and not disagreeable features'. She was reported to be terrified and trembling as she was led out. Phoebe mounted a stool, the noose was placed around her neck and she was allowed a few moments to pray with the Ordinary before her support was removed and she was left suspended. After hanging for half an hour until dead, the executioner put an iron chain around her upper body and fastened it to the stake with nails. Two cart loads of faggots were then piled around the stake and lit. After a while, the fire burnt through the rope and Phoebe's body dropped, remaining attached to the stake by the chain. It took over two hours to be completely consumed by the fire, which continued to burn until midday.

Margaret Sullivan and her co-accused, Jeremiah Grace, came to trial at the May Sessions of the Old Bailey in 1788. They were indicted as follows: 'For that they, on the 29th of April, a piece of base coin resembling the current silver coin of this kingdom, called a shilling, falsely and deceitfully, feloniously and traitorously did colour with materials, producing the colour of silver.' For this crime of high treason, Jeremiah was sentenced to be hanged and Margaret to be burned.

Catherine Murphy's execution on 18 March 1789 was to be the final burning of a woman in England. She was led from the Debtors' Door of Newgate past the nearby gallows from which four men, including her husband, were already hanging, to the stake. Her execution was similar to Phoebe Harris' described above.

On 10 May 1790, Sir Benjamin Hammett raised the issue of burning women in the House of Commons. He told fellow MPs that it had been his painful office and duty in the previous year to attend the burning of Catherine Murphy, as sheriff of London at the time, and he therefore moved to bring in a Bill to alter the law. He pointed out that the sheriff who refused to execute a sentence of burning alive was liable to prosecution, but thanked Heaven that there was not a man in England who would carry such a sentence literally into execution (see earlier references to strangling prior to burning). The Treason Act of 1790 was passed and Parliament substituted ordinary hanging for coining offences on 5 June 1790. Sophia Girton, a 25 year old, who had been convicted of coining at the Old Bailey on 24 April 1790, was thus saved from the fire and was in fact pardoned on condition of transportation for life to New South Wales on 12 June 1790. Her co-defendant, Thomas Parker, was hanged on 19 May 1790.

Executions by burning at Newgate were distinctly unpopular with the local residents of what was a respectable business area of the City. They had sent a petition to the Lord Mayor requesting that Phoebe Harris' execution be carried out elsewhere. This was an early version of 'not in my back yard' rather than a protest against the severity of her punishment. It was later reported that some locals became ill from the smoke from her body. There were similar protests over the Sullivan and Murphy executions and a great feeling of relief when Sophia Girton was reprieved, and the whole ghastly business passed into history. Even though by this time the condemned woman was dead before the faggots were lit, it must still have been a gruesome and revolting spectacle and one which conveyed a feeling of injustice. Men convicted of coining offences were hanged in the same way as other condemned males.

The Times newspaper took up this point after Phoebe Harris' burning and printed the following article: 'The execution of a woman for coining on Wednesday morning reflects a scandal upon the law and was not only inhuman, but shamefully indelicate and shocking. Why should the law in this species of offence inflict a severer punishment upon a woman than a man? It is not an offence which she can perpetrate alone – in every such case the insistence of a man has been found the operating motive upon the woman; yet the man is but hanged, and the woman burned.' Other London newspapers carried similar articles. Outrage was expressed again two years later at the burning of Margaret Sullivan, although strangely there was little media interest in Catherine Murphy.

6

English witchcraft executions

Writing in 2009, some 400 years later, it is hard to take seriously some of the accusations made against usually defenceless and poor old women. I do not therefore propose to offer any comment on the validity or fairness of their trials or the confessions that so many of the convictions were based upon. Nor do I seek to explain why certain areas of the country, particularly Essex and East Anglia, had so many more cases than other areas. It is interesting to note there were no witch trials in Wales.

Throughout Europe in the 16th and 17th centuries particularly, people certainly did believe in the power of witchcraft and this belief continued into the 19th century. Witch persecutions were prevalent at this time, especially in Germany, France and Scotland. Even in the early 19th century, after witchcraft had been effectively decriminalised, many still believed in it. Some thought that Mary Bateman, the murderous 'Yorkshire Witch' would be able to save herself by flying off the gallows at York in 1809. The people of Leeds had not wished to report her criminal activities to the authorities in case she put a spell on them. Witchcraft was a convenient scapegoat for unexplained illness and sudden deaths amongst people and livestock at a time when the medical profession did not have the knowledge to ascertain the proper causes of these.

It is estimated that fewer than 500 people were executed in England for witchcraft between 1566 and 1684, and that just six were put to death between 1066 and 1560. Of these six, only one is confirmed as having been burned at the stake, this being Margery Jordemaine on 27 October 1441. Margery was known as the 'Witch of Eye' and was convicted of treason for using sorcery to attempt to cause the death of Henry VI. She was executed at Smithfield. Three weeks later Roger Bolingbroke was executed for the same offence by hanging, drawing and quartering at Tyburn, these being the normal punishments for treason.

Henry VIII introduced a Witchcraft Act in 1542 which defined witchcraft as felony rather than a religious offence. It was to be tried by the normal Assize Courts and was punishable, like all other normal felonies of the time, with a maximum penalty of death by hanging. Burning at the stake was not permitted by this Act. Torture to obtain confession was prohibited.

The Act stated: 'It shall be felony to practise or cause to be practised conjuration, witchcraft, enchantment or sorcery, to get money; or to consume any person in his body, members or goods; or to provoke any person to unlawful love; or for the despight of Christ, or lucre of money, to pull down any Cross; or to declare where goods stolen be.'

Henry's statute was abolished just five years later by his son Edward VI and it is unclear whether anybody was actually executed in the intervening period. Elizabeth I passed a new Witchcraft Act in 1563 which came into force on 1 June that year. This Act specified a year's imprisonment plus pillorying on four occasions during the year for a first offence, with death by hanging for a second offence unless the person was convicted of murder by witchcraft, in which case the death sentence was mandatory.

The first recorded person to suffer under this Act was 64-year-old Agnes Waterhouse from the village of Hatfield Peverel, near Chelmsford in Essex, who confessed to murder by witchcraft. Agnes was tried at Chelmsford Assizes on 26 July 1566, along with her 18-year-old daughter Joan and one Elizabeth Francis. Agnes pleaded guilty, Joan was acquitted and Elizabeth convicted, being sentenced to the year in prison with pillorying. She was duly released but arrested and charged with witchcraft again in 1579. As it was her second conviction she was hanged.

There were 22 witchcraft trials at Chelmsford in 1579. One of the accused was Elizabeth Francis (see above) who confessed to being a witch and witching Alice Poole. Ellen Smith (or Smyth) from Malden was convicted of witching a 4-year-old child to death and was also hanged. A third woman to suffer was Alice Nokes of Lambourne who had been convicted of witching to death Elizabeth Barsett (or Barfoot). Richard and Joan Prestmary from Great Dunmow were convicted and condemned, but it seems that their sentences were not carried out.

The trial of the St Osyth witches was held at Chelmsford in 1582. St Osyth is a village near Brightlingsea, Essex. Fourteen women from the village were charged with witchcraft, of whom ten were charged with the capital felony of bewitching to death. Of these fourteen, two were not indicted, two were remanded to prison to face other charges, four were acquitted and four were convicted, sentenced to death but later reprieved. Just two of the defendants were to hang. They were Ursula Kempe and Elizabeth Bennet. They were duly executed at Chelmsford and their bodies returned to St Osyth for burial. In 1921, two female skeletons were discovered there who had had metal nails driven into their elbow and knee joints. This was believed at the time to be a way of preventing witches rising from the grave. Whether these were the skeletons of Ursula Kempe and Elizabeth Bennet is open to question.

In the year 1589, 31 women and six men were tried for witchcraft at Chelmsford Assizes. A triple hanging took place at Primrose Hill, Rainsford Lane, Chelmsford, when Joan Coney, Joan Upney (also given as Uptney) and Joan Prentice were executed a mere two hours after sentence. Joan Coney from Stisted was convicted of one murder by witching plus three instances where her victim became seriously ill. Joan Upney from Dagenham was convicted of the witching murders of Joan Harwood and Alice Foster. Joan Prentice from Sible Hedingham confessed to consorting with the devil, in the form of a ferret, which she had commanded to nip Sara Glascock who later died. A woodcut picture exists showing the three women hanging side by side from a simple gallows surrounded by cats or ferrets. It is unclear whether they were turned off ladders or the back of a cart.

In 1603, James VI of Scotland became James I of England on the death of Elizabeth I, thus uniting the kingdoms of England and Scotland. King James was very interested in witchcraft and took part in witch trials in Scotland. His statute of 1604 strengthened the law in England and made hanging mandatory for those convicted of witchcraft where the supposed victim was only injured rather than died. Strangely he did not introduce burning at the stake as was the Scottish practice.

The 'Witchfinder General'

Matthew Hopkins was the best-known witchfinder in England. The self-appointed 'Witchfinder General' lived at Manningtree in Essex and in the period from 1645 to 1647 set out to eradicate witchcraft in East Anglia with great zeal. He was assisted in this by John Stearne (or Sterne) and Mary Phillips. Estimates vary as to the number of witches that Hopkins and Stearne discovered from between 200 and 300. It is thought that he was born around 1620 and was the son of a church minister. He was an educated man who had some grasp of the law. Hopkins started his career in his home town of Manningtree accusing an elderly spinster called Elizabeth Clarke of witchcraft.

Thirty people, including those from Manningtree, were arraigned for this offence at the 1645 Essex Assizes at Chelmsford. Fourteen were to hang at Chelmsford on Friday 25 July. They were a Mrs Wayt, Jane Brigs, Jane Browne, Rachel Flower, Mary Greene, Mary Foster, Frances Jones, Mary Rhodes, Anne West, Mother Forman, Mother Clarke, Mother Miller, Mother Benefield and Mother Goodwin. The other five women were to be returned to Manningtree for execution and the hanging is thought to have taken place on the South Street Green there on 29 July 1645. In fact only four were to hang because Margaret Moone collapsed on the way to the gallows and is reputed to have cried out that the 'Devil had often told her she should never be hanged' with her dying breath.

Hopkins brought another group of witches to trial at the Suffolk Assizes at Bury St Edmunds the following month, resulting in the executions of 16 women and two men. His campaign continued into Norfolk, Cambridgeshire, Huntingdonshire, Bedfordshire and Northamptonshire.

Obtaining confessions by torture was illegal, so Hopkins and Stearne had to resort to other methods that were at least semi-legal and did not involve bloodshed. One was watching. The accused was stripped naked and examined, usually by Mary Phillips, for 'witch marks' such as a third nipple, then dressed in a loose shift and made to sit on a stool in the middle of the room watched round the clock to see if familiars or imps would come and suckle blood from them. When the victim dozed off their watchers would immediately rouse them and walk them around the room till they were fully awake again. This watching and walking could go on for several days and the victims became absolutely exhausted from sleep deprivation and would often confess.

Another method used was swimming. The accused was trussed up with the left thumb tied to the right big toe and right thumb to the left big toe and then lowered into water. If the person floated they were guilty because the Devil had saved them, whereas if they sank they were innocent. The small problem of their drowning didn't seem to bother Hopkins because he knew that the person would go straight to Heaven. Another method used in interrogation was pricking of the body to try and find any area of skin that did not cause the person to cry out. This area was where the witch's familiars sucked their blood from, according to Hopkins. Hopkins earned 20 shillings (£1) per witch, so he had a very lucrative business for the time. In 1647, shortly before his death, he published a pamphlet entitled *The Discovery of Witches*. He is thought to have died of tuberculosis later that year.

Although the persecution of witches was most widespread in East Anglia, it occurred in other parts of the country as well. One of the most famous cases was that of the Pendle Witches in Lancashire. A group of thirteen people living in and around the Forest of Pendle were accused of the murder by the witching of ten people. Twelve were tried at the Assizes at Lancaster Castle between 17 and 19 August 1612. Of these, ten were to be hanged on Lancaster Moor on 20 August. They were Elizabeth Device, her son James and daughter Alison (also Alizon), Anne Whittle, (aka Chattox), Anne Redferne, Alice Nutter, Katherine Hewitt, Jane Bulcock, her son John Bulcock and Isobel Robey. Elizabeth Southerns, who was also known as Old Demdike and was considered originally to be the ringleader of the group, died in prison. A thirteenth member of the group, Jennet Preston, was tried and hanged at York and Margaret Pearson was given a one-year prison sentence. Much of the evidence against them was given by 9-year-old Janet Device who was later to be tried and imprisoned for witchcraft. The Clerk of the Court, Thomas Potts, recorded the proceedings and later published a book on the case, entitled *The Wonderful Discoverie of Witches in the Countie of Lancaster*.

In Kent, Joan Cariden, Jane Holt and Joan Williford were hanged at Faversham on 29 September 1645. A further seven women were to hang for witchcraft at Penenden Heath near Maidstone in Kent on 30 July 1652. They were Mildred Wright, Anne Wilson, Mary Reade, Anne Ashby, Anne Martyn, Mary Browne and Elizabeth Hynes.

The number of trials and executions began to decline after the Restoration of the Monarchy in 1660. It is probable, but it cannot be confirmed, that Alice Molland was the last person to hang for witchcraft in England, at Heavitree near Exeter in 1684. The last confirmed executions were those of the 'Bideford Witches' also at Heavitree on 25 August 1682. They were three old women called Temperance Lloyd, Susannah Edwards and Mary Trembles. They had been convicted of bringing illness upon their neighbours. However, people were still charged with the offence. Jane Wenham of Walkern in Herefordshire became the last person to be convicted of witchcraft in England in 1712. She was condemned to death but reprieved. Jane Clerk, together with her son and daughter, was charged with witchcraft at Leicester in 1717, but the case against them was thrown out by the judge.

In 1736, a new Witchcraft Act was introduced in the reign of George II that read as follows: 'An Act to repeal the Statute made in the First Year of the Reign of King James the First, intituled, An Act against Conjuration, Witchcraft, and dealing with evil and wicked Spirits, except so much thereof as repeals an Act of the Fifth Year of the Reign of Queen Elizabeth, Against Conjurations, Inchantments, and Witchcrafts, and to repeal an Act passed in the Parliament of Scotland in the Ninth Parliament of Queen Mary, intituled, Anentis Witchcrafts, and for punishing such Persons as pretend to exercise or use any kind of Witchcraft, Sorcery, Inchantment, or Conjuration.'

This Act, which came into force on 24 June 1736, was aimed at those who pretended to be able to procure spirits, in other words, charlatans such as some fortune tellers and mediums. The punishment, upon conviction, was one year in prison plus quarterly exposure in the pillory for one hour on each occasion.

Scottish witchcraft executions

The situation in Scotland was different from that in England because witchcraft was deemed to be a quasi-religious crime, more akin to heresy, rather than an ordinary felony. Although the population of Scotland was far smaller, over 3,800 people were tried for witchcraft and as many as 1,500 people put to death between 1537 and 1722, compared to fewer than 500 executions in England.

A new Witchcraft Act was introduced in Scotland on 4 June 1563 in the reign of Mary Queen of Scots and remained in force until abolished by the 1736 Act (see above). Being a witch or consorting with witches was proscribed by this Act. Mary perceived witchcraft as a form of religious heresy and thus the punishment was strangulation at the stake followed by burning of the unconscious or dead body for both sexes. However, burning alive without strangulation could be ordered and there are credible records of this occurring. Additionally three people were beheaded for witchcraft – a man in 1613 and two women in 1614 – and there are one or two cases where the person is recorded as being hanged only.

There were three major witch hunt periods in Scotland. These were in the 1590s, under James IV, in the 1640s and finally in the 1660s. The last execution (see later) was carried out in 1727, some 43 years after the last English one. Burning at the stake was a rather expensive punishment as it required a considerable amount of materials that by definition could not be reused. Accounts exist to show that a burning could cost five to six pounds in the 17th century. Tar barrels were often used to place the unfortunate victim in and aid combustion. These are mentioned in some of the costed accounts.

One of the first recorded witch burnings took place at Castle Hill, Edinburgh, in 1479. James III's brother, the Earl of Mar, was accused of treason and sorcery against the king and was killed in his home without a trial. Twelve female witches and four male wizards were then hastily convicted and burned for their alleged parts in the conspiracy. The next documented burning took place on 17 July 1537 when Janet Douglas, Lady Glamis, was put to death on Castle Hill, Edinburgh, having been convicted of conspiring to poison James V. The charges against Janet, her husband and her son were trumped up for political reasons by the King. Her servants were tortured into giving incriminating evidence against them. Janet is still said to haunt Glamis Castle and her ghost is known as the 'Grey Lady'.

The records of the High Court of Justiciary show that one Janet Bowman was burned at Edinburgh in 1572 and a Bessie Dunlop four years later. In all, some 300 women shared Janet's fate on Edinburgh's Castle Hill and there is an iron fountain, the 'Witches Well', at the entrance to the Castle Esplanade commemorating their grisly fate.

One of the most famous Scottish cases was the North Berwickshire witch trials which took place in 1590/1. David Seaton, a deputy bailiff at

Tranent, a small town near Edinburgh, suspected one of his servants, a young girl called Gellie Duncan, of witchcraft. Gellie claimed to have some healing powers which certainly cast suspicion on her in the minds of some. Under questioning, she implicated many others and some 70 people in total were accused, including Francis, Earl of Bothwell; Dame Euphemia Macalzean (also given as McLean), who was the daughter of Lord Cliftonhall; a Dr John Fian (or Cunningham); Richard Graham; Barbara Napier; and Agnes Sampson. King James actually took part in the interrogation of the suspects and Agnes Sampson was questioned by him at Holyrood.

The Earl of Bothwell managed to flee the country and Barbara Napier, although condemned, pleaded pregnancy thus saving herself from the stake. The others were executed. Euphemia Macalzean was burned alive, without the mercy of strangulation, on the express order of the king on 25 June 1591. She was quite a wealthy woman and her estate was confiscated by the Crown. It is claimed by some writers that Gellie was hanged rather than burned at the stake, although in reality she was probably hanged and then burned. The alleged crime committed by the North Berwickshire witches was that they had conspired to cause the wreck of the ship bringing King James back from Denmark with his new bride to be, Anne, a Danish princess. The couple had by all accounts a very rough crossing from Denmark but did survive the voyage. James IV became obsessed by witchcraft and wrote a book on the subject, entitled *Daemonologie* in 1599.

The period from February 1597 to April 1597 saw the Aberdeen witch trials which resulted in the executions of 23 women and one man at Heading Hill by hanging and then burning. One of these women was Janet Wishart, 'Old Janet', convicted of the witching murder of James Lowe who had refused Janet the use of his barn. He accused Janet of killing him on his deathbed.

On 18 May 1671, Janet McMuldroche and Elspeth Thompson were strangled and burned at Dumfries. The following are the words of the warrant for their execution, dated two days earlier: 'Forsamuch as in ane court of Justiciarie holden be us within the Tolbuithe of drumfreis vpon the fyftein day of May instant Jonet McMuldroche and Elspeth Thomsone were found guiltie be ane ascyse of the se[ver]all articles of witchcraft spe[cif]it in the verdict given againest them theiranent Were decerned and adjudged be us the Lords Commissioners of Justiciarie to be tane vpon thursday next the eighteen day of May instant Betuixt tuo and foure houres in the afernoone to the ordinare place of executione the toune of drumfreis And their to be wirried at ane stake till they be dead And theirafter their bodies to be brunt to ashes And all their moveable goods and geir to be escheat.' (note: 'wirried' means strangled and 'escheat' means confiscated.)

The last person to be burned as a witch in Scotland was Janet Horne at Dornoch in Ross-shire in 1727. Janet had been accused of witching her daughter to make her hands and feet grow into horses' hooves, so that she could ride her. The daughter had a deformed hand, due to being 'shod by the Devil'! She was also tried but acquitted and later had a child who exhibited the same kind of congenital hand deformity.

A stone at the place of execution commemorates her death.

Witchfinders were also active in Scotland. John Kincaid, John Bain, John Dick and James Welsh were four of the most notable ones. They were known as 'common prickers' and would search women for the Devil's marks and prove their guilt by pricking the suspect mark. If the woman showed no reaction to the pin piercing her skin and the wound did not bleed she was guilty. John Dick and John Kincaid were later convicted of fraud and deceit, and James Welsh was flogged in Edinburgh for making a false accusation.

7

The Halifax Gibbet and the Scottish Maiden

One associates the guillotine with France and the French Revolution, but mechanised beheading had been going for several centuries previously in Britain. In Ireland there is record of a guillotine-like machine being used in 1307 for the execution of Murcod Ballagh. In England, the Yorkshire town of Halifax was unique in using decapitation as its sole form of capital punishment.

It is thought that Henry III granted permission to John de Warren, the lord of the manor, to carry out executions in 1286. John of Dalton became the first to die on a machine in the town in this year. It is unclear why it was invented, as hanging seemed to work perfectly well everywhere else in the country. One legend has it that Halifax could not find a hangman and so an execution engine operated by the community itself solved the problem. Initially the rope holding the axe had to be held by all those present. A further 10 executions are recorded between 1298 and 1505, although there is no means of knowing whether these were the only ones. Between 1541 and 1650, there are reliable records of 52 decapitations on the machine, which became known as the Halifax Gibbet.

The economy of Halifax was founded on the production of woollen cloth, and protecting this valuable commodity, known as the 'staple', from theft was of great local importance. The staple was washed and put out to dry on tent frames surrounding the town from where it could easily be stolen. In 1541, a law came into force which specified death by decapitation for theft of goods or animals in the parish of Halifax worth more than 13½ (old) pence or about 6p. The law was worded thus: 'If a felon be taken within the liberty of Halifax... either hand-habend (caught with the stolen goods in their hand or in the act of stealing), back-berand (carrying the stolen goods on their back), or confessand (having confessed to the crime), to the value of thirteen pence half-penny, he shall after three markets be taken to the Gibbet and there have his head cut off from his body.' Markets were held on Tuesdays, Thursdays and Saturdays (the main market day) and as Saturday was the third market of the week it was also the execution day. The practice of having executions on market day was common so that the greatest number of people could be deterred by them. The person was tried by the magistrate and the value of the goods allegedly stolen was assessed by four constables to see whether it amounted to 13½ pence. If so, they were condemned, provided that their conviction met the three other criteria above.

On 15 January 1539, the execution of Charles Haworth is recorded, and just over two years later, on 20 March 1541, Richard Beverley of Sowerby became the next. A further 44 men and six women were to follow him up the stone steps. The last two executions were carried out on 30 April 1650 when John Wilkinson and Anthony Mitchell were beheaded for the theft of 16 yards of cloth and two horses. They were executed on the day of their trial as it was a Saturday. After this the Halifax Gibbet fell into disrepair, although its stone base remained and the axe head was kept and is now preserved. The gibbet originally stood at Cow Green but was later moved nearer the town to a place that came to be called after it, Gibbet Street. This site was rediscovered in 1869 during excavations, along with the remains of two decapitated bodies, thought to be those of Wilkinson and Mitchell. There is an inscribed stone tablet detailing the gibbet at Shibden Hall, Halifax.

The machine stood on a thirteen feet square stone base some 4 feet high, reached by five stone steps. At one end were two wooden uprights of about 15 feet in height with a cross beam supporting a pulley. The pulley was attached by means of a rope 4' 6" high to a heavy wooden block that ran in grooves in the uprights and held an axe blade in its base. The blade weighs 7¾ lbs (17 kg) and is 10½" long, 7" wide at the top and 9" wide at the bottom. The rope was brought down to a pin at the corner of the stone platform furthest from the prisoner. When the pin was pulled out the blade was released and fell some 10 feet onto the neck of the condemned person who was lying over a wooden block set between the uprights.

Where the person being executed had stolen goods, as stated earlier, the blade was originally released by members of the community holding the rope. Where the person had been convicted of stealing an animal, it is claimed that the animal itself had the rope tied to it and then it was driven away from the structure thus releasing the pin.

It was possible to escape death on the machine if one was very quick and agile. If the condemned could get up and run as the blade was falling and get to Hebble Brook they were safe, but could never return to Halifax. In 1617, John Lacy achieved the feat, but foolishly thought that he would be pardoned having escaped and returned to Halifax in 1623. He was recognised and arrested, having his original sentence carried out on the same day, 29 January 1623. A pub called The Running Man in Pellon Lane commemorates Lacy's escape.

The contemporary 17th century poet John Taylor in 1622 penned the famous lines in his Beggar's Litany, 'From Hull, Hell and Halifax, Good Lord deliver us!' Apparently in Hull at the time there were very strict laws on begging, Halifax had the gibbet and in Hell he presumably imagined fire and eternal damnation. Not everyone shared Taylor's view of the Halifax Gibbet, though. The Regent of Scotland, James Douglas the 4th Earl of Morton, travelled through the town and witnessed a beheading on the machine. He was so impressed that he had a similar machine constructed for use in Scotland, which became known as the Maiden, apparently because its shape was similar to a contemporary clothes horse known by that name.

This machine was in use from 1564 to 1708 to replace manual beheading for those of high birth rather than thieves as in Halifax. It had more than 120 customers, including the Earl of Morton himself. It was somewhat different to the Halifax version in that the condemned person knelt and bent their neck over the block, rather than lying flat on the block. The Maiden can be seen in the Museum of Scotland at Edinburgh. The uprights house the sliding block and blade and are braced to the sides of the base and to the back of the machine at its base by a heavy pole. The iron blade is 13" tall by 10½" wide, weighted with a 75 lb block of lead, sliding in copper-lined grooves cut into the uprights. Again the blade is attached to a rope which was released by a lever on the back bracing pole. Contemporary woodcut illustrations show the Maiden was erected on a low wooden scaffold.

It is thought that the first persons to be decapitated by this device were several of the lower ranking murderers of Queen Mary's secretary, David Rizzio, on 9 March 1566. The killing is thought to have been at the instigation of her second husband, Henry Stewart, Lord Darnley. When

Mary Queen of Scots was forced to leave Scotland in 1567, her 1-year-old son James VI was crowned king. Scotland was therefore governed by a series of four Regents appointed by Parliament. James Douglas, Earl of Morton, was the last of these. It was the most powerful position in the country, but tended to be one that made enemies. The Earl of Morton was decapitated by the Maiden for treason on 2 June 1581 for his alleged part in the murder of James' father, Lord Darnley. Morton's severed head was placed on a spike on the Tollbooth in Edinburgh.

Several other famous persons were to be executed by the Maiden. At 4am on 5 July 1600, Jean Livingstone, Lady Warriston, was decapitated for the murder of her husband John. She was 21 years old and had persuaded her servants to carry out the actual killing in revenge for the abuse she had suffered at his hands. The murder had taken place just three days earlier, Jean being arrested at the scene with her nurse Janet Murdo and an unnamed female servant. All three were convicted after a brief trial and sentenced to be strangled and then burned at the stake. On account of her high birth, Jean's sentence was commuted to decapitation. In her few days in prison Jean confessed and repented her sins. Her family were ashamed of her crime and petitioned the authorities to bring the execution forward to the unusually early hour. Jean met her death with great courage and confessed her crime from each corner of the scaffold before submitting to the blade. Her execution took place at the Girth Cross of Holyrood in Edinburgh. Janet Murdo and the servant woman were less fortunate and were made to suffer their original sentence on Castle Hill on the same day. Because of her beauty, courage and youth Jean rapidly became romanticised in ballads. Whether these are factual we cannot know, but it seems everybody enjoyed this particular murder story.

Sir John Gordon, the 1st Baronet of Haddo, was beheaded at the Mercat (Market) Cross in Edinburgh for treason on 19 July 1644. Gordon was a Royalist, supporting Charles I during the Wars of the Three Kingdoms for which he received the Baronetcy in 1642. He was captured by Covenanters under the Marquis of Argyll in May 1644 and taken to Edinburgh where he was held in St Giles' Cathedral in what became known as 'Haddo's Hole' prior to his execution. The Covenanters were those who signed the National Covenant in 1638 confirming their opposition to the interference by the Stuart kings in the Presbyterian Church of Scotland.

Sir Robert Spottiswood was the second son of John Spottiswood who had been Archbishop of St Andrews and Primate of Scotland from 1615 and Lord Chancellor of Scotland from 1635 to 1638. Robert became a lawyer and was later appointed a judge. He was captured at the battle of Philiphaugh on 13 September 1645 and tried for appointing the Marquis of Montrose Lieutenant Governor of Scotland and for having taken part in the battle. Also captured were Colonel Nathaniel Gordon, the Hon. William Murray and Captain Cuthrie. All three were found guilty of treason for not withdrawing from the Covenant, which had been made a capital crime by an Act of 1644. Sir Robert's execution took place at the Market Cross at St Andrews on 16 January 1646. He was denied the opportunity to speak on the Maiden and threw his prepared speech into the crowd.

The Marquis of Argyll, Archibald Campbell, was put to death at Edinburgh on 27 May 1661. Campbell was convicted of treason for collaborating with Oliver Cromwell's government. His head was also displayed on a spike on the Tollbooth. Campbell's son, also Archibald, the 9th Earl of Argyll, shared his fate on the Maiden on 30 June 1685. He had led a rebellion against James VII and at the place of execution told the witnesses: 'I die not only a Protestant, but with a heart-hatred of popery, prelacy, and all superstition whatever.'

Lady Christian Nimmo was married to a wealthy merchant and suffered on the Maiden at the Mercat Cross in Edinburgh on 12 November 1679. She had been convicted of the murder of James Baillie, Lord Forrester, who was both her uncle by marriage and her lover. On 26 August 1679, James had gone to the Black Bull pub in the then village of Corstorphine (now a suburb of Edinburgh) and failed to make his appointment with Lady Christian. Angry, she sent a servant to the pub to fetch him, which in turn angered him. They quarrelled and Lady Christian stabbed him with his sword. She was arrested and pleaded that the death was accidental at her trial two days later, but this was not accepted and she was condemned for the murder. As many women did in this situation, she also 'pleaded her belly'. An examination by a panel of matrons dismissed this claim. She managed to escape from the Tollbooth prison disguised as a man but was soon recaptured. There was to be no second escape and her sentence was carried out. She reportedly wore a white dress with a white hood for her execution. Her ghost, known as the 'White Lady', is said to haunt Corstorphine at the spot where the couple used to meet beneath a dovecote and sycamore tree.

The Newgate Calendar records an execution on the Maiden in 1716 when John Hamilton was beheaded on 30 June of that year for the murder of Thomas Arkle, an innkeeper, in a quarrel over Hamilton's bill. As most historians give 1708 as the last year in which the Maiden was used, this execution is questionable; either the date or the method used may be incorrect.

8

On Tyburn Tree

Returning to the capital after our excursion to the North of England and Scotland, we find things were very much business as usual at London's Tyburn. The famous 'Triple Tree' gallows was set up at Tyburn in 1571, consisting of three tall uprights (approximately 12-18 feet high) joined at the top with three beams to form a triangle under which three carts could be backed at a time.

In 1605, Robert Dowe gave £50 for the ringing of the great bell of St Sepulchre's Church in Giltspur Street opposite Newgate prison on the mornings of executions and for other services concerning condemned prisoners, including the ringing of a hand-bell at midnight outside the condemned cell. For this 'service' a bellman was employed who entered Newgate via a tunnel between the church and the prison. On the night before a 'Hanging Day' he had to stand outside the Condemned Hold and give 'twelve solemn towles with double strokes' of a hand-bell and then recite the following:

> 'All you that in the condemned hold do lie,
> Prepare you, for tomorrow you shall die;
> Watch all and pray, the hour is drawing near
> That you before the Almighty must appear;
> Examine well yourselves, in time repent,
> That you may not to eternal flames be sent:
> And when St Sepulchre's bell tomorrow tolls,
> The Lord above have mercy on your souls.
> Past twelve o'clock!'

One somehow cannot imagine that this exhortation made the prisoners feel better about the events of the morrow. The hand-bell was preserved and is still on display in St Sepulchre's Church. Although a macabre ritual, it does show the importance the Church attached to repentance, a concept which continued well into the 20th century.

The largest ever mass execution at Tyburn took place on 23 June 1649 when 23 men and one woman were hanged for burglary and robbery, having been conveyed there in eight carts. On Sunday 2 September 1666, the Great Fire of London began, burning for three days before being finally extinguished on the Wednesday. People sometimes confess to high-profile crimes they did not commit and one Robert Hubert, a watchmaker from Rouen in France, did just that. Initially he claimed that he started the fire in Westminster, but when it was pointed out to him that the fire never reached there he changed his story and claimed that he firebombed the baker's shop in Pudding Lane. There was little or no evidence that the fire was anything other than an accident, although many people were ready to believe it was arson. So on the strength of his confession Hubert was hanged at Tyburn on 28 September 1666, even though he had not arrived in London until the Tuesday, two days after the fire started – it is amazing what some people will do to get themselves hanged! Hubert provided a convenient scapegoat for the authorities. Such was the level of public feeling that his body was torn apart by the crowd when it was taken down.

There is much made of highwaymen in folklore and there are a few individuals who stand out. Although Dick Turpin is probably the most well-known (see later), Claude Du Val or Duvall best epitomises the image of the daring, chivalrous highwayman. This gentleman also came from Rouen in France and is thought to have arrived in Britain in 1660. Du Val worked around London in places like Holloway and Blackheath and was known as the gentleman highwayman because of his chivalrous treatment of the ladies and forbearance of violence. Arrested whilst drunk at the Hole in the Wall pub in Chandos Street, London, he was allegedly visited by many ladies whilst awaiting his fate in Newgate. The Newgate Calendar tells us that his hanging at Tyburn on Friday 21 January 1670 was attended by 'ladies of quality' holding masks in the hope of remaining incognito. He is said to have died bravely, if only to please them, and afterwards was carried away from Tyburn in a mourning coach to lie in state overnight before being buried in Covent Garden under a white marble gravestone. The 27-year-old Du Val typifies the strange attitude of the time towards some criminals.

Although a notorious highwayman, there were considerable efforts made to get a reprieve for him and he was treated more like a folk hero than a common criminal when these failed.

Sessions, as London trials were known, were held at the Old Bailey, typically eight times a year. Death sentences were passed at the end of these trials and those condemned were returned to Newgate to await the outcome of the Recorder's Report to the King and the Privy Council who would decide their fate. Potentially there could be eight 'Hanging Days' at Tyburn to correspond with the Sessions, but in reality there were usually fewer, pre-1752. Sometimes if there were only a small number of death sentences at a particular Sessions, those not reprieved were held over for execution until after the following Sessions, presumably to make an economically viable group. One wonders also if the weather in January was often too poor to enable the journey to Tyburn.

Benefit of Clergy, touched on in earlier chapters, had developed into a legal loophole that saved many from the gallows, particularly first-time offenders. It was extended to women in 1624 and equalised between the sexes in 1691. The literacy test, typically reading from the 51st Psalm was abolished in 1706. However, its use was being progressively limited as a response to rising crime at this time. It was removed by the Robbery Act of 1691 for robberies of 5 shillings or more from a dwelling house, warehouse or shop. The Shoplifting Act of 1699 defined shoplifting to the value of 5 shillings (25 pence) as a capital crime without Benefit of Clergy. It was up to the jury to decide whether the goods allegedly stolen were worth 5 shillings or more, and it was not unknown for them to decide that they were not, despite evidence to the contrary.

The Larceny in a Dwelling House Act of 1713 removed Benefit of Clergy for stealing from a dwelling house or outhouse to the value of 40 shillings (£2). Sheep and cattle theft similarly ceased to enjoy this Benefit. The Riot Act of 1714 came into force on 1 August 1715. It was fully titled 'An Act for preventing tumults and riotous assemblies, and for the more speedy and effectual punishing the rioters'. Rioting that caused serious damage to churches, houses, barns and stables was henceforth to be punishable by death and be without Benefit of Clergy. Where a group of 12 or more persons were deemed to be behaving in a riotous fashion a Justice of the Peace read the Riot Act to them and ordered them to disperse. If they had not dispersed within one hour then force could be used and arrests made. In the next chapter we will look at the treatment of the Gordon Rioters. The last use of this Act was in Glasgow in 1919 and it was not abolished until 1973.

In the decade 1705–1714, a total of 446 death sentences were passed at the Old Bailey on 280 men, 112 women and 54 people whose sex was not recorded. Of these, 142 men, 36 women and possibly three others were subsequently hanged at Tyburn and one woman burned at the stake. This gave an overall reprieve rate of 59.87% – 49.29% of men being reprieved and 66.97% of women. Reprieve rates are based upon executions at Tyburn only. Six men and a woman were hanged in other locations and one woman burned at Smithfield.

Those not reprieved would be kept in the Condemned Hold of Newgate in abysmal conditions and it was not unusual for one or two to die of gaol fever or other illnesses before the next 'Hanging Day'. Something else they had to look forward to was the preaching of the condemned sermon on the Sunday prior to execution. They were given a separate area in the centre of the chapel with a coffin sitting on the table in front of them and subjected to pious exhortations by the Ordinary in the hope of saving their souls.

During the decade 1715–1724, 751 death sentences were passed on 587 men and 164 women. Of these 327 men and 24 women were put to death. The overall reprieve rate was 56.4%, with 44.3% of men and 85.37% of women being spared. Highway robbery was the most common offence for which people were actually executed, accounting for 104 of these 351 executions. Housebreaking came second with 89 executions, followed by burglary and stealing in a dwelling house with 45 hangings. Murderers accounted for just 26 executions. It should be noted that many of the cases of highway robbery amounted to no more than we would call street mugging today. In other words, the criminal had robbed a person on the King's highway, using force or the threat of force to obtain their valuables. A few of those hanged conformed to the traditional image of the highwayman on his horse holding a brace of pistols; a few were members of organised gangs; many were just opportunist muggers.

It is perhaps worth taking a moment to explain some of the other capital offences of the day whose names have long since disappeared from common usage. Privately stealing from a person is basically picking pockets, and by definition does not involve the use of force but rather the employment of stealth and nimble fingers. Robbery in a dwelling house (or shop or brothel) implies the use of violence or threat of it, whilst stealing in a dwelling house or shop is carried out without either forcible entry or violence (or threat of it) towards the occupants. Scams were often used to gain entry and then to distract attention whilst the criminal pocketed valuables. Stealing in a shop is the equivalent of shoplifting today. Housebreaking implies forcible entry to the premises. Personating was the crime of impersonating another person to gain pecuniary advantage. Uttering was the crime of passing forged bank notes or coins, wills, Letters of Attorney, etc.

Where women were sentenced to death they often 'pleaded their belly' i.e. that they were pregnant. The judge would order that they were examined by a panel of matrons and if found to be 'quick with child' they were respited until after they had given birth. If not 'quick' they could be hanged. Most of those respited were later reprieved, although in some cases, eg 31-year-old Deborah Churchill, they were called to former judgement and subsequently executed. She was hanged on 17 December 1708, having been originally condemned at the February Sessions of that year. The panel of matrons could not be sure whether she was or wasn't pregnant so she was respited for six months to make certain. She had been convicted of being an accessory to murder, despite having tried to prevent the murder by her boyfriend, Richard Hunt, who managed to escape to Holland. Paul Lorrain, the then Ordinary, took her to Tyburn in his coach and prayed with her to the end.

A strange event occurred in 1717. There should have been eight 'Hanging Days' that year and one was planned for Wednesday 6 November when three men were to die. However, William Marvell, London's then hangman, was arrested in Holborn and so the under sheriff asked for a volunteer from the crowd at Tyburn. One man volunteered but was set upon by those round him. In the end these three men had their sentences commuted. Theoretically the under sheriff should have carried out the execution himself, but not everyone had 'the stomach' for such work.

An important development in penal history occurred in 1718 with the passing of the first Transportation Act. Although criminals had been sent into exile abroad prior to this, there was no proper regulation or supervision of the process. The Act allowed prisoners to be sent to the American colonies, particularly Maryland and Virginia, for a period of seven years for lesser, non capital crimes. Condemned felons could be granted a reprieve on condition of transportation for 14 years or life. The convicts were handed over to companies who bore the cost of shipping them and sold them into servitude once they arrived at their destination. It is estimated that some 50,000 people were transported to America up to the outbreak of the American Revolution in 1776, many working on tobacco plantations. The same Act also made returning from transportation before the due time a capital crime.

On 1 June 1723, the 'Black Act' came into force which was defined by The Newgate Calendar as follows: 'After the first day of June, 1723, any person appearing in any forest, chase, park, etc, or in any highroad, open heath, common or down, with offensive weapons, and having his face blacked, or otherwise disguised, or unlawfully and wilfully hunting, wounding, killing or stealing any red or fallow deer, or unlawfully robbing any warren, etc, or stealing any fish out of any river or pond, or (whether armed or disguised or not) breaking down the head or mound of any fishpond, whereby the fish may be lost or destroyed; or unlawfully and maliciously killing, maiming or wounding any cattle, or cutting down or otherwise destroying any trees planted in any avenue, or growing in any garden, orchard or plantation, for ornament, shelter or profit; or setting fire to any house, barn or outhouse, hovel, cock-mow or stack of corn, straw, hay or wood; or maliciously shooting at any person in any dwelling-house or other place; or knowingly sending any letter without any name, or signed with a fictitious name, demanding money, venison or other valuable thing, or forcibly rescuing any person being in custody for any of the offences before mentioned, or procuring any person by gift, or promise of money, or other reward, to join in any such unlawful act, or concealing or succouring such offenders when, by Order of Council, etc, required to surrender, shall suffer death.'

The first to be convicted under its provisions were seven men who were tried at the King's Bench Session which opened on 13 November 1723.

They were Henry Marshall, Edward Elliott, Robert Kingshell, James Ansell, John Pink, Edward Pink, his brother, and Richard Parvin who were convicted of going armed with blackened faces and killing deer in Waltham Forest in Hampshire. These men became known as the 'Waltham Blacks' and were hanged at Tyburn on Wednesday 4 December 1723.

This Act and its subsequent extensions added 50 new capital crimes to the list and saw the start of what became known as 'The Bloody Code'. It also had the effect of depriving the poor of meat, poached at the expense of country landowners. The new laws did not actually lead to an upsurge in executions, which continued to average around 100 per annum in England and Wales, and dropped to an average of 67 per annum in the decade 1760–1769. Not quite the 'bloodbath' scenario that one might be led to believe by some books.

The talk of London in 1724 was the exploits of John Sheppard, better known as Jack Sheppard, who was a professional thief and an amazing escape artist. His forte was burglary, which was the crime for which he was finally convicted at the August 1724 Sessions of the Old Bailey. His first escape, soon after he was arrested, was from St Giles' prison, where he managed to make a hole through the ceiling and get out via the roof space. He was recaptured and taken to Newgate from which he managed to escape three times. On the first occasion he used a file to cut through his irons, made a hole through the wall and then descended to the street using knotted bedclothes. On 30 August he managed to escape from the Condemned Hold by removing a bar from the visitor's window and putting on women's clothes that had been brought in by his common law wife. He was rearrested on 9 September and chained to the floor in the 'Castle' at Newgate, the most secure part of the prison. On 14 October he undid his fetters using a nail then used an iron bar to break out onto the roof and escape. He was recaptured two weeks later and suffered alone at Tyburn on Monday 16 November 1724 before a huge crowd who had come to see the most infamous man in London die. Normally a single prisoner would have been held over until there was a batch to hang, but the authorities had had quite enough of his exploits. A sharp-eyed turnkey decided to search the 22-year-old before he was put into the cart and found a small knife on him with which he had intended to cut the cords binding his arms on the way to Tyburn and escape again. Sheppard became a folk hero and had plays and books written about him. Like Claude Du Val, Sheppard possessed the 'star qualities' that appealed to the 18th century public imagination. He never used violence, was said to be good-looking and faced his end bravely. He continues to be remembered today, a television documentary being made about him recently.

Another leading figure on the London crime scene of the day was the 'Thief Taker General' Jonathan Wild. Wild controlled a large number of criminals whilst at the same time operating as a thief taker. Both were lucrative jobs. He got a reward of £40 for each thief convicted whilst taking control of stolen property and then returning it to its owners for a reward. Where competing gangs or individual thieves would not give up their booty to Wild he informed on them and picked up the reward. He tried to do this with Jack Sheppard, who resisted Wild's advances, but was finally arrested by one of his men, James 'Hell and Fury' Sykes. For some years these scams worked well and Wild was very popular in London as he appeared to be actually doing something about crime. It should be borne in mind that there was no real police force at this time. Wild was attacked and stabbed in the throat in the Old Bailey by one of Sheppard's confederates, Joseph 'Blueskin' Blake, at the end of his trial in 1724. Blake was hanged at Tyburn on Wednesday 11 November 1724. This assault marked the start of Wild's fall from grace. Early in 1725, he was arrested for breaking one of his men out of prison and was also charged with theft. He was tried at the May Sessions of the Old Bailey, charged with 'feloniously receiving of Katherine Stetham the Sum of 10 Guineas, on account of recovering for the said Katherine Stetham 11 pieces of Lace, which had been privately stolen in her Shop by Persons unknown, and not at the same time apprehending, or causing to be apprehended the Felons concern'd in the said Robbery, so that they might be brought to Justice.' He was hanged with three other men on Monday 24 May 1725 amid scenes of public rejoicing at the downfall of this loathsome individual (compare Sheppard's execution). The night before the hanging Wild attempted suicide by drinking laudanum, according to the account of the Ordinary, the Rev Purney, and was not wholly recovered by the time of his execution.

A mass execution took place on 18 March 1741 when the famous pickpocket and thief, Mary Young alias Jenny Diver, was hanged before a huge crowd, together with 20 other criminals who had been condemned at the December 1740 and January and February Sessions of 1741. Mary was another celebrity criminal and hired a mourning coach for the trip to Tyburn. Once there, she joined two other women in the cart. The nickname Jenny Diver came from her ability as a pickpocket. She had previous form for this and had been reprieved to be transported from which she returned early, in itself a capital crime. She was finally caught by her last female victim, aided by passers-by, on 10 January 1741 and charged with the crime of privately stealing. Of these 20 criminals, 18 had been convicted of property crimes, one for forgery and one for returning from transportation.

So what was being hanged at Tyburn actually like at this time? The execution process began at around 7 o'clock in the morning when the condemned men and women would be led in fetters (handcuffs and leg-irons) into the Press Yard in Newgate. Here the blacksmith would remove their irons and the Yeoman of the Halter would tie the criminals' hands in front of them and put a cord around the body and elbows, so that they were able to pray when they reached Tyburn, and place the rope, or halter as it was known, round their necks, coiling the free end round their bodies. The noose was just a slip knot like the halter used on cattle and not the coiled type typically shown in films. When the pinioning was completed, they were placed in open horse-drawn carts, sitting on their coffins.

The procession, consisting of the City marshal, the court officer responsible for prisoners, the Ordinary, the hangman and his assistants, and a troop of javelin men started out for Tyburn about two and a half miles away. A stop was normally made at St Sepulchre's Church where the bell would be tolled and the minister would chant: 'You that are condemned to die, repent with lamentable tears; ask mercy of the Lord for the salvation of your souls.' As the procession passed on, the minister would tell the audience: 'All good people, pray heartily unto God for these poor sinners who are now going to their death, for whom the great bell tolls.' Here friends might present the criminals with small nosegays (bunches of flowers). The carts made their slow and bumpy passage along Holborn, St Giles and the Tyburn Road (now Oxford Street) to Tyburn itself. The narrow streets would be lined with crowds, especially if the criminals were notorious. Stops were made at two public houses along the way, thought to be the Bowl Inn at St Giles and the Mason's Arms in Seymour Place, where the condemned would be allowed an alcoholic drink. Once they left the second pub, it was but a short journey to the gallows.

On arrival at Tyburn around noon, some two to three hours after they had left Newgate, the prisoners were greeted by a large crowd of anything up to 100,000 people who had come to enjoy the spectacle. Amongst the crowd were hawkers selling food and souvenirs, and people selling broadsheets purporting to contain the prisoners' dying speeches and confessions of the condemned. It has often been said that pickpockets were operating among the crowd, despite the fact that it was frequently some of their number who were being hanged.

Wealthier spectators hired seats in Mother Procter's Pews which were open galleries like modern grandstands at a football stadium. A seat with a good view was much sought after and very expensive, costing 2 shillings (10p) which was a lot of money then. The poor just milled round the gallows held back by the javelin men. There was a house overlooking Tyburn, with iron balconies, from which the sheriffs of the City of London and County of Middlesex plus their invited guests watched the executions.

The carts were each backed under one of the three beams of the gallows. The hangman uncoiled the free end of the rope from each prisoner and threw it up to one of his assistants positioned precariously on the beam above. They tied the rope to the beam, leaving very little slack. The Ordinary would pray with the prisoners and when he had finished, the hangman pulled nightcaps over the faces of those who had brought them. As one can imagine, the preparations took quite some time when a large batch of prisoners were being hanged.

When everything was ready and from the signal from the City marshal, the horses were whipped away, pulling the prisoners off the carts and leaving them suspended, swinging like pendulums. They would have only a few inches of drop at most and many would writhe in convulsive agony, their legs kicking and bodies twitching, 'dancing the Tyburn jig' as it was known, until unconsciousness overtook them. The hangman, his assistants and sometimes the prisoners' relatives might pull on their legs to hasten their end.

After half an hour or so, the now lifeless bodies were cut down and claimed by friends and relatives or sent for dissection at Surgeons' Hall. Fights often broke out between the rival parties over possession of the bodies. Prior to the Murder Act of 1752, surgeons were allowed ten bodies per year. Wealthier criminals provided coffins for themselves; the poorer ones often could not afford these and it was not unusual for their friends and relatives to sell their bodies to dissectionists. The clothes of the executed belonged to the hangman; therefore some prisoners wore only their cheapest and oldest clothes, whilst others dressed to look their best for their final performance. It was normal for better-off criminals to wear their best clothes for their 'Hanging Match', as executions were known.

The whole execution was a leisurely and in some ways almost a theatrical process. Time seemed to matter very little, unlike 20th century hangings, and everyone went to enjoy the morbid entertainment. In some cases, even the prisoners seemed to enter into the spirit of the occasion. They were, after all, the stars of the show and behaved with as much courage as they could summon, joking and making speeches from the carts. Others seemed more affected by their situation and prayed fervently at the end with the Ordinary, no doubt afraid of what lay ahead in the afterlife which they would have believed in. It was widely believed at the time that the body of a newly hanged person had healing properties. People would pay the hangman to be allowed to stroke the hands of the executed person across their warts and injuries. From 1702, hangings were reported in the fledgling press, the *Daily Courant* being the first London daily newspaper. The Ordinary's reports of condemned criminals were also available. Crime was a major issue in the capital in the late 1600s and early 1700s and now at least some people could read about it, which did nothing to quell the fears of the property-owning middle classes.

On the night of Saturday 3 February 1733, three women were murdered at the Inns of Court. This was in itself unusual, but all the more so because their assailant was also female. Sarah Malcolm was a 22-year-old servant, but unlike most of her contemporaries she had come from a good background and was literate. She became a laundress and had several customers in the chambers above the Inns of Court, including an old lady named Mrs Duncomb who had a retired maidservant living with her and a younger maidservant looking after them both. The body of the younger woman, 17-year-old Ann Price, bore a stab wound to the throat, whilst Mrs Duncomb and Elizabeth 'Betty' Harrison showed ligature marks.

The motive for the crime was theft. Sarah Malcolm was arrested the next day and came to trial at the February Sessions. She denied the murders and defended herself robustly in court, but to no avail. She was taken back to Newgate and the following day, at the end of the Sessions, returned to court to be sentenced along with nine men. In Sarah's case it was ordered that her execution would take place as near to the crime scene as possible on Wednesday 7 March. The famous painter William Hogarth visited her in prison two days before her execution and sketched her prior to painting her portrait.

Newgate's portable gallows was set up in Fleet Street, in the square opposite Mitre Court, for the purpose. Sarah was prepared in the normal way in Newgate and placed in the cart with John Hooper, the hangman, to make the short journey to Fleet Street. She is said to have fainted in the cart and also to have 'wrung her hands and wept most bitterly'. When she arrived at the gallows, she listened carefully to the prayers of the Ordinary, John Gutherie, for her soul and again fainted. She was revived and just before the cart was driven from under her, she was reported to have turned towards the Temple and cried out, 'Oh, my mistress, my mistress! I wish I could see her!' and then, casting her eyes towards Heaven, called upon Christ to receive her soul. She was dragged off the cart by the rope and left kicking in the air, dying after a brief struggle. Her body was taken down and according to the parish records was buried in the churchyard of St Sepulchre's on 10 March. Strangely, it seemed that John Hooper was the only person present to have any real sympathy for her. Hogarth thought that 'she was capable of any wickedness' and the crowd surrounding the gallows were reportedly of the same view. Her case was reported in the *London Magazine* and *Gentleman's Monthly Intelligencer* for March 1733.

The Gregory Gang (or Essex Gang) were a group of highwaymen, thieves and housebreakers led by one Samuel Gregory, active in and around Epping Forest in the 1730s. It is thought that the gang numbered some 20 members, one of whom was Richard 'Dick' Turpin. Apprehended in Westminster, five of the gang stood trial for housebreaking at the February 1735 Sessions and were sentenced to death and afterwards to be gibbeted at Edgware. They included John Field, Joseph Rose, William Saunders and Humphrey Walker. Walker died in

Newgate before his execution, but was gibbeted with the others after they had been hanged on Monday 10 March 1735. Samuel Gregory, the gang's leader, was hanged and similarly gibbeted on Wednesday 4 June. Turpin had been with the others when the arrests were made but managed to escape.

With the break-up of the gang Turpin turned to highway robbery. A reward of £100 was being offered in 1737 for his capture. After a shoot-out with constables he made his famous journey to York on his horse 'Black Bess'. Here he lived under the name of John Palmer, making a living from horse theft. He was finally charged under that name with stealing a black gelding and a black mare worth £3 each and a filly foal valued at £1 from Thomas Creavy at Welton on 1 March 1739, according to the *York Courant* newspaper.

Three other men were condemned at the Yorkshire Lent Assize, namely Thomas Hadfield for highway robbery and John Stead who had also been convicted of horse theft. Burglar Lawrence Roberts was reprieved. In accordance with the normal York practice, one of the men had also to be reprieved on condition of hanging the other two. Thomas Hadfield was the lucky man and duly executed Turpin and Stead on Saturday 7 April 1739 at The Knavesmire outside the city, on what is now York racecourse. The gallows here was much like the one at Tyburn, having three beams. Turpin was a murderer, horse thief, highwayman and general thug, and his reputation as a dashing highwayman is ill deserved.

In the year 1749, Henry Fielding, a magistrate in Bow Street, started what would become the first real police force in London, the Bow Street Runners. This tiny force of just eight men was expanded under Henry's half brother John from 1754 and started to impact on the crime-ridden streets of the capital.

In the spring of 1752, the stories of two murderesses filled the newspapers. They were Mary Blandy and Elizabeth Jeffreys. Mary Blandy had poisoned her father at the behest of her lover, and Elizabeth Jeffreys had murdered her uncle. Mary died at Oxford on Monday 6 April 1752 on a gallows consisting of a wooden beam placed between two trees. At the place of execution she uttered the famous words, 'For the sake of decency, gentlemen, don't hang me high.' She was made to climb backwards up a ladder from which she was turned off, becoming still almost immediately. Elizabeth Jeffreys was hanged on Saturday 28 March, alongside her lover John Swan, near the sixth milestone in Epping Forest. The victim of the crime, Joseph Jeffries, was Swan's employer and thus Swan was guilty of petty treason. The trial judge ordered that the execution be carried out near the crime scene, which although not unusual in itself, was some 23 miles away. This required a 4am start from Chelmsford gaol with Elizabeth riding in the cart and Swan drawn along behind tied to a sledge. After hanging, Swan's corpse was gibbeted in another part of the forest, said to be near the Bald Faced Stag Inn in Hainault Road, Chigwell, as a warning to others.

Mary and Elizabeth were both reasonably educated and literate women who actually exchanged letters with each other from prison. From surviving woodcuts it seems Mary was very well looked after during her time at Oxford prison.

The murder rate in the 1740s and early 1750s was a cause for governmental concern and led to the passing of the Murder Act of 1752. The full title of it was 'An Act for the better preventing the horrid Crime of Murder'. From 1 June 1752, it mandated that the prisoner be kept fettered and fed only on bread and water, and be hanged within two days of sentence, unless that would fall on a Sunday, in which case the execution would take place on the Monday. It further prescribed the post mortem dissection of the bodies of all executed murderers, including females, or gibbeting for male murderers in particularly heinous cases.

Seventeen-year-old Thomas Wilford, who had stabbed to death his wife of just one week, was the first to suffer under this Act on 22 June 1752 at Tyburn. His sentence was as follows: 'Thomas Wilford, you stand convicted of the horrid and unnatural crime of murdering Sarah, your wife. This Court doth adjudge that you be taken back to the place from whence you came, and there to be fed on bread and water till Wednesday next, when you are to be taken to the common place of execution, and there hanged by the neck until you are dead; after which your body is to be publicly dissected and anatomised, agreeable to an Act of Parliament in that case made and provided; and may God Almighty have mercy on your soul.' His body was dissected at Surgeons' Hall in London.

The modern reader might wonder what was so dreadful about dissection after death, but in 1752 it was believed that the desecration of the body and the prohibition of Christian burial were great additional punishments. It was believed that one could not have an afterlife without a body. It was really quite a clever Act as it provided bodies for the medical schools and was a greater deterrent. In London, at least, it seemed to reduce the murder rate somewhat. In the decade 1755–1764, 25 persons were executed for murder, whereas in the previous decade it had been 32.

The 'Triple Tree' gallows at Tyburn remained in use until Monday 18 June 1759 when Catherine Knowland, convicted of highway robbery, became its last customer. The structure was removed during the summer, as it had become a cause of traffic congestion and was disliked by the residents of what was becoming a fashionable area of west London. It was replaced by a portable gallows which was first used on Wednesday 3 October 1759 for the hanging of four men, as reported in the Whitehall Evening Post of that day. It stood near the junction of Bryanston Street and Edgware Road and was dragged into position by horses for each execution. Surprisingly, there is no detail of what the new gallows looked like. The condemned were still transported to Tyburn in carts and turned off from them as previously, according to contemporary accounts.

9

The later 18th century

There was quite a sharp reduction in both death sentences and executions in England and Wales in the decade 1760–1769. A total of 670 executions were recorded – 621 men and 49 women – giving an average of 67 per annum compared with between 90 and 100 in previous and succeeding decades.

There were only five 'Hanging Days' at Tyburn in 1760, with nine men and a woman making the journey. Just ten men and two women were sentenced to death in London during this year. One of these executions was to be a unique event, as it was the last time a peer of the realm would be hanged for murder. The peer in question was Lawrence Shirley, the 4th Earl Ferrers, who was executed at Tyburn on Monday 5 May, having been tried and condemned by his fellow peers at Westminster Hall for the shooting dead of an old family steward named John Johnson in a drunken rage. Mr Johnson did not die immediately, being treated by the local doctor, Dr Kirkland, who was unable to save him.

As a peer, Ferrers could not be tried at the Leicestershire Assizes so he was transferred to the Tower of London and committed to the custody of Black Rod on 14 February. His case was heard at Westminster Hall on 16 April 1760 before the Lord High Steward, Lord Henley, and lasted two days. The Attorney General, Sir Charles Pratt, and the Solicitor General, Sir Charles Yorke, led the prosecution. They brought as witnesses Dr Kirkland, Sarah Johnson (the victim's daughter) and the three women servants who were present at the Hall at the time of the shooting. Ferrers conducted his own defence, as all defendants had to in those days. He had been dissuaded by his family from trying to claim that the shooting of John Johnson was justified. He therefore attempted a defence of insanity, a condition for which he was able to offer considerable evidence as just about everyone who knew of him thought he was mad. He later maintained, however, that he had done this only at the insistence of his family, and that he had himself always been ashamed of such a defence. It is easy to understand why the family were so concerned at the prospect of the damage to their reputation and the shame of having a prominent member of it hanged as a common felon.

One witness, Peter Williams, gave an account of what happened when the earl came to collect a mare that he had left in the care of the Williams family. Ferrers was unhappy with the way that the horse had been cared for and hit Mrs Williams and seriously injured Peter Williams with a sword. The Solicitor General pointed out that this was no proof of insanity or eccentric behaviour. He went so far as to say that if a man couldn't take such action against a negligent servant, then everyone present would be in the dock! This gives you an idea of the way the nobility of the time saw life – they were above the law. Ferrers clearly thought he was; he did not really seem capable of understanding that it was wrong for a man in his position to shoot Mr Johnson. At the end of the proceedings his fellow peers each individually rejected his defence and brought in a guilty verdict. The earl was given the same sentence as any other murderer: hanging followed by dissection. The thought of a public hanging at Tyburn appalled Ferrers. He was to suffer the death of a common criminal and he petitioned the king to be allowed to be beheaded instead, the death of a nobleman. Beheading was not a legally available punishment for murder, only for treason committed by a peer. Thus, the sentence had to stand and he remained in the Round Tower awaiting the trip to Tyburn. The only special treatment that Ferrers received was a delay in carrying out the sentence. Instead of the legal requirement of two days his execution was set for Monday 5 May 1760, almost three weeks after sentence.

A new form of gallows was constructed at Tyburn for the occasion. It consisted of a scaffold covered in black baize reached by a short flight of stairs. Two uprights rose from the scaffold, topped with a cross beam. Directly under the beam there was a small box-like structure, some 3 feet square and 18 inches high, which was designed to sink down into the scaffold and thus leave the earl suspended. There were even black cushions for Ferrers and the chaplain to kneel on to pray before the hanging. The hanging of a nobleman was a major public spectacle that attracted a huge crowd, with every seat in Mother Proctor's Pews taken.

At nine o'clock on the Monday morning, Ferrers' body was demanded of the keeper of the Tower by the sheriffs of London and Middlesex.

It had been agreed that Ferrers could make the trip to Tyburn in his own landau drawn by six horses. He was accompanied in this carriage by Mr Humphries, the chaplain of the Tower and Mr Vaillant, the sheriff. The procession to Tyburn was led by a troop of cavalry, with Ferrers' landau behind them, guarded on both sides, followed by the carriage of Mr Errington, the other sheriff; a mourning coach and six, containing some of his lordship's friends; and finally a hearse for the conveyance of his body to Surgeons' Hall after execution, with another contingent of soldiers guarding the rear of the procession. It took 2¾ hours to complete the journey to Tyburn.

Ferrers and Mr Humphries then knelt together on the cushions and said the Lord's Prayer. Ferrers concluded by saying: 'Lord have mercy upon me, and forgive me my errors.' He then mounted the 'drop' where his arms were tied with a black silk sash and the rope placed around his neck. His final words were to ask Thomas Turlis, the hangman: 'Am I right?' A white nightcap which Ferrers had brought with him was pulled down over his head. He had declined to give the signal to the hangman himself, so this was done by the sheriff. Some time around noon, the platform sank down, leaving the earl suspended. The mechanism had not functioned properly and Ferrers' feet were still just in contact with the platform. He writhed slightly for a short period before becoming still. Horace Walpole reported that it took four minutes for him to die. The body was left to hang for the customary hour before being taken down and placed in the coffin for transport to Surgeons' Hall and dissection. A woodcut was made of the body in its coffin. After being dissected, the body was put on display until the evening of Thursday 8 May, when it was returned to the family for burial in St Pancras' Church. Twenty-two years later Ferrers was reinterred in the family vault at Staunton Harold. It has been claimed that Earl Ferrers was hanged with a silken rope, but this is a myth. Ferrers' gallows, although not entirely successful, was the forerunner of the 'New Drop' that would become universal in the late 18th and early 19th centuries.

Thomas Turlis did not always have such co-operative prisoners as the earl. On 4 May 1763, he had two men and a woman to hang. The men behaved themselves at Tyburn, but the woman, Hannah Dagoe, attacked Turlis with great ferocity. She had been convicted at the April Sessions of stealing in a dwelling house. She managed to get the cords binding her arms undone and struck Turlis in the chest so hard that she nearly knocked him out of the cart. Having restrained her once more, he got the noose positioned and allowed her to cover her face with a handkerchief. Having done so, she jumped from the cart and, according to witnesses, her neck was broken by the fall.

Although the Ferrers execution had been an expensive one for the London authorities, ordinary executions in the shire counties could also be costly. Many counties had very few hangings. The county of Flintshire in Wales had just thirteen executions in the period 1735–1799. Edward Edwards was hanged there for burglary in June 1769 and the sheriff's pleadings detailed the cost of his execution. In Wales it was virtually impossible to obtain a hangman such was the stigma attached to the job at the time, so Ralph Griffin, the high sheriff of Flintshire had to send officials to Liverpool and Shrewsbury to find a man willing to do the job. The cost of this search was £15 10s and ultimately proved abortive. Finally a prisoner in Flint gaol, one John Babington, was persuaded by his wife to undertake the execution. For this they each got six guineas. Erecting the gallows cost a further £4 12s, and a cart to remove the body for burial afterwards cost £2 10s. Looking at some of the surviving accounts for executions I get the impression that local tradesmen were quite happy to 'rip off' the county for their services. The final bill for Edwards' hanging came to a whopping £102 17s, a lot of money in those days. Sheriff's Pleadings or Cravings were the strange terms used for the 'invoice' the high sheriff sent the Treasury for carrying out a death sentence passed by the King's judges. In view of the cost and aggravation of it, Mr Griffin might have been happier if Edwards had been reprieved.

There was usually a somewhat ambivalent attitude amongst the public towards criminals on their way to execution at Tyburn. Yes, they may have committed crimes, but everyone wanted to see them and watch the 'Hanging Match'. Often there was sympathy rather than enmity towards the sufferers as they were known. However, there was absolutely no public sympathy for the lone woman in the cart on the morning of Monday 14 September 1767. She was 47-year-old Elizabeth Brownrigg who had systematically tortured and abused her teenage apprentice girls, eventually killing one of them. Attitudes to the abuse and murder of children have not changed over the centuries and people expressed their abhorrence of her crime, praying for her damnation rather than her salvation and saying that 'the devil would fetch her'. In accordance with her sentence she was hanged and afterwards dissected at Surgeons' Hall where her skeleton became a permanent exhibit.

The building of a new prison at Newgate began in 1770 and finished in 1778, but it sustained severe damage in 1780 during the Gordon Riots (see below). This led to another rebuild which was finally completed in 1783 to the designs of George Dance.

The American Revolutionary War or War of Independence was fought between 1775 and 1783, causing the temporary suspension of transportation as an alternative punishment in 1776. This led to a sharp increase in executions in the 1780s. In the period 1770–1779, there had been an average of 85 a year, but in the following decade the average was 153 per annum. The peak years for executions were 1783 to 1787 – 184 people were put to death in 1783, rising to 191 the following year, 207 in 1785, 223 in 1786, and 226 in 1787, before dropping back to around 130 per annum for the next four years. The year 1793 was to be the first for a decade in which hangings dropped below 100, there being 92 executions in England and Wales that year. Those who escaped the rope during the years when transportation was unavailable were often sent to prison hulks moored in the Thames. These were retired warships whose masts and rigging had been removed. This could be a death sentence as conditions on them were appalling and as many as one in three prisoners died of disease. In May 1787, transportation to Australia began and would see an estimated 160,000 men, women and children sent there over the next 80 years.

One man who did not escape the noose at this time was the forger, 52-year-old Rev Dr William Dodd, who was hanged at Tyburn on 27 June 1777. Dr Dodd was a published author of books and poems and a popular chaplain, but he lived beyond his means and was convicted of forging a bond to the value of £4200 to clear his debts. An Old Bailey jury took just 10 minutes to convict him, although they also recommended him for mercy. It is unlikely in view of the normal treatment of forgers and the amount involved that there would have been a reprieve even if transportation had been available, although considerable efforts were made to win one by prominent people of the day such as Samuel Johnson. Alongside Dodd at Tyburn was Joseph Harris, who was to hang for highway robbery.

Parliament passed the Papists Act or Roman Catholic Relief Act in 1778 to repeal anti-Catholic laws enacted in the late 1600s. One of the provisions of this Act was to allow Catholics to serve in the armed forces. As the government was involved in three wars at the time, this had obvious benefits. However, not everyone applauded the new Act and 1780 saw the setting up of the Protestant Association by Lord George Gordon, a retired navy lieutenant, with the aim of getting it repealed. On Friday 2 June 1780, Gordon led a crowd of between 20,000 and 40,000 people to the House of Commons to present a petition against it. As is so often the way, what starts out as a peaceful protest quickly gets out of hand. Newgate prison and several Catholic churches were early targets for the rioters. The homes of known Catholics were also set upon as were public buildings such as the Bank of England together with the King's Bench, Fleet and Marshalsea prisons. A particular target was the house of the Lord Chief Justice, the 1st Earl Mansfield, who was blamed for not enforcing anti-Catholic laws. The rioting went on for five days, leaving a huge trail of destruction with 285 dead, 173 wounded and 139 arrested. Most of the dead had been killed after the army was ordered in to quell the riots on Wednesday 7 June. Of those arrested, 71 were tried at the June Sessions of the Old Bailey resulting in death sentences being passed on 32 men and three women. Fifteen men were subsequently reprieved, including Edward Dennis, London's only hangman. The rest were hanged at various places around London between 11 and 22 July, typically near where their crime had been committed. One woman, Mary Gardner, was respited and hanged at Tyburn on Wednesday 22 November. A further 50 rioters were tried at the Town Hall of St Margaret's Hill in Southwark. Surprisingly Gordon himself was acquitted and carried on his duties as an MP. He was later imprisoned for libelling Marie Antoinette and died in Newgate prison in 1793.

John Austin has the distinction of being the last person to be hanged at Tyburn. His execution took place on 7 November 1783. Austin had been convicted of highway robbery, having attacked a Mr John Spicer in Bethnal Green, stealing his watch, handkerchiefs, stockings, shirt and hat, in all valued at 41 shillings or £2.05. It is easy to dismiss cases like this as just another example of the judicial barbarism of the time, but it should be remembered that the victim was attacked by Austin and an accomplice and suffered a vicious assault with a sword as well as being tied up and robbed. The goods stolen from him would be worth nearer £500 at today's prices.

With the completion of rebuilding at Newgate it was decided to move the place of execution for London and Middlesex from Tyburn to the prison. Initially some hangings took place in the Old Bailey, but soon a spot immediately outside the Debtors' Door became the norm. On the eve of a hanging, the portable gallows was drawn into position in front of this door by a team of horses. This had two parallel beams from which a maximum of a dozen criminals could be hanged at once. The platform was 10 feet long by 8 feet wide and was released by moving the lever or 'pin' acting on a drawbar under the drop.

Large crowds still gathered and the gallows were guarded by javelin men. Wealthy people could pay as much as £10 for a seat in a window overlooking the gallows at the hanging of a notorious criminal. At around 7.30am the condemned prisoners were led from their cells into the Press Yard where the sheriff and the Ordinary would meet them. Their leg irons would be removed by the prison blacksmith, and the hangman and his assistant would bind their wrists in front of them with cord and also place a cord round their body and arms at the elbows. White nightcaps were placed on their heads. The condemned would now be led across the Yard to the Lodge and then out through the Debtors' Door where they would climb the steps up to the gallows. There would be shouts of 'hats off' in the crowd. This was not out of respect for those about to die, but rather because the people further back demanded those at the front remove their hats so as not to obscure their view. Once assembled on the drop, the hangman would put the nooses round their necks while they prayed with the Ordinary. Female prisoners might have their dress bound around their legs for the sake of decency but the men's legs were left free. When the prayers had finished, the hangman would pull the nightcaps down over their faces and at the signal from the under sheriff would move the pin, causing the drop to fall. The prisoners fell some 12-18" to about knee level and usually writhed and struggled for some seconds before becoming still. If their bodies continued to struggle, the hangman, unseen by the crowd, within the box below the drop, would grasp their legs and swing on them so adding his weight to theirs and thus ending their sufferings sooner. The bodies would be left hanging for an hour before being taken down.

The first executions at Newgate took place in the Old Bailey on 9 December 1783 when Edward Dennis and William Brunskill hanged nine men and a woman together. Between 9 December 1783 and 13 November 1799, 532 men and 19 women were executed at Newgate. Just 26 of these executions were for murder, although a further seven murderers were hanged near the scene of their crime. The largest number executed outside Newgate in a single day was 20, all men, who were hanged in two batches for a variety of offences, none of them murder, on 2 February 1785.

10

The early 19th century

The English penal system underwent massive changes in the first half of the 19th century, with whole swathes of crimes being reclassified as non capital and the introduction of imprisonment as a punishment instead of death or transportation for minor crimes. In 1816, the new Milbank prison opened in London as Britain's first national penitentiary. Other 'model' prisons followed, with Pentonville opening in 1842, based on the 'Panopticon' or radial principle, cell blocks radiating out from a central hub.

Initially the 'separate system' meant that each prisoner had his own cell and saw other prisoners only at work or during exercise periods. This was also referred to as the 'silent system' as communication between prisoners was forbidden. Sanitary conditions in these new prisons were vastly better and healthier than in the old county gaols with clean water and fresh air. At first many of them had sanitation in each cell, although this was usually removed later. Each inmate was made to undertake simple work such as picking coir and oakum (redundant ships' ropes) or weaving. Pentonville became the model for British prisons, a further 54 being built to the same basic design over the next six years. The Penal Servitude Act of 1853 formalised the use of imprisonment as a punishment in itself and introduced for the first time in the British penal system the concept of rehabilitation rather than mere retribution. Penal servitude reduced the use of transportation, which finally ceased in 1868.

Below is a listing of the last executions for various crimes in England. The year 1814 saw the last execution under the 'Black Acts'. This took place on 12 August when William Potter was hanged at Moulsham gaol in Essex for the crime of cutting down an orchard. Even the judge petitioned for a reprieve! The last record I have of an execution for cattle theft is on 2 April 1819 when John Northcott was hanged at Exeter.

It would seem that the death penalty for shoplifting was abolished in 1820, although different dates are given in other sources. A search of the

Old Bailey records reveals no death sentences for this offence after 1820 when 39-year-old Mary Green became the last to be condemned there on 28 June of that year. She was later reprieved. Subsequent trials for shoplifting resulted in sentences of whipping for males, prison or transportation. Whipping of females had ceased in 1805.

In 1828, the crime of petty treason was abolished, the offence being reclassified as ordinary murder by The Offences against the Person Act of that year. Hannah Reed was the last woman to die for this, at Leicester on 5 August 1825. The last person to hang for the high treason offence of coining was James Coleman at Newgate on 21 January 1829. Newgate also had the last hanging for forgery, which took place on 31 December 1829 when Thomas Maynard died there. The last executions for horse stealing took place at Leicester on 20 April 1829 and were those of Charles Forester, Henry Hinton and Joseph Varnham. It may come as a surprise to find that the last execution for sheep stealing took place in London rather than in, say, Wales or Cumbria. George Widget was hanged at Newgate on 25 May 1831 for stealing five sheep and 46 ewes at St Leonard's, Shoreditch.

Over the period 1832 to 1837, Sir Robert Peel's government introduced various Bills to reduce the number of capital crimes. Sheep, cattle and horse stealing were removed from the list in 1832, followed by sacrilege, letter stealing, returning from transportation (1834/5), forgery and coining in 1836, and arson, burglary and theft from a dwelling house in 1837. On 1 February 1832, three young men – George Beck, Thomas Armstrong and George Hearson – became the last to die for the crime of riot in England, having set fire to Beeston silk mill in Nottinghamshire. They were hanged on the steps outside what is now the Galleries of Justice museum at Nottingham. Four days earlier four men had been hanged at Bristol for riot.

The last executions for the crime of sodomy (buggery) took place on 27 November 1835 when 40-year-old John Smith and John Pratt, aged 30, were hanged at Newgate. They had been tried at the Old Bailey even though the offence had been committed in Surrey. Richard Smith, aged 45, was the last man to be executed for rape, at Nottingham on 30 March 1836. Rape ceased to be a capital offence in 1841. On 11 April 1836, William Harley became the last person to hang for burglary when he was executed atop Horsemonger Lane gaol in Surrey. The last hangings for robbery were carried out on the roof of the gatehouse at Shrewsbury prison on 13 August 1836 when Lawrence Curtis and Patrick and Edward Donnelly were put to death there. The last hanging for arson was that of Daniel Case at Ilchester in Somerset on 31 August 1836. This was to be the last execution in England and Wales for a crime other than murder or attempted murder.

Where a person was convicted of a capital felony the judge would have the nine inch square of silk, known as the 'Black Cap', placed on his head by the chaplain before passing the following sentence upon them: '(full name of prisoner) you will be taken hence to the prison in which you were last confined and from there to a place of execution where you will be hanged by the neck until you are dead and thereafter your body buried within the precincts of the prison, and may the Lord have mercy upon your soul.' The reference to burial within the precincts of the prison was as a result of the passing of the Anatomy Act of 1832, which determined that from 1 August 1832, the bodies of executed criminals would become the property of the Crown and were now to be buried in the prison grounds. Typically the person was placed into a cheap pine coffin or even a sack and covered with quicklime, which was thought at the time to hasten the process of decomposition. At the end of the Assize the judge had to sign the calendar, as the list of convicted prisoners' names was known. Where he had passed the death sentence, 'Hanged by the neck' or the Latin equivalent suspendatur per collum, normally abbreviated to sus per col, was written in the margin against the person's name.

The Trial for Felonies Act of 1836, better known as the Prisoner's Counsel Act, introduced by the Whig (Liberal) government, for the first time gave defence barristers access to pre-trial information and allowed them to address the jury and question the 'facts' of the case against their client. Previously the right to a defence barrister had been available only in treason trials. Also in 1836, the remaining provisions of the Murder Act of 1752 were repealed. A period of 14 to 27 days between sentence and execution for murderers now became normal.

In the first decade of the 19th century, 835 men and 36 women suffered the death penalty in England and Wales. In 1800, 125 men and 6 women were executed, but the peak year was 1801 with 219, a figure only previously slightly exceeded in 1785 and 1786. This number virtually halved the following year to 110, before declining to an average of 58.7 for the rest of the decade. The principal crimes for which people were actually executed were burglary, forgery, highway robbery and murder in that order. These were followed by horse and sheep theft, sodomy and attempted murder. Only 23 of more than 220 capital offences typically led to executions.

This high rate of executions reduced slightly over the next twenty years, with totals of 855 for the period 1810–1819, and 742 for the period 1820–1829. As stated earlier, there was a gradual reduction in the number of capital crimes over the same time, but it was not until the next decade, 1830 to 1839, that this really translated into a huge reduction in executions, the number of hangings in England and Wales falling to 297. Theft from property to the value of more than 40s (£2) was still a capital crime in the 1820s. The jury had to decide in each case whether the value of the goods stolen was above or below this figure. They often decided it was below, despite the evidence, and returned a 'partial verdict', i.e. that the person was guilty, but not of the capital offence. Many people escaped the death sentence as a result and ultimately the unwillingness of juries to send defendants to the gallows in these cases made the law unworkable.

Just to take a snapshot of the time, in the year 1810, 56 men and five women were hanged in England and Wales, of whom 26 had been convicted of property crimes and a further 18 of forgery or uttering forgeries. Only 11 of these executions were for murder or attempted murder and one for rape. Shooting at a person, although a separate offence distinct from attempted murder, often resulted in execution. Some small towns still retained the right to hang criminals and the city of Lichfield in Staffordshire had its last three executions in this year when William Weightman, John Neve and James Rich were taken from their cells in the Town Hall, seated in a cart to a field by what is now the link road to the A38 on the south-west of the town and hanged for forgery on 1 June 1810. The cells can still be visited. The year 1812 saw the only assassination of a British prime minister when John Bellingham shot and killed Spencer Perceval. For this he was hanged at Newgate on 18 May having attempted a defence of insanity. This is discussed more fully in Chapter 23.

A case that made headlines in 1815 was that of 20-year-old Elizabeth (Eliza) Fenning who was hanged outside Newgate for attempted murder on 26 July. There were serious doubts about her guilt which, combined with Eliza's looks and youth, ensured that considerable efforts were made to obtain a reprieve. Her case was discussed at the highest levels, including with the Lord Chancellor. She had been convicted of the non-fatal poisoning of her employer's household on rather flimsy evidence. William Hone, the owner of the *Traveller* newspaper, published editorials in Eliza's defence and demanded clemency. This is the first recorded instance I have found of a newspaper campaigning on behalf of a condemned person. Eliza chose her wedding dress for the hanging as she would not get to use it for its intended purpose, and behaved with courage and dignity on the gallows. As she had not been convicted of murder, her body was returned to her family for burial and her funeral was attended by a very large number of mourners.

Beside her on the gallows on Wednesday 26 July stood two men: William Oldfield, who had been convicted of the rape of 9-year-old Eliza Wills, and Abraham Adams for sodomy. A surviving broadsheet depicts the scene with a crude woodcut drawing. It tells us in the typical style of these publications that the prisoners 'seemed perfectly resigned to their unhappy fate'. The broadsheet also includes the text of a letter Eliza wrote to a Sunday newspaper protesting her innocence. It would be interesting to know what the reaction of the witnesses was to this triple hanging. It is hard to believe that they would have had any sympathy for the two men, but would have probably sympathised with the woman. The media, such as it was, reported the fact of the execution and a few minor details, especially words of repentance uttered by the prisoners, but would not have interviewed the general public as they do now.

John Cashman was hanged on 12 March 1817 in Skinner Street, London, opposite the house of a Mr Beckwith which Cashman had robbed and damaged during a riot. This was the last execution in London at or near the crime scene rather than outside Newgate.

Alongside the changes to the law and the use of capital punishment came the advent of hangings using the 'New Drop' gallows to replace the cart or ladder. Although the 'New Drop' concept had been introduced at Tyburn for the execution of Earl Ferrers as we saw in the last chapter, it was not immediately adopted nationwide but rather rolled out across the country as hangings were transferred to the newly constructed county gaols and away from the traditional places of execution. London led this trend with Essex following in 1785 when executions were transferred to Moulsham gaol in Chelmsford. Dorset executions were moved to a spot in front of the county gaol in Dorchester from March 1794.

The *Exeter Flying Post* newspaper records the last hanging at the old Heavitree gallows outside the town. This took place on Friday 4 April 1794 when Joan Stone was executed for arson, having maliciously set fire to an outhouse belonging to her master, John Burgain. Devon's next execution was carried out at the county gaol, almost a year later, on Friday 20 March 1795 when William Martinborough was hanged for the murder of Henry Smith.

Other counties followed suit as their new gaols were completed, eg Lancaster and Surrey in 1800. This move was an improvement in so far as it speeded up the execution process considerably by eliminating the lengthy cart ride or procession on foot to the gallows. This made security much easier and spared the condemned person the jeers and insults of the crowd along the way.

As murderers had to be executed within two (or three) days of sentence, it also helped to reduce costs as the number of 'Hanging Days' was increased. The Essex Lent Assizes which opened on 7 March 1785 led to the executions of five men. Robert Wright was hanged for the murder of Samuel Pewter on Saturday 12 March, having been sentenced on the Thursday. Two further hangings were carried out a week later when John Godfrey, aged 30, and William Dobson, aged 28, were put to death for burglary in a dwelling house, and the following week a further two when William Grace was executed for burglary alongside George Ingram for horse theft. It is probable that the gallows at Moulsham could accommodate only two prisoners at a time.

By definition all patterns of 'New Drop' gallows had the capacity to allow the condemned to fall through a single or double trap door or via a falling box mechanism. The gallows platform was typically reached by climbing a number of stairs. In some cases, e.g. Newgate, there were said to have been ten steps, whereas in other counties it was four or five, e.g. at Bodmin in Cornwall and Oakham in Rutland.

The amount of drop was typically between 12 and 18 inches and thus did not break the prisoner's neck but was sufficient to prevent survival. Some prisoners died almost without a struggle, while less fortunate ones could be observed writhing in the agonies of strangulation for two or three minutes after the drop fell.

Many of the new county gaols had their gallows set up on top of the flat roof of the gatehouse which had been specially designed for the purpose. Using the gatehouse roof had obvious advantages in terms of security and enabled the crowd to get a good view of the proceedings, but involved the prisoner climbing a considerable number of steps to get there. This concept was used in Staffordshire from 1793 to 1817, Surrey from 1800 and Shropshire from 1795, to give just a few examples.

Newgate, as the prison for London and the County of Middlesex, predictably had Britain's busiest gallows with 543 executions between 1800 and 1868. Almost all London's hangings took place in front of the Debtors' Door and continued there up to 25 May 1868. However, two people were hanged at Newgate using the old method of the cart in 1804. The unfortunate victims were Ann Hurle and Methuselah Spalding, who were executed on Wednesday 8 February, she for forgery and he for sodomy. A simple gallows was erected at the top of the Old Bailey, near to St Sepulchre's Church. Ann Hurle reportedly died in agony and struggled for two minutes or so. There was a scathing letter to *The Times* newspaper alleging that the authorities had been too idle to erect the normal gallows and commenting on the cruelty of these hangings. Whether or not it was idleness or due to a mechanical defect we do not know, but fortunately there was no recurrence and the 'New Drop' was back in action for Providence Hansard, another forger, on 5 July 1805. During the early 1800s, the original gallows with two parallel beams was replaced with a similar structure with a single beam which would still take up to six prisoners simultaneously.

The 'New Drop' arrived at Durham in 1816, but curiously was erected on the steps outside the courthouse rather than at the prison for each of the 14 public hangings there. The holes for the beams supporting the platform can still be seen in the wall, filled with stone plugs. The courthouse is next door to the prison and the prisoner was brought from the gaol through an internal passage that is now blocked off. The condemned person came out through a window onto the platform of the gallows set over the main door. This was simpler and more secure than bringing the person out of the prison gates and then making them climb steps up to the gallows platform, as happened at Bury St Edmunds, for instance. At Nottingham the gallows was similarly set up on the steps outside the court. In Derby it was set up on the pavement immediately outside the entrance to Friar Gate gaol.

Hangings in Hertfordshire were by no means a frequent event, the previous one having occurred in August 1822 when Charles Lee was executed for burglary. It was decided that a new gallows should be built, at considerable expense to the county, for the execution of John Thurtell. He had been condemned for the murder of fellow gambler William Weare on 24 October 1823 in a dispute over money. Construction began before the trial, so certain was everybody of the outcome! Mr Nicholson, the under sheriff of Hertfordshire, supervised the work and the structure was described as having a 'temporary platform with a falling leaf (single trap door) supported by bolts which could be withdrawn in an instant' so launching the criminal into eternity, as was the contemporary expression. The substantial cross beam was supported by two equally substantial uprights, about 8 feet high. The enclosure beneath the beam consisted of boards, 7 feet high, dovetailed into each other so that there were no gaps through which the body could be viewed. The new gallows was 30 feet long and 15 feet deep, with a short flight of steps up to the platform at the back leading directly from the prison door. The interior was painted black and presented 'a very gloomy appearance'. The outer walls of the enclosure rose approximately 3 feet above the platform, so the bulk of the prisoner's body was hidden from view after the drop. It appears to have worked satisfactorily as Thurtell reportedly died without struggling on Friday 9 January 1824. Madame Tussauds made a waxwork of him for display, having bought his clothes from the hangman.

Kent was the last county to move away from its old execution site, in its case Penenden Heath on what was then the outskirts of Maidstone, after the executions of Henry and William Packman there on Christmas Eve 1830 for arson. From then on the gallows was erected outside the main gate of the prison in County Road, Maidstone. The structure comprised a platform supported by beams, containing the trap doors and surrounded by a railing. In the centre was a simple gallows consisting of two uprights and a cross beam with an iron hook for attachment of the rope. The drop was reached by a short flight of steps, and the lower portion beneath the platform was draped with black cloth to prevent the crowd seeing the legs and lower body of the struggling prisoner. It was used for 28 public hangings, including four double ones, all carried out by William Calcraft. Fourteen-year-old John Amy Bird Bell became its first customer on 1 August 1831. See Chapter 11 for details of his case.

At Lincoln Castle executions took place on the roof of Cobb Hall, a large tower forming the north-east bastion of the Castle. Access for the prisoner and officials was via a spiral stone staircase within the tower leading up to the roof level. A total of 38 prisoners were to die here over the period from 1817 to 1859. The first was Elizabeth Whiting on 15 March 1817 for the murder of her infant child, the last being 20-year-old William Pickett and 24-year-old Henry Caret on 5 August 1859 for the murder of William Stevenson. Lincoln Castle can be visited, and Cobb Hall and the Lucy Tower are preserved. The graves of some of those executed at Lincoln are still visible at the base of the Lucy Tower.

Lancaster Castle had what became known as the 'Hanging Corner' where a total of 213 people were executed between 1800 and 1865. The 'Hanging Corner' is outside the small round tower on the east side of the building. On the ground floor of the tower is the 'Drop Room' where the prisoners were prepared and allowed final prayers with the chaplain before being led out through inward-opening French windows onto the balcony-style gallows. This would have been erected the previous afternoon and consisted of two uprights that were seated into holes cut into the flagstones of the courtyard. A heavy cross beam ran between the uprights with a platform containing the trap doors beneath it, level with the base of the French windows, draped in a black cloth. High railings surrounded the drop area, and the spectators were allowed up to these, within a few feet of the gallows. Many more crowded onto the opposite bank to get a good view of the proceedings. The tower and 'Drop Room' can still be visited today. It is quite an eerie feeling standing in this room looking at the exhibits and listening to what happened within. The French windows have also survived and one can look out to the bank opposite where the crowd would have stood.

Lancaster's gallows was very busy in its early days. Seven men were hanged together on 25 April 1801 as a result of convictions at the Lent Assize. Their crimes were forgery (1), housebreaking (3), highway robbery (2) and cattle theft (1). The highest single year total was 1817, with no fewer than 20 hangings. Nine of these executions took place on 19 April of that year. Eight women were put to death here between 1801 and 1828: Hannah Eastwood for forging bank notes in 1801, Mary Jackson for stealing in a dwelling house in 1806 and Margaret Chandler for the same offence two years later, Hannah Smith for the crime of riot in 1812, Susan Holroyd for murder in 1816, Margaret Dowd for uttering in 1818 and Rachael Bradley for murdering a child in 1827. The last was 22-year-old Jane Scott who was hanged on 22 March 1828 for poisoning her parents. She was so weak and in such a state of collapse that she had to be tied to a high chair and wheeled onto the drop. Here she was supported by two female warders whilst the final preparations were made. The specially adapted chair is still on display in the 'Drop Room'.

After 1835, Lancaster's role as an Assize town was reduced to serve just the northern areas of the county. Liverpool was allowed its own Assize, with those condemned there being hanged at Kirkdale prison. From 1864, Manchester also became an Assize town, its executions initially taking place at Salford. The last public execution at Lancaster occurred on 25 March 1865 when Stephen Burke was put to death for the murder of his wife.

The county of Rutland built a new gallows for the first executions at the new county gaol at Oakham, which took place on 5 April 1813 when William Almond and John Holmes were hanged for burglary. The gallows is a large and imposing black wooden structure with tall uprights and a wide beam. It was thought that this execution would be a triple hanging, but in the event it was only to be a double as a third man was reprieved. The platform was reached by five steps and was hinged to give two leaves. It was erected on the flat roof of the prison gatehouse for each execution and was to have just three more clients: Patrick Duffy for the rape of Elizabeth Robinson on 29 March 1824, Jacob Bozelander for the rape of Mary Waters on 20 March 1826 and 16-year-old John Perkins on 25 March 1833 for the crime of shooting at.

Fortunately it was stored well and is now on display at the County Museum, Oakham. It is probably the only surviving 'New Drop' gallows in Britain. The drop was operated not by a lever on the platform but by withdrawing a bolt from below. A similar arrangement is known to have been used at Dorchester, as is recorded in the execution of Elizabeth Brown in 1856. This meant that the prisoner had to stand pinioned, hooded and noosed for some time whilst the hangman descended from the platform and went under it to operate the mechanism.

The county gaol for Surrey was situated in Horsemonger Lane, Southwark, which was then in that county. Between 1800 and 1868, 128 people were hanged here, comprising 125 men and three women. The first executions took place on Friday 4 April 1800 when five men were hanged by William Brunskill, one each for coining, highway robbery and being at large, and two for burglary. A total of 12 men were executed on three occasions during 1800.

The gallows was erected on the flat roof of the main gatehouse in between the four lanthorns or skylights. The largest number hanged at one time was seven, on two occasions: Monday 21 February 1803 and Monday 4 April 1803. On the morning of Tuesday 4 April 1809, William Brunskill carried out a quadruple hanging. The prisoners were James Bartlett, who had been convicted of sodomy, highway robber Henry Edwards, and John Biggs and Samuel Wood who were to hang for burglary. A large crowd had assembled to watch and it is reported in the typical language of the time that 'the unfortunate men met their fate with great fortitude and died acknowledging the justice of their punishment.'

At around 9am on Monday 23 April 1827, Daniel Buckley and Jeremiah Andrews, both of whom had been convicted at the Surrey Assizes of the high treason offence of coining, were hanged by Thomas Foxen. Prior to the execution, they were drawn across the yard on a hurdle with Foxen standing behind them with a drawn sword to the foot of the staircase leading to the roof, up which they ascended for their brief walk to the gallows.

William Banks was executed on 11 January 1830 for the crime of housebreaking. Banks had been a member of the 'Molesey Gang', who had been convicted at the Surrey Assizes of breaking into the house of the Rev William Warrington at Grove Cottage, West Molesey, in Surrey.

He was a career criminal and his luck held out until July 1829 when he was informed on and he and his gang were arrested. However, his co-defendants were acquitted due to lack of evidence.

By 1837 just murder, attempted murder, piracy and high treason carried the death penalty. In this year there were only eight executions nationally, all for murder, whilst 1838 saw a reduction to six hangings, one of which was for attempted murder – the lowest annual total recorded up till then. There would be a further three executions for attempted murder, the last in 1861, after which it ceased to be a capital crime under the provisions of the Criminal Law Consolidation Act of that year. In London, the Recorder's Report was abolished and Old Bailey judges could commute the death sentence of non-murderers. In all, 350 people were publicly hanged between January 1837 and 26 May 1868. This figure comprises 318 men and 32 women and averages just over 11 executions a year. The lowest annual totals were just five, in both 1854 and 1855. The peak years were 1863 and 1864, with 21 hangings in each.

The proportion of female to male executions rose in the two decades 1830–1849, with 16 women being hanged in each in England and Wales. In the first 10 years 14 women went to the gallows for murder plus two for arson in 1833. Nationally, including Ireland, the numbers for female executions from 1830–1838 (there were none in 1839) were 30, with ten in Ireland and four in Scotland. In the succeeding decade 15 women were executed for murder and one for attempted murder in England and Wales, with a further four women hanged in Ireland, all for murder. There were no female executions in Scotland at this period. This gave the highest proportion of female executions recorded, with women representing over 14.5% of the total for England and Wales; typically they had always been in the 4-5% range. There was a spate of poisoning murders committed by women at this time, their husbands frequently being the victims. This occurred at a time of reluctance on the part of the authorities to hang women in public, and many more were reprieved if their crime did not involve the use of poison.

In Chapter 9 we looked at the cost of executions in the 18th century. They do not appear to have been any cheaper in the 19th century. The hanging of Jane Jameson for the murder of her mother on Town Moor, Newcastle upon Tyne, on 7 March 1829 cost the county £28 13s 3d

(£28.67). This figure breaks down as follows. The joiner's bill for making and erecting the gallows was £8 5s 3d, plus an allowance to the joiners of 6s. On the day of execution seven police sergeants cost 5s each, 20 constables were 3s 6d each, 16 javelin men to guard the cart cost 5s each, plus 10s for summoning the constables and an allowance of £2 18s for javelin men, sergeants, constables, etc. For the tolling of the bell of St Andrew's Church, 2s 6d; hangman's fee, 3 guineas; for the hanging rope and pinioning cords, 3s; a cart and driver to convey Jane to the place of execution, 15s; a mourning coach to bring her body back, 15s 9d; horses for the officials, 5s each; and for the Rev Green attending her to the place of execution, 5s. It appears that Jane was made to stand on a stool placed in the cart which was pulled from under her when she finished her prayers, rather than being dragged off the cart. She reportedly died easily. As the first woman to hang at Newcastle for over 70 years her execution drew a huge crowd, estimated at 20,000.

The situation in Scotland was rather different from that in England and Wales. Scottish law had far fewer capital crimes than English law at the beginning of the 19th century: just 50 as compared to 220. However, Scotland did have two offences that were not recognised in English law, namely hamesucken and stouthrief. Hamesucken is 'the seeking and invasion of a person in his dwelling house', whilst stouthrief is a form of robbery taking place in a dwelling house. Bryce Judd and Thomas Clapperton became the last to hang for hamesucken on Wednesday 5 January 1820 at Calton Hill, Edinburgh; David Little was the last to be executed for stouthrief, at Glasgow on Wednesday 27 January 1831. Between 1800 and 1868, 273 people went to the gallows in Scotland, comprising 259 men and 14 women. A further 207 were sentenced to death but reprieved or respited. Scotland had a system of Assize courts with four circuits, one each for the east, west, south and north of the country. In addition, the High Court of Justiciary sat in Edinburgh. It acted as an independent court for that city and could hear the more complex and difficult cases from the Circuits.

As in England, the King and Privy Council had to approve Scottish death sentences, so there tended to be a greater time between sentence and execution or reprieve due to the difficulty of communication. Surviving records for Dundee show the cost of hanging Arthur Wood on 25 March 1839 for the murder of his son came to more than £60. A new gallows was erected on the second floor of the Hospital Buildings in front of the new gaol and cost £40 7s 11d (£40.40). John Scott, Edinburgh's hangman, was brought in to perform the hanging and was paid £17 5s, with a further £2 10s for travelling expenses and 15s for food whilst at the prison. Additionally there was the cost of two companies of cavalry who had come from Edinburgh to keep order among the large crowd that witnessed this rare event in Dundee.

11

The execution of children and teenagers

A number of books convey the impression that large numbers of children were hanged for minor crimes such as theft during the 18th and 19th centuries, but the surviving records, such as the Ordinary's Reports from Newgate, do not support this.

There was a different concept of the criminal responsibility of children and at this time the age of criminal responsibility was originally just seven. The law did not see children as distinct from adults until much later (1933) and did not accept that they did not know the difference between right and wrong. It still mandated the death sentence for children above the age of seven convicted of a capital felony. It would also punish teenagers just as severely as their adult counterparts for the most serious offences, particularly murder, rape, arson and highway robbery. There was a strong presumption against reprieving those who committed murder for gain, murder by poisoning or brutal murders, especially of their superiors or those who murdered their own children. Careful study of surviving records does seem to indicate a disparity of actual punishment, as distinct from sentence, between the sexes. Girls were generally executed only for the most serious crimes, whereas teenage boys could hang for any capital felony. Death sentences were certainly routinely passed on 8-13 year olds, but equally routinely commuted. Elizabeth Fry, the celebrated prison reformer, visited a woman named Elizabeth Fricker in Newgate in 1817. She recorded the meeting in her diary and noted that she also saw six men and seven young children in the Condemned Hold with Fricker. All the adults hanged, but all the children were reprieved.

Allegedly the youngest children ever executed in Britain were Michael Hamond and his sister Ann, whose ages were given as 7 and 11 respectively in *The History of Lynn* written by William Richards and published in 1812 (page 888). They are also referred to as being 'under age', without specifying what this term actually meant, and as 'the boy and the girl' as they were both small. Their executions are supposed to have taken place outside the South Gate of (King's) Lynn on Wednesday 28 September 1708 for an unspecified felony. It was reported that there was violent thunder and lightning after the execution and that their hangman, Anthony Smyth, died within a fortnight of it. A woodcut picture of them in the cart has survived, but it is unclear whether they really were hanged or what their ages were. There are no other contemporary records of children of this age actually being executed, although as stated earlier, it was legally possible.

Court records often did not give the age of defendants sentenced to death, as presumably age was not always considered to be relevant, if it was obvious that they were over seven. In some cases the only guide to their age is how old they told the chaplain or Ordinary they thought they were. The legal requirement to register a birth did not come in until 1837, and even the children themselves were not always sure exactly how old they were. Again the age of executed criminals was often not reported in the early newspapers, so it is not easy to trace all of the executions of juveniles in the 18th century. Below are some reliable examples of the execution of youngsters, rather than a conclusive list.

On Monday 12 March 1716, William Jennings (also given as Jenkins and Atkins) was hanged at Tyburn for housebreaking. His age was reported as just 12 in a contemporary newspaper. Sixteen-year-old Thomas Smith was hanged at Tyburn on 25 April 1716 together with William King who was 18, also for housebreaking. Edward Elton was hanged there the following year for the same offence. He told Paul Lorrain, the Ordinary, that he was 16, although there is no official confirmation of this. At this time there was no official record of the prisoner's name either as there was no proof of identity. They were tried under the name they had given when arrested. This may often have been an alias if they had a previous conviction because they might well escape the noose if they could convince the court that they were first-time offenders.

Five teenagers were hanged at Tyburn on Monday 20 May 1717. They were Martha Pillah (also given as Pillow) for stealing to the value of six guineas, who told Paul Lorrain that she was about 18; even she was not certain. With her in the cart were 17-year-old Thomas Price and 18-year-old Josiah Cony (alias Conyhatch) who were to die for housebreaking and

John Lemon, alias Lament, who claimed to be 18, together with his partner in crime, 17-year-old Christopher Ward, who were to suffer for burgling the home of Mr George Emmerton and stealing £4 worth of goods.

James Booty died at Tyburn on Monday 21 May 1722 for the rape of 5-year-old Anne Milton. He told the Ordinary that he had reached the age of 16. In Chapter 5 we read about 16-year-old Mary Groke (or Grote) who was burned at the stake for the petty treason murder of her mistress in March 1738. As we saw in Chapter 2, 16-year-old rapist William Duell was hanged at Tyburn on 24 November 1740, but survived and later had his sentence commuted to transportation. Seventeen-year-old Catherine Connor went to the gallows at Tyburn on Monday 31 December 1750 for publishing a false, forged and counterfeit will, purporting to be that of Michael Canty. She told the court that she could neither read nor write and that the forgery was made by a Mr Dunn, although she was present at the time. Catherine was one of 15 prisoners to hang that day.

As reported by the *York Courant* newspaper, 17-year-old Bezaleel Knowles was hanged at York on Saturday 28 April 1753. He was guilty of the brutal murder of Dorothy Gibson, whose throat he had cut in the parish of Knaresborough, to the extent of nearly decapitating the poor girl. Thursday 19 April 1759 saw the execution of 16-year-old John Morgan at Heavitree, near Exeter. According to the *Western Flying Post* newspaper he had stolen a pair of silver studs valued at 1s 6d (7½p) and other goods and money belonging to William Lowman. Elizabeth Morton, aged 15, was hanged at Gallows Hill, Nottingham, on 8 April 1763 for the murder of the 2-year-old child of her employer, John Oliver. Her execution was reported in the Leicester and Nottingham Journal.

In Chapter 9 we saw an increase in executions during the years 1776–1783, when transportation was unavailable. This trend was also reflected in juvenile executions.

Eighteen-year-old John Shepherd was hanged at Stafford on 29 March 1783, having been found guilty of the highway robbery of John Holmes, taking his watch valued at £3. John Cunningham, who was 16, was hanged near the scene of his crime at Halldown, near Kingsteignton in Devon, on 18 August 1783 for having strangled to death one John or James Pratt at Plymouth Dock. It is not known whether he was dissected afterwards or gibbeted. Thomas Walkins, aged 17, was executed at Hereford on

Friday 2 April 1784 for breaking into the dwelling house of Robert Jauncey in Lugwardine in February 1784 and stealing a bag, valued at 2d, and 40s in money (£2.01 in total).

Four prisoners were to die on Tuesday 28 March 1786 at Fisherton Anger near Salisbury, of whom one was a 17-year-old named William Hiccock who was executed for a house burglary that netted him some £25. The Reading Mercury records the execution of 18-year-old William Guest on Tuesday 6 April 1784 on Kennington Common. He had been convicted of the highway robbery of Mary Southouse in the parish of Wandsworth on 5 December 1783, robbing her of a silk purse, valued at 6d, and 10s in cash – a total haul of just 52½p. James Herslake, aged 17, was hanged at Heavitree, near Exeter, on Friday 7 April 1786 for stealing two oxen valued at £15. On Saturday 8 April 1786, two teenagers dangled side by side from the Leicestershire gallows. They were 19-year-old John Figures for a house burglary in Syston and 17-year-old Thomas Torville for horse theft.

Two 17-year-old boys were amongst a group hanged at Ilchester in Somerset on Wednesday 19 April 1786. William Norman was guilty of breaking into the dwelling house of Edmund Oland in the parish of Exford and stealing a pound of butter and other goods valued at 2s 2d (11p) plus a pair of breeches and other goods valued at 10s 2d (51p) and a silver half crown (12½p). John Smith had broken into the dwelling house of Henry Pinn and stolen two silver teaspoons and other goods valued at 30s, and £28 in money. Their executions were reported in the Western Flying Post. On Saturday 16 September 1786, 17-year-old Susannah Minton was executed for arson at Hereford before a large crowd. She had been convicted of 'voluntarily and maliciously setting fire to and burning a barn, the property of Paul Gwatkin, in the parish of Kilpeck on 11 November 1785'. She had been tried at the Lent Assizes but was respited to the Summer Assizes, probably because she had claimed that she was pregnant.

Six men were to suffer at Kennington Common on 11 April 1786, including 15-year-old James Coussins, who had been found guilty of setting fire to an outhouse belonging to Hannah Pool in Bermondsey in February of that year. Friday 16 March 1787 saw the hanging of 18-year-old John Lewis at Fisherton Anger, who had confessed to the murder of his wife Sarah by poisoning her. He also admitted poisoning his

9-month-old son in 1786. It is almost certain that unless he had severe mental problems, he would not have been reprieved at any period in history. Seventeen-year-old Anthony Farnsworth was hanged with his co-defendant, 21-year-old Samuel Martin, on Wednesday 24 March 1790 at Nottingham for robbing the warehouse of Messrs John Heard and Co in Nottingham.

Sarah Shenton, an 18 year old, was hanged at Moor Heath on the outskirts of Shrewsbury on Thursday 22 March 1792. She had been convicted of the murder of her male bastard (illegitimate child) whose throat she had cut immediately after birth on 30 September 1791 at Albrighton. The last executions at Moor Heath were a quadruple hanging carried out on Saturday 10 August 1793. Those executed comprised three teenagers: William Richards, aged 18; John Mumford, also 18; and Richard Sinister, aged 19. With them was 29-year-old Daniel Sheldon. They had all been convicted of a stealing a large amount of goods from the dwelling house of John Jackson at Halesowen on 7 May 1793. At the Dorset Lent Assizes in Dorchester in March 1794, 15-year-old Elizabeth Marsh was convicted of the murder of her grandfather, John Nevil. She died on Monday 17 March and was the first person to be executed outside the new county gaol in Dorchester. Her body was given to local surgeons for dissection. Betty Limpany, whose age is recorded as being about 18, was hanged at the county gaol, Exeter, for arson on Friday 5 April 1799 for maliciously setting fire to the dwelling house of William Leach.

19th century public hangings

Children, like adults, continued to be sentenced to death for a very large number of felonies up to 1836. It seems there was increasing public disquiet about hanging children and there is no evidence of anyone under 14 years old being hanged in the 19th century. The following are confirmed cases of the execution of young people in the 19th century, but cannot be considered definitive as the ages of prisoners were still not always recorded.

Eighteen-year-old Sarah Lloyd was executed at Bury St Edmunds on 23 April 1800 for stealing in the dwelling house of her mistress, Mrs Sarah Syer, at Hadleigh in Suffolk on 3 October 1799. She and her boyfriend had stolen some jewellery and also started several fires in the house. There was local agitation for a reprieve for Sarah, but not everyone thought that she deserved one. *The Times* newspaper published an editorial that was very critical of her, and other publications were similarly hostile. One wonders if it was because it was her mistress who was the victim and her crimes were therefore considered almost treasonable. No one was actually injured by the fires. In court Sarah was said to be 22 years old, but to be only 18 according to her supporters. At this remove we cannot know which is the correct figure.

Ann Mead, aged 16, was found guilty of the murder of Charles Proctor, aged 16 months, by feeding him a spoonful of arsenic at Royston in Hertfordshire. A large crowd witnessed her death outside Hertford prison on Thursday 31 July 1800. There would have been little sympathy for her in view of the nature of the crime. Seventeen-year-old Thomas Chalfont was put to death at Newgate on 12 November 1800 for stealing from a post office. Chalfont worked in the post office and stole a package containing £10. The jury recommended him for mercy at the end of the trial. David Duffield, aged 17, was hanged at the Bowling Green, Haverfordwest in Pembrokeshire on 6 April 1801 for the murder of 11-year-old Anne Morgan. Duffield was gibbeted at Tavernspite. He was the last juvenile to suffer this fate in the 19th century. Duffield's execution and gibbeting cost the County of Pembrokeshire £20 6s 4d.

Mary Voce was hanged at Gallows Hill, Nottingham, on Tuesday 16 March 1802 for poisoning her child. It is thought that she was born in 1788, which would make her only 14. It is interesting that the newspapers of the day found little noteworthy in the execution of a 14-year-old girl and gave her story very little coverage. *The Times* reported the execution of 17-year-old John Fisher at Horsemonger Lane gaol on Monday 4 April 1803. He was executed for robbery in the dwelling house of John O'Neill in the parish of St John, Southwark: stealing six shirts valued at 12s, a curtain valued at 7s and a child's shift valued at 6d, in total worth under £1. Eighteen-year-old Thomas Hillicker (or Hillaker) was executed at Salisbury on 22 March 1803, having been convicted of riot and maliciously pulling down and burning Littleton Mill at Steeple Ashton on 27 July 1802. This was the last case of a juvenile being hanged for riot.

The 'murder of a bastard' child, i.e. infanticide, by its mother was not an uncommon crime and often led to execution. This was despite the girl's frequently desperate circumstances and lack of any capacity to look after the baby. Such was the case of 17-year-old Mary Morgan who was hanged for the murder of her bastard at Presteigne in Radnorshire in 1805. She had become pregnant after being seduced by a member of the local gentry in Presteigne and then abandoned by him. She was tried and condemned to death on Thursday 11 April, her execution taking place two days later, at noon on the Saturday. Her body was buried in unconsecrated ground close to the churchyard at Presteigne, in which there are two memorial stones to her. On 6 May 1806, 15-year-old Peter Atkinson was executed at York Castle for cutting and maiming Elizabeth Stockton. Sixteen-year-old Thomas White and 42-year-old John Newball Hepburn were convicted of an 'unnatural crime', sodomy, at the December 1810 Sessions of the Old Bailey. They were hanged at Newgate on 7 March 1811. It is unclear from surviving records whether the act was consensual, as no victim's name is given.

On 22 March 1819, 16-year-old Hannah Bocking probably became the youngest girl to be executed in the 19th century when she was publicly hanged outside Derby's Friar Gate gaol for the murder, by poisoning, of Jane Grant. She was 15 at the time of the crime which took place in a meadow in sight of a gibbet from which hung the body of murderer Anthony Lingard, which sadly did not deter her. Three teenage boys were executed together for highway robbery outside Newgate on 31 March 1821, the youngest being John Davis who was 16 and had robbed a Mr George Barritt of his watch, seal and a ribbon. The value of the items was given as £3 10s 1d. The other two lads were 17-year-old James Reeves and his 19-year-old co-defendant, Joseph Johnson, who had robbed a Mr George Tucker at St Martin in the Fields and stolen his watch and other items, together valued at £3 11s (£3.55). Seventeen-year-old William Thompson was hanged at Newgate for highway robbery on 25 September 1821, and William Harding, also 17, for sheep stealing on 21 November 1821. He had taken six sheep valued at £10.

Benjamin Glover, aged 16, was hanged at Ilchester in Somerset on 1 May 1822 for stealing in a dwelling house. Giles East was also 16 when he was executed at Surrey's Horsemonger Lane gaol on 20 January 1823 for raping a little girl. Seventeen-year-old Charles Melford was executed together with his 21-year-old brother, William, for housebreaking on 12

March 1828 at Newgate. Three days later 18-year-old Moses Angel was hanged at Fisherton Anger near Salisbury for the murder of Daniel Blake. James Cook, aged 16, was hanged at Chelmsford's Springfield prison on 27 March 1829 for arson, having set fire to the premises of William Green, the farmer for whom he worked as a cow hand. Sixteen-year-old William Jennings became the last person to be hanged at Gallows Hill, Appleby in Westmorland, on 23 March 1829, for the rape of Agnes Corothwaite. A boy of just 9 was reputed to have been hanged at Chelmsford for arson on 5 August 1831, but it is probable that William Jennings was actually 19.

Seventeen-year-old Thomas Turner was executed for the rape of 9-year-old Louise Blisset at Worcester on 13 August 1830. The following year, on 25 March 1831, Thomas Slaughter, another 17 year old, was hanged there for setting fire to a hayrick.

John Amy Bird Bell, aged 14, was executed on Monday 1 August 1831 at Maidstone in Kent for the premeditated murder of 13-year-old Richard Taylor in a wood near Chatham. John and his 11-year-old brother, James, killed Richard for the sum of 9s (45p) which he was collecting from the Parish on behalf of his disabled father. Richard had been stabbed in the throat and his body thrown into a ditch. James Bell was reprieved. John became almost certainly the youngest male to be hanged in the 19th century. In 1833, a boy of 9 was sentenced to death at Maidstone Assizes for housebreaking but was reprieved after public agitation. March 1832 saw two 18 year olds hang in four days. Daniel Middleton was one of three men to die for the rape of Sarah Kempster at Salisbury on the 20th, while James Addington was executed for arson at Bedford on the 24th.

On 25 March 1833, 16-year-old John Perkins was hanged at Oakham in Rutland for the crime of shooting at. Sixteen-year-old Sylvester Wilkes was executed at Dorchester on 30 March 1833 for arson. Thomas Knapton, aged 17, was hanged at Lincoln Castle on 26 July 1833 for the rape of 19-year-old Frances Elstone. He was the last juvenile to hang for a crime other than murder. Seventeen-year-old William Marchant was executed at Newgate on 8 July 1839 for the murder of Elisabeth Paynton. Joseph Wilkes, aged 17, was hanged at Stafford also for murder on 2 April 1842. Another 17-year-old murderer, Charles Powys, died on the same gallows on 25 January 1845. Catherine Foster was one of two teenage girls publicly hanged in the period from 1840–1868. She was just 17 years old when she poisoned her husband, John, to whom she had been married for only three weeks, at Acton near Sudbury in Suffolk. Her execution was carried out on Saturday 17 April 1847 by William Calcraft in the meadow outside Bury St Edmunds gaol. A crowd of some 10,000 people had turned up to see it and Catherine reportedly made a speech from the platform imploring other girls not to follow her example and to stick to their marriage vows.

The year 1849 saw four teenage executions out of a total of 17 in England and Wales. The first was 17-year-old Thomas Malkin who was hanged at York Castle for the murder of Ester Hannan on 6 January 1849. George Millen, also 17, was executed at Maidstone on 28 March for the murder of 82-year-old Mr Law. James Griffiths, who was 18, was hanged at Brecon on 11 April for killing Thomas Edwards. The fourth of this series of executions was to be the last of a teenage girl in England. On 20 April 1849, 18-year-old Sarah Harriet Thomas was hanged at Bristol for the murder of her mistress. She was hysterical at the end, the governor of the gaol fainted and even the hangman was noticeably upset by her execution. This would be the City of Bristol's final public hanging and was carried out on the flat roof of the gatehouse of New Gaol in Cumberland Road. Three 18-year-olds were to hang for murders between 1853 and 1857. They were William Flack, at Ipswich on 17 August 1853, for killing Maria Steggles; Thomas Munroe, at Carlisle on 13 March 1855, for the murder of Isaac Turner; and George Edwards, at Maidstone on 20 August 1857, for killing his brother, Thomas.

Seventeen-year-old Charles Normington was hanged at York on 31 December 1859 for killing Richard Broughton. He was the last person under 18 to hang in public. On 11 April 1863, Robert Alexander Burton, aged 18, was hanged at Maidstone for killing 8-year-old Thomas Houghton. Wanting to be publicly hanged by the short drop method would seem a strange ambition to most people, but this was seemingly what Burton did want. His first employment was as an apprentice before joining the West Kent Militia in Maidstone, from which he deserted with his bounty money. He then worked briefly for a shoemaker from whom he stole and for which he received a two months' prison sentence.

As a result he became embittered and decided to commit murder, his first choice of victim being the shoemaker, whom he blamed for his spell in prison. However the shoemaker had moved and Burton could not locate him, so he considered killing a woman who had refused to serve him alcohol in a Chatham pub, but feared she would put up too much of a fight. Eight-year-old Thomas Houghton seemed a far safer bet, so Burton lured him from outside his home to a nearby railway tunnel ventilation shaft where he cut his throat. He then gave himself up and led police to the body. Burton came to trial at the Lent Assizes where he pleaded guilty to the murder. He was advised to change his plea and a defence of insanity was attempted, but his mental state was not sufficient to warrant this under the McNaughten Rules. He was thus convicted and sentenced to death, for which he thanked the trial judge. He willingly, almost eagerly, accompanied Calcraft to the gallows three weeks later on 11 April 1863 and was observed smiling as he was prepared. Unusually for the time, he died without a perceptible struggle.

Charles Robinson, another 18-year-old, was executed at Stafford on 9 January 1866 for killing Harriet Seager.

Private hangings 1868–1899

Between 1868 and 1899 there were a total of 446 executions in England and Wales, of which nine were of 17- and 18-year-old boys. The first private hanging in Britain was that of 18-year-old Thomas Wells at Maidstone prison on 13 August 1868. Details of this case will be found in Chapter 14. On 4 January 1875, 17-year-old Michael Mullen was executed at Liverpool. Michael McLean, also 17, was hanged there on 10 March 1884 for the murder of Jose Jimenez. Seventeen-year-old Joseph Morley was executed at Chelmsford on 21 November 1887 for the murder of his landlady, Mrs Rogers.

On 2 January 1889, 18-year-old William Gower and 17-year-old Charles Dobel were excuted at Maidstone for the murder of Mr Bensley Lawrence. Dobel's was the last execution of a 17-year-old in England and Wales. Eighteen-year-old Richard Davis was executed by James Berry at Knutsford in Cheshire for patricide on 8 April 1890. There was a triple execution at Winchester on 21 July 1896, one of the prisoners being 18-year-old Samuel Smith who had murdered Corporal Robert Payne.

The final teenager to hang in the 19th century was 18-year-old George Nunn, at Ipswich on 21 November 1899, for the murder of Eliza Dixon.

The 20th century

The Children's Act of 1908 stipulated for the first time a minimum age for execution of 16 years. However, there is no record of anyone aged under 16 being hanged since 1833 (see earlier). As was often the way, the law was simply catching up with established practice. Three 16-year-old and nine 17-year-old males would be given the death sentence between 1901 and 1932, but not one would hang. The last of these was Harold Hayward Wilkins, aged 16, who was condemned at Stafford Assizes on 18 November 1932 for the sexually motivated murder of Ethel Corey at Streetly, near Sutton Coldfield. The law was changed the following year by the Children and Young Persons Act in 1933 which raised the minimum age to 18 years. This same Act also raised the age of criminal responsibility from seven to eight years old. It was later raised to ten by the Children and Young Persons Act of 1963. This concept is known as doli incapax, which translates from Latin as 'incapable of crime' (below the specified age).

Seven teenage girls were condemned to death during the 20th century, although all were reprieved. Seventeen-year-old Eva Eastwood was convicted of murder and robbery in December 1902. Susan Chalice, also 17, was convicted of the murder of an infant child in July 1904. Eighteen-year-old Catherine Smith was sentenced in Scotland in 1911, also for the murder of an infant child, as was 18-year-old Rosalind Downer for the same offence in London in 1918. Elizabeth Humphries, also 18, was convicted of child murder in 1933. Another 18 year old, Elizabeth Maud Jones, was convicted with her American soldier boyfriend of a robbery murder in London in 1945, for which he was hanged. In 1952, Edith Horsley, also 18 years old, spent time in the condemned cell at Birmingham's Winson Green prison for murdering a child.

Three 18 year olds were hanged in the 20th century. They were Henry Julius Jacoby on 7 June 1922 at Pentonville, for the murder of Alice White (see Chapter 18); Arthur Bishop on 14 August 1925, also at Pentonville, for the murder of Francis Rix; and Francis 'Flossie' Forsyth, who became the last teenager to be executed in England and Wales.

He was hanged by Harry Allen, assisted by Royston Rickard, at Wandsworth on 10 November 1960 for the (capital) robbery murder of Allan Jee. One of his co-defendants, 23-year-old Norman Harris, was executed at the same time in Pentonville prison. There were two other men involved: 17-year-old Terrence Lutt and 20-year-old Christopher Darby. Lutt was too young to be sentenced to death and Darby was convicted only of non-capital murder.

The last teenage execution in Scotland took place at Glasgow's Barlinnie prison on 29 December 1960 when Anthony Miller, aged 19, was executed for the murder of John Crimin. The penultimate death sentence in England was passed on a teenager, 19-year-old David Henry Wardley, at Birmingham on 27 October 1965. He was automatically reprieved.

12

Execution Dock and post mortem punishments

The High Court of Admiralty was established by Edward III around 1360, having jurisdiction over civilian crimes committed at sea and directly offshore. It tried the cases of merchant seamen accused of murder, mutiny and piracy and also resolved 'prizes' which were ships and goods captured at sea. The court had the services of a marshal and court officers and sat at the Old Bailey. By the 16th century it had responsibility for trying all crimes that were committed at sea or along the English coast outside the borders of individual counties, involving English merchant ships' crews but not Royal Naval seamen. It functioned as a criminal court up to 1834 when this role was transferred to the Central Criminal Court. However, it continued to try cases involving shipping, collisions and salvage. The Judicature Acts of 1873 and 1875 saw the High Court of Admiralty merged with the other courts into the High Court of Justice.

In its role as a criminal court it passed death sentences which were carried out at Execution Dock, rather than at Tyburn. This was located between Wapping Old Stairs (off Wapping High Street) and Wapping Dock Stairs in east London. Hangings took place here for over 400 years. The gallows was erected on the foreshore at low tide and executions had to be timed to fit in with this. For instance, that of Captain John Sutherland (see later) was postponed from Monday to Thursday 29 June 1809 to coincide with a suitable low tide time. Time and tide wait for no man, so we are told!

Persons accused of crimes under the jurisdiction of the Admiralty were normally remanded to Marshalsea prison in Southwark to await trial. Those condemned were taken either from the Marshalsea, across London Bridge and past the Tower of London to Execution Dock, or alternatively from Newgate prison whence they went via Cornhill, Whitechapel Road and Commercial Road to Wapping. The procession to the gallows was led by the marshal on horseback (or his deputy) carrying a silver oar, representing the authority of the Admiralty. The prisoner travelled in a cart with a chaplain and the hangman (normally London's civilian executioner of the day). Crowds lined the shoreline and the wealthy hired boats moored in the Thames to get a better view of the proceedings. Hangings were carried out in the same way as on land, and in later times a 'New Drop'-style gallows was used.

After execution the bodies were chained to a stake at the low water mark and left there until three high tides had washed over them. Sometime between 1786 and 1814, this practice ceased. In particularly serious cases of piracy the court could order gibbeting after execution, in which case the body was covered in pitch and gibbeted lower down the Thames on the Isle of Dogs or Bugsby's Hole or Reach, near Blackwall, as a deterrent to passing merchant sailors. In cases of murder, after 1752, the court would order dissection or gibbeting as with civilian murders. If the criminals were to be dissected they were taken down from the gallows when the tide had come in far enough for the water to touch their feet before being removed and sent to Surgeons' Hall. Just as in the procession to Tyburn, those going to Execution Dock were allowed to stop for a drink, and the landlord of The Turk's Head pub supplied them with a quart of ale.

Perhaps one of the best-known pirates to die at Execution Dock was Captain Kidd. William Kidd had been born in Scotland around 1645. He moved to America as a child and lived in New York. Later in life he became a privateer and helped to suppress piracy in the Caribbean and the Indian Ocean. He is known to have commanded a ship called the *Adventure Galley* whose purpose was to capture French naval vessels and pirate ships. This mission was not greatly successful and as many of his crew were ex-pirates he turned to piracy himself in order to prevent a mutiny. He also murdered a member of his crew, William Moore, during an argument. His last act of piracy was committed against the *Quedagh Merchant* which was transporting gold and valuables for the British East India Company. When Kidd returned to New York he was arrested and later returned to England in 1700 to stand trial for piracy and murder. He was tried with other members of the crew but was the only one to hang, the rest being reprieved. The execution took place on 23 May 1701 and the first time he was suspended the rope broke, so he had to endure a second execution, after which his body was gibbeted.

Captain John Gow was a noted 18th century seafarer who became known as the 'Orkney Pirate'. He took part in a mutiny on board the *Caroline* during a voyage to Santa Cruz in which the ship's captain, surgeon and first mate were murdered. Gow assumed the captaincy and renamed the ship *Revenge*. In this guise it preyed upon merchant shipping plying off France, Portugal and Spain for a year or so before returning to Scotland. Gow altered the name to the *George* and told locals that he had been blown off course on a voyage to Scandinavia. In Stromness, Gow and his men were recognised by the crew of another ship, who persuaded one of his gang to inform on them to the magistrates. They were eventually arrested, but not before plundering several local houses. They were transferred to Marshalsea prison and Gow and seven members of the gang were condemned at their subsequent trial. They were hanged on 11 June 1725. Gow had asked the executioner to pull on his legs to hasten his demise. Hangman John Price did as requested but with such force that the rope broke and Gow had to be hanged again a few minutes later. His body and that of his first mate were afterwards gibbeted on the river bank, one at Deptford and the other at Greenwich.

Prior to 1735 records of hangings at Execution Dock are incomplete. Between 1735 and 1830 there were 78 confirmed executions and six probable ones. Of these, 29 were for murder, 18 for piracy, eight for mutinies on five different ships resulting in three double executions, and seven for treason including serving with the French. Three men were hanged for stealing from ships, another for stealing the complete vessel and two for destroying their own ships.

On 25 March 1752, Captain James Lowry was executed for beating a seaman named Kenneth Hossack to death on board the *Molly* returning from Jamaica in December 1750. Lowry had shown sustained cruelty towards his crew and may well have killed two others, although he was not tried for or convicted of these crimes. When the *Molly* docked in Lisbon, ten members of the crew managed to get ashore and see the British Consul there, swearing an affidavit to him regarding the murder of Hossack. This led to an advertisement in the press offering a reward for Lowry's capture. He responded to this by accusing the ten of piracy. They were sent back to England by the Consul to potentially stand trial. Lowry was arrested on his return and stood trial at the Admiralty sessions of the

Old Bailey on 18 February 1752. Here his accusers gave evidence against him and he was convicted. Lowry was not a popular criminal and was subjected to abuse and insults on the journey from Newgate to Execution Dock. After the hanging his body was gibbeted at Blackwall. This is not the only instance of a captain going too far with his own brand of discipline. The law gave captains, including merchant ones, a considerable amount of power in handing down punishments to men at sea, but did not allow them to kill their crew. A picture of Lowry's execution is in the National Maritime Museum.

Captain John Lancey was hanged on 7 July 1754 for scuttling the brig *Nightingale*. It is probable that Thomas Powe perished alongside him for his role in the crime. Another captain who committed murder was David Ferguson, killing Peter Thomas, a cabin boy, aboard the *Betsey* during a voyage to Virginia. He was hanged on Thursday 3 January 1771, having been tried the previous year. It is reported that this execution drew a huge crowd, both on the shoreline and on barges and ships on the river. The Gentleman's Magazine of 4 February 1796 describes the executions of Michael Blanche, Francis Cole and George Colley that took place on Thursday 28 January 1796 as follows:

'This morning, a little after ten o'clock, Colley, Cole, and Blanche, the three sailors convicted of the murder of Captain Little, were brought out of Newgate, and conveyed in solemn procession to Execution Dock, there to receive the punishment awarded by law. On the cart on which they rode was an elevated stage; on this were seated Colley, the principal instigator in the murder, in the middle, and his two wretched instruments, the Spaniard Blanche, and the Mulatto Cole, on each side of him; and behind, on another seat, two executioners. Colley seemed in a state resembling that of a man stupidly intoxicated, and scarcely awake, and the two discovered little sensibility on this occasion, nor to the last moment of their existence, did they, as we hear, make any confession. They were turned off about a quarter before twelve in the midst of an immense crowd of spectators. On the way to the place of execution, they were preceded by the marshal of the Admiralty in his carriage, the deputy marshal, bearing the silver oar, and the two City marshals on horseback, sheriff's officers, etc. The whole cavalcade was conducted with great solemnity.'

The captain of the ship *Adventure*, 46-year-old William Codlin, was hanged at Execution Dock on Saturday 27 November 1802. He was convicted of deliberately scuttling the ship by ordering the crew to bore holes in the wooden hull. The motive for this was to collect the insurance money. Codlin's trial lasted from 9 o'clock in the morning until midnight at the Old Bailey on 26 October 1802. Somehow one cannot imagine a modern court having this much stamina. After execution his body was taken down by friends in a boat and given a proper burial. Captain John Sutherland, a 46-year-old married man, was the commander of a transport ship named *The Friends* who was convicted of stabbing to death his 13-year-old cabin boy, William Richardson, (also given as Richard Wilson) on the River Tagus near Lisbon in Portugal in November 1808. His trial took place at the Old Bailey on Friday 22 June 1809, before Sir William Scott, the President of the Court of King's Bench. Sutherland was hanged on Thursday 29 June 1809 and dissected afterwards.

On Thursday 9 December 1830, George James Davis, alias Huntley, aged 27, and William Watts, alias Charles Williams, aged 32, became the last to die here for acts of piracy committed aboard the brig *Cyprus*. Today, the original location of Execution Dock is overlooked by a pub named the Captain Kidd.

Post mortem punishments

As you will have read above and in previous chapters, courts could order post mortem punishments in addition to hanging. The Murder Act of 1752 mandated these for murderers, but they could also be awarded for other crimes, notably robbing mail coaches. After 1752, the court could choose between dissection and gibbeting for murderers and would choose the latter where it wished to make a particular example of a criminal.

Dissection was the most frequent additional punishment and it was not unusual for the public to be admitted to watch the proceedings for a small fee. Leeds Royal Infirmary raised £30 from those who came to see the body of Mary Bateman, the 'Yorkshire Witch' in 1809. (Mary's skeleton is still on show at the Thackray Medical Museum in Leeds.) Before 1752, medical schools were always short of bodies on which to practise anatomy, and the regular supply of bodies of condemned murderers was very useful in furthering anatomical knowledge and surgical skills. It is unclear when gibbeting came into use, although there are records of it happening in the 13th century during the reign of Edward II. The first recorded instance of it in Scotland was in March 1637 when a man called McGregor, who was a robber and murderer, was ordered to stay on 'the gallowlee till his corpse rot'.

Gibbeting, or hanging in chains, was normally inflicted only on men, although there is evidence that both Evan Hugh Jones and his wife, Margaret, suffered this fate for the murder of a peddler named John Rea near Manafon in Montgomeryshire in August 1735. It appears that their bodies were hung on the branches of a large oak tree on the top of a hill near their home where the murder was committed. It is probable that Rea was not their only victim and that they had killed other men who had stayed with them, hence the severity of the punishment.

Murderers were typically gibbeted at or near the crime scene, highwaymen and pirates in prominent places such as crossroads or hill tops or the banks of the Thames. After the hanging, the prisoner would be stripped and their body dipped into molten pitch or tar and then, when it had cooled, dressed again and placed into an iron cage that surrounded the head, torso and upper legs. The cage was riveted together and then suspended from either the original gallows or a purpose-built gibbet. Here it would stay until the body rotted away or was stolen by relatives and friends for burial. Quite a few sets of gibbet irons have survived and can be found on display in museums. It could take several years for the flesh to rot away or be eaten by birds, and the scene was supposed to act as a powerful deterrent. It has been said that criminals were more horrified by being measured for their cages than they were at the thought of their hanging.

Edward Miles was hanged on Lancaster Moor on Saturday 14 September 1793, having been found guilty of robbery of the Warrington to Manchester mail near Warrington two years earlier, taking three bags containing letters from Chester, Liverpool and Warrington that were bound for Rochdale and one bag containing letters from Chester that was going to Manchester. He was reportedly gibbeted near 'The Twysters', Manchester Road, Warrington. Again his gibbet irons survived. Highway robbery of His Majesty's mail was considered to be almost treasonable and was thus punished more severely. In 1800, three men were ordered to be gibbeted at Ashton-under-Lyne after execution at Lancaster. They were John Brady (also given as Ready) and John Burns who had robbed mail man, Edward Burrell, at Ashton and Donald McDevatt, alias James Weldon, who had taken part in the Burrell robbery and also a similar one against another mail man, Michael Motter, at Warrington. These three were among a group of six men who were executed on Saturday 19 April 1800 in the first hangings at Lancaster Castle.

William Jobling was gibbeted after his execution at Durham, on 3 August 1832, for the murder of Nicholas Fairles, a local magistrate and a policeman during a riot. His gibbet was erected at the place of the crime at Jarrow Slake and is described as being formed from a piece of oak, 21 feet long and about 3 feet in diameter with strong bars of iron up each side. The post was fixed into a 1½-ton stone base, sunk into the slake. The cage and the scene were described thus: 'The body was encased in flat bars of iron of two and a half inches in breadth, the feet were placed in stirrups, from which a bar of iron went up each side of the head, and ended in a ring by which he was suspended; a bar from the collar went down the breast, and another down the back, there were also bars in the inside of the legs which communicated with the above; and crossbars at the ankles, the knees, the thighs, the bowels, the breast, and the shoulders; the hands were hung by the side and covered with pitch, the face was pitched and covered with a piece of white cloth.' Jobling's body was hoisted up to the top of the post and left as a warning to the populace. Sadly, Jobling was not actually the perpetrator of this murder. Before he died, Fairles was able to identify his killer, a friend of Jobling's, one Ralph Armstrong. However, Armstrong had managed to escape, leaving Jobling, who had been present but had done nothing to prevent the killing, to be convicted.

Twenty-one-year-old James Cook became the last man to be gibbeted, having been hanged at Leicester on 10 August 1832 for the murder of John Paas. The gibbet was erected in Saffron Lane near the Aylestone Tollgate and drew large crowds. Its forbidding presence was unpopular with the local residents, so unusually the body was taken down within the week. It was not at all unusual for gibbets to draw local protests; there were also protests about those on the Thames. One William Sykes wrote to Sir Robert Peel about this in 1824, saying that ladies travelling down the Thames would ask if they had passed the gibbets before coming on deck. Gibbeting was finally abolished in 1834 for both civil and nautical crimes.

13

The ending of public executions

Witnessing punishments such as whippings, the stocks, the pillory and particularly executions was always very popular with the general public. In the days before newspapers and when few of the populace could read, they also served a practical purpose of allowing the inhabitants of a town to see justice done. As we have seen, the execution could be carried out at the scene of the crime for this reason. Up to the end of the 18th century, executions were a spectator sport for all classes of society – the wealthy as well as the poor. When London executions moved to Newgate at the end of 1783, they continued to attract large numbers of spectators and the better-off would rent roof tops and rooms in houses opposite the Debtors' Door to get the best view.

Where the criminal was unusual, the execution could be guaranteed to draw huge crowds. Such was the case with 39-year-old Henry Fauntleroy who was the managing partner at Marsh, Sibbald & Co, a failing Marylebone bank, who had been convicted at the Old Bailey on 30 October 1824 of large-scale forgery. Fauntleroy was convicted of trying to defraud the Bank of England of £5000 in 3% annuities belonging to a Mr Francis Young. His case got wide coverage in the newspapers due to his social status and his alleged immoral behaviour. Fauntleroy confessed to the crime and claimed his motive was to try to prop up the bank. It was claimed by others that the motive was to support his lavish lifestyle and many girlfriends. It is thought that the crime for which he was executed was just one of many similar offences that had netted him a huge sum of money over several years.

There was considerable effort made to secure a reprieve and unusually further legal argument prior to his execution, but to no avail. This hanging of a 'gentleman' at Newgate, just after 8 o'clock on Tuesday 30 November 1824, was watched by an estimated 100,000 people. It was reported that just three minutes elapsed between Fauntleroy leaving his cell and being suspended. He writhed on the rope for a moment before James Foxen, the hangman, pulled down on his legs, so ending his suffering.

Five broadsheets were printed, one giving an 'Account of the Execution & Dying Behaviour' of Fauntleroy, whilst another purported to be his 'Sorrowful Lamentation' and a third was an account of his trial. Two more gave details of the execution, such was the interest in the case. It is claimed in some publications that Fauntleroy was the last person to be hanged for forgery in England, which is incorrect. This particular dubious honour fell to Thomas Maynard as mentioned in Chapter 10. Nationally, seven men were to die for this crime between Fauntleroy and Maynard: five at Newgate, one at Exeter and one at Stafford.

Ordinary people would walk for miles to watch an execution, and by the 1850s, special trains were laid on to take them to the county town, as happened at Stafford on Saturday 14 June 1856 for the hanging of the 'Rugeley Poisoner', Dr William Palmer. Owing to concern that he might not get a fair trial in Staffordshire, Parliament passed the Trial of Offences Act in April 1856 that allowed Palmer to be tried at the Old Bailey. He was kept at Newgate during the trial and returned to Stafford after conviction. This Act became known as 'Palmer's Act'.

In many counties, executions were held on market days to get the largest audience, and school parties would be taken to see them as a moral lesson, something which is certainly recorded as happening at Lancaster Castle. Public houses and gin shops always did a very brisk trade on a 'Hanging Day'. Executions were often carried out around noon to give the local people time to get there. Such was the case at Bury St Edmunds when William Corder was executed (see below). Thus, many were more or less inebriated before the proceedings began, still a recipe for rowdiness and bad behaviour.

By the 19th century, newspapers had become more widely available and would carry detailed accounts of trials and executions. There was the flourishing trade in execution broadsheets as noted above. These were normally single sheets of paper with the details of the crime, trial and punishment of the criminal, often including the 'last true confession' and lament of the condemned person. They generally had a stylised woodcut picture of the execution scene, modified as required to suit the sex and number of prisoners. The only problem with them is that as they were usually printed before the execution, they could not accurately describe an event that had not yet happened and indeed may not actually happen at all, as it was not unknown for the criminal to be reprieved after the broadsheet had gone to print. One wonders how much of the other verbiage they contained was pure speculation and invention on the part of the printers, particularly the 'last true confession'.

I have included one in the illustrations to give an idea of what they were like. This one is from Scotland and is dated December 1821, reproduced with the permission of the National Library of Scotland. It is interesting to see the writer's attitude to the public hanging of a woman by this time. Margaret Shuttleworth had murdered her husband, but was not treated to the execration that she would have been a few decades earlier. If the broadsheet is to be believed, there seemed to be considerable public sympathy for her. It is worth noting the almost theatrical nature of the proceedings, with a psalm being sung, prayers offered on the gallows and a speech being made by Margaret herself.

The *Illustrated Police News*, first published on 20 February 1864, was a very popular tabloid-style publication in the later Victorian era, largely replacing the broadsheet and packed with prurient details of the latest murder cases and executions. High-quality drawings were included of the murder scene, the criminal and the execution. Sometimes there were also little tableaux of the crime or the murderer's supposed dreams prior to their hanging.

Photography was only just coming into existence in the 1850s, but it was not possible to print photographs in newspapers of the day. In fact, I am not aware of any photograph of a British public execution. To compensate for this lack of pictorial information, death masks were made of famous criminals after execution and put on display. William Corder, who was hanged on 11 August 1828 for the shooting of Maria Marten in the famous 'Red Barn Murder', had a cast taken of his head after death, which can be seen at the Moyses Hall Museum, Bury St Edmunds, the town where the execution took place. A book about his trial was bound in his own skin which had been removed during his dissection and tanned. The *Sunday Times* reported this execution and had a woodcut picture of the scene.

William Palmer's death mask can still be seen in the County Museum of Staffordshire at Shugborough Hall. The death mask of William Burke, who was executed in Edinburgh on 28 January 1829, clearly shows the indentation in the neck left by the noose. The mask of Robert Smith, the last man publicly executed in Scotland, is preserved in the collection of a museum in Dumfries. A contemporary newspaper court reporter described Smith thus: 'His face indicates susceptibility to fits of extreme passion; it is not of the low criminal type.'

Phrenology was very much in vogue in the 19th century, although it was considered by many to be a pseudo-science. The concept was that the shape of a person's head and the lumps and bumps of their skull would give an insight into their personality. Studying casts of the heads of executed murderers would tell us more about them. It didn't! Madame Tussauds waxworks would buy the prisoner's clothes from the hangman, as well as other artefacts to display in order to add reality to the wax figures. The Chamber of Horrors was very popular with visitors, then as now, and new figures were put on display with amazing rapidity whilst there was still public interest in their case. This continued well into the 20th century.

The move to abolish public executions

Efforts to reduce the number of capital crimes and executions had been going on from the end of the 18th century, and during the first 40 years of the 19th century had met with considerable success. In the five years from 1828–1833, executions still averaged over one a week in England and Wales, although the distribution of them throughout the country was very uneven. London and the Home Counties had the most, whilst there were just two in the whole of Wales.

However, there was little mood in the country for outright abolition of capital punishment. So, as this was clearly unattainable, the next step of the anti-capital punishment lobby was to campaign for the ending of public executions, something strongly supported by the Quaker movement and influential people such as the authors Charles Dickens and William Thackeray as well as much of the press. The 'great and the good' have never been happy about the ordinary people enjoying overtly morbid pastimes such as watching a criminal strangling on the end of a rope!

There is no doubt that both sexes did enjoy a 'good hanging' and there was general disappointment expressed if the criminal died too easily, as William Palmer did. Where the criminal was female, the proportion of women in the crowd seemed typically to be higher. One gets the impression that the campaign to abolish public executions had far more to do with the fact that the lower classes enjoyed them, than out of any consideration for the feelings and sufferings of the prisoner.

It was not unknown for public hangings to end in tragedy and not just for those being hanged. Crushing injuries and fainting were quite commonplace as the crowd pressed forward to get a better view. On Monday 24 February 1807, however, things were going to be very much worse. Three murderers were to die at Newgate that morning: Owen Haggerty, John Holloway and Elizabeth Godfrey. The two men had been convicted of killing John Cole Steele, whilst Elizabeth Godfrey had fatally stabbed her neighbour Richard Prince. The trio had been tried at the Old Bailey Sessions on 18 February 1807 and the execution proceeded quite normally with the drop falling at around 8.15am.

The execution of three murderers, one of whom was female, was an unusual event and had attracted a larger than usual crowd. As they surged back and forth, there were cries of 'Murder, Murder' as people began to be trampled and crushed. The worst affected area was Green Arbour Lane, nearly opposite the gallows. As was normal at hangings, there were various street vendors selling refreshments. One pie seller had his basket of pies perched on a stool which was overturned in the mêlée, causing more people to fall and be trampled. A 12-year-old boy by the name of Harrington, who had gone to watch the execution with his father, died here, although his father survived and was taken to St Bartholomew's Hospital. A woman who was nursing a baby passed it over the heads of the crowd, enabling it to be rescued. Sadly, she was trampled to death a few moments later. In another part of the crowd, a cart collapsed under the weight of spectators and several of its occupants died.

The authorities were powerless to help the injured and dying because they simply could not reach them. It was only after the gallows was drawn back into Newgate that the area could be cleared to reveal the full extent of the tragedy. No fewer than 27 bodies were discovered at the scene and there were a further 70 people requiring hospital treatment. A temporary mortuary was set up at St Bartholomew's Hospital to enable relatives and friends to identify their loved ones. An inquest opened the following day which concluded on the Friday with a verdict 'that several persons came by their death from compression and suffocation'. It is unclear whether the authorities took any action to prevent a recurrence of this tragedy, but no similar problems were subsequently reported.

It has often been stated that public executions encouraged crime, particularly offences such as pickpocketing, then known as privately stealing from a person. It seems reasonable to believe this as when individuals are concentrating on the drama unfolding on the gallows above, they are off their guard and thus easy prey. Prison chaplains claimed that many of those they ministered to in the condemned cell had previously witnessed one or more executions. Clearly they did not have the deterrent effect that had originally been hoped for.

Victorian England was full of hypocrisy and whilst there might be publicly expressed disgust in the press at the behaviour of spectators at executions, privately people were lapping up every prurient detail. Executions had several obvious advantages for the individual observer's conscience: they were a perfectly legal form of sadistic and voyeuristic entertainment as the victims were criminals after all and one could justify taking the family to watch the hanging because one was going to see justice done. It was also a good moral lesson for the children!

Progressively, attitudes to public hangings were changing between 1800 and 1868. Initially all social classes enjoyed them, but by the end of the period it was no longer fashionable for the better-off to be seen at these events. Whether the propaganda of the abolitionists was having the desired effect on the middle and upper classes is unclear; perhaps it was the Victorian notions of morality that had come to the fore and people had become embarrassed to admit to going to watch a hanging.

There were exceptions to this, though, such as the execution of 23-year-old Swiss-born valet François Benjamin Courvoisier at Newgate on 6 July 1840. He had murdered Lord William Russell and his execution was attended by members of the nobility. The author and novelist William Makepeace Thackeray attended Courvoisier's hanging and spent some hours prior to it in observing what he described as a good-natured crowd. There were many young people of both sexes present and he formed the opinion that some of the teenage girls were prostitutes. Charles Dickens was also there and had hired a spot with a good view of the gallows. The crowd's excitement rose as the hour of execution arrived and there were the usual shouts of 'hats off' when Courvoisier was brought out. Thackeray records in 'Going to see a man hanged' that he could not bring himself to look upon the final scene and that he had flashbacks of the execution for two weeks afterwards, such was the impression it had made on him. This was to be the sole hanging at Newgate in 1840. As hangings had become rare events they were probably of far greater public interest. Again several broadsheets were printed in this case. Charles Dickens seemed to enjoy watching executions and had attended a guillotining in Rome on Saturday 8 March 1846. He railed against the behaviour of the crowd, but it did not stop him going to witness such spectacles himself.

The most famous execution at Horsemonger Lane gaol in Surrey was that of Maria and Frederick Manning who were hanged there on the morning of Tuesday 13 November 1849. They had been condemned for the murder of Patrick O'Connor. Maria was interested in Patrick but had married Frederick instead and was determined to kill Patrick for his money. She invited him to dinner and shot him in the head in the kitchen of their house in Miniver Place, Bermondsey. The bullet did not prove fatal, so Frederick finished Patrick off with a crowbar. They buried Patrick's body in a pre-dug grave below the kitchen flagstones, covering it with plenty of quicklime, which was thought at the time to speed decay of the flesh. Ironically it was what they too were to be buried in.

The following day Maria managed to get into O'Connor's lodgings which she looted, taking everything of value including his share certificates. She paid a further visit the following day to see if there was anything she had missed. These share certificates were to be her undoing. She travelled to Edinburgh where she was arrested when she tried to sell them to a stockbroker who had heard that they had been stolen. Frederick had travelled to Jersey where he was soon arrested.

Their execution took place on the flat roof of the prison gatehouse and was attended by a huge crowd, estimated at between 30,000 and 50,000 people. It was reported that some of the wealthier women present used opera glasses to get a better view of the proceedings. There was considerable comment on what Maria wore – a fashionable black satin dress and veil. Black satin apparently went out of fashion and stayed that way for the next thirty years! They were hanged side by side a little after 9 o'clock by William Calcraft. The execution passed off without incident, but led to angry outbursts in *The Times* newspaper from Charles Dickens deploring the behaviour of the crowd. In one letter to the paper he wrote: 'I was a witness of the execution at Horsemonger Lane this morning.' 'I believe that the sight so inconceivably awful as the wickedness and levity of the crowd collected at that execution this morning.' 'When the two miserable creatures who attracted all this ghastly sight about them were turned quivering into the air, there was no more emotion, no more pity, no more thought that two immortal souls had gone to judgement than if the name of Christ had never been heard in this world.' It is reported that some 2,500,000 broadsheets were printed for this execution.

The hanging of William Bousfield outside Newgate on 31 March 1856 did not go well. Twenty-nine-year-old Bousfield had killed his wife, Sarah, and their three children with a cut-throat razor which he then turned on himself sometime in the night of the Saturday or Sunday, 2/3 February. Finding that he had not been able to commit suicide, he went to Bow Street police station and gave himself up, telling a startled PC Fudge that he had murdered his wife. An investigation of their home revealed the dead children. Bousfield was tried and convicted at the Old Bailey a month later, on 3 March. On Sunday 30 March, the eve of his execution, he again attempted suicide by throwing himself on the fire in the condemned cell, sustaining facial burns before he could be removed by warders. His face was bandaged up and he had to be carried to the scaffold the following morning for his appointment with Calcraft. The drop fell as usual, but somehow his feet managed to get back onto the side of the platform and had to be pushed down by one of the warders because Calcraft had gone from the gallows as a threat had been made to kill him the previous day. He was called back to find that Bousfield had again got his feet back onto the platform and in the end had to jump down and hang onto Bousfield's legs to complete the execution. Hardly a dignified ending and not one that went down well with spectators.

Famous author-to-be, Thomas Hardy, was just 16 when he first went to watch a hanging and was able to secure a good vantage point in a tree close to the gallows.

The criminal was Elizabeth Martha Brown(e) who was to die for the murder of her husband, John. She was hanged by Calcraft outside Dorchester gaol at 9 o'clock on a rainy Saturday morning, 9 August 1856, before 3-4,000 spectators. If this does not sound a large number, it is worth noting that at the 1801 census, the population of Dorchester stood at 2,402 and had risen to only 9,000 by the end of the century.

Elizabeth behaved with courage and dignity at the end and was still a good-looking woman at 45 years old. Hardy recalled 'what a fine figure she showed against the sky as she hung in the misty rain, and how the tight black silk gown set off her shape as she wheeled half round and back'. It made an impression on him that lasted until old age. He still wrote about the event in his 80s. It was to provide the inspiration for his novel *Tess of the D'Urbervilles*, first published in 1891. It seems possible that Hardy found something erotic about the execution and particularly her writhing body in the tight dress and facial features partially visible through the rain-soaked hood. This execution caused a leading article to be written in the Dorset County Chronicle advocating the abolition of the death penalty. She was the last woman to be publicly executed at Dorchester and only three more men were to suffer here in public.

The year 1864 was an unusually busy one for hangings at Newgate. Firstly, there were the five 'Flowery Land Pirates' on 22 February, followed by John Devine on 2 May, and 23-year-old Charles Bricknell on 1 August. But the case that was to make the headlines and capture the public's interest was Britain's first railway murder which occurred on 9 July 1864. There was considerable concern about the safety of train travel at this time. The person convicted of the crime was a German tailor called Franz Muller, a man in his early 20s. Sixty-nine-year-old banker Mr Thomas Briggs was travelling from Fenchurch Street station by the North London Railway to Hackney on that Saturday evening after dining with relatives. Two clerks travelling home got into a first class carriage at Hackney and noticed that it was empty and that there was blood on the window and floor. They alerted the guard and a search of the compartment revealed a bloodstained hat, a bag and a walking cane. In the meantime, a body had been discovered on the tracks. At this point, Mr Briggs was still alive, although unconscious, and was taken to a nearby pub for attention. Sadly, he never recovered consciousness. He was identified and it was found that his gold pocket watch and chain were missing, but strangely there was quite an amount of money still on him. The pocket watch was found by police at a jeweller's shop in Cheapside, the owner, Mr John Death, remembering that it had been brought in by a young man with a German accent. The hat was also traced directly to its purchaser, Franz Muller.

The police went to Muller's address and found that he had escaped on a ship bound for the USA. Chief Inspector Richard Tanner and his sergeant George Clarke took a faster ship and arrived in New York two weeks before Muller got there. Here he was arrested and, after some negotiation with the American authorities, returned to Britain to stand trial at the Old Bailey on 27 October 1864 before Mr Baron Martin. The jury took just 15 minutes to find Muller guilty. He was hanged outside Newgate on 14 November 1864 by William Calcraft. The execution went smoothly and was attended by a huge multitude, whose behaviour was, as had now become the norm, condemned at least by *The Times* and the *Sporting Times* newspapers.

There was always the danger that public executions would make martyrs of the victims, and this was to be the case in the hanging of three young Fenians (Irish Republicans) at the New Bailey prison in Salford on Saturday 23 November 1867. William Allen, William Gould and Michael Larkin had been convicted by a Special Commission of the murder of police sergeant Charles Brett during a successful attempt to release two Fenian leaders, Thomas Kelly and Timothy Deasy, from a prison van transporting them across Manchester on 18 September. Sergeant Brett was in reality shot by accident. He was inside the van and his assailants demanded that he open the door, which he refused to do. Instead, he looked through the keyhole to get a view of the situation just as one of them fired a bullet into the lock which passed though his head. Although there seems adequate proof of this chain of events, it does not amount to manslaughter in law as the killing occurred as part of another serious crime.

On the eve of the execution, large crowds gathered just to see the gallows which had been erected on the Friday morning immediately outside a large gap that had been made in the prison wall. It had to be protected by police and the 72nd Highland Regiment was on hand the following morning to ensure that there would be no rescue for the three condemned men. In all, it is estimated that there were 2,500 police and soldiers on duty. Calcraft officiated as usual and the three men became still soon after the drop fell. It is interesting to note from a contemporary drawing of the scene how little the 8,000 or more spectators would have actually been able to see of the hanging bodies. The front of the gallows had a fence up to about chest level and the area beneath the platform was draped in black cloth to hide their struggles from view. Once the drop had fallen, all that would have remained visible would have been the hooded heads and shoulders of the three men. This arrangement was quite typical.

These executions provided the Fenian movement with the martyrs they sought and also brought wide press coverage, mostly condemnatory. The three became national heroes in Ireland and America and were dubbed the 'Manchester Martyrs'. There were huge funeral processions across Ireland for them, with an estimated 60,000 people attending the one in Dublin. In conclusion, it is fair to say that at best these public displays were a source of ribaldry, drunkenness and crime, and at worst, the cause of serious loss of life. One tends to feel that Charles Dickens' comments on the execution of the Mannings summed up the situation very well.

The last public executions and the legal changes that led to their abolition

The decade from 1850 to 1859 had just 95 executions, the lowest 10-year total yet. A further 115 men and 5 women were to die in public between 1 January 1860 and 26 May 1868. Twelve men and one woman were hanged within prisons in the remainder of the decade, giving a total of 133 for the 10 years. The Criminal Law Consolidation Act of 1861 reduced the number of capital crimes to four: murder, high treason, piracy and arson in a Royal Dockyard (this was a separate offence, not high treason). In reality, except for four executions for attempted murder, this Act was more of a tidying-up exercise as nobody else had been hanged for a crime other than for murder since 1837. The last execution for attempted murder took place on 27 August 1861 when Martin Doyle was put to death at Chester. Doyle was hanged after Royal Assent was given to the 1861 Act, but his execution was legal as the offence was committed and the indictment signed before the Act came into force on 1 November of that year.

The 1864 Royal Commission on Capital Punishment sat for two years and concluded that there was no case for abolition of the death penalty, but did recommend ending public executions. (Franz Muller, above, was hanged while the Commission was sitting.) In the spring of 1868, England and Scotland carried out their last public executions. In Wales, the last one had been two years earlier when Robert Coe was executed outside Cardiff prison on 12 April 1866 for the murder of John Davies. Joseph Bell became the last person to die in public view in Scotland when he was hanged at Perth on 22 March of that year.

The last public hanging of a woman and last public execution at Maidstone prison took place at midday on Thursday 2 April 1868 when 25-year-old Frances Kidder was executed for the murder of Louisa Kidder-Staples, her 12-year-old step-daughter. Frances had married William Kidder, who had Louisa and a younger child by his previous relationship and whom Frances deeply resented. Only Louisa lived with them and Frances consistently abused her. On 24 August 1867, she had taken Louisa to visit her parents in New Romney and also took one of her own children with her. Frances' parents went out and while they were away, Frances drowned Louisa in a ditch, having to hold the struggling child under as the water was only a foot deep. She claimed afterwards that they had fallen into the ditch together when they were frightened by passing horses. She came to trial on Thursday 12 March 1868 at the Spring Assizes in Maidstone before Mr Justice Byles. The prosecution brought in evidence of the abuse of Louisa and of previous threats to drown her. Frances maintained her story of the two of them being frightened by the horses and of Louisa falling into the water, from which she claimed she had tried to rescue her. This was rejected by the jury after just 12 minutes' deliberation.

The execution was set for exactly three weeks later. In the condemned cell she confessed to the prison chaplain. Kidder had to be helped up the steps onto the gallows and held on the trap doors by two warders where she prayed intently while Calcraft made the final preparations. She struggled hard for two or three minutes after he released the trap and was described by the reporters who witnessed the scene as having 'died hard'. An estimated 2,000 people, many of them women, had come to watch her final agonies.

Maidstone prison had also been the location of the previous female public hanging in Britain, that of 29-year-old Ann Lawrence who was put to death alongside 20-year-old James Fletcher on 10 January 1867, having both been convicted at the same Assizes. He had battered warder James Boyle to death with a hammer in Chatham prison, while she had murdered her baby son Jeremiah and attempted to kill her lover Walter Highams at Tunbridge Wells. Ann Lawrence told the governor of Maidstone prison, Major Bannister, that she hoped her execution would be carried out despite the petition for her reprieve.

The Capital Punishment (Amendment) Act received its third reading in Parliament on 11 May 1868. The following day Robert Smith was executed outside Dumfries prison, but the authorities ensured that the public saw very little. This was the last nominally public hanging in Scotland. Nineteen-year-old Smith had raped and strangled 9-year-old Thomasina Scott in a wood near Annan.

England's last fully public hanging was to be that of Michael Barrett at Newgate. Twenty-seven-year-old Michael Barrett originated in County Fermanagh, Ireland, and was another member of the Fenians. He was convicted of causing an explosion at the Clerkenwell House of Detention in London on 13 December 1867 in an attempt to free Richard O'Sullivan Burke, a Fenian Brotherhood member. The bomb blew a huge hole in the prison wall, destroying and damaging several houses opposite the prison in Corporation Lane. The blast killed seven people, injuring many more, and was one of the first Irish bombings on English soil. Six people were arrested but Barrett was the only one to be convicted at the Old Bailey on 6 April 1868 on one specimen charge of murder in respect of the death of Sarah Ann Hodgkinson who lived at 3a Corporation Lane, the house most severely damaged by the blast. Sarah had received a huge cut to her neck that extended from in front of her right ear to the cheek, her scalp was cut with glass and one of her major veins severed, causing death from haemorrhage and suffocation. Unusually for the time, a government commission was set up to review the case prior to the execution, hence the abnormally long period between the trial and the hanging. This concluded that Barrett had been correctly convicted and that his alibi defence of having been in Glasgow at the time was false.

Barrett was hanged by William Calcraft shortly after 8am on Tuesday 26 May 1868, dying without a struggle. It was reported in *The Times* newspaper that there were a great many members of the lower classes, including young women with children, present at this execution and that the crowd stretched past St Sepulchre's Church and almost into Smithfield, such was the interest in it. In its editorial, *The Times* celebrated the fact that this hanging would be the last such vulgar public display. Barrett's body was buried that evening under the flagstones in 'Birdcage Walk', the corridor linking the Old Bailey to Newgate, and later reburied in a mass grave in the City of London Cemetery in 1902 when Newgate closed.

Three days later, on 29 May, the Capital Punishment (Amendment) Act came into force, ending public hanging as such, and requiring all future executions to be carried out within prisons. It further required that the sheriff or under sheriff, the governor, the prison doctor and such other prison officers had to be present. The prison doctor was required to examine the prisoner after execution to verify that life was extinct and to sign a certificate to that effect to give to the sheriff. The sheriff, the governor and the prison chaplain were required to sign a declaration to the effect that judgement of death had been executed on the prisoner. This Act allowed the governor of the prison and the sheriff of the county in which the execution took place the discretion to admit newspaper reporters and other witnesses, including the victim's relatives, to the hanging.

In the drafting of the Act, no thought had been given to the Channel Islands and so it was just over seven years later when Britain's last public hanging took place. On 12 August 1875, Joseph Philip Le Brun was executed by William Marwood in St Helier, Jersey, for the murder of his sister, Nancy. This was the only public execution using a measured drop ever seen in Britain. The law in Jersey did not fall into line with that of England until 1907 for the island's next execution, that of Thomas Connan at St Helier on 19 February of that year for the murder of Pierre Le Guen.

There can be little doubt that the prison and police authorities were very pleased to see the end of public executions as they required considerable crowd control. There was also a large financial saving for individual county authorities since they no longer had to provide police and javelin men or meet the costs of erecting the gallows for each execution.

14

Within the walls – the early private hangings

From the beginning of June 1868 all executions had to be carried out within prisons. The first was that of 18-year-old Thomas Wells at Maidstone prison. Although the law had changed the location, it had not changed the method of execution nor had it laid down any specific protocols for carrying out private executions. It was still up to the sheriff or under sheriff and the governor of the prison to determine the precise details. The governor of Maidstone decided to have the gallows erected in the former timber yard within the prison grounds, out of sight of the cell blocks and nearby houses. It was the same one that had been used for Frances Kidder earlier in the year.

Thomas Wells had been employed as a carriage cleaner at Dover Priory railway station and had taken his gun to work, where his boss, Mr Edward Walshe, the station master, had caught him firing at birds. He was offered two alternatives: either to make a full apology for his actions and promise never to repeat them or be dismissed. He was given ten minutes to consider this offer but declined to make the apology, shooting Mr Walshe in the head instead. He was captured minutes later and was sent for trial at the Kent Summer Assizes of 1868 before Mr Justice Wills. His defence was to be one of insanity due to the effects of a serious accident he had had whilst at work at the station, being nearly crushed by a train. The jury did not accept this and took just five minutes to convict him. He was therefore returned to the condemned cell at Maidstone to await execution on 13 August 1868. As usual, William Calcraft was to be the hangman and was assisted by George Smith of Dudley for this novel occasion. Although the proceedings were now hidden from the general public, they were hardly private. Guests of the sheriff and sixteen newspaper reporters were permitted to witness it. Wells was led to the gallows at 10.30am and had to be supported on the trap doors by two warders. When the drop fell, Wells, like so many of

Calcraft's victims, died visibly struggling against the pinioning straps over the ensuing two or three minutes. *The Times* newspaper noted afterwards that there had been no protests over the move from public to private hangings, at least not from its readers. It is not known whether the ordinary folk of Maidstone actually shared the paper's lofty opinion, as theirs were not canvassed.

The next private execution was that of another teenager, 19-year-old Alexander Arthur Mackay. Mackay was employed by George Grossmith as a general servant at his eating house at 11 Artillery Passage, London. He had an argument with George's wife Emma on the morning of Friday 8 May after George had left the shop, as a result of which he attacked her with a rolling pin, an iron bar and items of crockery in the kitchen. She died nine days later from her head injuries, but had recovered consciousness sufficiently on the first day to make a statement to the police.

Mackay was able to escape from London and was captured in Maidstone some five weeks later and returned to the capital for trial. He appeared at the Old Bailey before Mr Justice Lush on 17 August, represented by two defence counsel. He was convicted, but the jury recommended him to mercy on account of his age, 18 at the time of the offence.

The Home Secretary, Earl Cranbrook, saw no reason for a reprieve and 8 September was the date set for the execution. The gallows was erected in an enclosed yard near the chapel and the hanging was attended by representatives of the press. A little before 9am, Mackay was led into the yard supported by the Ordinary, the Rev Jones, and ascended the steps up onto the platform where he joined in with Rev Jones' prayers. Calcraft pulled the lever and Mackay dropped the customary few inches, taking several minutes to become still, according to contemporary reports. The black flag was raised over the prison after the trap had opened and the bell of St Sepulchre's Church tolled. His body was left hanging for an hour before being taken down and prepared for the formal inquest, which took place that afternoon. Mackay was then buried in an unmarked grave within the prison.

The third and last private execution of 1868 took place at Lincoln Castle on 28 December. The condemned was 29-year-old Priscilla

Biggadyke who had been convicted of the murder by arsenic poisoning of her husband, Richard, on 1 October 1868. This case was dubbed 'The Stickney Murder' by the press. Richard and Priscilla had not been on good terms and it was suspected that she was having an affair with their lodger, Thomas Proctor. Thomas was also charged with the murder, but his indictment was thrown out by the judge, Mr Justice Byles, before the start of her trial at Lincoln on 11 December. Once again the jury made a recommendation to mercy, this time on the basis that the evidence had been circumstantial. However, there was to be no reprieve.

On 27 December, the gallows was erected close to the court building on the Castle Green. Thomas Askern, Yorkshire's hangman, was appointed to carry out the execution at 9 o'clock on the Monday morning. Askern, like Calcraft, used the short drop and Priscilla took three minutes to struggle into unconsciousness on the rope after he released the trap, according to newspaper reports. As became the custom, and one which was to continue up to abolition, a small crowd of people had assembled to see the black flag raised over the castle tower. After the inquest Priscilla's body was buried within the Lucy Tower. She was the last person to hang at Lincoln Castle. A new county gaol opened in Greetwell Road in Lincoln two years later. Thomas Askern had decided to experiment with a new position for the eyelet of the noose for this execution, positioning it under the chin, causing her head to be thrown back. In this position, he claimed, which seems reasonable, the noose would not strangle her. One assumes that it took three minutes for the rope to so constrict the major blood vessels of the neck as to cut off the blood supply to the brain. Both 1870 and 1871 were to be lean years for Calcraft and his fellow executioners, with just seven and three hangings respectively.

One of the first Victorian 'baby farmers', 34-year-old Margaret Waters, met her end at Horsemonger Lane gaol on Wednesday 11 October 1870. She had been charged with five counts of wilful murder of children in the Brixton area of London, as well as neglect and conspiracy. Metropolitan Police Sergeant Richard Relf became the first specialist investigator of baby farming murders. He examined the cases of 18 infant deaths locally, leading to the arrest of Waters. She was convicted of the murder of an infant named John Walter Cowen. Her sister, Sarah Ellis, was convicted in the same case for obtaining money under false pretences and sentenced to 18 months' hard labour. As was usual for Surrey, William Calcraft carried out this hanging.

In the spring of 1872, a young man was occupying one of Lincoln Castle's two male condemned cells. Twenty-eight-year-old Frederick William Horry had been convicted at the Lent Assizes of the shooting murder of his wife Jane at Boston in Lincolnshire. Frederick and Jane had run the George Hotel in the village of Wolstanton in the Staffordshire Potteries and all had gone well until Frederick began to drink heavily. Jane left him in 1871 and went to live with his father in Boston. Frederick moved to Nottingham and at some point bought a gun. He visited Jane a few times and on the last occasion used the gun to kill her, his motive being jealousy. He pleaded insanity at his trial, which the jury refused to accept, and was duly condemned.

The murder, trial and forthcoming execution were big news locally. One resident of the Lincolnshire village of Horncastle was even more interested in the story. He was William Marwood, the local cobbler. Fifty-four-year-old Marwood had taken a great interest in the process of execution by hanging over the years and knew that he could improve on the way it was carried out by Calcraft et al. He had never hanged anyone or even assisted at or witnessed an execution but had read a great deal on the subject, including the work of doctors in Ireland, which had convinced him that if an accurately calculated drop was given that related to the prisoner's weight, then the neck should be broken and death be fast and pain free.

Amazingly he persuaded the authorities at Lincoln prison to let him carry out the hanging of Horry on 1 April 1872. Perhaps after the execution of Priscilla Biggadyke, Lincoln's previous hanging, the governor there was only too willing to give Marwood a try so as to avoid the wholly distressing scene that he had had to witness then. A pit was dug and the gallows erected over it for this execution. When Marwood released the trap doors Horry dropped from view leaving just the still taught rope in view. There was no struggling, no choking sounds and the whole process was far less unpleasant for all concerned. Thus a new dawn was to be ushered in. Although this execution was judged a success, the county sheriffs did not immediately move en masse to use Marwood.

William Calcraft, Thomas Askern and Robert Anderson still continued to be appointed and it was not until Calcraft retired in mid-1874 that William Marwood was appointed executioner for the City of London and County of Middlesex and effectively began to take the national role.

Askern carried on in the north until 19 December 1876, his last execution being that of James Dalgleish at Carlisle for the murder of his landlady, Sarah Wright. The reason that Askern was given this job was that Marwood had an appointment at Horsemonger Lane on the same day to execute Silas Barlow for the murders of his former girlfriend Ellen Soper and their child at Battersea. Robert Anderson carried out the triple hanging of Charles Edward Butt, Mary Anne Barry and Edwin Bailey at Gloucester on Monday 12 January 1874, due to the unavailability of the now 74-year-old Calcraft. Short drops were used and although the two men became still almost immediately, Mary Anne Barry struggled hard for some time. Anderson had to press down upon her shoulders to quicken her death. This execution was attended by some forty people, including representatives of the press, so although not public, could hardly be described as private either.

Edward Butt, aged 22, had shot and killed 20-year-old Amelia Selina Phipps out of jealousy because she would not have a long-term relationship with him. They were near neighbours on adjoining farms at Arlingham. Edwin Bailey and Mary Anne Barry were convicted of causing the death of 9-month-old Sarah Jenkins by poisoning. Sarah's mother, 17-year-old Mary Susan Jenkins, claimed that Bailey was Sarah's father and wanted maintenance payments from him. He persuaded Mary Anne Barry to help him poison the baby using strychnine disguised in the outer wraps of packets of Steedman's Soothing Powders which were used to comfort teething babies. The hangings took place at 8 o'clock in the morning and when the prisoners had been pinioned in their cells they were led out in a procession, headed by the chaplain. Butt and Bailey were wearing suits and Barry a long print dress. She was accompanied to the gallows by the matron of Gloucester. As required by law, the under sheriff, the governor, Captain H. K. Wilson, the deputy governor, the chaplain, the prison doctor and several warders were present.

The three condemned prisoners knelt on the platform and recited the Lord's Prayer with the chaplain before Anderson made the final preparations. Barry was placed between the men on the trap, their legs were tied and the white hoods placed over their heads, followed by the nooses. The chaplain and the hangman shook hands with each prisoner and then Anderson withdrew the bolt releasing the trap doors, causing the prisoners to drop below the level of a calico screen which had been set up on the platform to hide the hanging bodies. A black flag was hoisted over the prison to show that the executions had been carried out. After the formal inquest, their bodies – that were still wearing the clothes that they were hanged in – were placed in coffins with quicklime and buried in unmarked graves in the execution yard. This would be the last short drop hanging of a woman in Britain.

William Calcraft probably performed his last hanging at Newgate, that of James Godwin, on 25 May 1874. Godwin had pleaded guilty to the murder of his wife Louisa. After this, Calcraft retired as the executioner for London and Middlesex on a pension of 25 shillings (£1.25) per week provided by the City of London. There is, however, some evidence in the form of sheriff's pleadings, that he may have hanged John MacDonald at Exeter on 10 August 1874. MacDonald was executed for the murder of his girlfriend, Bridget Walsh.

Marwood's first execution at Newgate was to be that of 48-year-old Frances Stewart on Monday 29 June 1874. Stewart had drowned her grandson, Henry Ernest Scrivener, in the River Thames after a quarrel with her son-in-law. She became the first woman to be hanged using a measured drop. On the morning of her death she was pinioned in the condemned cell and then led in a procession of two matrons, the under sheriff and the chaplain to the gallows. Here Marwood made the necessary preparations and released the trap doors. According to a report from the *Echo* newspaper the execution was bungled because the noose was not tightened sufficiently and she struggled somewhat. Whether this is actually true we cannot know as reporters were not allowed inside the shed and had to watch the proceedings from outside. The entrance to the shed had two pairs of half doors and only the upper pair were left open after the prisoner and officials had entered. Thus with a long drop all that would be seen was a taut rope hanging down from the beam; the prisoner's body would have been completely below the level of the trap doors. Having taken over from Calcraft at Newgate, William

Marwood was soon working all over the country, including Ireland.

At this time there was no standardisation of equipment or execution protocols between individual counties. Some counties had purpose-built execution sheds, as in Warwickshire, and London and Middlesex, while others set up the gallows in one of the yards in the open air, for instance Durham, Sussex and Gloucestershire. In some counties witnesses and newspaper reporters were invited to watch; in others hardly anyone other than the officials required by law was present. Equally there was a mixture of short drop and long drop hangings. All eight executions in England in 1873 used the short drop, and ten of the 19 hangings in 1874 did. Marwood carried out all 22 executions in 1875 by the latter method. Generally no assistant executioner was used at this time, the hangman either doing everything himself or relying on a volunteer prison officer for help with pinioning the legs. This was not invariably the situation as the next case shows.

On 1 May 1876, the trial of the '*Lennie* mutineers' took place at the Old Bailey. The accused were all members of this vessel's crew and comprised Matteo Cargalis, aged 36; Giovanni Cacaris, 21; Paroscos Leosis, 30; Pascales Caludis, 33; George Kaida, 22; Charles Renken, 27; George Green, 34; and Georgios Angelos, 19. They had been charged with the wilful murder of the ship's captain, Stanley Hatfield, 'on the high seas within the jurisdiction of the Admiralty of England'. The *Lennie* was a 950-ton sailing cargo ship on a voyage from Antwerp to New Orleans with a crew of sixteen. Hatfield was set on and had his throat cut on the morning of 31 October 1875, six days into the voyage, in the Bay of Biscay. Friction arose between the captain and the crew over a tacking error which caused the captain to be severely critical of one of the Greek sailors. As well as killing the captain, the mutineers also shot the first mate and the second mate but were not tried for these crimes. All three bodies had been thrown overboard. They were caught due to the quick thinking of the ship's steward, Belgian-born Constant Von Hoydonck. They wanted to sail the ship to Greece but had no navigational skills and had to rely on Von Hoydonck who sailed it to the Isle de Re off the coast of France where he sent out distress messages in bottles and by using flag signals. The accused were persuaded to go ashore in France in one of the ship's boats where they were duly arrested and brought back to England for trial.

At the end of the trial Cargalis, Cacaris, Caludis and Kaida were found guilty and sentenced to death, while Angelos, Green, Leosis and Renken were acquitted. The four condemned were returned to Newgate to await execution where they were visited in prison by the Greek Orthodox Bishop of London and the Greek Vice-Consul. In view of the number of prisoners to be hanged simultaneously it is thought that it was George Incher from Dudley in the Midlands who was hired to assist Marwood with this execution, which took place on Tuesday 23 May 1876. This case was widely reported in the press and was to be Newgate's only quadruple private execution.

An important piece of legislation passed in 1877 was the Prisons Act which transferred control of 113 local gaols to the Home Office. This led to the immediate closure of 38 prisons with another 19 following over the next 11 years. Many were old and dilapidated and not fit for purpose. When Horsemonger Lane gaol closed in 1878, Surrey executions were transferred to Wandsworth prison which had opened in November 1851. An execution shed was constructed near the coal yard at the end of A Wing and contained the white-painted gallows transferred from Horsemonger Lane gaol. The beam was 11 feet above the trap doors which opened into a 12-feet deep brick-lined pit dug into the ground. This facility was to remain in use up to 1911, during which time 28 men and one woman would die here.

William Marwood carried out the first hanging at Wandsworth on 8 October 1878, that of 31-year-old Thomas Smithers for the murder of his girlfriend Amy Judge, whom he stabbed to death out of jealousy at 30 Cross Street, Battersea, on 22 July 1878. Smithers reportedly died without a struggle. A crowd of a thousand or so people had gathered outside the prison to see the black flag raised just after 9 o'clock.

Multiple murders were rare events in the late 1800s, especially in rural communities. A particularly tragic case occurred on Wednesday 17 July 1878 when all five members of the Watkins family were found murdered in their cottage at Llangibby, two miles south of Usk in Monmouthshire. Downstairs lay the bodies of 40-year-old William and his wife Elizabeth, whilst in the upstairs bedrooms were discovered the bodies of their children, eight-year-old Charlotte, five-year-old Frederick, and four-year-old Alice. All had been stabbed repeatedly and the upstairs rooms had been set alight, the fire having already burnt parts of the children's bodies. It seemed apparent from the state of the house that robbery had been the perpetrator's initial motive and that the fire had been started in the hope of destroying the evidence of the murders.

The previous day a 21-year-old Spaniard named Joseph Garcia had been released from nearby Usk prison after serving a nine-month sentence for house breaking. He had decided to walk to Newport and was offered a lift by the driver of a cart, which he refused. The driver was later to identify him from his appearance and unusual accent. Later that afternoon he was spotted at Newport railway station where he was arrested. He was found to be carrying a knife and there were blood stains on his clothes which he had attempted to wash and which were still damp. The police also found items belonging to William Watkins on Garcia. He was committed to the next Monmouth Assizes for trial. After an application by the defence who were concerned that Garcia would not get a fair trial in the rural community, the venue was moved to Gloucester and his case was heard there on 28 October 1878. Garcia spoke very little English and was represented by a Spanish-speaking barrister at the trial, throughout which he maintained his innocence. He was convicted of the murders and returned to the small prison at Usk, the county gaol for Monmouthshire which had opened in 1844, to await execution. He was hanged by William Marwood on 18 November 1878.

One of the most infamous Victorian criminals was Charles Peace who was hanged at Armley prison, Leeds, by William Marwood on Monday 25 February 1879, 'For what I done but never intended,' as Peace said. Peace was a violent career criminal who was born in Sheffield in May 1832. His first recorded conviction was for house burglary in 1851, for which he served a month in prison. His next conviction for the same offence came in October 1854, when he was sentenced at Doncaster Sessions to four years' penal servitude. This was followed by a six-year sentence in 1859 and an eight-year sentence in 1866. He tried to escape during this, but was recaptured and was to spend the next six years in various prisons up to 1872. On his release he returned to Sheffield.

In 1875, Peace moved out of Sheffield into the suburb of Darnall where he met a Mr and Mrs Arthur Dyson. Peace was a womaniser and began having an affair with Mrs Dyson, or at least so he claimed and she denied. She had certainly gone out with him to music halls and pubs, but it seems that she had rejected his sexual advances and this was something he was not happy about. Peace threatened to kill Mr Dyson and he, in turn, took out an injunction against Peace in the hope that he would leave the couple alone. Peace did for a time, moving to Hull and opening a café. His burglaries continued and one night he went to Manchester, armed as usual with his revolver. Peace was spotted by two policemen in the grounds of a house at Whalley Range, around midnight on 1 August 1876. Constable Cock tried to arrest him, but Peace drew his gun and warned Cock to stand back, firing a warning shot at the officer. Cock took out his truncheon and advanced towards Peace, who fired a second time, killing him. Peace was able to escape and return to Hull. Two local villains, brothers John and William Habron, were arrested for the crime. Habron was convicted and sentenced to death but fortunately reprieved.

Peace's second murder was to be that of Arthur Dyson on 29 November 1876, whose wife he still desired. He went to the Dysons' home and during an argument shot Mr Dyson through the head, killing him instantly. Once again, he was able to escape back to Hull where he was nearly arrested as Mrs Dyson had been able to identify him as her husband's killer. A reward was offered for his capture. He was now the nation's most wanted man, moving constantly from one town to another, eventually ending up in London, where he was to evade capture for over two years.

Peace had always had a love of music and musical instruments and set up as a dealer in them, partially as a front to his usual business of house burglary. He sometimes carried his burglary tools in a violin case when he went out on a job. He was able to live in some style from the proceeds of these activities, with a 'Mrs Thompson' as his mistress. This married lady's real name was Susan Bailey, and she was eventually the one who betrayed him. His career as a burglar in London lasted from the beginning of 1877 until 10 October 1878 when he was finally caught red-handed by three policemen in Blackheath trying to rob a house. Peace fired several shots at one officer before he was overpowered. When he was questioned he gave his name as John Ward. Susan Thompson was also arrested for trying to sell stolen property and identified Ward as

Peace, hoping to obtain the reward. An officer was sent down from Yorkshire and was able to positively identify Peace in Newgate prison.

He stood trial at the Old Bailey in November 1878 on the charges of burglary and attempted murder and was sentenced to life in prison. However, Peace had now to answer to the charge of the murder of Mr Dyson and so was moved by train to Sheffield where he was charged with the murder of Arthur Dyson on 18 January 1879. During the journey north he attempted to escape by throwing himself out of the carriage but was quickly recaptured. His trial before Mr Justice Lopes began on 4 February 1879. Mrs Dyson was the principal witness for the Crown and described the murder of her husband to the court. Forensic evidence was able to show that the bullet that killed Mr Dyson was fired from the revolver recovered from Peace when he was arrested in London. Late in the afternoon the jury retired and took just 10 minutes to convict Peace. *The Times* newspaper reported that since Franz Muller murdered Mr Briggs on the North London Railway and the poisonings of William Palmer, no criminal case had created such excitement in the public mind as that of Charles Peace.

In the condemned cell Peace confessed to the murder of PC Cock and thus William Habron was given a pardon and £800 compensation. The hanging was scheduled for Tuesday 25 February and was attended by four newspaper reporters. As Marwood attempted to place the white hood over Peace's head, he asked for a glass of water which was refused. Peace then spoke to the journalists, which he was allowed to do before Marwood pulled the lever. His last words were reported to be: 'My last thoughts are for my children and their mother, a wonderful woman; they mustn't worry about me. I know where I am going. I am going to Heaven.' A large tableau of Peace and Marwood soon appeared in Madame Tussauds waxworks, depicting the execution scene.

Wandsworth's next hanging was that of Kate Webster, the only woman to be executed there. Kate Webster was born Catherine Lawler in 1849 in Killane, County Wexford, Ireland, and had got into crime quite early in life, serving several prison terms for various thefts and offences of dishonesty, including 12 months in Wandsworth in 1877. On 13 January 1879, Kate began working for Mrs Julia Martha Thomas at 2 Vine Cottages, Park Road, Richmond. Initially the two women got on well and Kate recorded that she felt she could be happy working for Mrs Thomas, who was a comfortably off although rather eccentric woman in her mid-50s. The relationship quickly soured due to the poor quality of Kate's work and pub-going habits. Mrs Thomas decided to dismiss Kate and she was to leave her employment and house on Friday 28 February 1879. On the Friday Kate pleaded to be allowed to stay in the house over the weekend which Mrs Thomas allowed. A quarrel ensued on the Sunday afternoon because Kate was late returning from visiting her son which in turn made Mrs Thomas late for church. The quarrel reignited when Mrs Thomas got home, culminating in her death. Kate claimed that her employer had fallen down the stairs and that to prevent her crying out she had strangled her. The precise cause of death was impossible to ascertain because Kate decided to dismember the body and burnt some of it on the stove, throwing the remains into the River Thames from Richmond Bridge. She put Mrs Thomas' head into a bag and kept it for a day or two before disposing of it. She also assumed her former employer's identity and began wearing her clothes and selling off her furniture.

The box containing Mrs Thomas' remains was found the next day and, although without the head she could not be positively identified, it led to a search of 2 Vine Cottages which revealed an axe, a razor and some charred bones. On 23 March, a full description of Kate Webster was circulated by the police in connection with the murder of Mrs Thomas and the theft of her effects. Kate fled to Ireland but was arrested on 28 March, being brought back to England by two detectives from Scotland Yard. She was taken to Richmond police station where she made a statement on 30 March and was formally charged with the murder.

Kate came to trial on Wednesday 2 July 1879 before Mr Justice Hawkins at the Central Criminal Court. Her trial concluded with a guilty verdict and death sentence on Tuesday 8 July. Before she was sentenced she was asked if she had anything to say and claimed to be pregnant. A jury of matrons was empanelled and Kate was examined by Newgate's doctor who concluded that she was not pregnant. As the crime had been committed in Surrey, Kate was transferred back to Wandsworth for execution. This was carried out by William Marwood at 9 o'clock on Tuesday morning, 29 July 1879. Kate was given a drop of 8 feet. Some 200 to 300 people had gathered to see the black flag hoisted at 9.05. After the formal inquest she was interred in plot No 3. This plot was never reused.

Executions at Lewes prison, the county town of East Sussex, were rare events. Martin Vinall had been hanged there on 18 January 1869 for the murder of David Baldry. The next hanging here took place on 29 November 1881 when another 22-year-old man was to die.

The case of Percy Lefroy, whose real surname was Mapleton, received a great deal more press coverage as he was another railway murderer and his execution was attended by reporters. Mapleton was convicted of the murder of Isaac Gold on a London, Brighton and South Coast Railway train at Preston Park on the outskirts of Brighton on Monday 27 June 1881. At first he told the station staff that he had been the victim of an attack and was taken to the police station to make a statement. An examination of the carriage that he had emerged from revealed bullet holes and a great deal of blood in the compartment. Although the police were suspicious of him, there was no evidence at the time to hold him, so after giving his statement and receiving some medical attention Mapleton was allowed to return to London in the company of a policeman. In the meantime staff searched the track and came across the body of a man in Balcombe Tunnel who was later identified as Mr Gold. He had been shot and robbed of his gold watch and chain and his money. Mapleton managed to give his police escort the slip, despite Detective Sergeant Holmes having been informed that Mr Gold's body had been found. For the first time a newspaper (the *Daily Telegraph*) was able to print a picture of Mapleton which led to innumerable sightings of similar-looking men all over England. The real Mapleton was arrested on 8 July, living under an assumed name at a house in Stepney in London, and was subsequently tried for the murder at Maidstone Assizes. In view of its importance at the time, his case was heard by the Lord Chief Justice, Lord Coleridge.

The gallows at Lewes was erected in one of the yards over a newly constructed brick-lined pit. It consisted of two stout uprights and a cross beam set over a double door trap and painted black. Mapleton's newly dug grave was visible nearby and would have been seen by him as walked to his doom. Marwood chatted to reporters prior to the execution. He told them that the rope he was going to use that morning had hanged nine people and had been used the previous day at Manchester's

Strangeways prison for the hanging of 21-year-old John Simpson who had murdered his girlfriend, Ann Ratcliffe. A little before 9 o'clock Marwood's conversation was interrupted by a warder telling him that he was required to pinion Mapleton. He used a heavy leather body belt round the young man's waist which had straps at the side for his wrists. The prisoner was led into the yard supported by a warder on either side and with Marwood holding the belt from behind for the 60-80 yard walk to the gallows. Once on the trap Marwood strapped his legs and put the white hood over his head, followed by the noose. A drop of 10 feet was given which instantly broke Mapleton's neck. There were no movements observed and he died without any sign of struggle. He was left on the rope for the normal hour before being taken down for viewing by the inquest jurors, officials and pressmen. This execution took some 3-4 minutes. Although Mapleton's execution seems unnecessarily cruel by modern standards with his grave visible clearly visible as he was led to his execution, his actual death was quick. The next execution at Lewes took place on 29 August 1887 when William Wilton was executed for the murder of his wife.

Between 14 May and 9 June 1883, William Marwood visited Kilmainham gaol in Dublin to carry out the executions of five men condemned for their parts in the Phoenix Park murders. 'The Invincibles' as they called themselves, were a previously unknown Irish Nationalist group who had stabbed to death the Permanent Under Secretary for Ireland, Thomas Henry Burke, and Lord Frederick Cavendish, the Chief Secretary for Ireland, as they walked through Dublin's Phoenix Park on the evening of Saturday 6 May 1882. This high-profile case was put in the hands of Superintendent John Mallon who rounded up a number of known Fenian activists. He persuaded the leader of 'The Invincibles', James Carey (see Chapter 15) and Michael Kavanagh, to testify against the others, and in due course Joseph Brady, Thomas Caffrey, Daniel Curley (who was alleged to have masterminded the murders), Michael Fagan and Timothy Kelly were tried separately. A temporary gallows was built for what were to be Kilmainham's first private hangings in one of the prison's yards.

Twenty-two-year-old Brady was the first to die on 14 May with Curley following on the 18th. It was a busy period for Marwood. He returned to

England to carry out the hangings of Joseph Wedlake and George White at Taunton on 21 May, then travelled to Glasgow to execute Henry Mullen and Martin Scott on 23 May at Duke Street prison for the murders of gamekeepers Robert Fyfe and David McCaughtrie before returning to Dublin for the executions of Fagan on 28 May and Caffrey on 2 June and finally Kelly on 9 June. A metal plaque bearing the names of the five 'Invincibles' can still be seen close to where the gallows stood in Kilmainham.

Things did not always go to plan as our next case shows. Marwood travelled to Durham for the execution of murderer and bigamist James Burton, aged 33, on 6 August 1883. He had battered 18-year-old Elizabeth Ann Sharpe to death out of jealousy on 8 May after she had left him because of his foul temper and drug taking. Burton could not come to terms with this rejection and stalked her. He was arrested and tried at the Summer Assizes and was convicted after the jury had deliberated for just 23 minutes. In the condemned cell, he made a full confession to the crime.

The press were allowed to witness the hanging which, as at Lewes, took place in the prison yard. A drop of 7' 8" had been calculated by Marwood and just before 8 o'clock Burton was led out for his execution. He was pinioned and hooded in the normal way and the free rope allowed to loop down behind his back. Just as Marwood was operating the trap Burton fainted and began to fall sideways, causing the loop of rope to catch on his elbow and preventing him falling straight. It was obvious to the reporters that something had gone badly wrong. Burton was swinging violently to and fro in the pit. Marwood, assisted by two warders, dragged the poor man out and got the rope disentangled before pushing him off the edge of the platform through the still open trap doors. This drop was inadequate and it took two minutes for Burton to become still. His face was badly contorted and his neck very swollen when his body was viewed by the coroner's jury at the inquest later in the day. It was clear that he had been strangled to death.

Hansard records that questions were asked in the House of Commons on 9 August as to whether the Secretary of State, Sir William Harcourt, had ordered an inquiry into this bungled execution. He assured the House that he had. There were further questions regarding Marwood's competence. It is interesting to see how in just eight years the official attitude to executions had changed. When Calcraft was in charge, most of his victims were strangled, but by the 1880s this was no longer acceptable. However, it all rapidly became irrelevant as this was to be William Marwood's last hanging. A month later he too was dead.

15

A time of change and many unfortunate incidents

When William Marwood died an amazing 1400 applications were received to replace him. Two men were seriously considered for the post: James Berry and Bartholomew Binns. Binns had assisted at a small number of executions whereas Berry had not, although he had discussed the process of hanging with Marwood on occasion.

Binns was appointed and carried out his first execution on 6 November 1883 when he hanged 24-year-old Henry Powell at Wandsworth for the murder of John Briston. The execution went without a hitch and Powell's neck was broken by the 7' 6" drop given.

Binns' most notable executions were those of Catherine Flannigan and Margaret Higgins who were hanged side by side on 3 March 1884 at Liverpool's Kirkdale gaol for the arsenic poisoning of Thomas Higgins, Margaret's husband. They had been convicted of killing Thomas for his life insurance. However, he was not their only victim. There were at least three others and they were not the only female poisoners operating in this area of Liverpool in the 1880s. As was the norm, the Crown simply prosecuted one capital case at a time, holding the other charges in reserve in case it did not get a conviction in the first.

The execution of Henry Dutton at Kirkdale on 3 December 1883 was botched by Binns. The 22-year-old was to die for the murder of Hannah Henshaw, his wife's grandmother, on 6 October at their home in Athol Street, Liverpool. Dutton weighed just 128 lbs and was given a drop of 7' 6" using an over-thick rope with the eyelet positioned at the back of his neck. Death resulted from strangulation. Dr James Barr, the prison doctor, was dissatisfied with the way Binns had conducted the hanging and again there was a strong suspicion that he had been drinking beforehand.

Binns hanged 48-year-old Patrick O'Donnell, an Irish Republican, who had shot the chief witness in Dublin's Phoenix Park murder case which had led to the execution of 'The Invincibles' described earlier. The shooting had been committed aboard the SS *Melrose* sailing from Cape Town, South Africa, in front of several witnesses, including both men's wives. James Carey was using the name James Power, having been given a new identity in exchange for the conviction of 'The Invincibles' of which he had been a former leader. O'Donnell was brought back to England and stood trial at the Old Bailey before being transferred to Newgate to await execution.

Binns' last job was the hanging of Michael McLean at Walton on 10 March 1884. He was deemed to be the worse for drink and the execution was judged to have been bungled as it took 13 minutes for McLean's heart to stop. After a formal complaint from the prison authorities concerning this and his behaviour, Binns was sacked. In all he hanged just eleven people: nine men and two women. Binns' departure opened the way for his previous competitor, James Berry, who carried out his first execution at Edinburgh's Calton prison on 31 March 1884. It was the double hanging of William Innes and Robert Vickers. They were two poachers who had shot and killed two gamekeepers, John Fortune and John McDairmid.

Berry's first execution in England was that of 44-year-old Mary Lefley at Lincoln on 26 May 1884. She had poisoned her husband with arsenic in a rice pudding and had to be dragged to the gallows screaming 'murder, murder' and struggling with the warders. Two days later, at Durham, Berry executed Joseph Lowson for the 'Butterknowle Murder'. Initially three men – Joseph Hodgson, William Siddle and his 25-year-old brother-in-law Joseph Lowson – had been arrested and charged with the murder of acting police sergeant William Smith at Diamond Pit in the village of Butterknowle on the night of Saturday 23 February 1884. The sergeant had been found dying in the road having been literally stoned to death. Joseph Hodgson was acquitted and at the last moment, after a confession from Lowson, William Siddle was reprieved. The prison bell began to toll at 7.45am; Berry entered the condemned cell and pinioned Lowson at 7.55. The usual procession formed up and proceeded to the gallows set up in the open air in the prison yard. Berry made the preparations and Lowson dropped out of sight. His body was viewed by reporters and the inquest jury later in the morning and his face was said to look calm. The rope mark visible on his neck was the only outward sign of his violent end.

Berry did have some rather problematical hangings, however. The most famous was that of 20-year-old John Henry George Lee. He was convicted of the murder of his elderly employer Emma Anne Whitehead Keyse, for whom he worked as a footman at 'The Glen', a beach-front home in the village of Babbacombe in Devon. On Saturday 15 November 1884, Emma's body was discovered in the dining room. Her throat had been cut, she had head injuries and an attempt had been made to burn her body, the house having been set on fire with paraffin in three different places. Only one man was in the house at the time of the murder – Lee. He had a cut on his arm which he claimed to have done when breaking a window to allow smoke to escape. The paraffin can which had been full the day before was found to be empty. It was stored in Lee's pantry as it was one of his duties to top up the lamps.

He was arrested and charged with his employer's murder, coming to trial before Sir Henry Manisty at the next Devon Assizes, where he continued to protest his innocence. He was convicted on circumstantial evidence and sentenced to death. The execution was set for Monday 23 February 1885 at Exeter prison and James Berry was appointed to carry it out. The gallows was set up in the shed that normally housed the prison van. Lee was led in just before 8am and the usual preparations made, but when Berry pulled the lever, nothing happened; the trap doors just dropped an inch or so. Berry stamped on them and tried the lever again, but to no avail. So the hood, noose and straps were removed and Lee was then taken back to his cell whilst the trap release mechanism was checked and retested. It worked perfectly.

The process was now repeated but with the same result and yet again the trap worked as soon as Lee was removed. After the third unsuccessful attempt, the governor took the decision to halt the execution whilst he obtained directions from the Home Office. Lee's death sentence was later commuted to life in prison by the Home Secretary, Sir William Harcourt, and he served 22 years before being released from Portland prison in 1907. He became known as 'The man they could not hang' and the case received widespread publicity. Conspiracy theories abounded as to why the trap would not open with Lee on it, ranging from divine intervention through the wood swelling in the damp weather, to one of the prisoners who had helped to erect it placing a wedge between the leaves of the trap which he removed again as soon as Lee was taken off and reinserted at each new attempt. The reality was much more prosaic. The gallows had last been used in a different location in the prison for the hanging of Annie Tooke in 1879 and had been erected in the coach house for Lee's execution. The frame had not been installed correctly and one of the long hinges fouled on the side of the pit when there was weight on the trap doors. Once again questions were raised in the House of Commons on the failure of this execution and an official inquiry was instigated.

Moses Shrimpton was a 65-year-old poacher who had been convicted of stabbing to death police constable James Davies at Beoley, near Redditch in Worcestershire, on 28 February 1885. Davies had apprehended him stealing chickens from a local farm. PC Davies was the first police officer to be murdered on duty in Worcestershire. The gallows was set up on 20 May 1885 in Worcester prison's treadmill house. Berry released the trap and Shrimpton disappeared from view. When the witnesses and newspaper reporters looked down into the pit they were horrified by what they saw. Shrimpton had been all but decapitated by the fall and there was blood running down over his body and splashes of it on the brick lining of the pit. At 65 years old, Shrimpton's neck muscles had weakened and Berry claimed the weight he was given for Shrimpton by the prison authorities had been incorrect.

On 7 October 1885, the Home Office wrote to the Prison Commission advising them that the hangman should be required to lodge within the prison on the night before an execution to avoid getting drunk and entertaining the locals in hotels and pubs with stories of their executions. This was advisory rather than mandatory as the Home Office recognised that it was the sheriff who appointed the hangman and oversaw the execution. In Berry's case drunkenness was not an issue at this time as he was a teetotaller. Problems were to arise again at the execution of Robert Goodale at Norwich Castle on 30 November 1885. Forty-five-year-old Goodale had been condemned for killing his wife Bathsheba. Goodale weighed 15 stone (95 kg) but due to the fact that he was in poor physical condition, Berry reduced the length of the drop from 7' 8" to 5' 9". This still proved to be far too much and he was decapitated by the force.

Again representatives of the press were present to witness this ghastly spectacle. It led to editorials attacking capital punishment which would not have been appreciated by the Home Office of the day.

The government was concerned about these incidents as they resulted in bad publicity and raised questions over the continuing use of hanging as the form of capital punishment. So, in 1886, the Conservative Home Secretary, Sir Richard Assheton Cross, commissioned a former Liberal Home Secretary, Lord Aberdare (Henry Austin Bruce), who had held the office from December 1868 to August 1873, to chair a committee. Its brief was to inquire into and report to the Home Secretary upon 'the existing practice as to carrying out the sentence of death and the causes which in several recent cases have led either to the failure or to unseemly occurrences and to consider and report what arrangements may be adopted (without altering the existing law) to ensure that all executions may be carried out in a becoming manner without risk of failure or miscarriage in any respect'. The committee took two years to issue its report in June 1888, partially due to Lord Aberdare becoming ill during the proceedings and having to go abroad to recuperate. Much of its work had been of a largely technical nature, looking at the 'nuts and bolts' of hanging and trying to find detail improvements to the equipment and process that were for the first time to be used nationally. None of its recommendations required any legislation to allow them to be implemented.

The Capital Sentences Committee, to give its full title, took evidence from James Berry in June 1877 which included a discussion of the elasticity of the ropes supplied by the government. The elasticity issue was very important because if the rope stretched significantly the condemned got a greater drop and therefore an increased chance of decapitation. There was also discussion of the correct position for the eyelet or thimble of the noose. Berry was of the view that it should be placed behind the left ear, the sub-aural position. It could be equally well positioned under the right ear if the hangman was left handed.

The committee heard a lot of medical evidence and one witness, Dr Marshall, described the hanging of Edward Hewitt at Gloucester on 15 June 1886 for the murder of his wife, Sarah Ann, as follows:

The balcony-style gallows used at York Castle for nineteenth-century private hangings. *Author's photo*

Beheading on Tower Hill
The execution of Kilmarnock and Arthur Lord Balmerino in 1746.

Beaumaris Prison
A montage of the gallows showing the bridge from the prison across to the outer wall, the noose and the trap door. *Author's photo*

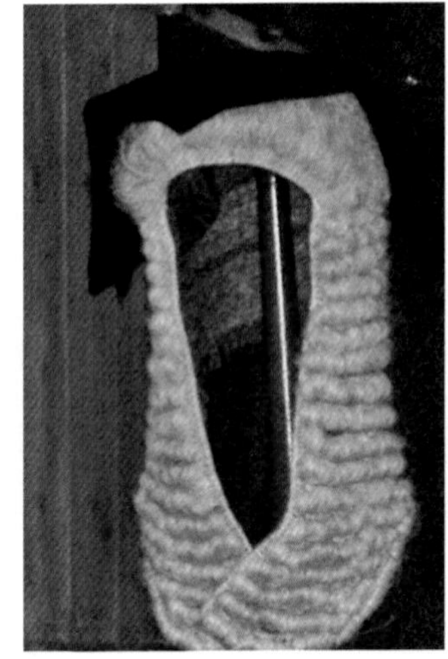

Black cap
The judge's wig with the black cap; worn when pronouncing the sentence of death. *Author's photo*

Block and axe

Beheading block and axe at the Tower of London as used for the execution of Simon Fraser, Lord Lovat, in 1747. *Author's photo*

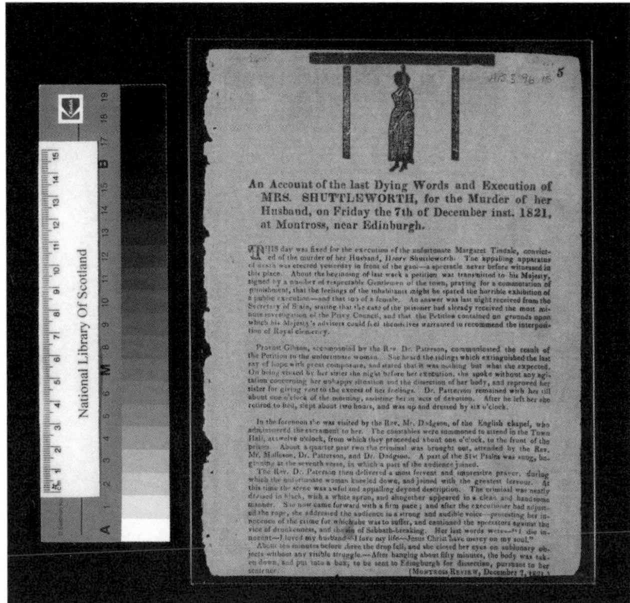

An Account of the last Dying Words and Execution of MRS. SHUTTLEWORTH, for the Murder of her Husband, on Friday the 7th of December inst. 1821, at Montross, near Edinburgh.

THIS day was fixed for the execution of the unfortunate Margaret Tindale, convicted of the murder of her Husband, Henry Shuttleworth. The appalling apparatus of death was erected yesterday in front of the gaol—a spectacle never before witnessed in this place. About the beginning of last week a petition was transmitted to his Majesty, signed by a number of respectable Gentlemen of the town, praying for a commutation of punishment, that the feelings of the inhabitants might be spared the horrible exhibition of a public execution—and that too of a female. An answer was last night received from the Secretary of State, stating that the case of the prisoner had already received the most minute investigation of the Privy Council, and that the Petition contained no grounds upon which his Majesty's advisers could feel themselves warranted to recommend the interposition of Royal clemency.

Provost Gibson, accompanied by the Rev. Dr. Patterson, communicated the result of the Petition to the unfortunate woman. She heard the tidings which extinguished the last ray of hope with great composure, and stated that it was nothing but what she expected. On being visited by her sister the night before her execution, she spoke without any agitation concerning her unhappy situation and the direction of her body, and reproved her sister for giving vent to the excess of her feelings. Dr. Patterson remained with her till about one o'clock of the morning, assisting her in acts of devotion. After he left her she retired to bed, slept about two hours, and was up and dressed by six o'clock.

In the forenoon she was visited by the Rev. Mr. Dodgson, of the English chapel, who administered the sacrament to her. The constables were summoned to attend in the Town Hall, at twelve o'clock, from which they proceeded about one o'clock, to the front of the prison. About a quarter past two the criminal was brought out, attended by the Rev. Mr. Molleson, Dr. Patterson, and Dr. Dodgson. A part of the 51st Psalm was sung, beginning at the seventh verse, in which a part of the audience joined.

The Rev. Dr. Patterson then delivered a most fervent and impressive prayer, during which the unfortunate woman kneeled down, and joined with the greatest fervour. At this time the scene was awful and appalling beyond description. The criminal was neatly dressed in black, with a white apron, and altogether appeared in a clean and handsome manner. She now came forward with a firm pace; and after the executioner had adjusted the rope, she addressed the audience in a strong and audible voice—protesting her innocence of the crime for which she was to suffer, and cautioned the spectators against the vice of drunkenness, and that of Sabbath-breaking. Her last words were—"I die innocent—I loved my husband—I love my life—Jesus Christ have mercy on my soul."

About ten minutes before three the drop fell, and she closed her eyes on sublunary objects without any visible struggle.—After hanging about fifty minutes, the body was taken down, and put into a box, to be sent to Edinburgh for dissection, pursuant to her sentence.

(MONTROSE REVIEW, December 7, 1821.)

Broadside

Broadside of the execution of Margaret Shuttleworth.
Reproduced with the kind permission of the National Library of Scotland

Burning at Tyburn
A woodcut picture of an execution by burning at the stake.

Cato St. Conspirators
The hanging and decapitation of the Cato Street Conspirators.

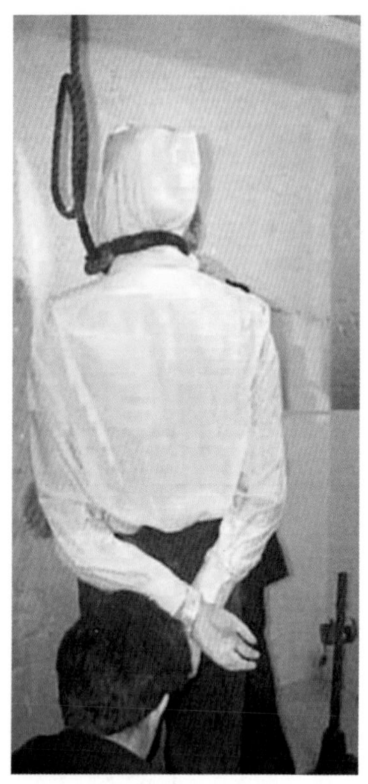

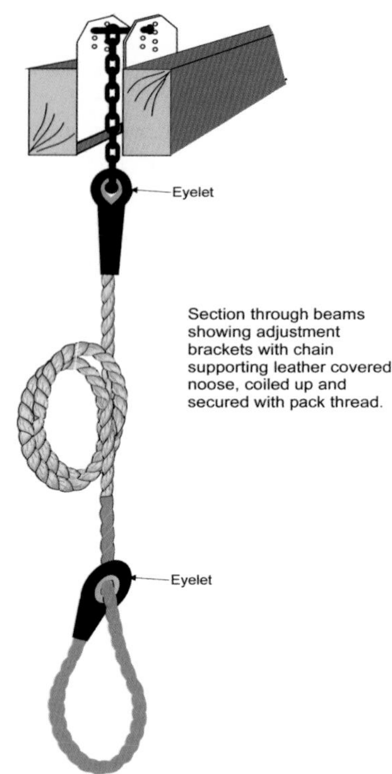

Above left: What one would have seen as a witness to a 1950s hanging.
Author's photo

Above right: Author's drawing showing the rope, noose and means of adjustment of the drop.

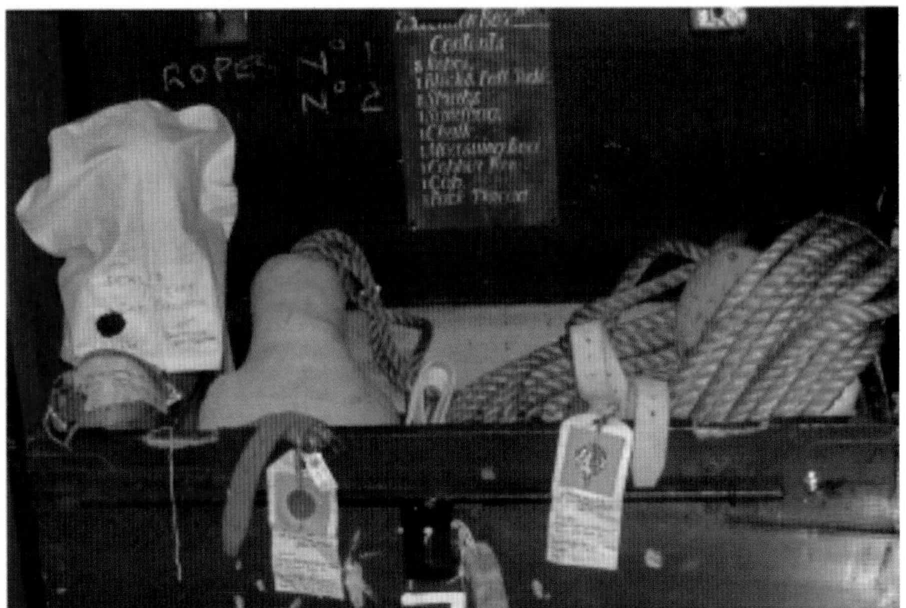

Above: The contents of a modern execution box sent to county prisons from Pentonville. *Author's photo*

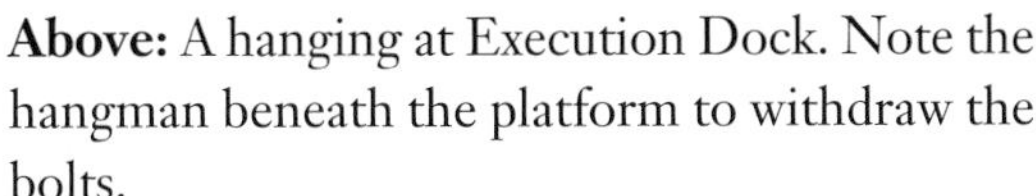

Above: A hanging at Execution Dock. Note the hangman beneath the platform to withdraw the bolts.

Left: The hanging of the Earl Ferrers at Tyburn in 1760 using a new drop gallows.

Above right: The body of the Earl Ferrers in its coffin awaiting dissection.

Above: Halifax Gibbet.

Above: The burning of Catherine Hayes at Tyburn in 1726.

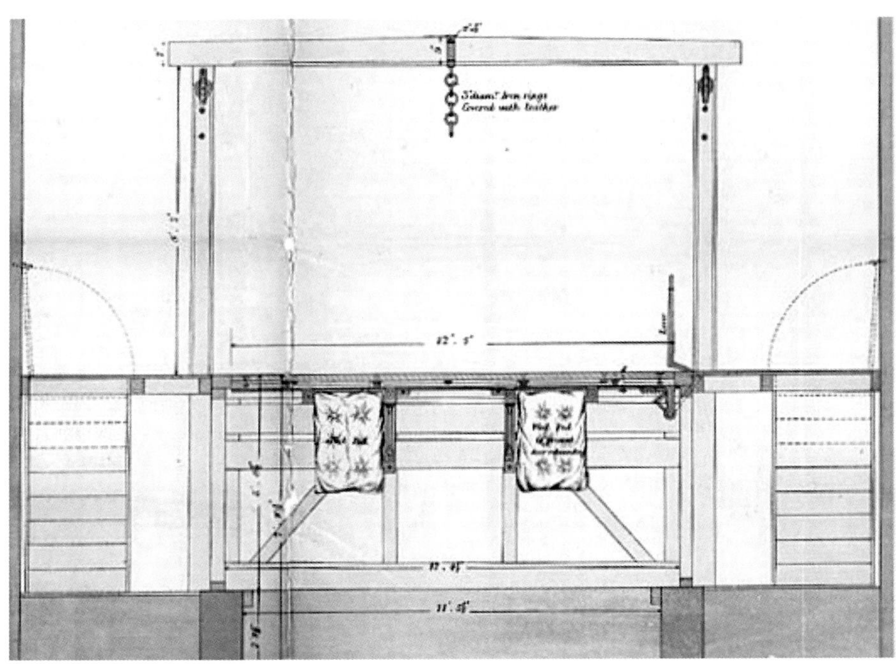

Newgate later gallows
Plans for the new gallows installed in the execution shed at Newgate in 1881.

Woodcut drawing of a hanging outside what is now the Galleries of Justice in Nottingham.

Peine forte et dure
Prisoner in Newgate undergoing pressing for refusing to plead.

Recorder's report
The recorder of the Old Bailey presents his report to the king and privy council.

Ruthin
The condemned cell at Ruthin gaol with model figures of the prisoner and chaplain. *Author's photo*

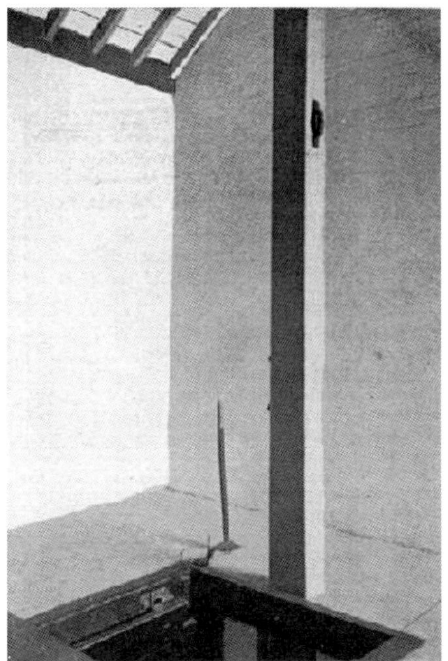

Above left: Interior of the first execution shed at Wandsworth, circa 1880, showing the lever, trap doors and the pulley for raising them set into one of the uprights.

Above right: John Smith being taken down from the gallows in 1705. He was later revived.

Below: Drawing of a modern condemned suite in the 1950s. *Author's drawing*

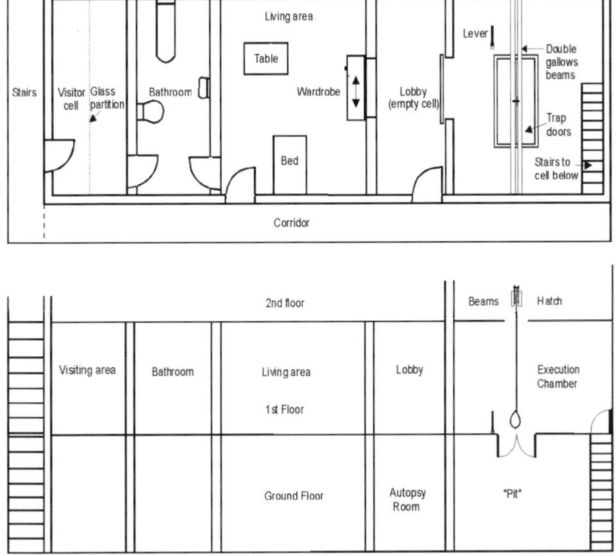

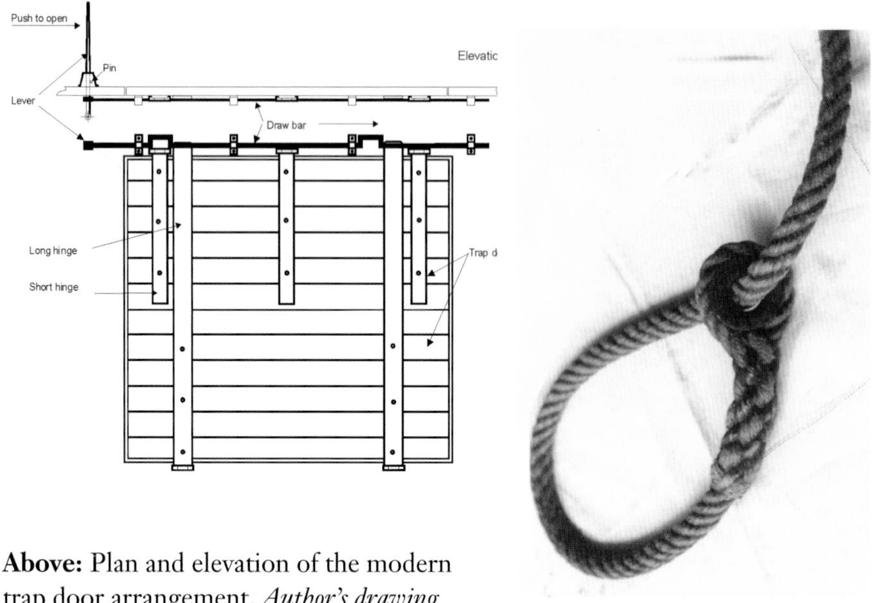

Above: Plan and elevation of the modern trap door arrangement. *Author's drawing*

Above right: Victorian noose showing eyelet and leather washer. *Author's photo*

Below: The execution of William Corder outside Bury St. Edmunds Gaol for the 'Red Barn Murder'.

> 'I descended immediately into the pit where I found the pulse beating at the rate of 80 to the minute and the wretched man struggling desperately to get his hands and arms free. I came to this conclusion from the intense muscular action in the arms, forearms and hands, contractions, not continuous but spasmodic, not repeated with any regularity but renewed in different directions and with desperation. From these signs I did not anticipate a placid expression on the face and I regret to say my fears were correct. On removing the white cap about 1½ minutes after the fall I found the eyes starting from the sockets and the tongue protruded, the face exhibiting unmistakable evidence of intense agony.'

Hewitt weighed 144 lbs (65 kg) and Berry had given him a drop of 6 feet. It took 2½ minutes for Hewitt to become still. The same problem had occurred at Cardiff on 2 March 1886 with the hanging of 30-year-old David Roberts who was condemned for killing David Thomas. Roberts was clearly strangled to death due to the length of drop being insufficient. Part of the committee's remit was to produce an official table of drops, which was finally issued in 1892. It specified shorter distances than Marwood and Berry had typically used to avoid the possibility of decapitation, although it considered this to be preferable to strangulation. Marwood had devised the first drop table and Berry's was based upon it. The new table would provide for a drop that produced 840 pounds force and is reproduced below.

Weight of prisoner, lbs	Drop in feet & inches
105 & under	8' 0"
110	7' 10"
115	7' 3"
120	7' 0"
125	6' 9"
130	6' 5"
135	6' 2"
140	6' 0"
145	5' 9"

Weight of prisoner, lbs	Drop in feet & inches
150	5' 7"
155	5' 5"
160	5' 3"
165	5' 1"
170	4'11"
175	4' 9"
180	4' 8"
185	4' 7"
190	4' 5"
195	4' 4"
200 & over	4' 2"

The weight is that of the clothed prisoner in pounds, recorded the day before execution. It should be noted that these drop lengths were starting points that could be increased or decreased by the executioner in consultation with the prison doctor.

A number of other recommendations were made by the Capital Sentences Committee. Executioners were no longer to be paid a salary as Calcraft had been, but rather hired by the individual county sheriffs on a job-by-job basis. Properly trained assistants were to be used, who would be able to take over if the hangman became ill or fainted and would also be available to carry out an execution if the 'No 1' was busy elsewhere. This particular recommendation did not really take effect until James Berry resigned. The sheriffs were to be able to choose from a list of hangmen and assistants approved by the Prison Commissioners. The suggestion that the hangman and assistant should stay in the prison from 4 o'clock in the afternoon prior to an execution was endorsed by the committee and became standard practice.

From 1878, a standard pattern of noose with a metal eyelet was available from the Prison Commissioners. The 'government rope', as it was known, was made by John Edgington & Co Ltd of 48 Long Lane in east London, formed from a 10' 2½" length of ¾"-diameter Italian hemp with a metal eyelet for the noose and another for attachment to the beam by means of a 'D' shackle and chain. A rope could be ordered from Newgate prison by the sheriff of the county requiring it. Up to this time hangmen had supplied their own ropes, but this was no longer considered satisfactory. Nor was their propensity for showing off and indeed selling off used ones for profit. The committee recommended that in future only government supplied ropes were to be used.

A report was to be completed after each execution (Form LPC4) and among other details such as the drop given, would contain the governor's comments on the conduct of the execution by the hangman and his assistant. After execution the prisoner's clothes were no longer to be the property of the hangman and were to be burnt. Once these various recommendations had come into practice the Home Office had effectively taken control of the administration of executions. Much of what was recommended continued to be the practice up to abolition. However, the Home Office was not willing to take responsibility away from the sheriffs for the appointment of the hangman as was made clear by the Home Secretary of the day, Henry Matthews, later Viscount Llandaff, in a parliamentary debate on 12 April 1889.

Prior to 1884, each county was responsible for providing its own gallows so that there was no standardisation. Some had single trap doors, some double traps. Some were housed in purpose-built sheds; others were erected in the open air in the prison yard. Some had the platform set level with the floor or ground, whilst others required the prisoner to climb steps. Many were deemed unsatisfactory. To overcome these problems, in 1885 the Home Office commissioned Lieutenant Colonel Alten Beamish to produce a standard design for use throughout the country. This consisted of two uprights with a cross beam in 8" section oak. The beam was long enough to execute three prisoners side by side and was set over a 12' long by 4' wide two-leaf trap set level with the surrounding floor. The trap doors were made from 3" thick oak and were released by a metal lever set into the floor of the execution chamber. The one nearest the lever was conventionally hinged, whilst the other had extended hinges that ran under the first leaf and were held on top of an iron drawbar which had three slots. The doors fell against bales of cotton to reduce the noise. Below the platform was a 13' deep brick-lined pit. This design was a great improvement and helped to speed up the process. The beam had one or more iron bands attached to it from which hung lengths of chain for attachment of the rope. In the thoughtful way of the Home

Office, at least some of these gallows had the Royal Coat of Arms displayed on the beam, which must have been a great comfort to the condemned!

The first person to die on the new style gallows was 28-year-old Matthew William Chadwick at Liverpool's Kirkdale prison. Chadwick was convicted of stabbing Walter Davies to death during an attempted robbery at the pawnbroker's shop that Davis worked in. The execution was carried out by James Berry on 22 March and was judged to be entirely satisfactory.

As a result of another recommendation by the Capital Sentences Committee the design of the gallows beam was to be improved. The single beam was replaced by two beams of 8" x 3" section oak, running parallel to each other about 2" apart. Over the centre of the beams were positioned three metal brackets, each having four holes offset at half inch centres through which a cotter pin was inserted, supporting the chain which hung down between the beams and terminated in a 'D' shackle. This allowed very much more accurate adjustment of the drop. The beams were 8' above the trap doors and were generally set into the wall at each end, there being no uprights. It took until the end of the 19th century for the new standard to become universal.

Sadly the committee's recommendations did not prevent further mishaps occurring. Robert Upton was nearly decapitated at Oxford prison on 17 July 1888. Sixty-one-year-old Upton was hanged for the murder of his wife, Emma. It seems likely that Berry actually gave Upton a considerably greater drop than he had originally calculated. Although Upton died easily enough, it created another gruesome scene for the attending newspaper men to report. On 10 August 1888, Arthur Delaney, aged 31, was to suffer for the murder of his wife at Derby prison. Delaney died from asphyxia rather than the effects of a broken neck and again it seems that Berry miscalculated the length of the drop. The same was to happen at the execution of wife murderer 45-year-old Henry Delvin, who was hanged on 23 September 1890 in Glasgow's Duke Street prison. Delvin had beaten his wife to death with a poker in front of their children.

The case of Mary Eleanor Wheeler is almost certainly unique in having a father and daughter both hanged, just over a decade apart, for two completely separate murders. Mary's father, Thomas Wheeler, was executed by William Marwood at St Albans prison in Hertfordshire on 29 November 1880 for the murder of a local farmer, one Edward Anstee. In the condemned cell, Thomas had written a letter to the farmer's widow apologising for what he had done and asking her forgiveness and prayers that his sins should not be visited on his wife or their then 14-year-old daughter, Mary. Sadly this was not to be the case.

Mary Wheeler had been convicted of the murder of her lover's wife, 32-year-old Phoebe Hogg, on 24 October 1890. Phoebe was found with her throat cut and other serious injuries, lying on a pavement in Crossfield Road, London. Later that day, a bloodstained pram was discovered in Hamilton Terrace containing the body of a small child, later to be identified as Phoebe Hanslope Hogg, the daughter of the murdered woman. The baby had died from suffocation, possibly deliberately or due to the body of her mother being placed in the pram on top of her.

Wheeler was tried for the murder of the mother at the Old Bailey before Mr Justice Denman, the case opening on 1 December. She was convicted after a three-day trial and returned to Newgate to await execution on Tuesday 23 December. There was no possibility of appeal, but her solicitor made considerable effort to obtain a reprieve for her on the grounds that she was not in control of herself at the time of the crime due to epilepsy, something that she had suffered from since birth. The Home Secretary, Henry Matthews, declined a reprieve and there was little public sympathy for her, probably due to the extremely violent nature of the mother's murder and the fact that a baby had died too. The execution went ahead as planned, the governor of Newgate deciding to exclude newspaper reporters completely. She weighed 126 lbs and was given a drop of 6' which broke her neck. Some 300 people had gathered outside the prison on a bitterly cold December morning to hear St Sepulchre's Church bell tolling and witness the black flag being hoisted above the prison, which evoked a cheer from the crowd. Many artefacts from the murder scene were purchased by Madame Tussauds and put on display, including the pram. The *Illustrated Police News* did an article on the case, complete with one of their famous pictures of how they imagined her execution. This was one of 16 executions in England in 1890.

Berry's penultimate execution in England was to be that of John Conway, a 62-year-old bachelor at Liverpool's Kirkdale prison on 20 August 1891. Conway had confessed to the brutal murder of a young boy named Nicholas Martin so he could watch him die. The boy's body was found floating in the River Mersey, wrapped in a sailor's kitbag together with a saw and knife and other items that could be traced back to Conway. Once again the prisoner was nearly decapitated by the drop and the Liverpool press were there to witness the horrible bloody mess. Whose fault it was is a matter of debate. Berry blamed Dr Barr, the prison surgeon, for insisting on an over-long drop for an elderly and relatively heavy prisoner, but it seems that everybody else blamed Berry.

No mishap was reported at Berry's final execution, that of Edward Fawcett at Winchester just five days later. However, Berry had decided that he had had enough and decided to resign. This was probably a sensible decision because the Prison Commission had had enough of him too. There was increasing concern over the number of incidents at hangings and his behaviour in hotels and pubs before and after executions. His conduct after a double hanging at Hereford caused questions to once again be raised in the House of Commons. Sir Edmund Lechmere, the MP for Bewdley in Worcestershire, questioned the Home Secretary, Henry Matthews, on 11 and 12 April 1889, about Berry's behaviour, stating that he had taken part in a show in Hereford the night before the execution and had held a 'levee' in a pub in Worcester after it, before going to Kidderminster where he visited three pubs and gave lectures 'on morality and phrenology' to the disgust of the Mayor of that town.

In the decade from 1 January 1883 to 31 December 1892, there were 153 executions in England, including those of seven women, with exactly one-third being for wife murder. There were just four hangings in Wales and eight in Scotland, of which two were for wife murder. A further 29 men were put to death in Ireland during the period.

16

Into the 20th century

The county of Yorkshire had tended to employ James Billington, rather than James Berry, from 1884 to carry out its executions. His first job was the hanging of Joseph Laycock, a Sheffield hawker, at Armley prison in Leeds for the murder of his wife and four children. Laycock was reported to have asked just before being hanged: 'You will not hurt me?' to which James Billington replied: 'No, thaal nivver feel it, for thaal be out of existence i' two minutes.' Apparently Billington was correct in this assertion and continued to be appointed in Yorkshire. There were to be a further nine executions in the county between Laycock on 26 August 1884 and 25 August 1891 when James Berry finished. Two of these were at York Castle and the rest were at Armley, including one double hanging. This occurred on 31 December 1891 when two wife murderers, 45-year-old Robert West and 39-year-old Frederick Brett, were hanged side by side.

After Berry's departure Billington took over the 'No 1' position and was soon working nationwide, although Thomas Scott of Huddersfield usually got the jobs in Ireland. There were eleven executions in 1891, of which Billington carried out four. One was in Yorkshire and one each in Somerset, Durham and Herefordshire, all in December. Harry Dainton was executed at Shepton Mallet prison on the 15th for the murder of his wife, John Johnson was hanged at Durham for killing Margaret Addison, and Charles Saunders at Hereford on the 28th for killing 2-year-old Walter Steers.

In December 1891, the Home Office issued a 'Memorandum of Instructions for carrying out the details of an Execution'. This was a confidential document that explained how the gallows should be tested and prepared. Firstly the trap doors were to be tested without any weight on them and then again with a sandbag at least equivalent in weight to the prisoner. This would be left on the rope overnight and the execution shed locked up until the following morning. On the morning of the execution the sandbag was to be raised and then dropped again to remove any further stretch from the rope. The drop that had been calculated for the prisoner was now to be accurately set and a 'T' chalked on the trap doors where the person was to stand. By now the free rope was to be fastened to the chain with pack thread to enable the noose to be at chest height and avoid it fouling on the prisoner's arms as happened to James Burton at Durham. The prisoner was to be pinioned in the cell or in a room adjacent to the gallows and then brought in and placed directly under the beam on the chalk mark. Their legs were to be strapped and the white hood applied, followed by the noose. The eyelet was to face forwards and be held in place by a leather or rubber washer. Once the trap doors had been released, the person was to be left suspended for one hour before being taken off the rope and prepared for inquest. The body was lifted using a separate rope and a block and tackle, and not 'cut down' as one might read elsewhere. This was Britain's first formal execution protocol.

1892 was a busy year for the hangman with 17 executions in England and Wales, three in Ireland and one in Scotland. It was also the year that the Register of Execution LPC4 form came into use, recording the details of each execution and permitting comment on the behaviour of the hangman and his assistant. The prisoner's weight and height were recorded, together with the length of drop set and the final length afterwards. The cause of death was also given.

Possibly one of the strangest occurrences at a hanging took place in the execution shed at Newgate on 15 December 1892. The man standing pinioned, hooded and noosed on the trap doors was Dr Thomas Neill Cream and the man with his hand on the lever was James Billington. In the split second as Billington went to push the lever, Cream said from under the hood: 'I am Jack the...' at which point he plummeted down into oblivion. Afterwards Billington said that if he had known Cream was going to speak he would have waited, but other accounts tell of Cream deliberately waiting to hear the mechanism begin to move so that he would not finish the sentence. It seems a strange thing to do with one's last second of life! Possibly it was done just to taunt the authorities, particularly Sir Henry Smith, the recently appointed Commissioner of the City of London Police who was present at the hanging. In reality Cream was not and could not have been Jack the Ripper as he was serving a sentence in Joliet Penitentiary in the American state of Illinois at the time of the 'Ripper' murders. Neill Cream was born in Scotland in 1850 and moved with his family to Canada in 1854 where he later studied to become a doctor, graduating in 1876. He moved back to England in 1881 and was convicted at the Old Bailey, under the name of Thomas Neill, on 17 October 1892 of the murder of a prostitute, 27-year-old Matilda Clover, by poisoning with nux vomica (the alkaloid poison strychnine) on 20 October 1891. He was also responsible for the poisoning deaths of three other prostitutes: 19-year-old Ellen Donworth on 13 October 1891, and 21-year-old Alice Marsh and 18-year-old Emma Shrivell, both on 11 April 1982.

The perpetrators of the Muswell Hill murders, 31-year-old Henry Fowler and 33-year-old Albert Milsom, were hanged at Newgate on 9 June 1896. They had been convicted of beating to death a 79-year-old widower called Henry Smith. A third person was to be hanged with them: William Seaman, who had killed Jonathan Goodman Levy and Sarah Ann Gale in Turner Street, Mile End, London. To avoid trouble between Fowler and Milsom it was decided to place Seaman between them on the drop. When Fowler was bought into the shed the other two were already hooded and he asked: 'Is Milsom there?' Having been assured that he was, he said: 'Very well, you can go on.' Billington did. Fowler and Milsom had killed Mr Smith during a robbery at his home, Muswell Lodge, on the night of 13/14 February 1896. The pair had tied the old man up and beaten him severely, leaving him to die on the kitchen floor. Milsom confessed to the burglary in a written statement whilst on remand in Holloway prison and implicated Fowler in the murder, which he denied being involved with. However, under the doctrine of common purpose if they had both gone there to rob Mr Smith then both were responsible for his death and thus equally guilty.

This was the last triple hanging at Newgate and Billington was assisted by William Warbrick who reputedly went through the trap with the prisoners as he was still pinioning the legs of one when Billington operated the trap. He held on to the man's legs to save himself.

'Baby farming' was prevalent in the late Victorian era. It was a time when there was no effective contraception available and great social stigma attached to having a child out of wedlock. There were no official adoption agencies and social services did not exist. So a number of untrained women filled the vacuum by offering fostering and adoption services to unmarried mothers who would hand over their baby plus, say, £10 to £15 (a significant sum of money then) to them in the hope that the child would be rehomed. These services were not illegal and unmarried mothers were often desperate to get rid of babies. They would answer newspaper adverts placed by seemingly reputable motherly women who would take the child with no questions asked. There were few easy alternatives as abortion was illegal and the back street abortions that were carried out were a very high-risk alternative. Abandoning a baby was similarly illegal and little sympathy was extended by the courts to women who murdered their unwanted children. Selina Wadge was hanged by William Marwood on 15 August 1878 at Bodmin for the murder of her illegitimate son, and Louisa Masset (see later) became the first person to be executed in the 20th century for murdering her young son. If a baby disappeared, its mother was often too frightened or ashamed to report it missing so it was very easy for the unscrupulous baby farmers to kill off unwanted or hard to foster (or sell?) babies. At least six baby farmers found killing their charges easier than rehoming them and doing so yielded a quick profit without the cost of caring for the child for some weeks or months. In an age of high infant mortality, deaths of babies and small children were quite common and attracted little attention. Where a baby's body was found, it was often impossible to trace the mother as the authorities did not have the advantage of modern methods such as dental records or DNA tests.

One of England's most notorious baby farmers met her end at the hands of James Billington at Newgate on 10 June 1896. She was 57-year-old Amelia Dyer who had been condemned for the murder of 4-month-old Doris Marmon, a baby entrusted to her care, having received £10 to look after her. It is thought that Dyer had murdered at least six other babies for money. Each baby had been strangled with white tape. As Mrs Dyer said, that was how you could tell it was one of hers. At 57, she was the oldest woman to go to the gallows since 1843. Her ghost was said to haunt Newgate prison. Dyer had made two suicide attempts in Reading police station prior to her trial before Mr Justice Hawkins at the Old Bailey on 21 May 1896. The defence tried to prove insanity, which would have saved her from the gallows, but failed to convince the jury who took just five minutes to convict her. During her three weeks in the condemned cell, she filled five exercise books with her 'last true and only confession'. The chaplain visited her the night before her execution and asked her if she had anything to confess. She offered him her exercise books, saying: 'Isn't this enough?'

There were just seven men hanged in England in 1897, five of which were for wife murder, one for the murder of a cousin and the other for the killing of his father. There were no executions in Ireland or Wales and just one in Scotland, where 31-year-old George Paterson was executed in Glasgow on 17 June for the murder of Mary Ann McGuire. In 1898, there were ten English executions of which five were for wife murder. There were two hangings in Ireland but none in Scotland or Wales. The youngest woman to be hanged in private in the UK was Mary Ann Ansell who, at the age of 22, was executed at St Albans prison on Wednesday 19 July 1899 for the murder of her sister Caroline. Caroline was a mental patient detained within the Leavesden Asylum in Abbots Langley and it was here that her sister sent a cake laced with phosphorus. The cake was traced back to Mary Ann and the alleged motive for the crime was to obtain Caroline's life insurance money to enable Mary Ann to marry. She was found guilty but unusually where a young woman was in the dock the jury made no recommendation to mercy.

The Metropolitan Asylums Board that ran Leavesden passed a resolution asking for clemency and the *Daily Mail* newspaper also campaigned for a reprieve on the grounds that she too was mentally ill, as mental problems ran in the family. A petition was drawn up in the House of Commons and signed by some 100 MPs asking for a delay of one week in carrying out the execution whilst her mental state was further investigated. Sir Mathew Ridley, the Home Secretary, decided against this and was unmoved by the other representations, as it was a poisoning case. Her execution drew a crowd of some 2000 to see the black flag hoisted over the prison. St Albans prison had not had an execution since 1880 when Thomas Wheeler (the father of Mary Eleanor Wheeler) was hanged there. As it did not have its own gallows it borrowed Bedfordshire's.

Unusually the first two executions of the new century were both women. On Tuesday 9 January 1900, James Billington hanged 36-year-old French-born Louisa Masset at Newgate for the murder of her illegitimate son, 4-year-old Manfred. She had battered and suffocated the little boy to death and dumped his body in the ladies' toilet at Dalston Junction railway station in London. The most likely motive for the murder seemed to be that Manfred was a hindrance to her relationship with her boyfriend. The next execution was that of Ada Chard-Williams, also at Newgate, on 6 March for the baby farming murder of Selina Ellen Jones. In fact, the next three English executions were to be at Newgate. Of the 13 hangings in England in 1900, seven were for killing either a wife or girlfriend as was the single execution in Wales. Thomas Scott carried out the only hanging in Ireland during this year, that of 34-year-old Patrick Dunphy at Waterford who had murdered his sons, Eddie and John.

French-born Marcel Fougeron stabbed 64-year-old Hermann Francis Jung to death at 4 Lower Charles Street, Clerkenwell, London, in the course of robbing him. Mr Jung was a member of the Swiss Benevolent Society which helped foreigners in England and had given Fougeron money. He was tried at the Old Bailey on 21 October 1901 where he claimed that Mr Jung was an anarchist and had tried to persuade him to help kill the Colonial Secretary. The two got into an argument over money that Mr Jung had lent to Fougeron and in the ensuing fight Fougeron claimed he killed Mr Jung in self defence. His story was not accepted by the jury and Fougeron was hanged on 19 November by James Billington, assisted by a new man, Henry Pierrepoint. This was to be his first job as an assistant.

In late May 1902, Newgate prison closed for good and was demolished by 1904 to make way for the new Central Criminal Court. Between 17 November 1783 and 6 May 1902, there had been 1,194 hangings at Newgate, of which 50 were of women. Of the total hangings, 58 men and 5 women were executed in private from September 1868. Since 1877, as a result of the Prison Act of that year, Newgate had been used only as a remand prison for those awaiting trial at the Old Bailey and those subsequently condemned to death there. The last execution at Newgate was that of 21-year-old George Woolfe who was hanged on 6 May 1902 for the murder of his girlfriend Charlotte Cheeseman. It seems that he wanted to end the relationship and so had stabbed her to death on Tottenham Marshes after a quarrel on Saturday 25 January 1902. The execution was carried out by William Billington, assisted by John Ellis. Newgate's gallows were then transferred to Pentonville prison and John Macdonald became the first to die there on 30 September 1902 for the murder of Henry Groves whom he had stabbed to death in a dispute over 5s (25p). He was executed by William Billington, assisted by Henry Pierrepoint.

In early 1903, Holloway prison became an all-female institution and also the place of execution for women condemned in London and Middlesex who had previously been dealt with at Newgate. The first women to be hanged at Holloway were the 'Finchley Baby Farmers', 29-year-old Amelia Sach and 54-year-old Annie Walters, on Tuesday 3 February 1903, in what was to be Holloway's only double execution and the last double female hanging in Britain. They were executed for the specimen crime of killing a 3-month-old boy by the name of Galley. It is thought that they may have murdered as many as 20 infants. William Billington and Henry Pierrepoint officiated.

James Billington carried out his last execution on 3 December 1901, with the hanging of 53-year-old Patrick McKenna at Strangeways prison in Manchester for stabbing his wife, Anna, to death during an argument. McKenna and Billington both came from Farnworth near Bolton and had known each other in happier times. Billington died 10 days later of bronchitis and was succeeded by his two sons, William and John, who had assisted him at various hangings, and by Henry Pierrepoint.

On 5 January 1902, the Home Office issued another set of rules for carrying out executions, which read as follows. (The use of upper case letters is as in the original document)

> For the sake of uniformity it is recommended that Execution should take place in the week following the third Sunday after the day on which the sentence was passed, on any week day but Monday, and at 8am.
> The mode of execution and the ceremonial attending it is to be the same as heretofore in use.
> A public notice, under the hand of the Governor of the Prison, of the date and time appointed for the execution to be posted on the Prison Gate not less than twelve hours before the execution and to remain until the inquest has been held.
> The Bell of the Prison, or if arrangements can be made for the purpose, the Bell of the Parish or neighbouring church to be tolled for 15 minutes after the execution.
> The person or persons engaged to carry out the execution should be required to report themselves at the Prison not later

> than 4 o'clock on the afternoon proceeding the completed the execution and until permission is given them to leave.

The document finished with 'Approved by the Secretary of State'.

The requirement for the prison or nearby church bell to be rung before and during an execution was thus amended to require it only to be tolled after the hanging had been carried out. The practice of raising a black flag on the prison flag pole ceased. Those who gathered outside prisons on the morning of execution now had to content themselves with the posting of the official notice on or by the main gate after the prisoner's death had been certified.

Samuel Herbert Dougal, the 57-year-old 'Moat Farm' murderer, was hanged at Chelmsford prison on Tuesday 14 July 1903. He had been convicted of shooting 55-year-old Camille Cecile Holland at the farm in Clavering, Essex, on 19 May 1899 over his affair with a new servant girl. Over the next few years he helped himself to Camille's money and was finally caught when trying to change high-value bank notes for ones of smaller denomination at the Bank of England. The cashier recognised the serial numbers on the notes as ones that had been circulated by the police.

Led to Chelmsford's gallows a few moments before 8 o'clock, Dougal was prepared in the usual way and standing on the trap, hooded and noosed, was asked repeatedly by the chaplain, the Rev J. W. Blakemore, if he was guilty. On the third occasion Dougal replied 'guilty' and William Billington was finally able to push the lever. The chaplain's behaviour was reported by the attending press representatives and led to a question being raised in the House of Commons on 16 July by H. D. Greene, the member for Shrewsbury. The Secretary of State, Mr Akers Douglas, told Mr Greene that there were no statutory rules governing the relationship between the chaplain and the condemned. Apparently Dougal had promised to make a full confession but had not done so. The chaplain's explanation was reported to the House thus: 'As the last moment approached, my spiritual anxiety became intense. I prayed earnestly with him during the last quarter of an hour, during which he sobbed, but he seemed unable to unbend and make a confession. I knew not what to do more, so, under strong impulse, and quite on the inspiration of the moment, I made the strong appeal at the scaffold.' As a result, the Home

Office issued instructions to chaplains to avoid such acts in the future.

However, conversations on the gallows could not be entirely prevented by Home Office edict. Another equally unusual one was to take place at Armley prison in Leeds on 29 December 1903. Forty-two-year-old Emily Swann and 30-year-old John Gallagher had been condemned for beating to death Emily's abusive husband, William, on 6 June after he had left Emily with two black eyes from their latest fight. The case was known as the 'Wombwell Murder' from its location at Wombwell near Barnsley. On the eve of her execution Emily was prostrate with fear, but a glass of brandy revived her sufficiently for her to walk to the gallows. She was led in to the sight of her boyfriend standing pinioned, hooded and noosed on the trap and her own noose hanging down in front of her. Instead of fainting she calmly said: 'Good morning, John.' He was not aware that she was there and was completely taken aback by this, but managed to reply: 'Good morning, love.' As the noose was placed round her neck, she said: 'Goodbye. God bless you.' At this point Billington released the trap. This would be the last occasion that a man and woman would die side by side in Britain. There were to be a total of five double executions in 1903, including Sach and Walters and Gallagher and Swann mentioned above.

An extraordinary case opened at St George's Hall in Liverpool on 12 May 1903. It was the trial of Gustav Rau, Otto Monsson (both German) and Willem Schmidt (Dutch) for mutiny and murder on the high seas. The three were accused of killing Alexander Shaw, the captain of the sailing cargo ship *Veronica*, in December 1902 at sea off the coast of South America. They had also been charged with killing six other crew members who they had variously shot, beaten or stabbed to death. A British freighter, the SS *Brunswick*, was anchored off the coast of Brazil waiting to pick up its cargo when its first officer, William Watson, noticed a ship's boat approaching, bearing the name of the *Veronica* and containing five men. These were the above defendants together with Henry Flohr and Moses Thomas.

Gustav Rau told an amazing story of misfortune. The *Veronica* had started its voyage to Montevideo on 11 October with a crew of twelve, two of whom had died in accidents at sea. They then had a fire on board and had to abandon ship, in one of the two lifeboats, losing contact with the remaining members of the crew in the other boat. It was noted that

Moses Thomas seemed afraid of the others and asked to be separated from them. It was also observed that Gustav Rau had some of the captain's clothing which seemed odd to the captain of the Brunswick. On the voyage back to Liverpool, Thomas told the captain that the missing crew of the *Veronica* had really been murdered by the other four, which they vehemently denied, sticking to the story of the fire and accusing Thomas of inciting the mutiny and killing the rest of the crew. The captain of the Brunswick was deeply suspicious and handed all five over to the police when he docked in Liverpool in January 1903.

Henry Flohr decided to support Thomas' version of events. It seemed that the first mate, Alexander Macleod, was the first to be murdered by Schmidt and Rau, who had quarrelled with him over his authoritarian management style. Macleod was battered to death and thrown overboard. Once they had murdered Macleod, they were then at serious risk, so it was decided to kill any other member of the crew who would not join them. Thus, four other men were battered and thrown into the sea while the captain of the *Veronica*, Alexander Shaw, and another man were shot prior to being thrown overboard. A final man, Alexander Bravo, jumped over the side and was shot at in the water. The trial before Mr Justice Lawrence lasted three days and, on 14 May, all three defendants were found guilty and sentenced to hang. Otto Monsson was reprieved following the jury's recommendation to mercy on account of his age. Three weeks later, at 8 o'clock on the morning of Tuesday 2 June 1903, Rau and Schmidt were hanged side by side by William Billington, assisted by John Billington. This was to be the first double execution at Liverpool's Walton prison.

The next double hanging took place at Leicester prison on Tuesday 21 July when two poachers, 29-year-old Thomas Porter and 24-year-old Thomas Preston, were executed for the murder of William Atkinson at Sileby on 25 May. On 16 December, William Brown, aged 27, stood on the gallows beside 36-year-old Thomas Cowdrey at Winchester prison. They had been found guilty of battering to death a prostitute, named Ester Atkins, to steal her night's takings. Once again William and John Billington carried out the execution. The year 1903 saw no fewer than 27 executions, including those of three women, the highest annual figure in the 20th century, in a year when 312 homicides were recorded and the population of England and Wales was just over 33 million.

17

The early 1900s

The concept of fingerprinting came into being at the beginning of the 20th century, having been invented, almost by accident, in India some years earlier as a way of ensuring that contracts were adhered to. Mr Edward Richard Henry, later Sir Edward and Commissioner of the Metropolitan Police, had written a book entitled *The Classification and Use of Fingerprints* in which he defined a system for taking and using them. He made a presentation of his system to a Home Office committee, under the chairmanship of Lord Belper, which examined the 'Identification of Criminals by Measurement and Fingerprints' in 1900. This led to the setting up of a Fingerprint Bureau at Scotland Yard in July 1901. The first conviction to rely on the new evidence came a year later in a burglary case.

The first capital conviction where fingerprint evidence played a significant part was that of the Stratton brothers in 1905. Twenty-year-old Albert Ernest and 22-year-old Alfred Stratton were found guilty of the robbery murders of an elderly couple, Thomas and Ann Farrow, at their paint shop in Deptford High Street in London on 27 March 1905. In the course of robbing the shop the Strattons had battered the owners to death. They had also left a bloody fingerprint on the cash box. The pair were tried at the Old Bailey on 5 and 6 May before Mr Justice Channell who in his summing up told the jury not to rely on the fingerprint evidence alone. The jury did convict the pair and they were returned to Wandsworth prison to await execution. This took place on 23 May and as it was a double execution John Billington was given two assistants, Henry Pierrepoint and John Ellis. Albert Stratton weighed 172 lbs and was given a drop of 6' 6", whilst his lighter brother Alfred was given a drop of 7' 6" as he weighed 147 lbs. In Albert's case the drop was sufficient to cause fracture dislocation of the neck, but in Alfred's case, although there was dislocation of the neck, there was also evidence of asphyxia. Both men had been given slightly longer drops for their weights than specified in the official 1892 table of drops, but even so it was not sufficient to break Alfred's neck cleanly.

The Court of Criminal Appeal was created by the Criminal Appeal Act of 1907 for England and Wales. It was to be 1927 before a similar court came into being in Scotland and 1930 for Northern Ireland. In capital cases the defendant was limited to appealing against their conviction for murder, there being no scope for appealing the mandatory death sentence.

Rhoda Willis, also known as Leslie James, became the last baby farmer to be hanged when she was executed by Henry and Tom Pierrepoint at Cardiff prison on Wednesday 14 August 1907, her 44th birthday. She had been convicted of the murder of a 1-day-old baby girl called Treasure on a train between Llanishen and Cardiff. She was tried at Swansea before Mr Commissioner Shee on 23 and 24 June 1907. She denied the murder and claimed that the child had been ill and had died of natural causes. The prosecution showed that she had died from asphyxia. She made a full confession to her solicitor in the condemned cell on the morning of her death. Although middle aged, Willis was still an attractive woman, and her blaze of golden hair glinting in the morning sunshine as she was led across the yard to the execution shed was noted by Henry Pierrepoint. She stood 5' 2" tall and weighed 145 lbs, her drop being calculated at 5' 9". Death was, as usual, recorded as being 'instantaneous'.

Although the practice of admitting the press to executions was diminishing rapidly in the 20th century, it was still permitted in some counties. Thus we have the details of the hanging of 29-year-old Abel Atherton on 8 December 1909. Atherton had been convicted at Durham Assizes before Mr Justice Walton of the shooting of 33-year-old Elizabeth Ann Patrick. He maintained throughout that it was an accident and that he had not meant to kill Elizabeth. At 7.50 that Wednesday morning, the under sheriff entered the prison with three newspaper reporters who were allowed to stand in front of the execution shed. Atherton was brought to the doctor's room by two warders, where his hands were pinioned by Henry Pierrepoint, and then led forward to the gallows in a procession consisting of the chief warder, the chaplain, Atherton (held by a warder on either side), Pierrepoint and his assistant William Willis, the principal warder, the governor, the prison surgeon and finally another warder. All but the chaplain entered the shed and once Atherton was on the drop, Willis knelt down behind him to pinion his legs while Pierrepoint placed the noose over his head and adjusted it before pulling the white hood over him. (Henry Pierrepoint did do it in this order, unlike most other hangmen.) On the gallows, Atherton exclaimed: 'Yer hanging an innocent man!'

The clock of the nearby Assize Courts was striking the hour when Pierrepoint released the trap giving Atherton a drop of 7' 3". The execution was over before the clock finished striking and the press men who looked down into the pit reported that Atherton's death was 'instantaneous' and that he was hanging perfectly still. The execution shed was locked up and Atherton was left on the rope for the customary hour. The official notice of the execution was posted on the prison gate and the inquest carried out later in the morning.

One of the most famous cases in the early part of the 20th century was that of American-born 48-year-old Dr Hawley Harvey Crippen. He was convicted of murdering his domineering wife, also American, Cora Turner (stage name Belle Elmore). The crime took place at the Crippens' house at 39 Hilldrop Crescent in London on or about 1 February 1910. The marriage was not a happy one and she belittled him at every turn. Eventually Crippen, who was having an affair with his secretary, Ethel le Neve, unable to stand her behaviour any longer, poisoned her with hyoscine and then dismembered the body and buried it in the cellar. After being interviewed by the police over the disappearance of his wife, Crippen and Ethel le Neve decided to leave the country. They went first to Antwerp in Belgium where they boarded the steamship SS *Montrose* bound for Canada. Ethel shared Crippen's cabin and masqueraded as his son. Captain Kendall, the master of the Montrose, recognised Crippen from a newspaper photograph and sent a ship-to-shore telegraph from the *Montrose* to its owners who alerted Scotland Yard. This was the first time a ship-to-shore telegraph had been used in a criminal case.

Inspector Drew of Scotland Yard set sail for Canada on the faster steamship, the SS *Laurentic*, and was able to catch up with the *Montrose* in Canadian waters. He boarded the ship from the pilot's launch on 31 July 1911 and arrested Crippen and le Neve. This drama on the high seas filled the newspapers of the time and, together with the sinister sounding name of the prime suspect, made it the 'crime of the century' in the press during that summer. Crippen came to trial at the Old Bailey on 18 October before Lord Alverstone, the then Lord Chief Justice. The trial ended on 22 October with the jury taking less than 30 minutes to convict him. A clandestine photo of Crippen in the dock was taken and this has appeared in many books (it was then, and still is, illegal to photograph a prisoner in the dock). Crippen was returned to Pentonville to await his appointment with the hangman. His last request, which was allowed, was to have a photo of Ethel le Neve in his top pocket when he was hanged at 9 o'clock on the dark and foggy morning of Wednesday 23 November 1911 by John Ellis. He was 5' 4" tall and weighed 136 lbs so Ellis gave him a drop of 7' 9". In his memoirs, Ellis recalls that Crippen smiled as he walked towards him. A large crowd had gathered outside the prison to see the execution notice posted. Ethel le Neve was charged with being an accessory to the murder, but was acquitted at her trial.

Frederick Henry Seddon was a 40-year-old superintendent of collectors for a large insurance company who was hanged at Pentonville prison on 18 April 1912 for the murder of 49-year-old Eliza Mary Barrow. Miss Barrow was quite wealthy and rented the second floor of Seddon's house at 63, Tollington Park, London. Seddon set about obtaining Miss Barrow's money and property and had persuaded her to sign over her several properties to him in return for an annuity for the rest of her life. As he did not want to wait that long he poisoned her with arsenic in September 1911, conveniently inheriting her wealth. Her cousins, Albert and Amelia Vonderahe, had expected to inherit and went to the police who they persuaded to obtain permission to exhume the dead woman's body. Arsenic was discovered in the corpse and evidence came to light of the purchase by Seddon of fly papers containing arsenic.

He was tried and convicted at the Old Bailey on 27 February 1912. The jury took an hour to find him guilty although he maintained his innocence until the end. Seddon was 5' 3" tall and weighed 136 lbs and was given a drop of 7' 1" by John Ellis, which again was more than indicated by the official table. Approaching the gallows in the execution shed in the prison yard, Seddon was somewhat unnerved by the sight of the noose and the sudden sounding of a loud horn of a tourist coach passing the prison. Ellis was afraid Seddon was going to faint and got the execution over as quickly as he could – in just 25 seconds, a record at that time.

In 1913, the Home Office issued a second and final table of drops, which continued in use until abolition. This table is still used by some other countries today, e.g. Singapore. As a comparison both the 1892 and 1913 tables are reproduced below. The 1913 table is designed to produce a final force of 1000 foot pounds and the length of drop is calculated by dividing the prisoner's weight in pounds in their clothes into 1000. If there were special reasons, such as the prisoner having a diseased or weak neck, the governor and prison medical officer would advise the executioner on the length of drop to be used. Drops in excess of 8' 6" were not to be used.

It will be seen that the drops specified in the 1913 table are longer than those in the 1892 one, as in some cases the prisoner's neck had not been broken by the shorter fall (see Alfred Stratton, above).

1892 table		**1913 table**	
Weight of prisoner lbs	Drop in feet & inches	Weight of prisoner lbs	Drop in feet & inches
105 & under	8' 0"	-	-
110	7' 10"	-	-
115	7' 3"	118 & under	8' 6"
120	7' 0"	120	8' 4"
125	6' 9"	125	8' 0"
130	6' 5"	130	7' 8"
135	6' 2"	135	7' 5"
140	6' 0"	140	7' 2"
145	5' 9"	145	6' 11"
150	5' 7"	150	6' 8"
155	5' 5"	155	6' 5"
160	5' 3"	160	6' 3"
165	5' 1"	165	6' 1"
170	4' 11"	170	5' 10"
175	4' 9"	175	5' 8"
180	4' 8"	180	5' 7"
185	4' 7"	185	5' 5"
190	4' 5"	190	5' 3"
195	4' 4"	195	5' 2"
200 & over	4' 2"	200 & over	5' 0"

On November 1914, Charles Frembd became the oldest man to be hanged in Britain in the 20th century. Frembd was a 71-year-old German-born grocer who had cut his wife Louisa's throat at their shop in Harrow Road, Leytonstone. Louisa was found dead on their bed with her husband beside her, having inflicted a minor wound to himself with the knife. This execution was carried out by John Ellis at Springfield prison in Chelmsford. At the inquest a bruise was noted on Frembd's face which had been caused by the trap door rebounding and hitting him. It was to be the last execution at Springfield. The army took it over during World War 1 and future Essex hangings were carried out at Pentonville.

On 8 August 1914, Herbert Asquith's government introduced the Defence of the Realm Act as a wartime measure. Among its many provisions this Act made espionage a capital crime and permitted trial by court martial for those accused, unless they were British. Eleven men were to be executed by firing squad and two hanged. The first of these was Robert Rosenthal, who was to die for spying. Rosenthal had been passing coded messages relating to the movements of ships from the ports of Edinburgh, Hull and Portsmouth and was caught when he returned to Britain from Denmark. He was tried on 6 July at the Westminster Guildhall and convicted of espionage, being hanged at Wandsworth prison by Thomas Pierrepoint and Robert Baxter on the morning of Thursday 15 July 1915.

The defendant in the second case is probably far better known. He was 51-year-old Roger Casement. Sir Roger, as he was entitled to be called, was a retired diplomat and Irish by birth, although a British citizen, as all of Ireland was part of the UK at this time. He was a supporter of Irish Nationalism and after the outbreak of war he moved from Ireland to Germany. Here he tried to get the German government to support a rebellion against British rule and recruit Irish-born prisoners of war into an Irish Brigade to fight against the British. The Germans sent a shipment of arms to Ireland to be used in the Easter Rising of 1916, but these were intercepted at sea aboard a German freighter disguised as a Norwegian vessel. Casement was captured soon after being put ashore from a German U-boat in Tralee Bay on 21 April 1916. He was taken to London and stood trial at the Old Bailey between 26 and 29 June. He was convicted of treason as he was a British subject and the Treason Act applied irrespective of where the treasonable acts had been committed. As part of his conviction he was stripped of his knighthood and other honours. He appealed without success, and despite considerable activism on his behalf, was hanged by John Ellis and Robert Baxter at Pentonville prison on Thursday 3 August 1916. It has been reported that Casement's body was not given a coffin before burial but simply placed in the grave and covered with quicklime and then soil. His last wish was that he be buried in Ireland and in 1965 this was finally granted by the Labour government under Harold Wilson. He was given a state funeral and reburied with full military honours in Glasnevin cemetery in Dublin.

Perhaps the most notorious criminal to end his days at Maidstone prison was George Joseph Smith who was dubbed the 'Brides in the Bath' murderer. Smith was not only a serial killer but also a serial bigamist. He was a career criminal who had been in trouble with the law since childhood and had served several prison sentences during his 43-year life.

Smith was always able to attract the opposite sex and in 1898 was married for the first time under the assumed name of Oliver Love to a Miss Caroline Thornhill. He wrote false references for Thornhill to enable her to get jobs as a domestic servant in houses in London and Sussex and then persuaded her to steal items for him. When she was arrested in Worthing and jailed for 12 months, Smith left her and moved to London where he was married for the second time to his landlady. In 1900, after her release from prison, Thornhill spotted Oliver Love, as she knew him, in London and reported him to the police. He was arrested and given a two-year sentence for receiving stolen property. He was duly released and travelled the country as a dealer in second-hand goods. His next marriage was to a widow named Florence Wilson in 1908. He persuaded her to draw out her life savings and give them to him before he vanished from her life. In July 1908, he married yet again, this time a lady called Edith Pegler in Bristol. The following year he married Sarah Freeman and was able to steal her savings. In 1910, he met his first murder victim, Beatrice Mundy, known as Bessie, in Bristol. He married the unsuspecting woman in August of that year in the name of Henry Williams. Beatrice had a large sum of money tied up in a trust which could be released only upon her death. The trust had been set up to provide her with a monthly income. So Smith persuaded Beatrice to make a will in his favour before he drowned her in the bath in at their home in Herne Bay, Kent. Smith called the doctor, who tried to save her, but it was too late. It appeared to be just a tragic accident, although it aroused the suspicion of Beatrice's relatives. Smith got his money – some £2500 – a huge sum in those days, and returned to Edith Pegler.

Like so many murderers he could not stop while he was still ahead. He would have almost certainly got away with Beatrice's murder and her money. But he continued with his trail of marriages and murders. His next victim was 26-year-old Alice Burnham whom he met in Southsea in Hampshire. He married her and took her on holiday to Blackpool on 10 December 1913 where they stayed in a guesthouse. Two days later, Alice was found drowned in the bath. His next marriage came the following year to Alice Reavil whom Smith relieved of her savings and some furniture before abandoning her. He struck again in December of 1914 when he met, and of course married, 38-year-old Margaret Lofty in Bath. Margaret had a life insurance policy for £700 (enough to buy a good house at the time) and this was an opportunity too good to miss for Smith. He persuaded her to make a will in his favour, and two days later Margaret was found drowned in the bath.

After her death, Smith returned to the long-suffering Edith Pegler, who as usual accepted him back. Alice's death made headline news and the article was read by Joseph Crossley, the husband of the Blackpool landlady with whom Smith had stayed with Alice Burnham, and by Alice's father. Both reported their suspicions to the police who arrested Smith and charged him with bigamy while they delved further into the trail of suspicious drownings.

He was to be charged with all three murders and came to trial at the Old Bailey on 22 June 1915 before Mr Justice Scrutton for the murder of Beatrice Mundy (Bessie Williams). Mr Justice Scrutton permitted evidence of the two other murders to be admitted as they proved a pattern of crime. The famous barrister Sir Edward Marshall Hall defended Smith, but even he could not save him from the evidence of the equally famous pathologist, Bernard Spilsbury. Spilsbury demonstrated to the court that the drownings could not have been accidental due to the victim falling asleep as they would not slide down the bath and under the water of their own volition. They had to be pulled down by lifting up the knees with one hand while pushing the head down with the other. The lady who had volunteered to assist Spilsbury in this demonstration became almost immediately unconscious and had to be revived. The jury were convinced by this remarkable demonstration and the other evidence, taking just 20 minutes to return a guilty verdict on 1 July. Smith was hanged by John Ellis, assisted by Edward Taylor, on Friday 13 August 1915, protesting his innocence until the end.

Smith was one of just nine men hanged in England during 1915, of whom all but one had been convicted of killing wives or girlfriends. The year 1916 was even quieter for civilian executions, with just eight in England and Wales. Of these, five were for the murders of girlfriends or ex-girlfriends, and one in Wales was for wife murder. There were no civilian executions in either year in Scotland or Ireland. However, in May 1916, 14 men were shot by firing squad in the Quarry Yard at Dublin's Kilmainham gaol and one more (Thomas Kent) at Cork Barracks, having been convicted of treason for their parts in the 1916 Easter Rebellion. Kilmainham gaol has been restored and is now open to the public. Plaques mark the place where these executions were carried out. They were: Tom Clarke, Thomas MacDonagh and Padraic Pearse on Wednesday 3 May; Joseph Mary Plunkett, William Pearse, Edward Daly and Michael O'Hanrahan on Thursday 4 May; John MacBride on Friday 5 May; Eamonn Ceannt, Michael Mallin, Conn Colbert and Sean Heuston on Monday 8 May; Thomas Kent on Tuesday 9 May; and finally Sean MacDiarmada and James Connolly on Friday 12 May.

Louis Marie Joseph Voison was a 42-year-old French butcher who lived in the basement of 101 Charlotte Street, London. He had two lady friends: 32-year-old Belgian-born Emilliene Gerard and French-born Berthe Roche. Mme Gerard had sought shelter from a German air raid in Voison's basement apartment on the night of 31 October 1917. Roche was also present and it is thought that a fight broke out between the two women which led to Roche attacking Gerard with a poker. To stifle her cries Voisin suffocated her and then decided to dismember the corpse. Parts of the mutilated body were found in a local park on 2 November wrapped up in meat bags. With the grisly find was a scrap of paper on which had been handwritten the words 'Blodie Belgiam' and a bed sheet with a laundry mark that was traced back to Mme Gerard. In her house they found a photograph of Voison and other links to him, which led to the arrest of both him and Berthe Roche. It was the scrap of paper with its misspelled wording that was to give him away. He had presumably intended it to throw the police off the scent, but when he was asked to write the same words as spoken to him he made the same spelling errors. His handwriting also matched that on the scrap of paper. He was tried at the Old Bailey in January 1918 before Mr Justice Darling and was convicted of the murder. Although Berthe Roche had been involved in the fight and it was held that she had struck Mme Gerard, she was convicted only of being an accessory to murder and sentenced to seven years in prison. Voison's hanging was carried out by John Ellis and Edward Taylor at Pentonville prison on 2 March 1918.

There had been nine executions in England and Wales in 1917, and just seven in 1918. Scotland had one hanging in 1917, that of Thomas McGuiness at Glasgow's Duke Street prison on 16 May for the murder of Alexander Imlach. This was Scotland's first hanging for four years. There were no executions in Ireland for civilian offences in this period.

18

The inter-war years

Lord Birkenhead, the Lord Chancellor, was instrumental in framing the provisions of the Infanticide Act of 1922. This made the killing of a newborn baby under 35 days old by its mother no longer a capital crime if it could be shown that the balance of her mind was impaired. The impairment was a partial defence to murder, so that where it could be proved that it was the mother who killed the baby she would be guilty of manslaughter and liable for a term of imprisonment at the judge's discretion, up to life imprisonment. In reality this was another instance of the law catching up with judicial practice as most probably the last woman to be executed for infanticide was 24-year-old Mary Smith who went to the gallows at Stafford on 19 March 1834.

It is not always possible from surviving records to know whether a child murder fell into this category or not. Large numbers of women and girls continued to be sentenced to death after 1840 for killing their infant children, but all were reprieved. Fifteen women who had been convicted of murdering their babies were reprieved in the first decade of the 20th century.

One of the youngest men to suffer at London's Pentonville prison was Henry Julius Jacoby, aged just 18. Jacoby worked as pantry boy at the Spencer Hotel in Portman Street, London. Among the guests on the night of Monday 13 March 1922 was 66-year-old Lady Alice White. Her body was discovered the next morning by a chambermaid who, unable to get an answer from Room 14, let herself in with the master key. The poor girl was confronted by a horrible sight. Lady Alice had been severely battered around the head, although she was still alive and survived for a further two days. The police naturally interviewed all the hotel's staff and suspicion quickly fell on Jacoby who confessed to them that he had hit Lady Alice with a hammer when, on entering her room, he had disturbed her and caused her to let out a shriek. He later withdrew this confession and instead claimed that he saw an intruder strike the blows. The jury at his Old Bailey trial on 28 April 1922 were not impressed with this version and convicted him with a recommendation to mercy, as they were not convinced that the lad had intended to kill but rather that he did so in panic when Lady White woke to find him in her bedroom and screamed.

Jacoby was hanged by John Ellis on 7 June 1922. Ellis recalls that Jacoby seemed completely unconcerned about his impending fate and when Ellis went to have a look at him on the afternoon before his execution, he was playing a makeshift game of cricket with one of the warders in the exercise yard. After his wrists had been pinioned, Jacoby made a point of thanking the governor and prison officers for their kindness to him in the condemned cell. He was described by Ellis as the calmest person in the execution shed that Wednesday morning.

One case that has never disappeared is that of 28-year-old Edith Thompson and 20-year-old Frederick Bywaters who were jointly convicted of the murder of Edith's husband, Percy, on 4 October 1922. This case has been written about in many books and there have been screenplays based upon it. It was the major news in the autumn of 1922. It is felt by many that Edith Thompson was hanged more for adultery than for murder, a murder which it is very unlikely she took any active part in. The brief facts of the case are that Edith and Percy were returning home to Ilford in Essex after a night out at the theatre in London when Edith's lover, Frederick Bywaters, attacked Percy and stabbed him to death. Edith was said to have shouted at Frederick: 'Oh don't! Oh don't!' Sadly for her, Bywaters had kept the 62 letters she had written him, which described Percy's murder by various means such as poison and putting ground glass in his food. The question the Old Bailey jury had to decide was whether there was common purpose between Frederick and Edith to kill Percy. Mr Justice Shearman instructed the jury: 'You will not convict her unless you are satisfied that she and he agreed that this man should be murdered when he could be, and she knew that he was going to do it, and directed him to do it, and by arrangement between them he was doing it.' This was his explanation of the doctrine of common purpose. The jury took just over two hours to find them both guilty on 11 December 1922. Edith collapsed in the dock and cried out: 'I am not guilty. Oh God, I am not guilty!' as she was sentenced.

There was huge media interest in the case worldwide and a petition was drawn up with nearly a million signatures to spare Edith. There was considerable pressure in the media for a commutation. However, this, together with Bywaters' repeated confession that he and he alone killed Thompson, failed to persuade the Home Secretary, William Clive Bridgeman, later 1st Viscount Bridgeman, to reprieve her. This would be the first occasion when a man and a woman convicted of the same murder would be held at and hanged at separate prisons. Edith was taken to Holloway and Bywaters to Pentonville, less than a mile apart. Both appealed their convictions, but these were turned down. This was the first female hanging in Britain since Rhoda Willis in 1907. At 9am on Tuesday 9 January 1923 the usual processions left the condemned cells of the respective prisons. Bywaters was executed by William Willis, assisted by Seth Mills, still protesting Edith's innocence. At Holloway it was a very much more distressing scene. A few minutes before he entered the condemned cell, Ellis records hearing a ghastly moaning coming from Edith's cell. When he and Seth Mills entered she was reportedly semi-conscious and in a state of total collapse. According to Ellis' biography, she looked dead already.

Edith was carried from the condemned cell to the execution shed by two warders and had to be held up on the trap whilst the preparations were completed. It has been alleged that there was a considerable amount of blood dripping from Edith's lower body after hanging for the regulation hour. Two theories have been speculated for this. Bernard Spillsbury, who carried out the autopsy, felt it was caused by her being pregnant and miscarrying, whilst others claim it was due to inversion of the uterus, and the prison authorities claim that nothing untoward happened at all. It will be 2023 before the case papers are released into the public domain to enable any accurate information to be uncovered, such was the sensitivity of the case. In any event, after this, future female prisoners were made to wear canvas underpants for their execution. Whatever really happened, this hanging seemed to have a profound effect on all those present. Several of the prison officers involved took early retirement and her executioner, John Ellis, retired at the end of the year.

On 10 October 1923, Susan Newell made history as the only woman to be hanged in 20th century Scotland. In fact, she was the first to be executed in Scotland since Jessie King on 11 March 1889. She had murdered a young boy called John Johnson who had refused to give her an evening newspaper when she could not produce the money to pay for it. She was arrested in Glasgow's Duke Street with the boy's body hidden under a rug in a pram. Her daughter, who had seen John murdered and was accompanying her mother when arrested the morning after the killing, was the main witness against her at her trial at Glasgow on 18 September 1923 before Lord Alness.

She was to be hanged by John Ellis, assisted by Robert Baxter, at Duke Street prison in Glasgow (the same Duke Street in which she was arrested). Ellis was noted for the speed at which he conducted executions and it is perhaps his wanting to get the procedure over with quickly and not wanting to hurt Susan that caused him not to strap her wrists tightly. Ellis used the leather body belt that he had used for Edith Thompson which had an additional strap to go round the thighs. This was necessary because as skirts got shorter over the years, there was concern that they would billow up as the prisoner dropped.

On the gallows, Susan allowed Baxter to strap her legs and thighs without protest, but was able to get her hands free from the loose wrist straps and defiantly pulled off the white hood, saying to Ellis: 'Don't put that thing over me.' Rather than risk another trying scene, Ellis decided to proceed without it as the noose was already in place, so he simply pulled the lever and Susan went through the trap with her face uncovered. She was said to be the calmest person in the execution chamber, accepting her fate with both courage and dignity, although she never confessed to the killing.

Multiple murders were rare events in the early part of the century and where they did occur, they often involved members of the same family. However, Alfred Burrows did things slightly differently. He had been in a relationship with Hannah Calladine for some two years and married her, even though he was already married. He served a prison sentence for bigamy as a result and moved in with Hannah on his release. The couple had a child whom they christened Albert Edward. Burrows was in dire financial straits and decided to solve the problem by murdering Hannah and Albert on 20 January 1920. He disposed of their bodies in an old mine shaft on the moors near Glossop in Derbyshire. Hannah's 5-year-old daughter by a previous relationship, Elsie, lived with them and Burrows rid himself of her the following day, dumping her body down the shaft too. After this Burrows told his real wife that he and Hannah had split up and they resumed their marriage.

Nothing further was heard of Burrows until 4 March 1923 when 4-year-old Thomas Wood was reported missing and Burrows was questioned as he had been seen with the boy. He took the police onto the moors and they were able to recover Thomas' body from the mine shaft that showed evidence of strangulation and sexual abuse. He was thus charged with this murder and later with the other three as the police excavated bodies from the shaft. He was tried at Derbyshire Assizes on 3/4 July and hanged at Nottingham prison, as Derby no longer had execution facilities, by John Ellis assisted by William Willis on Wednesday 8 August 1923.

On 3 September 1925, Tom Pierrepoint and Robert Wilson carried out a double hanging at Armley and on the following day a further single execution. The first two prisoners were Alfred Bostock who had killed his mistress, Elizabeth Sherratt, and 23-year-old Wilfred Fowler, who was a Sheffield gangster who had taken part in the murder of William Plommer. Fowler's brother and leader of the gang, Lawrence, was to die the following day for the same crime. Lionel Mann assisted Tom Pierrepoint at this hanging.

Alfred Bostock and Elizabeth Sherratt both worked for the Parkgate Ironworks in Rotherham and had fallen for each other virtually on sight. Albert was married, but had a passionate affair with Elizabeth which progressed well until Elizabeth announced that she was pregnant, a setback that Alfred could simply not accept. On 3 May 1925, her battered body was found floating in the River Don near Rawmarsh. Bostock was the prime suspect and was quickly arrested for the murder. He presented a weak alibi in his defence and, although the evidence against him was circumstantial, it took the jury only 15 minutes to convict him. It is unclear why he was hanged alongside William Fowler and not alone. One surmises that the prison authorities thought there would be trouble between the Fowler brothers so had decided to hang them separately.

The Fowlers were members of a Sheffield gang that had been terrorising the city for some time and who considered themselves beyond the law. One of the gang's members, Trimmer Welsh, had got into a fight with William Plommer over his treatment of the barmaid in the pub where they were both drinking, which Plommer had won. This led to his ambush by two members of the gang, including youngWilfred Fowler, but they were no match for this powerfully built and courageous ex-boxer. Two defeats for the gang were more than its pride and arrogance could stomach, so a mob of a dozen or so went to Plommer's house and when he came out to face them, they beat, stabbed and kicked him to death. They were soon rounded up, some receiving prison sentences; Lawrence and William, being convicted of murder, received death sentences. Their executions brought to an end the gang terror in Sheffield in the 1920s.

The last civilian execution at Shepton Mallet in Somerset took place on Tuesday 2 March 1926 when Tom Pierrepoint and Lionel Mann hanged John Lincoln for the murder of Edward Richards at Trowbridge in Wiltshire. A very much more sad case of multiple murder than Alfred Burrows above occurred on 2 December 1925 at the Birkenhead home of 54-year-old Lock Ah Tam. Liverpool, being a major port and entry point into the UK, had a large Chinese community. Tam was Chinese by birth and had been a successful and well-respected businessman in Birkenhead. He ran the European branch of the Jack Ah Tai organisation for Chinese dock workers, the Chinese Progress Club and was superintendent of Chinese sailors for three steamship companies in Liverpool. He had a reputation as a peacemaker, being able to sort out conflicts between dockers.

Tam received head injuries in a fight at the Chinese Progress Club in 1918 from a group of foreign sailors and, although he recovered, it left him with emotional problems and violent mood swings. He had never previously been violent towards his family, but began to quarrel with his wife, son and two daughters. The situation was exacerbated by his deteriorating business affairs and came to a head on the Wednesday evening when Tam shot his wife, Catherine, and daughters, Doris and Celia. Having done so he phoned the police to tell them to come and arrest him. Tam came to trial at Chester Assizes in February 1926 and was defended by Britain's foremost counsel, Sir Edward Marshall Hall. The defence was one of insanity due to automatism caused by an epileptic seizure brought on by the blow to the head seven years earlier. This failed as it could be shown that Tam understood what he had done and that it was wrong because he had telephoned the police immediately afterwards. The jury returned a guilty verdict after 12 minutes of deliberation and tears were seen running down the face of Mr Justice McKinnon as he sentenced Tam to death. He was duly executed by William Willis, assisted by Henry Pollard, on the morning of Tuesday 23 March 1926 at Liverpool's Walton prison.

In 1927, there were eight hangings nationally (England, Scotland and Wales) with a sharp rise in 1928 to 24, of which three were in Scotland. The year 1929 saw a return to a more typical eight. In 1929, a Select Committee on Capital Punishment was set up under the chairmanship of the Labour member for Motherwell, the Rev James Barr. He was an outright abolitionist and as a result six Conservative MPs left the committee before it published its report on 9 December 1930. The 98-page report cost more than £1200, according to a parliamentary answer on 24 July 1930.

Its main recommendations, which were ignored by the government and savaged by the press, were:

> a suspension of the death penalty for five years, with reprieves being granted until this was approved by Parliament,
> an extension of the provisions of the McNaughten Rules governing capital crimes committed by the mentally ill, to give more weight to medical opinion,
> greater use of the Royal Prerogative, i.e. reprieves, and
> the raising of the minimum age for execution from 16 to 21, and that women should be treated equally in deciding whether or not to reprieve.

One gets the impression from examining the statistics for female death sentences and reprieves that women were much more likely to be reprieved than men. In the first 30 years of the 20th century there were a total of 751 death sentences passed in England and Wales. Of these 88 were on women which resulted in just six executions. (Louisa Masset is excluded from this total as she was sentenced in 1899.) In the same period, 414 men had gone to the gallows, so the reprieve rate for men was 37.5%, whilst for women it was 93.2%. As a result of this committee sitting there were just three executions in 1930, rising to 10 in 1931.

Twenty-six-year-old Frederick Parker and 21-year-old Albert Probert were convicted of the robbery murder of 80-year-old Joseph Bedford at his shop in Clarence Street, Portslade near Brighton in Sussex. Although they were tried and convicted in Sussex, Lewes prison, like Springfield prison in Essex, no longer had an execution facility, so they were hanged together at Wandsworth prison at 9am on 4 May 1934 by Thomas Pierrepoint, assisted by his nephew, Albert. This was to be the last time a newspaper reporter was admitted to an execution and prompted a stiffly worded letter from the Home Office essentially banning the practice. One assumes that the Prison Commissioners did not feel that it was worthwhile building modern execution suites at every county prison to replace the old execution sheds as hangings were very infrequent in most counties, and with good rail links the families of the condemned could easily get to London to visit their relatives. Percy Clifford, aged 32, had been the last to hang at Lewes, on 11 August 1914 for the murder of his wife, Maud.

The final execution of 1934 was that of 43-year-old Ethel Lillie Major at Hull prison at 8 o'clock on the morning of 19 December. She had poisoned her husband, Arthur, at Horncastle in Lincolnshire, where William Marwood had lived. As a young woman Ethel had got pregnant by a boyfriend and had given birth to a daughter who was named Auriel and brought up by Ethel's parents as her younger sister. Ethel married Arthur Major who initially accepted Auriel as Ethel's sister but in due course found out the truth, which caused quarrels. Arthur began an affair with a neighbour and the marriage went from bad to worse. Ultimately Ethel laced some corned beef with strychnine and gave this to Arthur on 22 May for his evening meal. Arthur did not like the taste of his dinner and threw the remains out for the next door's dog to eat, which died soon after. Arthur expired two days later after suffering what appeared to be a severe epileptic fit. An anonymous letter was sent to the local police linking the two deaths and it was decided to postpone Arthur's funeral and exhume the dog. Both bodies were found to contain the poison. When questioned, Ethel denied that she had had any strychnine, but this was before she was told what poison had been used. She was found to have a key that fitted her gamekeeper father's poison cabinet. As a result of the foregoing she was tried at Lincoln Assizes between 29 October and 1 November 1934. After conviction she was transferred to Hull to await execution. This was to be the last hanging at Hull and the only female one there. Her ghost is said to haunt the prison.

In 1936, two women were executed. The first of these cases was that of self-styled nurse, 36-year-old Dorothea Waddingham, who had poisoned two residents with morphine in her nursing home at 32 Devon Drive, Nottingham. They were Louisa Baguley, a widow of 89, and her 50-year-old disabled daughter, Ada. The trial opened in Nottingham on 27 February 1936 and lasted three days. Waddingham performed badly in the witness box and the jury took just two hours to find her guilty. Nottingham no longer had an execution facility so she was transferred to the modern condemned suite at Winson Green prison in Birmingham where she was hanged by Thomas Pierrepoint, assisted by his nephew Albert on Thursday 16 April. She was a small woman, 4' 11" tall and 123 lbs in weight, so was given a drop of 8' 5". It was estimated that as many as 5000 people, led by the well known anti-capital punishment campaigner, Mrs Elsie Van der Elst, had gathered outside Winson Green to protest against the execution.

The second case was that of 33-year-old Charlotte Bryant who was hanged at Exeter. She too had been convicted of poisoning, in this case her husband, Frederick, with arsenic. Her four-day trial opened at Dorchester on 27 May before Mr Justice MacKinnon and the forensic evidence was presented by Dr Roche Lynch. This was later found to be flawed as he had claimed that the level of arsenic found in the ashes of the stove was abnormally high. This factual correction was not permitted to be heard by the Appeal Court, as introducing new evidence after a guilty verdict was banned in law. As the appeal had been turned down, Charlotte's fate lay in the hands of the Home Secretary, John Allsebrook Simon, who refused to intervene.

For reasons that are not clear, Charlotte was transferred to Exeter prison in Devon for execution. (Dorchester continued to have an execution facility which was last used on 24 July 1941 for the hanging of David Miller Jennings.) Charlotte was led to the gallows at 8am on Wednesday 15 July 1936 by Tom Pierrepoint assisted by Thomas Phillips. By an odd coincidence, a man also called Bryant (no relation) had been hanged the previous day at Wandsworth. In the condemned cell she had been ministered to by a Catholic priest, Father Barney. He was not bound by Home Office rules of secrecy and described her last moments as 'truly edifying', reporting that 'she met her end with Christian fortitude'. She never confessed to the murder.

Although there were only seven hangings in 1936, two of which are detailed above, the third case to make the headlines that year was that of 36-year-old Dr Buck Ruxton, which was one of the first cases where new forensic techniques played a major part in securing a murder conviction in Britain. Ruxton had been born Bukhtyar Rustomji Ratanji Hakim in Bombay in 1899 and had studied medicine as a post-graduate student in Edinburgh before setting up practice as a GP in Dalton Square, Lancaster. In Edinburgh he had met and fallen for Isabella Kerr. He was insanely jealous of Isabella and during a row over an alleged lover in September 1935 it is thought that he strangled her in front of their housemaid, Mary Jane Rogerson. As Mary had seen all, she too had to be eliminated and was either strangled or suffocated. After killing the two women, Ruxton carried their bodies into the bathroom and surgically dismembered them, removing all their distinguishing features in the hope of making it impossible to identify the bodies or determine the cause of death. He wrapped the body parts in sheets of newspaper, including a special edition of the *Sunday Graphic* newspaper sold only in the Lancaster area, and then drove to Scotland where he threw the bodies into a ravine at The Devil's Beeftub near the town of Moffat in Dumfriesshire. On returning to Lancaster he put about the story that Isabella had gone on holiday and taken Mary with her, a story that the girl's parents did not believe.

The body parts were found by a walker and it was soon realised that there were two separate sets of remains. The newspaper that they were wrapped in gave the police Lancaster as a clue as to their origin, where two women had been reported missing. Ruxton was questioned and arrested on 13 October 1935. The Glasgow Police Identification Bureau used fingerprints to help identify the bodies and also the then new technique of photographic superimposition, matching a photo of Isabella to the shape of one of the skulls found. The match was perfect. This pioneering forensic work was carried out by pathologist Professor John

Glaister and Professor of Anatomy James Couper Brash. Ruxton was tried at Manchester Assizes in March of 1936 before Mr Justice Singleton, the jury taking just over an hour to convict him. Amazingly, a petition for clemency was organised prior to the execution and signed by some 10,000 people. He was hanged at Strangeways by Thomas Pierrepoint, assisted by Robert Wilson, at 8am on 12 May 1936. The police had to deal with a very large crowd of people who had gathered outside the prison on that Tuesday morning. A few days after his death, his signed confession was published, dated 14 October 1935. It said: 'I killed Mrs Ruxton in a fit of temper because I thought she had been with a man. I was mad at the time. Mary Rogerson was present at the time. I had to kill her.'

During the 1930s, the Prison Commissioners issued revised instructions for the burial of executed persons.

'Instructions to be observed in burying the bodies of executed prisoners:

1. All the clothing, with the exception of the shirt or similar garment, will be removed from the body, which will be placed in a coffin made of ½ inch wood, deal or pine.

2. The sides and ends of the coffin will be well perforated with large holes.

3. Lime will not be used. (See note below.)

4. The original size of the plot of ground will be 9 feet by 4 feet, and the grave will be from 8 to 10 feet in depth.

5. When the coffin has been covered with 1 foot of earth, charcoal to the depth of 3 inches will be thrown into the grave, which will then be filled in. The top coffin will not be less than 4 feet below the ground surface.

6. Arrangements will be made for the grave sites to be reused in sequence, in such wise that no grave shall be used over again until 7 years have elapsed. When a grave is reopened the charcoal and the foot of earth above the last coffin will not be disturbed.

7. A register of graves will be kept, containing the name of each convict buried, the date of burial, the site of the grave, and the position of the coffin in the grave.'

Note: It had been the practice to bury bodies with quicklime as this had been thought to speed the process of decomposition, but in fact was found to preserve the body.

A new gallows was installed at Wandsworth prison in 1937. This had the beam concealed above the ceiling of the execution room and accessed through small traps in the ceiling. The beam was of the double pattern with three metal chain brackets straddling the top surfaces. For a single execution the centre one was used with ropes attached to the outer two for the warders supporting the condemned man to hold on to so as to avoid falling through the trap with him. Where a double execution was to be carried out the outer brackets were used and there were small handrails on the side walls for the warders to hold on to. The main trap doors were 9' long and 4' 6" wide and were large enough to be used for double executions. The trap doors, lever and beam are now on display at the Galleries of Justice in Nottingham, having been previously stored out of sight at the Police Service Museum at Rugby.

Just 15 people would be executed in 1938 and 1939 in England, with Wandsworth having seven of these hangings and Durham three. The last execution at Gloucester prison took place on 7 June 1940 when 40-year-old Ralph Smith was hanged for the murder of his ex-girlfriend, Beatrice Baxter. Future Gloucestershire executions were carried out in Bristol. There were no executions in Scotland or Wales in this two-year period.

19

World War 2 and its aftermath

Britain was at war with Germany from September 1939, but this did not lead to a sharp rise in executions for ordinary capital crimes. During the period from September 1939 to July 1945, 140 people were sentenced to death in England and Wales. Of these, 69 were to hang for civilian murders, an average of 11.5 per annum. There were no wartime executions in Scotland and just one in Northern Ireland. Fifteen men were hanged and one shot for espionage and treason during the war, and a further three men were hanged for treason after the war.

The first civilian execution during the period was that of 30-year-old Leonard Hucker at Wandsworth on 10 October 1939. Hucker had stabbed 60-year-old Mary Moncrieff to death at Willesden in the August of that year. The last two executions of the year were also carried out at Wandsworth on two consecutive days.

Mabel Mundy, who was 44 years old, had been raped and battered to death at Hindhead in Surrey on the evening of 4 July 1939; three soldiers who had been seen with her were charged with the murder. They were 27-year-old Stanley Ernest Boon, 26-year-old Arthur John Smith and Joseph William Goodwin, all of whom were stationed at Aldershot Barracks. All three were found to have blood and/or semen on their clothing and were committed for trial at the Old Bailey on 16 September. At the end of the proceedings on 21 September, Goodwin was acquitted and the other two were found guilty. Both men's appeals were turned down. They blamed each other for the murder and it was thus decided to execute them separately. Thomas Pierrepoint, assisted by Stanley Cross, hanged Boon at 9am on Wednesday 25 October and Smith at the same time the following morning, but assisted by Thomas Phillips.

Peter Barnes and James Richards were to be the first men to suffer the death penalty in 1940. This was for an IRA bombing in Coventry that claimed the lives of a woman and four men on 25 August 1939. A huge explosion occurred in Broadgate when a bomb left in a bicycle basket went off in the crowded shopping area at around 2.30 on that Friday afternoon, injuring some 70 people and causing a lot of damage. The dead were John Corbett Arnott, aged 15; Elsie Ansell, aged 21; Rex Gentle, aged 33; Gwilym Rowlands, aged 50; and James Clay, aged 82. The bomb had been assembled at a safe house at 25 Clara Street in the Stoke area of Coventry and then brought into the city on the bike. Peter Barnes was charged along with Joseph and Mary Hewitt, her mother Brigid O'Hara and James Richards who lodged with the Hewitts. The defendants came to trial at Birmingham from 11 to 14 December 1939. The Hewitt family were acquitted of all charges leaving just Barnes and Richards to face the guilty verdicts. When asked if they had anything to say before sentence, Barnes continued to assert his innocence whilst Richards admitted his part in the crime, seeing himself as a freedom fighter. Their appeals were dismissed and both were hanged at Winson Green prison on 7 February 1940 by Tom Pierrepoint, assisted by his nephew Albert, Thomas Phillips and Stanley Cross.

On the evening of Thursday 29 February 1940, a robbery took place at a shop in Cuxhoe, County Durham. Two young men, 24-year-old Vincent Ostler and 27-year-old William Appleby, had broken into the Co-op store there in the early hours of the morning. A passing cyclist, Jesse Smith, noticed the light was on, which was unusual in a shop at night in those days and thought he saw a person inside. He decided to report this immediately to the police and constables William Shiell and William Stafford went back with Smith to see what was going on. When they heard the police, the robbers made a break for it and were chased by Shiell. One of the men shot Shiell in the stomach. He remained conscious long enough to tell Stafford that there were two assailants and that one of them had said 'Let him have it' before the shot was fired. Shiell was able to describe one of his attackers to colleagues before he died later the next day in hospital.

Ostler and Appleby were arrested on 4 March, both blaming the other. The words 'Let him have it' were to prove significant at their trial at Leeds before Mr Justice Hilbery in May. It was shown that Ostler had fired the fatal shot, but by saying 'Let him have it', which PC Shiell had insisted Appleby had said, Appleby was held to have incited Ostler and was therefore equally guilty. Their appeals were dismissed and the law took its course on Thursday 11 July 1940 when Thomas Pierrepoint, again assisted by his nephew, hanged them side by side.

The next execution of 1940 was a rather more unusual case – one that might be described as a political assassination. The victim was Sir Michael O'Dwyer who had been mistaken by the perpetrator for General Reginald O'Dwyer, who was the general who had given the order for soldiers to fire upon Sikh protestors during the Amritsar riots of 1919 in India. Sikh extremist 37-year-old Udam Singh attended a meeting of the East India Association at Caxton Hall in London on 13 March 1940 and as the meeting broke up discharged all six shots from a revolver at those on the stage, hitting four people. Sir Michael was the only one fatally injured, dying at the scene. Singh was overpowered and arrested and came to trial at the Old Bailey on 5 June 1940. His appeal was dismissed on 15 July and he was hanged by Stanley Cross and Albert Pierrepoint on 31 July at Pentonville. As normal, his body was buried within the prison, but at the request of the Indian government his remains were exhumed and returned to India for cremation and scattering on the River Ganges as a national hero in July 1974. This was to be Stanley Cross' first time as 'No 1' and he did not perform to the satisfaction of the officials. However, he seems to have got away with it on this occasion and his name remained on the list of qualified hangmen.

On 1 August 1940, the Emergency Powers (Defence) Act (2) came into force which broadened the scope of its predecessor, the Emergency Powers (Defence) Act of 1939. Among the provisions of this new Act were non-jury trials for British citizens as well as foreign nationals accused of espionage. During World War 2, six spies were hanged at Pentonville prison under the provisions of Section 1 of the Treachery Act 1940. This stated: 'If, with intent to help the enemy, any person does, or attempts or conspires with any other person to do any act which is designed or likely to give assistance to the naval, military or air operations of the enemy, to impede such operations of His Majesty's forces, or to endanger life, he shall be guilty of felony and shall on conviction suffer death.' It came into law on 23 May 1940.

The first to be charged under this Act were Sjoerd Pons, Carl Heinrich Meier, Jose Waldeburg and Charles Albert Van Den Kieboom. Waldeburg was German, while Meier and Van Den Kieboom were

Dutchmen. All had landed on the South Coast on 3 September 1940 and were caught almost immediately in possession of a short wave radio transmitter and a quantity of pound notes. They had intended to pose as refugees and feed information back to Germany on military installations and troop movements. They were tried 'in camera' at the Old Bailey on 22 November 1940 before Mr Justice Wrottesley, sitting with a conventional 12-person jury but without representatives of the press or public who were excluded from the trial in case sensitive information leaked out. Sjoerd Pons was acquitted, but the other three were convicted and sentenced to hang. Waldeburg and Meier were hanged by Thomas Pierrepoint on Tuesday 10 December 1940 and Kieboom a week later on the 17th by Stanley Cross after his appeal had been dismissed.

British-born George Johnson Armstrong had offered to spy for Germany whilst in America and was arrested and deported to Britain. He was convicted of sending a letter to Dr Herbert Scholz, the German Consul in Boston, Massachusetts, in which he had offered assistance and information to the Nazis. He was tried at the Old Bailey on 8 May 1941. His appeal was dismissed on 23 June and he was hanged at Wandsworth prison by Tom Pierrepoint and Steve Wade on 9 July 1941. The next two months saw three more executions for spying. Twenty-five-year-old Swiss-born Werner Henrich Walti and 34-year-old German Karl Druke were hanged on the morning of 6 August 1941. They had been landed by seaplane off the Scottish coast and paddled ashore in a rubber dinghy. Walti was soon apprehended at Edinburgh's Waverley rail station and Druke sometime later. They were tried together at the Old Bailey on 12 and 13 June before Mr Justice Asquith. Their appeals were dismissed by the Court of Criminal Appeal on 21 July, both men being hanged at Wandsworth by Thomas Pierrepoint, assisted by Albert Pierrepoint, Stanley Cross and Harry Kirk. Interestingly, the mandatory notice of execution that had to be put up on the prison gate the day before the hanging had the word 'murder' crossed out and 'treason' handwritten above.

14 August 1941 saw the only execution by firing squad during World War 2 on English soil. The prisoner was Josef Jakobs, a German citizen who had been convicted of spying by a court martial. Jakobs was not the luckiest of men. Parachuted into England on the morning of 1 February

1941, he broke his leg and was immediately spotted by two workers at Dovehouse Farm in Ramsey Hollow, Huntingdonshire. He had a pistol, a helmet, a map of a British airfield, a radio transmitter and a quantity of cash on his person. Jakobs' trial took place at the headquarters of the Duke of York's Regiment in Chelsea on 4/5 August 1941. He pleaded not guilty, but in view of the overwhelming evidence was convicted and sentenced to suffer death by shooting. He claimed to have come to England to help with the British war effort and petitioned the king to this effect. The only facility for carrying out Jakobs' sentence was the Tower of London and he was transferred there to await execution on 14 August. As had been the practice in World War 1, he was tied to a chair on the miniature rifle range with a target pinned over his heart. At 7.12am on 14 August, a volley of shots from the rifles of the 8-man Scots Guards firing squad ran out and Jakobs slumped forward. After the inquest his body was buried in an unmarked grave at St Mary's Roman Catholic Cemetery in Kensal Green, London.

In his autobiography, Albert Pierrepoint recalls how one of the spies that he hanged put up a serious fight in the condemned cell. This was 29-year-old Karel Richard Richter who was executed at Wandsworth on 10 December 1941. Richter, a large and powerful man, threw himself head first against the cell wall when he realised that his time had come. Then, when he had recovered somewhat, he fought with Pierrepoint, Harry Allen and the warders until Pierrepoint managed to get his hands strapped behind him and began to lead the procession out to the gallows. Richter's arms were so strong that he managed to burst the leather strap and had to be further restrained. Just as Pierrepoint had finished the preparations on the gallows and was in the act of pushing the lever, Richter jumped and loosened the noose causing it to catch under his top lip instead of remaining under his jaw. However, his neck was still broken by the force of the drop.

A serial killer who murdered four women over a six-day period stalked the streets of London in February 1942. The first victim was 40-year-old Evelyn Hamilton whose body was discovered in an air raid shelter at Montagu Place on Sunday 9 February. Evelyn had been strangled and robbed. The corpse of 35-year-old Evelyn Oatley was discovered in her flat in Wardour Street the following day. She too had been strangled and had had her throat cut and been sexually assaulted. A prostitute named Margaret Florence Lowe was next on the following day; her mutilated body was also found in her flat and she too had been strangled and seriously sexually assaulted. Doris Jouannet was the final victim, her body being discovered in her Paddington flat, also strangled and mutilated. The killer struck again on Friday 14 February, but the intended victim, Greta Hayward, was saved by a passing delivery boy as she was about to be strangled. Her attacker left behind his gas mask, which enabled identification. Another prostitute, who went by the name of Kathleen King, was attacked a few days later but managed to fight off her assailant.

The perpetrator was soon traced through the number on the gas mask. He was a 28-year-old airman named Gordon Frederick Cummins. The police had fingerprints from the crime scenes and found various items of the women's property in Cummins' possession which helped to ensure a conviction at his Old Bailey trial on 27/28 April. The prosecution proceeded only with the murder of Evelyn Oatley and it took the jury just 35 minutes to bring in a guilty verdict. He was hanged at Wandsworth by Albert Pierrepoint, assisted by Harry Kirk, on Thursday 25 June 1942 during an air raid. On the morning of the execution, he wrote to his wife asking her forgiveness and saying: 'Although I don't know, I think I must be guilty – the evidence is overwhelming.' Other than a hatred of women in general and prostitutes in particular, his motives for this killing spree seem unclear. It is thought that he may have killed two other women in late 1941 although this cannot be proven.

At 9am on Tuesday 7 July 1942, two hooded and pinioned forms plummeted through the trap doors at Wandsworth. They were Alphonse Timmerman and Jose Estella Key, aged 28 and 34 respectively, who had been convicted of unrelated acts of espionage at the Old Bailey in May 1942. Albert Pierrepoint officiated, assisted by Harry Kirk, Steve Wade and Henry Critchell. Key was Gibraltarian and thus a British subject. Duncan Scott Ford was the next spy to hang, again at Wandsworth, on 3 November 1942. Scott Ford was a 21-year-old British merchant seaman who had served in the Royal Navy before being court-martialled and discharged. Whilst in port in Lisbon, he was approached to provide detailed shipping movements for the Germans and was arrested on his return to England as the British authorities had been tipped off about his activities. He was sent to Camp 020 at Latchmere House on Ham Common in Surrey for interrogation. He was tried 'in camera' and condemned on October 16.

Just two more foreign spies would hang at Wandsworth before espionage executions were moved to Pentonville. They were 46-year-old Johannes Dronkers on 31 December 1942 and 40-year-old Franciscus Winter on 26 January 1943. Three men were executed for espionage at Pentonville prison. The first was 58-year-old Oswald John Job on 16 March 1944, followed by 28-year-old Pierre Neukermans on 23 June, and finally 27-year-old Joseph Van Hove on 12 July.

Between March 1943 and June 1945, 16 US servicemen serving in the European Theatre of Operations were hanged and two shot at Shepton Mallet prison in Somerset under US jurisdiction for murder, rape or both crimes. Hanging was the preferred method by the US Military as it was considered a more ignominious death for a soldier than shooting. Tom Pierrepoint was contracted to carry out the hangings and his nephew Albert assisted him. Those executed were condemned under the provisions of the Visiting Forces Act of 1942 that allowed American Military justice to be enacted on British soil. To enable the hangings to take place, a new brick-built extension was added to one of the prison's wings. The two-storey red brick structure looks totally out of place against the weathered grey stone walls of the original 17th century building. A new British-style gallows was installed on the first floor of the building and two cells within the main building were converted into a condemned cell.

Of these 18 men, nine were convicted of murder, six of rape and three of both offences. The rape executions would be the first on British soil since 30 March 1836 when Richard Smith had been hanged at Nottingham. Rape still carried the death penalty in US Military law and was still punishable by death in most of the southern states of America. The last execution of a rapist in the USA did not take place until May 1964 when Ronald Wolfe was gassed in Missouri. Execution by shooting was not permitted for murder in Britain but was under US Military law.

The normal US Army method of hanging was not permitted in England; this was confirmed by Albert Pierrepoint in his autobiography. Most of the typical American execution customs were allowed, however.

He commented adversely upon the delay to the execution process caused by the reading of the death warrant on the gallows and allowing the condemned man to make a final statement. Neither of these things occurred in British executions but was standard practice in America. Typically there were up to 20 witnesses and officials in the execution chamber. After execution, the bodies were buried in Brookwood Cemetery in Surrey. Many were later reburied in France.

Hangings were normally carried out at 1 o'clock in the morning of the specified day. Shooting executions were carried out around 8am. The British method of hanging was used. There was no standard drop of four to six feet and no hangman's coiled noose, but an accurately calculated drop using a British noose. US Army regulations laid down that a condemned prisoner at execution 'will be dressed in regulation uniform from which all decorations, insignia, or other evidence of membership therein have been removed. Likewise, no such evidences will appear on any clothing used in burial.' In all cases the condemned men had the services of the prison chaplain in the days leading up to their execution. They were housed in a condemned cell adjacent to the execution chamber for the last three or four days of their lives.

Records of these hangings indicate that the time between releasing the trap doors and confirmation of death varied considerably. David Cobb's execution took only 3½ minutes until he was officially pronounced dead by three US medical officers. He was left hanging for one hour, as was the norm in England. It took 22 minutes before George Smith could be certified dead. The average time for 15 of the 16 hangings was 14.8 minutes. (The data is not available for one hanging.) It is presumed that the time was from the moment of the drop until no further heartbeat could be detected by the attending medical officer. This would tally with the time it took for the heartbeat to stop in civilian hangings at the time.

Pte David Cobb, a 21-year-old GI, was the first to be hanged on 12 March 1943. Cobb was stationed at Desborough Camp in Northamptonshire and had been on guard duty for some time during Sunday 27 December when he was reprimanded by 2nd Lieutenant Robert Cobner. He protested and Cobner ordered the sergeant of the guard to arrest him. Cobb threatened the man, who backed off, so Cobner unwisely decided to attempt the arrest himself. Cobb fired his rifle at Cobner, fatally injuring him. He was tried by US court martial at Cambridge on 6 January 1943, the trial occupying less than a day. His death sentence was reviewed and in due course confirmed by the authorities.

Pte Harold Smith had gone AWOL (absent without leave) in London in January 1943, and with another young soldier was staying in a hotel enjoying the town until their financial resources dried up. He then returned to Chisledon Camp near Swindon to find his own unit had been posted elsewhere. He found a loaded pistol and then got into an altercation with Pte Harry Jenkins whom he shot dead. He also fired at another soldier before escaping back to London, where he was arrested by a British policeman. He was handed over to American authorities and was court-martialled at Bristol on 12 March. He made a full statement admitting his guilt and was duly hanged on 25 June 1943.

Lee A. Davis was another young soldier who was convicted of rape and murder. The crimes took place near Marlborough in Wiltshire, as two young women walked back from the cinema. Davis asked the girls what they were doing and one, Muriel Fawden, said she was returning to the hospital where she worked as a nurse. They tried to get away from Davis who shouted after them: 'Stand still or I'll shoot.' He then instructed the terrified girls to go into some bushes beside the footpath. Muriel's companion, Cynthia Lay, decided to make a run for it and Davis shot her dead. He then forced Muriel into the bushes and raped her but surprisingly did not kill her. She was able to give a full statement to the police and, as a result, all rifles of the American soldiers stationed nearby were examined. Davis' was found to have been fired and forensic tests matched it to the shell cases found near Cynthia. Davis admitted he had been at the scene of the crime but said he had only meant to fire over the heads of the girls. He was court-martialled at Marlborough on 6 October for the murder and rape, being hanged on 14 December.

John Waters, aged 39, had been seeing a local woman, 35-year-old Doris Staples, in Henley-on-Thames where he was stationed. Their relationship was deteriorating and on 14 July 1943 he went to the draper's shop where she worked and shot her five times. The police arrived while Waters was still on the premises and a short siege began, which ended when the police threw a tear gas canister into the shop and broke down the door. Seeing that he was cornered, Waters shot himself, but did not make a very good job of it. In due course he came to trial at Watford, Hertfordshire, on 29 November 1943 and was convicted and sentenced to death for Doris' killing. He was hanged on 10 February 1944.

J. C. Leatherberry was executed for the murder of Colchester taxi driver Henry Hailstone in Essex on the evening of 5 December 1943. Hailstone's taxi was found abandoned and parked facing the wrong way which the police thought unusual and made them wonder if it had been parked by a foreigner who drove on the other side of the road. In the car was a bloodstained jacket with Hailstone's driving licence in the pocket. When the area round the car was searched a bloodstained overcoat was found with a name tag inside of Captain Walker. When Walker was interviewed he told police that the coat had been stolen along with his Rolex watch by a soldier on the day of the murder. However, a gas mask had been left during the robbery and this bore the identifier of J. Hill. Hill was traced and said he had lent the gas mask to fellow soldier George Fowler. Fowler was arrested and when his belongings were searched a pawn ticket was found for the missing Rolex. Fowler also admitted that he and Leatherberry had been involved in the murder. Their motive appeared to be to steal the car. Fowler maintained that it was Leatherberry who had strangled the driver. Both were convicted at their court martial at Ipswich on 19 January 1944 and both received the death sentence. However, Fowler's was commuted as the court accepted that Leatherberry was the principal and because he had given evidence. Fowler was returned to military prison in the USA to serve his life sentence while Leatherberry was sent to Shepton Mallet to be hanged by Tom Pierrepoint on 16 March 1944.

Pte Wiley Harris was stationed at Belfast in Northern Ireland. He had gone out with his friend Pte Robert Fils to a bar for the evening where they met a pimp called Harry Coogan who offered them the services of a young woman. Harris accepted, and he and the girl went to a nearby air raid shelter to have sex, Coogan keeping watch outside as this sort of activity was illegal. As they were getting started Coogan shouted to them that the police were approaching. Harris and the girl got dressed and emerged from the shelter to find that there were no police. Harris then demanded his money back and a struggle ensued between Harris and Coogan in which Coogan punched Harris. This caused the fight to escalate to the point where Coogan was stabbed 17 times. The court martial was not prepared to accept self defence in view of the number of stab wounds, so Harris was convicted and hanged on 26 May 1944.

Alex Miranda, aged 20, became the first American serviceman to suffer death by shooting at Shepton Mallet. He had been convicted of violation of the 92nd Article of War (murder) and was executed by an 8-man firing squad in the prison grounds on Tuesday 30 May 1944 for the murder of his sergeant, Thomas Evison, at Broomhill Camp in Devon. Miranda had gone out drinking and had been arrested by the civilian police and taken back to the camp. Here he became aggressive, the object of his aggression being Sgt Evison who was reportedly asleep at the time. Getting no response from the sleeping man, he shot him dead. The location of Miranda's court martial is unknown as is the reason why he was sentenced to be shot rather than hanged, bearing in mind that both David Cobb and Harold Smith had also killed other US soldiers.

Eliga Brinson and Willie Smith were hanged by Albert Pierrepoint on 11 August 1944 for the rape of Dorothy Holmes after a dance at Bishop's Cleeve in Gloucestershire. Dorothy left the dance with her boyfriend and both were ambushed and assaulted by Brinson and Smith. After the boyfriend ran to get help, they both raped Dorothy. They were caught through the bootprints they left in the field where the rape took place. They came to trial at Cheltenham on 28 April 1944, their case taking two days to complete.

Madison Thomas was another soldier convicted of rape. His victim was Beatrice Reynolds, who was returning home after helping out at the British Legion hall at Gunnislake in Cornwall on the evening of 26 July 1944. Thomas accosted her on her way home and she tried to get rid of him by talking to her friend Jean Blight, but without success. He hit her and pulled her into a field where he raped her and robbed her of her watch. Thomas had also spoken to Jean Blight and she was able to positively identify him the next day when the entire camp at Whitchurch Down near Tavistock was put on parade. Blood on Thomas' trousers was shown to be of the same group as Beatrice's. He was court-martialled at Plymouth on 21 August and hanged by Albert Pierrepoint on 12 October 1944.

Benjamin Pyegate was the second and last US soldier to face a firing squad at Shepton Mallet. The crime took place at Tidworth Barracks in Wiltshire on 15 July 1944. Pyegate became involved in an argument with three fellow soldiers in his hut and kicked James Alexander in the groin prior to stabbing him to death. On 28 November 1944 he was duly executed by shooting, or musketry as the Americans rather quaintly called it. He was led out and tied to a post. A black hood was placed over his head and a 4"-diameter white target placed over his heart. Eight soldiers stood 15 yards away with their rifles, one of which contained a blank round. The officer in charge of the execution gave the regulation commands as detailed in the US Army Manual: 'At the command READY, the execution party (firing squad) will take that position and unlock rifles. At the command AIM, the execution party will take that position with rifles aimed at target on the prisoner's body. At the command FIRE, the execution party will fire simultaneously.' The medical officer then examined the prisoner and, if necessary, could direct that a 'coup de grâce' be administered. The sergeant of the execution party was responsible for administering this with 'a hand weapon, holding the muzzle just above the ear and one foot from the head'. It is not known whether it was required in Pyegate's case.

Ernest Clarke and Augustine Guerra were jointly convicted of the rape and murder of 15-year-old Elizabeth Green at Ashford in Kent on 22 August 1944. They had been drinking in a pub in Ashford and left at closing time to walk back to their barracks. On the way they encountered Elizabeth whom they raped and strangled. Hair and fibre samples taken from the scene matched those found on the prisoners. Faced with this evidence they confessed to the rape, but claimed that they had not intended to kill Elizabeth. They were tried on 22 September 1944 at Ashford and hanged side by side on 8 January 1945.

Robert Pearson and Parson Jones were convicted by court martial of the rape of Joyce Brown at Chard in Somerset on 3 December 1944. Joyce was heavily pregnant at the time of her rape, which must have been obvious to her assailants. However, she was dragged into an orchard where both men raped her. After the crime was reported, the clothes of all the men on the base were searched and Pearson's and Jones' were found to be muddy. They both admitted to having sex with Joyce but claimed that she consented. Her pregnancy, bruising and statement to the police told a different story. They were tried at Chard on 16 December 1944 and hanged side by side on 17 March 1945.

William Harrison sexually assaulted and strangled 7-year-old Patricia Wylie in Killycolpy, County Tyrone, Northern Ireland. Patricia was the daughter of a couple who had shown friendship to him. On the pretext of buying them a thank you present, he took Patricia shopping with him on the afternoon of 26 September 1944. His trial took place on 18 November 1944 and he was hanged on 7 April 1945.

George Smith had gone hunting on private property (Honingham Hall in Norfolk) with fellow soldier Leonard Wojtacha, both armed with service carbines. They were challenged by the owner, Sir Eric Teichman, and in the course of this confrontation Smith shot Sir Eric once through the head, killing him. The court martial took place at Attlebridge in Norfolk, commencing on 8 January 1945, and lasted five days due to the repeated hospitalisation of Smith. He had made a confession when he was arrested but claimed it had been made under duress and withdrew it at his trial. He was convicted and hanged on 8 May 1945 (VE Day) despite requests for clemency, including one from Lady Teichman.

Aniceto Martinez, a young Mexican-American soldier, was working as a guard at a prisoner-of-war camp near Rugeley in Staffordshire. On the night of 6 August 1945, he broke into the house of 75-year-old Agnes Cope in Rugeley where he raped her. She survived to tell the police of her ordeal and the prisoner-of-war camp became the focus of their enquiries. Only Martinez had been out of the camp the previous night and when questioned he confessed to the rape. Fibre samples taken from his clothing and those in Agnes' house matched, adding forensic evidence to the confession. Martinez was tried at Lichfield, Staffordshire, on 21 February 1945 and became the last person to be hanged for rape in the UK when he went to the gallows on 15 June of that year.

Thomas Pierrepoint and his nephew Albert hanged most of these men, Tom doing the first three, with Albert acting as assistant. Albert did only three as 'No 1'. Tom claimed 13 in total. There would typically have been two assistants at each of the three double hangings. Herbert Morris assisted at three, Alexander Riley assisted at three and Steve Wade at the rest.

All of these men were tried by courts martial under specific procedures laid down in the 1928 American forces Manual for Courts Martial. The court was normally composed of legally trained officers and usually the prisoner was defended and prosecuted by officers at the rank of captain or above. After a guilty verdict where a death sentence was passed it had to be confirmed and reviewed by a Board of Review. If confirmed it was normally carried out in about three months. (Under British law three clear Sundays had to elapse between sentence and execution at this time.) Amongst all these spies and US Service personnel, normal civilian executions continued during the war. In England and Wales there were 12 in 1940, 11 in 1941 and 15 in 1942. There were 15 again in 1943, of which seven were for the murders of wives or girlfriends.

One of the more unusual cases, and the first execution of 1943, was that of 49-year-old Harry Dobkin who had murdered his wife Rachel in April 1941. A body discovered by workmen demolishing a burnt-out church in Kennington was found to be that of a female buried there for 12-18 months. The famous pathologist Dr Keith Simpson was able to determine that the woman had been strangled and that she was around 40-50 years old, just over 5 feet tall and had brown hair. A search of missing persons threw up the name of Rachel Dobkin and a photograph provided by her sister enabled the features to be superimposed over a photo of the skull. Her dental records matched the fillings found in the dead woman's teeth.

Rachel had left Harry Dobkin after just three days of marriage, but was pregnant by him and obtained a maintenance order against him when the child was born. It is thought that this was the motive for murdering her. Dobkin was charged with and convicted of the killing at the Old Bailey in November 1942 and hanged at Wandsworth on 27 January 1943 by Albert Pierrepoint, assisted by Herbert Morris. Dobkin stood 5' 4½" high, weighed 204 lbs and was described as 'strong and muscular' according to the LPC4 form. He was given a drop of 5' 9" which resulted in fracture dislocation of the second and third cervical vertebrae.

It is notable that of the 15 civilian hangings in 1943, 10 took place in London. Pentonville had three and Wandsworth had seven; the remainder taking place in Birmingham, Exeter, Leeds and Liverpool. Gordon Horace Trenoweth, aged 33, had been convicted of the murder of 61-year-old Albert James Bateman, whom he had battered to death at Falmouth in Cornwall on Christmas Eve 1942. Bateman was a tobacconist who had a shop at Commercial Chambers in the town. He is thought to have been killed around 6pm, his murder being discovered by his wife who went to the shop after he failed to come home for dinner. The killer had left a revolver on the counter.

Trenoweth was a married man with five children and a criminal record. When he was arrested he was found to have two packets of cigarettes on him. His clothes had traces of gun oil on them and fibres from the crime scene. He was tried before Mr Justice Tucker at Exeter and defended by Mr J. Scott Henderson, the trial lasting from 11 to 16 February. Both his father and sister gave alibi evidence for him, but the jury did not accept this. However, they did recommend him to mercy. Obviously the judge and Home Office did not concur in this as he was hanged at Exeter by Thomas Pierrepoint assisted by Herbert Morris on Tuesday 6 April 1943, the last hanging at Exeter.

1944 saw nine civilian hangings including a double execution at Leicester at 8 o'clock on the morning of 8 August – the last executions of the year. The prisoners were William Alfred Cowle, aged 31, and William Frederick Meffen, aged 52. Cowle had stabbed his ex-girlfriend Nora Payne to death, and Meffen had cut his stepdaughter's throat. The executions were carried out by Tom Pierrepoint, assisted by his nephew Albert, Harry Kirk and Alexander Riley, two assistants being the norm where there were two prisoners.

One American soldier who was not hanged at Shepton Mallet was 22-year-old Karl Hulten who, with his 18-year-old girlfriend Elizabeth Marina Jones, was convicted of the murder of George Edward Heath, a 34-year-old taxi driver at Chiswick in west London on 7 October 1944. Hulten had planned to rob Mr Heath and when they reached the requested destination in Heath's taxi, Hulten shot him and then deposited his body in a ditch, making off with the taxi and its owner's belongings. The vehicle was spotted and Hulten arrested. He incriminated Elizabeth Jones and she too was arrested. Both were charged with the murder under the doctrine of common purpose. As a gesture of goodwill the US authorities permitted their citizen to be tried under British law. The pair were duly convicted at the Old Bailey on 16 January 1945 and both condemned. Jones was taken back to Holloway but was subsequently reprieved due to her age whilst Hulten paid for his crime at Pentonville on Thursday 8 March in the company of Albert Pierrepoint and Henry

Critchell. The immature Jones seemed to fancy herself in the role of gangster's moll and was lucky to escape the noose. She served nine years in prison for her part in the crime.

A unique event in modern Britain occurred on Saturday 6 October 1945 when five young men went to the gallows, one at a time, at London's Pentonville prison. Their names were Joachim Palme-Goltz, aged 20; Kurt Zuchlsdorff, also 20; Heintz Brueling, aged 22; Erich Koenig, aged 20; and Josep Mertins, aged 21. All five were German prisoners of war and had been convicted of the murder of fellow prisoner of war, Sergeant Major Wolfgang Rosterg at Comrie prisoner-of-war camp in Perthshire. They suspected that Rosterg had given away their plans to escape from their previous camp at Devizes in Wiltshire to the British authorities and decided to court-martial and execute him. This they did by beating him and then hanging him. Eight men were arrested for the crime of whom two were found not guilty, one sentenced to life in prison and five to hang by a British court martial at Kensington between 2 and 12 July. Albert Pierrepoint was assisted by Steve Wade and Harry Allen for this task, which most unusually was carried out on a Saturday.

The last few days of 1945 and the first few days of 1946 were a busy period for Britain's hangmen with seven executions in less than three weeks. John Amery, aged 33, was hanged for treason at Wandsworth on 19 December by Albert Pierrepoint, assisted by Henry Critchell. Amery, the son of a cabinet minister, pleaded guilty to treason at his eight-minute trial at the Old Bailey on 28 November 1945. He had broadcast German propaganda and had tried to organise British prisoners of war in Germany to fight for the Nazis. It is said that Amery spoke the following words to Albert Pierrepoint as he went to pinion him: 'I have always wanted to meet you, Mr Pierrepoint, but not under these circumstances.'

Two men convicted at the Essex Assizes in November went to the gallows at Pentonville on 21 December. The first, at 8am, was 40-year-old John Riley Young who had been convicted of the brutal robbery murders of Frederick and Cissie Lucas at their home at Leigh-on-Sea in Essex on 6 June 1945. He confessed to the murders when he was arrested. Albert Pierrepoint and Steve Wade carried out Young's execution and then after taking down and removing the body, reset the trap doors and the rope for the hanging of James McNicol at 9.30am in which Herbert Morris assisted.

Thirty-year-old James McNicol had shot Sgt Donald Kirkaldie in the sergeant's hut at Thorpe Bay military base near Southend in Essex on the night of 16 August 1945. Kirkaldie was a good friend of McNicol and was not the intended victim, if indeed there really was one. McNicol had got very drunk during the VJ celebrations on the camp and after an altercation with another sergeant had stolen a rifle and fired into the shared hut from outside, sadly killing his friend. He was tried as a civilian at Chelmsford on 13 November and his appeal was heard on 5 December. McNicol was hanged on 21 December 1945. There is good reason to believe that he should not have been executed for a crime that was probably manslaughter, due to the effects on his judgement of the army-prescribed malaria medication that he was taking, combined with the large quantity of beer he had consumed. It is not obvious from studying the case papers how the mens rea or criminal intent was proven at his trial. For a killing to be murder there has to be proof of intent.

On 29 December, the last execution of 1945 took place when 24-year-old Robert Blaine was hanged at Wandsworth by Albert Pierrepoint and Harry Kirk. Blaine had killed John Ritchie, a captain in the Canadian army, in Soho on the night of 14 September.

The year 1946 started with the executions of two traitors. William Joyce, better known as Lord Haw-Haw, was hanged at Wandsworth on Thursday 3 January and Theodore Schurch at Pentonville the following day. Joyce – of Irish birth but a British passport holder – was convicted of high treason for his propaganda broadcasts from Germany to Britain during the war. He was tried at the Old Bailey on 17-19 September and appealed his conviction at the end of October. The courts held that as he was a British passport holder he owed allegiance to the King and was therefore guilty. Albert Pierrepoint and Alex Riley carried out the 39-year-old's execution, giving him a drop of 7' 4".

Theodore Schurch, aged 27, became the last man to die for treason in Britain. He was born in Britain of Swiss parents and had been active in the British Union of Fascists before the war. He joined the army and was captured by the Italians in North Africa whereupon he offered his services to them, reporting back information gleaned from fellow British prisoners of war. He was hanged at Pentonville by Albert Pierrepoint and Alex Riley on Friday 4 January 1946. Finally William Batty was hanged at 8am on 8 January at Armley prison in Leeds by Tom Pierrepoint and Harry Allen for the shooting murder of Samuel Grey, whose wife he wanted as a lover.

Although strictly outside the scope of this book, it is worth noting that a total of 190 men and 10 women were hanged for war crimes at Hameln (Hamlin) prison near Hanover in Germany under British jurisdiction. The executions were carried out by Albert Pierrepoint who was flown in especially for each set of hangings between 13 December 1945 and 6 December 1949. Generally he was assisted by Regimental Sergeant Major O'Neil who was a member of the Control Commission there. The hangings took place in a purpose-built execution room at the end of one of the prison's wings, the gallows having been specially constructed by the Royal Engineers to allow the execution of prisoners in pairs. As many as 15 executions could be carried out on a single day as happened on 26 February 1948.

20

The post-war period

After the turbulent times of World War 2 life soon settled back to normality in the late 1940s. There were 22 executions in Britain during 1946, of which eight were for the murders of wives and girlfriends. Three executions took place in Scotland, all at Glasgow's Barlinnie prison. The following year the total reduced to 12 in England and Wales, and there were none in Scotland.

Twenty-eight-year-old Neville George Clevelly Heath murdered two women – his girlfriend Margery Gardner, aged 32, and 21-year-old Doreen Marshall – both in the summer of 1946. Heath had previous convictions and had been court-martialled three times while serving in the forces during the war. Margery Gardner enjoyed masochistic sex and Heath was a sadist, so there was an obvious bond. They acted out their fantasies in the Pembridge Court Hotel in London's Notting Hill Gate where Heath tied Margery up and whipped her with a diamond weave pattern leather whip. He had also bitten her breasts and inserted an object into her vagina causing heavy bleeding, all before suffocating her, probably to stifle her screams on the evening of Friday 21 June. Her body was discovered in Room 4 of the hotel by staff the following morning. Heath had left the hotel and gone to stay with his fiancée, Yvonne Symonds, at Worthing in Sussex. Heath told Yvonne about the murder in the hotel and said that Margery had gone there with a man named Jack and that he had let them use his room. He also said that he had seen the body, although he did not tell her that he had been in any way involved in the killing. After leaving her, he wrote a letter to Scotland Yard telling them the same story.

Passing himself off as Group Captain Rupert Brooke, he met his second victim, Doreen Marshall, at a dance in Bournemouth at the beginning of July 1946. He invited her to dinner at his hotel and later murdered her. Again, her breasts were savagely bitten and a sharp object had been thrust into her vagina. He hid her naked body in bushes and covered it over with her clothes. The hotel manager asked him to contact the police who were looking for Yvonne (as a missing person) and he went voluntarily to Bournemouth police station for an interview, where the sharp-eyed detective noticed his strong resemblance to the photograph of Neville Heath wanted in connection with Margery Gardner's murder. He was duly arrested and charged with her murder and later with Yvonne Symonds' murder as well. He was tried at the Old Bailey before Mr Justice Morris on 24 September 1946 and put forward a defence of insanity which was rejected. Three weeks later on Wednesday 16 Octobers he kept his 9am appointment with Albert Pierrepoint. His last request was for a large whisky.

At this point it might be worth examining the procedure for a typical execution of the period. By this time the remaining prisons that carried out hangings had purpose-built execution suites with the gallows between 10 and 20 paces from the condemned cell.

Executions were normally carried out at 9am in London and 8am in the rest of the country. These times could be varied where for instance two men were to be hanged, one at 8 o'clock and one at 9.30, as happened in the case of John Riley Young and James McNicol mentioned previously. The procedure was governed by a standard set of rules laid down by the Home Office. The same officials were required by law to be present: the governor of the prison, the sheriff or under sheriff of the county, the prison doctor, the chaplain or a priest of the prisoner's religion, two or more warders plus, of course, the hangman and his assistant. Not all prisons had a permanent gallows beam so, where required, this would be sent by train from Pentonville and erected in the execution room. An execution box containing two ropes, one new and one used, a white hood, pinioning straps, block and tackle, etc was also sent.

The prisoner was weighed and their height measured the day before the execution, the hangman surreptitiously viewing the person to enable him to calculate from their weight and physical appearance the correct drop, using the official table of drops as a starting point. The length of the drop was carefully set and the gallows tested whilst the prisoner was out of their cell on the evening before the execution, using a bag of sand of approximately the same weight as them, which would be left on the rope overnight to remove any stretch. Around 7am, the executioners would reset the trap doors and make a final adjustment to the length of the drop to allow for the amount the rope had stretched. The rope was coiled up and secured with a piece of pack thread so that the noose dangled at chest level. Outside the prison a notice of the execution had been put up. On the morning of execution the prisoner would be attended by the chaplain and permitted to wear his or her own clothes. If the condemned person appeared to need it, the prison doctor could give them a glass of brandy or whisky to help them cope, but they were not given tranquillisers.

Just before the appointed hour the execution team formed up outside the condemned cell and, on the signal from the governor, the hangman entered and strapped the prisoner's hands behind his back with a leather strap. The hangman went straight to the gallows, turning to face the condemned prisoner who followed, supported by a warder on each side. The assistant and the chaplain brought up the rear. All typically went through a second door in the condemned cell which was normally hidden by a wardrobe and either straight into the execution room or across an adjoining lobby. The other officials entered the execution room via another door and lined up along the back wall.

The prisoner was led onto the trap doors which had the letter 'T' chalked on them to position their feet exactly over the middle of the trap. In case they fainted at the last moment, they were supported by the two warders standing on boards across the trap and holding onto ropes attached to the beam with their free hands. The hangman pulled the white cotton hood over the prisoner's head and positioned the noose round the neck whilst the assistant strapped their ankles. As soon as all was ready, the hangman removed the safety pin from the base of the operating lever and pushed it to release the trap doors. The prisoner dropped through the trap and would be left hanging motionless in the cell below, unconscious, with their neck broken. The whole process would have occupied about the same length of time as it has taken you to read this paragraph – somewhere between 15 and 20 seconds.

Everything was done to make the execution as speedy and humane as possible, so as to spare both the prisoner and the staff who had to witness it any unnecessary distress. Once the signal had been given by the governor to enter the condemned cell, the hangman was in total charge of the proceedings and did not have to wait for a further signal from the governor before the releasing the trap. Thus the prisoner did not to have to spend a moment longer than was necessary, hooded and noosed. The prison doctor listened to the chest of the suspended prisoner with a stethoscope and would expect to hear an abnormal heart rhythm and progressively weakening heartbeat for a few minutes. When he was satisfied that they were dying, the execution cell was locked up for an hour before the executioners returned to undress and take down the body using the block and tackle and prepare it for an inquest later in the morning. In some cases the body was washed before it was readied for the inquest. Up to 1955, the executioners had to measure how much the neck had been stretched by the hanging. It was often 1-2" (25-50 mm) and was recorded in the Execution Register. The body would show marks of suspension, elongation of the neck and occasionally traces of urine, faeces and semen.

Spectators and/or protestors usually gathered outside the prison on the morning of a hanging to see the notice of execution posted on the main gate once death had been certified. At the three hanging prisons in London – Holloway, Pentonville and Wandsworth – an autopsy was carried out in an adjoining area under the gallows after the body was taken down. After the inquest, the body was buried within the walls of the prison, usually at lunchtime on the day of execution.

A murder that made the headlines in the spring of 1947 was that of 31-year-old Alec de Antiquis. He was a father of six and owned a motorbike repair business in London. It was one of those situations of being in the wrong place at the wrong time. He happened to be in the vicinity of a jeweller's shop in Charlotte Street on the afternoon of 29 April. Three young men had decided to rob the shop and had struck the manager when he closed the safe and shot at another employee before fleeing empty-handed, only to find their getaway car blocked in by a truck. Alec de Antiquis tried to stop the men by riding his motorbike into their path and was shot through the head. His crumpled body lying on the pavement was photographed by Geoffrey Harrison, a press agency photographer. Coincidentally, Albert Pierrepoint happened to be passing Charlotte Street at the time of the incident on his way to an appointment.

The three men arrested for the crimes were 21-year-old Charles Jenkins, 23-year-old Christopher Geraghty and 17-year-old Terrence

Rolt. All three were convicted at the Old Bailey on 28 July after a week-long trial. The older two got the death sentence; Rolt was sentenced to be detained at His Majesty's Pleasure as he was under 18, being released in 1956. It could be shown that it had been Geraghty who had killed Mr de Antiquis, but once again the doctrine of common purpose meant that all were equally guilty as they had taken part in the robbery, each armed with a gun. The appeals were dismissed and Jenkins and Geraghty were hanged at 9 o'clock on the morning of Friday 19 September at Pentonville by Albert Pierrepoint, assisted by Harry Allen and Henry Critchell. This execution led to the break-up of their gang.

There was a surge in gun crime, particularly in London, in the immediate post-war period when guns were very easy to obtain and the American gang culture was proving popular amongst some young people of the time. It is notable how history repeats itself when one compares the situation in the late 40s to that of London now.

In 1948, the words of the death sentence were modified by the judiciary. Up to this point the judge would pass the following sentence: '(full name of prisoner) you will be taken hence to the prison in which you were last confined and from there to a place of execution where you will be hanged by the neck until you are dead and thereafter your body buried within the precincts of the prison, and may the Lord have mercy upon your soul.' Thereafter the sentence was modified by the substitution of the words 'suffer death by hanging' for 'be hanged by the neck until dead', and this sentence continued to be used for those convicted of capital murder up to 1956.

In April 1948, the House of Commons voted in favour of a Bill introduced by Sidney Silverman to suspend the death penalty for five years. The Labour Home Secretary, James Chuter-Ede, announced that he would reprieve all murderers until the future of the Bill was resolved. This resulted in 26 reprieves and no executions between March and October 1948, giving a total for the year of just eight for England and Wales, and one in Scotland. The House of Lords rejected the Bill, so in November 1948, the Home Secretary promised to set up a Royal Commission to examine the subject.

Thus, on 20 January 1949, prime minister Clement Atlee announced to Parliament: 'The King has been pleased to approve the setting up of a

Royal Commission on Capital Punishment with the following terms of reference: To consider and report whether liability under the criminal law in Great Britain to suffer capital punishment for murder should be limited or modified, and if so, to what extent and by what means, for how long and under what conditions persons who would otherwise have been liable to suffer capital punishment should be detained, and what changes in the existing law and the prison system would be required; and to inquire into and take account of the position in those countries whose experience and practice may throw light on these questions. I am glad to be able to announce that Sir Ernest Gowers (a senior civil servant) will act as chairman of the Royal Commission.' It should be noted the Commission was not asked to decide whether the death penalty should be abolished, but rather whether it should be limited or modified. This was not what many on the Labour benches wanted, but it was felt that abolition was a matter for Parliament, not a Royal Commission. The Commission, comprising ten men and two women, had 63 meetings over the next four years and took evidence from a wide range of people with expertise in the field, including prison governors, chaplains, staff and Albert Pierrepoint.

From 1900 to the end of 1948, 1178 death sentences had been handed down in England and Wales, including 123 passed on women. Of these 617 had been carried out, including 14 on females. The overall reprieve rate was thus 47.6%, with 88.6% for women. Part of the Commission's brief was to look at whether so many death sentences should be passed when there was a serious probability of a reprieve. It noted that out of 129 people who had been reprieved and served a 'life sentence', only one had been convicted of another murder. When one examines the crimes for which people were hanged at this time, with the large preponderance of domestic murders as highlighted in previous chapters, this does seem reasonable. The Commission examined the various methods of execution as an alternative to hanging, including shooting, electrocution, gassing and lethal injection. The latter was opposed by the British Medical Association on the grounds that its members would be involved in carrying out executions, rather than in just certifying death, and was considered as impractical and not necessarily humane by the Commission. Shooting was rejected it on the grounds that 'it does not possess even the first requisite of an efficient method, the certainty of causing immediate death'. This is interesting in the light of the then recent execution of Josef Jakobs in 1941.

Those giving evidence to the Commission frequently emphasised their belief that execution should be rapid, clean and dignified. It concluded that hanging as described and demonstrated by Albert Pierrepoint to the Commission members on a visit to Pentonville in November 1950 came closest to this model. They determined that British-style hanging was still the best available method of execution, but thought that it had no particular unique effect as a deterrent to murder. Their 506-page report was published in September 1953 and led to some slight modifications to various aspects of the system. Some of these concerned improvements to the condemned cell and the prisoner's regime in it. One major recommendation was the compulsory psychiatric examination and the taking of an electro-encephalograph of the brain of all persons convicted of murder. The report also recommended improvements to the actual execution process. Prisoners were to be removed from the rope once certified dead and no longer left hanging for an hour. The morbid and irrelevant practice of measuring how much their neck had stretched was also ended.

The Commission recommended retention of capital punishment unless there was overwhelming public support for abolition, which there was not. Most of the Commission's other recommendations were not taken up by what was then the Conservative government under Winston Churchill, e.g. the abolition of capital punishment for a trial period of five years and the removal of the doctrine of constructive malice (which is that if a person is killed during the commission of another felony such as rape or robbery then the killing is automatically deemed to be murder). Again there was a recommendation that the minimum age for execution be raised from 18 to 21 and that juries might be given the power to recommend life sentences instead of death sentences. In reality there was little significant change as a result of the Commission's painstaking and highly detailed analysis of the system of capital punishment in Britain.

Fifteen men and one woman were to go to the gallows in 1949. The most notable of these was John George Haigh, the infamous 'acid bath' murderer. He was hanged at Wandsworth by Albert Pierrepoint, assisted by Harry Kirk, on Wednesday 10 August 1949. Pierrepoint obviously considered Haigh as a special case and used his special calf leather wrist strap to pinion him before giving him a drop of 7' 4".

Thirty-nine-year-old Haigh possessed a great deal of natural charm and passed himself off as an engineer. He battered or shot three men and three women to death between 1944 and 1949, all for financial gain, disposing of the bodies by dissolving them in sulphuric acid which quite reduced them to a liquid sludge that he could pour down the drain. His victims were William Donald McSwann and, later, his parents William and Amy McSwann. They were followed by Dr Archibald Henderson and his wife Rosalie, and finally by Mrs Olive Durand-Deacon for whose murder he was to hang. Mrs Durand-Deacon lived, like Haigh, at the Onslow Court Hotel in South Kensington, and he interested her in a factory he claimed to own in Leopold Road, Crawley, Sussex, which he told her was going to make cosmetics. He persuaded her to go with him to look at the factory, which was little more than a store room. When they got there, he shot her in the neck. He had previously equipped the building with a carboy of acid, a 40-gallon drum and rubber gloves and apron. He took Mrs Durand-Deacon's jewellery and other valuables, including her fur coat, which he had cleaned to remove the bloodstains prior to sale and then put her body into the acid to dissolve.

One of the other residents at the Onslow Court, who was a friend of Mrs Durand-Deacon, was greatly concerned by her disappearance and asked Haigh to go with her to Chelsea police station to report her missing. The police became suspicious of Haigh and obtained a search warrant for his factory where they were to discover a revolver and the acid drum together with human remains including bone fragments, Mrs Durand-Deacon's false teeth and her gallstone. When they arrested Haigh and put this evidence to him, he told them: 'Mrs Durand-Deacon no longer exists. I have destroyed her with acid. You can't prove a murder without a body.' He went on to admit to eight other killings, of which only five could be substantiated. He was tried at Lewes Assizes before Mr Justice Humphreys in July 1949 and put forward a defence of insanity, claiming that he was also a vampire and had drunk a glass of the blood of each of his victims. This made sensational headlines in the newspapers. However, the jury were less impressed and took just 17 minutes to find him guilty.

It is often said that the bodies of the hanged were buried in unmarked graves. In one sense this is true – they certainly did not have a headstone – but the location of each was known as noted earlier. On 17 May 1950, the Prison Commission issued revised guidance on burials as detailed in Standing Order SO 184. The information contained in the Register of Graves was to be increased to include the following:

Number of grave space (as authorised plan)
Name
Date of interment
Depth of interment
Whether first, second or third interment in grave
Remarks (if any).

This was a response to the fact that a number of prisons were running out of room to bury the bodies of executed criminals, having done so for 116 years. As you can see, it was not unusual to have as many as three coffins on top of each other.

The record for the fastest-ever hanging was made on 8 May 1951 when Albert Pierrepoint, assisted by Syd Dernley, hanged 29-year-old James Inglis at Manchester's Strangeways prison. The whole procedure took just seven seconds from the time Pierrepoint entered Inglis' cell to the actual hanging.

To the Old Bailey jury on the afternoon of 13 January 1950, it must have seemed an open and shut case. Before them stood a pathetic little man, 25-year-old Timothy John Evans, who had apparently murdered his baby daughter, Geraldine, and who had confessed to the killing of his wife as well. There appeared to be a strong prosecution case which the jury accepted. Evans was condemned, his execution taking place at Pentonville at 9am on Thursday 9 March 1950. It was one of those cases which would have faded almost instantly from the public memory were it not to be for the gruesome discovery of more bodies at Evans' erstwhile home, 10 Rillington Place, Ladbroke Grove, three years later.

Evans had rented rooms at Rillington Place from John Christie, a short and insignificant man, bald and bespectacled, who was nicknamed 'Reggie no dick' by local children and who had a criminal record stretching back some years. Christie murdered at least seven women: Ruth Fuerst in 1943, Muriel Eady in 1944, Beryl Evans (Timothy's wife) in 1949, Ethel Christie (his own wife) in 1952, and Kathleen Maloney, Rita Nelson and

Hectorina MacLennan in 1953. In most cases he had lured these women to the house and had then gassed them into unconsciousness before strangling them. It is thought he indulged in sex acts with them before burying their bodies in the garden or hiding them around the house.

By early 1953, the house was somewhat crowded with corpses, so Christie decided to move and sublet the property to a Mr and Mrs Reilly who noticed a foul smell in the kitchen. When the owner investigated it he discovered three of the women's bodies hidden in an alcove off the kitchen that had been wallpapered over. As one can imagine, this discovery made headline news. Christie had left his lodgings and was wandering the streets before being apprehended on London's Embankment on 31 March 1953. Under questioning, he admitted to the murders except Geraldine Evans and seemed to be working on the theory of 'the more the merrier,' probably in the hope of being found guilty but insane. Christie would not, however, admit to killing the baby despite repeated questioning and only admitted killing her mother after some time in custody.

He came to trial at the Old Bailey on 22 June 1953 before Mr Justice Finnemore and his counsel offered the expected defence of insanity. The jury took just under an hour and a half to reject this and reach a guilty verdict after a three-day trial. Three weeks later, Christie stood under the same beam as Evans had done and at 9 o'clock on the morning of Wednesday 15 July 1953, was also hanged by Albert Pierrepoint. The Home Office allowed for the reburial of Timothy Evans' body in consecrated ground in late 1965 and he was granted a posthumous pardon on 18 October 1966, as Christie had given evidence against him and had admitted killing Beryl. However, controversy still continues as to whether Evans killed either his wife or daughter or both. Professor Keith Simpson, the famous forensic pathologist who was involved in the cases, does not believe that Evans was innocent of both crimes. Ludovic Kennedy's book entitled *10 Rillington Place* and the subsequent film of the same title provide a valuable insight into the cases.

Derek Bentley was hanged by Albert Pierrepoint on Wednesday 28 January 1953 for his part in an armed robbery at a Croydon factory which resulted in the murder of PC Sidney Miles. This case aroused much controversy at the time and became a cause célèbre to the anti-capital punishment lobby. Derek Bentley was finally granted a well-deserved posthumous pardon in 1998. On the evening of Sunday 2 November 1952, he went out with his friend, 16-year-old Christopher Craig, to carry out a burglary. Bentley was armed with a knife and a knuckle-duster which Craig had given him. Craig had a similar knife as well as a .455 Ely revolver. They chose to break into the warehouse of Parker & Barlow in Croydon, Surrey. As they climbed onto the roof of the warehouse they were spotted by a little girl who lived opposite and whose mother phoned the police. The nearest patrol car arrived very quickly containing detective constable Fairfax and a uniformed constable. Craig and Bentley were on the roof as the police arrived and attempted to run. DC Fairfax grabbed Bentley, but did not formally arrest him. This was crucially important to Bentley's subsequent conviction. Craig decided to shoot his way out and fired at DC Fairfax, wounding him in the shoulder. At some time during the shooting, Bentley is alleged to have said the now famous words 'Let him have it, Chris.' Sound familiar? See the case of Ostler and Appleby in Chapter 19.

Bentley offered no resistance to Fairfax and stood by the injured policeman without any restraint for the next 30 minutes or so; hardly the action of a desperate young thug who could have easily overpowered the wounded and unarmed Fairfax. Other officers arrived on the scene within minutes, some of them armed. Craig continued shooting at anyone that moved, and as the first of the reinforcements, PC Sidney Miles, came up the stairs and through the door onto the roof he was shot through the head and died almost instantly. Craig eventually ran out of bullets and threw himself off the roof in a vain attempt to avoid capture. He landed on a greenhouse roof 30 feet below and broke his back. Both Craig and Bentley were charged with the murder of PC Miles. They came to trial at the Old Bailey on Thursday 9 December 1952 before the Lord Chief Justice, Lord Goddard, and both pleaded not guilty. The case against Craig was not actually as conclusive as one would imagine. There was some debate as to whether the bullet that had killed PC Miles had been fired from a .455 revolver and the bullet exhibited in court had no traces of blood on it. It has been claimed that Lord Goddard was biased against them and his summing up was certainly not sympathetic to their case. It took the jury just 75 minutes to return guilty verdicts against both youths. In view of his age, Craig was sentenced to be detained at Her Majesty's Pleasure and served just over 10 years whilst Bentley received the mandatory death sentence. The jury had made a recommendation to mercy in respect of Bentley. Bentley's appeal was heard and dismissed on 13 January 1953.

Bentley's fate now rested entirely with the Home Secretary, Sir David Maxwell Fife. There was a considerable campaign against the execution led by Bentley's father and also in Parliament who, in law, were unable to debate the individual case until after the execution had been carried out! A petition was signed by 200 MPs calling for a reprieve, but all to no avail. Bentley was hanged at Wandsworth on 28 January 1953, at the age of 19, by Albert Pierrepoint, assisted by Harry Allen. It is hardly difficult to see why this case became a cause célèbre. A somewhat retarded 19-year-old is hanged on a legal technicality for a crime that he did not commit and was never even alleged to have committed, whilst the actual culprit escapes the noose because of his age. As to the now famous words 'Let him have it, Chris,' even if they were actually uttered (itself a matter of contention) what did Bentley mean by them? These words are clearly open to two meanings: hand over the gun, or shoot him. Had it been alleged that Bentley had shouted 'Shoot the bastards, Chris,' his intentions would have been all too clear. Bentley was not given the benefit of this doubt and the case was perceived as a clear injustice by the public at large.

Britain's last double side-by-side hanging took place at Pentonville on Thursday 17 June 1954 when 22-year-old Kenneth Gilbert and 24-year-old Ian Grant were executed by Albert Pierrepoint, assisted by Royston Rickard, Harry Smith and Joe Broadbent, for the murder of 55-year-old George Smart in the course of a robbery. George Smart was the night porter at Alban Court Hotel in Kensington and on the night of Tuesday 9 March caught Gilbert and Grant breaking into the hotel. They attacked Smart and then tied him up and gagged him, ultimately causing his death by asphyxia. They blamed each other at the trial and assured the jury that they had not intended to kill Mr Smart. The jury did not accept this argument and neither did Lord Goddard when he dismissed their subsequent appeal. They had stolen just £2 and a quantity of cigarettes. Double hangings were later banned by the Homicide Act of 1957 as they took longer to carry out.

The early 1950s saw an unusually high level of executions, with 18 in England and Wales, and two in Scotland in 1950, 15 the following year, and 23 in England and Wales, and two in Scotland in 1952. The years 1953 to 1955 also saw the executions of three women, which had not happened since the beginning of the century. The first of these was 46-year-old Louisa Merrifield who had been convicted of poisoning Sarah Ricketts. Mrs Ricketts was a 79-year-old bedridden widow who lived in Blackpool. She had hired Louisa and her husband Alfred to look after her in March 1953 and soon made a new will leaving her bungalow to Louisa. Sarah Ricketts had some rather strange dietary habits. Apparently, she was fond of very sweet jams which she ate directly from the jar by the spoonful, washed down with rum or a bottle of stout. Louisa, having got the will made in her favour, capitalised on these peculiar habits by adding Rodine, a phosphorus-based rat poison, to the jam.

Mrs Ricketts' death was considered suspicious and so a post mortem was carried out which revealed the presence of the poison. A local chemist had recorded the sale of Rodine to Louisa. The police could not find the poison container which she had purchased, but felt that they had enough circumstantial evidence to charge both her and Alfred. She had talked openly of inheriting the bungalow and this also threw suspicion on her. The pair came to trial at Manchester Assizes on 20 July 1953. Alfred was acquitted, there being no real evidence that he was part of the plot, but Louisa was found guilty. She was duly hanged by Albert Pierrepoint on the morning of Friday 18 September 1953. Several hundred people gathered outside the prison gates that morning to see the death notice displayed.

The next woman to be hanged was Styllou Pantopiou Christofi, a 53-year-old Greek Cypriot. By 1953, she had not seen her son Stavros for 12 years and had saved up sufficient money for the passage to Britain in July of that year. Stavros had married a German girl called Hella Bleicher and they lived together in Hampstead, London. He worked as a waiter and she as a shop assistant and they had three children and a happy marriage. But all of that was to change with the arrival of his mother. Christofi continually picked on Hella and found fault with everything she did. Having enough, Hella decided to go to Germany with the children for a holiday on the understanding that Stavros would convince his mother to leave for Cyprus before she returned. Before Hella could leave, tragedy struck. On the night of 29 July, her mother-in-law came into the bathroom and hit her over the head with a heavy ash pan from the boiler. Having knocked Hella unconscious, Christofi then dragged her into the kitchen and strangled her. In an attempt to dispose of the body, she poured paraffin over Hella and lit it, setting fire to the house in the process. In panic and fearing for her grandchildren, she ran into the street and raised the alarm. The police and fire brigade turned up to find Hella's partly burnt corpse in the kitchen. One of the police officers noticed the marks of strangling on her neck and Christofi was arrested. She told him: 'Me smell burning, me come down, me pour water, but she be died.'

Christofi was tried at the Old Bailey on 28 October 1954. Her counsel put forward a defence of insanity which the jury rejected. She was therefore sentenced to death and returned to Holloway to be hanged by Albert Pierrepoint, assisted by Harry Allen, on Monday 13 December 1954. She asked for a Maltese Cross to be put on the wall of the execution chamber opposite to where she would stand and this wish was granted – it remained there until the room was dismantled in 1967. Her motive for the killing appears to have been jealousy over what she saw as Hella replacing her in Stavros' affections. It is believed that she had also committed an earlier murder in Cyprus.

The third and last female hanging was to be a much more famous and contentious case. It was, of course, that of Ruth Ellis, just eight months later. She too was hanged by Albert Pierrepoint at Holloway, this time assisted by Royston Rickard, on Wednesday 13 July 1955, for the murder of her boyfriend, David Blakely. He had refused to see her over the Easter holiday so she lay in wait for him outside the Magdala pub and when he came out, shot him five times with a revolver on the Easter Sunday evening. She was arrested at the scene by an off-duty policeman and never denied the crime. She was convicted by an Old Bailey jury after deliberating for only 23 minutes and refused to appeal her sentence. Ellis' execution caused a great deal of public controversy, both at home and abroad. There was a huge demonstration outside Holloway and much adverse comment in the press over the hanging. It was widely felt that her execution was unjust because Blakely had been mentally and physically abusive to her. Pierrepoint remarked to waiting journalists afterwards that for all their interest in Ruth, they had shown scant interest the previous year when he had hanged Styllou Christofi. Several books and films have been made about this case. It should be noted that a further four women received death sentences after Ruth Ellis, but all were reprieved.

The period covered by this chapter saw some very controversial cases. At least three – Derek Bentley, Timothy Evans and Ruth Ellis – were perceived to have been miscarriages of justice or at least unjust in the public mind and there was great pressure for reform of the system to make it fairer. All of this was to lead to the government introducing the Homicide Act of 1957, which became law on 21 March of that year. Between 15 September 1955 and 16 May 1957, whilst the Act was being formulated and debated, all persons convicted of murder (47 men and three women) were reprieved.

The Act created a new offence of capital murder that was defined as:

murder in the course or furtherance of theft
murder by shooting or causing an explosion
murder while resisting or preventing an arrest, or while rescuing someone from lawful custody
murder of a police officer
murder of a prison officer or other member of prison staff by a prisoner or by a person unlawfully at large.

Section 6 of the Act also mandated the death penalty for anyone convicted of two murders committed on two separate occasions within Great Britain. This Act did reduce the number of death sentences. It also introduced the notion of diminished responsibility into English law and redefined the concept of provocation as a defence to a murder charge. The Act abolished the concept of constructive malice and also reduced killing in a suicide pact from murder to manslaughter. It was considered an unworkable shambles by almost everyone, however, as there were some strange inconsistencies in the Act. Murder by shooting would still be capital, whereas murder by poison would not. Murder in the course of theft was capital, but not in the course of rape. Murder of a single police or prison officer would bring a death sentence, but the murder of two or three people on the same occasion would not necessarily do so. In the next chapter we will look at the practical effects of the Act.

21

The effects of the Homicide Act of 1957

A total of 65 people were sentenced to death in England and Wales for crimes committed after March 1957 and, of these, 29 were hanged, giving a reprieve rate of 55.4%. The Act was supposed to eliminate unnecessary death sentences, yet reprieves continued at only a slightly reduced rate.

The first man to be condemned under the Act was Ronald Patrick Dunbar for a murder committed during the course of a robbery in 1957. He was reprieved. Only one woman was sentenced to death under the provisions of the 1957 Act. She was Mary Wilson, at Durham on 29 March 1958, who was dubbed by the press as the Widow of Windy Nook. She was reprieved, probably because of her age (she was 66 years old), even though she had poisoned two husbands and the two murders were committed on different occasions. Age was not typically a bar to execution, however. Of those hanged, 18 were aged 25 or under, one being only 18. Three men were hanged in Scotland, two in Northern Ireland and one on the island of Jersey after 1957.

Twenty-two-year-old John Wilson Vickers became the first person to hang in England and Wales under the new law, having been convicted of the murder of 72-year-old Jane Duckett. She owned and ran a small grocery shop in Carlisle and Vickers decided to rob her on Monday 15 April 1957. She heard the sound of someone on her premises and put up a fight, in the course of which he battered her to death. Vickers was arrested and tried at Carlisle on 23 May 1957. He was convicted and sentenced to death but appealed on the grounds that there was no constructive malice in the killing. The appeal was dismissed and after an unsuccessful attempt to take the case to the House of Lords, he was hanged at Durham on Tuesday 23 July 1957 by Harry Allen and Harry Smith.

The wording of the death sentence was further modified after 1957: '(full name of prisoner) you will be taken hence to the prison in which you were last confined and from there to a place of execution where you will suffer death in the manner authorised by law, and may the Lord have mercy upon your soul.' The references to hanging and to burial were removed.

Wales had its last execution on 6 May 1958 when Vivian Teed was hanged by Robert Leslie Stewart, assisted by Harry Robinson, for the murder of William Williams at Swansea.

One of the first capital cases that I remember as a boy was that of Guenther Fritz Podola in 1959. Podola had been born in Berlin in 1929 and came to Britain in the spring of 1959 after deportation from Canada where he had been convicted of theft and burglary. In July 1959, he was once again engaged in crime in London's South Kensington. He tried to blackmail his victim, a Mrs Schiffman, by claiming to have embarrassing photos and tape recordings of her. As she knew she had nothing to hide, she reported the phone call to the police who tapped her line. When Podola rang again they were able to trace the call to a nearby call box where the police found him moments later. He ran away from the detectives and was chased and caught near a block of flats in Onslow Square. While the one policeman went to fetch the car, Podola produced a gun and shot the other policeman, Detective Sergeant Raymond Purdy, and fled. Purdy had taken Podola's address book when he arrested him, and it was discovered by his widow when Purdy's belongings were returned to her. This pointed the police towards the Claremont House Hotel in Kensington where Podola was staying in Room 15. Armed police assembled outside the room and at the signal, forced the door. Podola, who was probably listening at the door, was hit on the head by it as it flew open. He was hospitalised for four days as a result and claimed to have no memory of his arrest or the shooting of DS Purdy.

Podola was tried at the Old Bailey, the jury rejecting his defence of memory loss. Even though it could be proved that he had shot Purdy, if he genuinely could not recall doing so and was not mentally fit to stand trial he would have had to be acquitted. Podola was hanged by Harry Allen and Royston Rickard on 5 November 1959 at 9.45am, the last person to die for the murder of a police officer in Britain.

Bedford prison did not have many executions; in fact, it had not had a hanging since 26 November 1942 when William Cooper was executed for murdering John Harrison. This was about to change with two executions taking place in just over a year. The first was that of Jack Day, aged 31, who was executed by Harry Allen, assisted by Harry Roberts, at 8am on Wednesday 29 March 1961, having been convicted of the murder of 25-year-old Keith Godfrey Arthur on Tuesday 23 August 1960 at Edward Street in Dunstable. Jack Day was a second-hand car salesman and was very jealous of his wife. The murder occurred in Day's house on the Wednesday evening when he came home to find Arthur talking to his wife. Also present was 13-year-old Patricia Dowling. Day demanded to know why Arthur was there and he replied that he had come round to see if Day wanted to go out for a drink. Day pulled out a revolver and shot him in the throat and then disposed of the body in a barn on Dunstable Downs where it was found two days later. The crime was traced back to Day and there was very strong witness evidence from Patricia Dowling. He was charged with capital murder as he had used a gun and came to trial at Bedford before Mr Justice Streatfield on 18-20 January 1961. Day appealed but this was dismissed on 6 March.

Just over a year later there was to be another and far better known case that ended on the same gallows. James Francis Hanratty, aged 25, was hanged on 4 April 1962 for the murder of Michael Gregsten on the A6 road near Bedford on the evening of 22 August 1961. Michael Gregsten and Valerie Storie were having an affair and had parked up in a field near Slough in his grey Morris Minor. They were interrupted by a man who tapped on the car window and got into the car, threatening them with a gun and robbing them of their money and jewellery. Gregsten was ordered to drive off and later to stop in a lay-by on the A6 where he was shot and Valerie Storie raped and then also shot. She survived but was left paralysed. Hanratty had previous convictions for housebreaking and car theft for which he had served prison terms, but none for violent offences. Two 38-calibre shell cases were found in a hotel room that he had occupied under a false name, and this led to his arrest after Valerie Storie picked him out at an identity parade from his voice with its distinctive Cockney accent. He claimed to have been in Liverpool at the time of the shooting, but at his trial he changed this to being in Rhyl in North Wales. Hanratty was tried at Bedford between 22 January and 17 February before Mr Justice Gorman in what was then the longest murder trial ever. The jury took over 9 hours to convict him. After his appeal had been dismissed he was hanged on 4 April 1962 by Harry Allen, assisted by Royston Rickard. Controversy continued over this case, however, particularly with the partial 'confession' of Peter Alphon and over the validity of Valerie Storie's identification evidence. This led to the Home Office granting permission for Hanratty's remains to be removed from Bedford prison and reburied by his family at Carpenders Park Lawn Cemetery at Watford in Hertfordshire in 1966.

By the end of the 20th century DNA testing had advanced considerably, so it was decided to test DNA from Hanratty's mother and his brother Michael. This was compared to semen found on Valerie Storie's underwear and to a sample taken from a handkerchief in which the murder weapon was found. The matches tied these items to Hanratty with a probability of 2.5 million to one. So in March 2001, Hanratty was once again exhumed so that a DNA sample could be taken directly. This test gave an even stronger match. The family had taken the case to the Criminal Cases Review Commission who recommended an appeal court hearing. In the light of the DNA evidence, on 10 May 2002, at the Court of Criminal Appeal in London, the Lord Chief Justice, Lord Woolf, sitting with Lord Justice Mantell and Mr Justice Leveson, ruled that Hanratty's conviction was not unsafe and that there were no grounds for a posthumous pardon.

Twenty-one-year-old Edwin Albert Arthur Bush became the last man to hang at Pentonville on 6 July 1961 when he was executed for the murder of shop assistant Elsie Batten. He had battered and stabbed her to death in order to steal a sword from the antiques shop where she worked. A half-caste Indian, Bush sought to use racism as a defence to killing Elsie, who he said had made racist remarks to him, causing him to lose his temper and lash out at her. The Old Bailey jury did not accept this and he was duly executed by Harry Allen, assisted by John Underhill.

The final murderer to stand on Wandsworth's gallows, and indeed to be executed in London, was 49-year-old Henryk Neimasz on Friday 8 September 1961. Neimasz had been convicted at Lewes Assizes of the murder of Hubert Buxton and his wife, Alice, who he had shot and battered to death respectively in their home on the night of 12 May 1961. Neimasz had been having an affair with Alice Buxton, who wanted him to leave his wife for her, something he refused to do. Sadly, he resolved the problem by killing both of them. He was hanged by Harry Allen, assisted by Samuel Plant. As he had used a gun to kill Hubert Buxton he was guilty of capital murder.

The last hanging in Northern Ireland was that of 25-year-old Robert Andrew McGladdery on 20 December 1961 at Crumlin Road prison in Belfast. It was carried out by Harry Allen, assisted by Samuel Plant. McGladdery had been convicted of the murder of 19-year-old Pearle Gamble near Newry. On the eve of his execution he allegedly confessed to strangling and stabbing Miss Gamble on the night of 28 January as she walked home from a dance.

Russell Pascoe, aged 24, and 22-year-old Dennis John Whitty, were jointly convicted of the murder of 64-year-old William Garfield Rowe at Nanjarrow Farm near Falmouth in Cornwall on 14 August 1963. They had battered and stabbed the elderly farmer to death in an attempt to steal his alleged fortune. In reality they managed to find just £4 in the house, although the police later located a further £3000 hidden away. They were tried at Bodmin between 29 October and 2 November 1963 and on conviction, Pascoe was sent to Bristol to await execution and Whitty to Winchester as Bodmin had long since ceased to have an execution facility. Simultaneously at 8 o'clock on the morning of Tuesday 17 December they were led to the gallows. Pascoe was hanged by Harry Allen and Royston Rickard, and Whitty by Robert Stewart and Harry Robinson. Outside Horfield prison in Bristol there was a considerable demonstration with Tony Benn, the MP for Bristol South East, and the Bishop of Bristol, the Right Rev Oliver Tomkins, present.

Twenty-one-year-old Henry Burnett was the last person to be hanged in Scotland in the newly constructed Condemned Suite at Craiginches prison in Aberdeen on 15 August 1963 for the murder of Thomas Guyan. Burnett wanted Guyan's wife, Margaret, and after she threatened to leave him and return to her husband Burnett went to Guyan's flat at 14 Jackson Terrace in Aberdeen and shot him in the face. He attempted to escape by stealing a car, but was captured within the hour as police followed the vehicle. This was the only execution carried out at Aberdeen in the 20th century. Harry Allen was the hangman, assisted by Samuel Plant.

The last hangings of all in Britain were two carried out simultaneously at 8am on Thursday 13 August 1964 at Walton prison, Liverpool, and Strangeways prison in Manchester, when Peter Anthony Allen and Gwynne Owen Evans (real name John Robson Walby) were executed for the robbery murder of laundryman John West at King's Avenue, Seaton in Workington on 7 April 1964.

Allen, aged 21, was hanged at Walton by Robert Leslie Stewart, assisted by Harry Robinson, whilst 24-year-old Evans was dealt with by Harry Allen, assisted by Royston Rickard. At the time it was not realised that these would be the last executions in England and so they passed with very little publicity. Indeed, a further 17 men were sentenced to death after this, the last being 23-year-old David Stephen Chapman on 1 November 1965, for a murder committed during the course of a robbery. On 9 November 1965, the Murder (Abolition of Death Penalty) Act suspended the death penalty for murder in Britain for a period of five years.

22

The road to abolition of the death penalty

It might be thought that the abolition campaign was a post-World War 2 phenomenon, but this is very far from the truth. Capital punishment has in fact been abolished twice in England, the first time in the 11th century by William the Conqueror. One of his earliest decrees was: 'I forbid that any person be killed or hanged for any cause.'

Serious efforts to have the death penalty abolished had been going on since the late 1700s. Large numbers of crimes were being made capital offences under the 'Bloody Code'. To many educated people this was an increasingly ridiculous situation, especially when so many reprieves were given and many of the crimes were of a minor nature. It is notable that there were no executions for many of the more obscure capital felonies, such as impersonating a Chelsea Pensioner or begging on the street by a soldier without prior permission from his commanding officer.

Typical of the worst aspects of the 'Bloody Code' was the case of Mary Jones who was hanged at Tyburn for shoplifting on 16 October 1771. Mary was thought to be about 18 or 19 years old and was already married with two children when her husband, William, was press ganged into the navy, leaving her destitute. She had stolen a roll of muslin which was valued at £5 10s (£5.50). In 1777, her case was raised in Parliament by Sir William Meredith, the MP for Liverpool, who was opposing a motion to add yet another offence to the list of capital crimes. He told the House that he did not believe 'a fouler murder was ever committed against law, than the murder of this woman by law'. His eloquence was to no avail, however, and the Bill was carried. Sir William suggested that Parliament consider the use of 'more proportionate punishments' instead of the death penalty or at least the mandatory death sentence for most felonies. His proposal was rejected, but it opened up the debate. With over a thousand people being sentenced to death each year, even though only a small proportion was actually executed, it was clearly a debate that was needed.

Burglary and highway robbery were two of the most comn that led to the gallows in the late 17th and early 18th centuries. In the 28-year period from 1800 to 1827, the crimes which led to over a hundred executions in England and Wales were: burglary – 442, murder – 380, highway robbery – 288, forgery – 211, horse theft – 145, uttering (passing forgeries) – 144 and sheep theft – 130. Rape accounted for 98 executions. The famous lawyer Sir Samuel Romilly (1757–1818) constantly attempted to get Parliament to de-capitalise minor crimes. On 17 January 1813, he introduced a Bill in the House of Commons 'to repeal so much of the Act of King William as punishes with death the offence of stealing privately in a shop, warehouse or stable, goods of the value of 5s' (25p). This is what we call shoplifting now. This Bill was rejected by the House of Lords.

After Romilly's death, Sir James Mackintosh took up the abolitionist cause. Mackintosh (1765–1832) was a Scottish-born lawyer and author who had served as a judge in India. On 2 March 1819, he carried a motion by a majority of 19 against the government for a committee to consider capital punishment. He chaired a House of Commons Committee set up to examine capital punishment in 1819 and this led to six Bills embodying the recommendations of the committee put forward in May 1820, only three of which became law. Lord Eldon, the Lord Chancellor, secured an amendment to keep the death penalty for stealing to the value of more than £10, which would be about £250 today. On 21 May 1823, Mackintosh put forward a further nine proposals to Parliament for removing the death penalty for less serious offences. He wanted to make forgery a non capital crime, but this was opposed by Sir Robert Peel, even though the government did reduce the number of capital crimes significantly. As we saw earlier, a conviction for forgery frequently resulted in an execution.

In 1810, there were no fewer than 222 individually defined capital crimes, this number being steadily reduced between 1813 and 1861. By 1861, the number of capital crimes were reduced to just four by the Criminal Law Consolidation Act of that year. In effect there was really only one crime – murder – for which people would continue to be put to death in Britain. Over the first 68 years of the 19th century, individuals and pressure groups were to lend their voices to the argument in favour of abolition with some success. Several, including author Charles Dickens and the Quaker movement, campaigned for ending of public executions as detailed in Chapter 13. In the period from January 1868 to December 1899, 988 people were condemned to death, of whom 454 were executed, 446 in private and 8 in public, prior to abolition of public executions. All were murderers.

The early part of the 19th century saw great efforts for prison reforms from people such as Elizabeth Fry and John Howard. Prison conditions were generally appalling at the time as they were mainly used to hold people awaiting trial, execution or transportation. Elizabeth Fry worked tirelessly for prison reform, helping to found the Association for the Improvement of the Female Prisoners in Newgate. This group campaigned for better conditions for these women, a school for their children and a woman matron to look after them. Its activities spread to other towns and represented the first real attempt to treat criminals as human beings rather than vermin to be eradicated. Elizabeth Fry commented unfavourably on the attitudes of some of the condemned women she met in Newgate, who seemed more concerned about what they would wear on the gallows than in the salvation of their souls.

In 1925, the National Campaign for the Abolition of Capital Punishment was formed and this continued to campaign for abolition up to the end. Several then well-known left-wing politicians were members of this group at various times, including prime minister-to-be Harold Wilson. It would be wrong to omit mention of one of the most tireless campaigners against capital punishment in the period from 1935 to 1960. Violet Van der Elst (1882–1966) was also known as 'Sweet Violet' and less flatteringly as 'VD Elsie'. Although she came from a humble background, she became very wealthy and would arrive outside prisons on the eve of an execution in her Rolls-Royce. Here she would play hymns through loudspeakers and distribute leaflets to the crowd. She was considered as an annoyance by the authorities and an object of amusement and derision by the public. It was not at all unusual for her to be fined for causing an obstruction or for some other minor public order offence.

Her first major demonstration took place outside Wandsworth on 2 April 1935 at the hanging of Leonard Brigstock. As usual, it was both spectacular and futile. She received a hostile response from the crowd outside Strangeways a year later at the execution of Buck Ruxton (see Chapter 18). She wrote a book entitled *On the Gallows* in 1937 that was an apologia for some recently hanged criminals both in Britain and the USA. It is unclear whether her campaigning really had any effect. The public could tell the difference between cases such as Buck Ruxton and Neville Heath as compared to Derek Bentley, for instance, and were much more sympathetic to the latter. Social attitudes in Britain were changing in the 1940s. Class barriers were beginning to come down and people felt sickened by the wholesale slaughter of World War 2 and the holocaust of Nazi Germany. Labour was elected to Parliament in July 1945 and the Prime Minister, Clement Attlee, appointed a known abolitionist, James Chuter-Ede, as Home Secretary. Abolition of capital punishment was not included in their manifesto but was close to the hearts of many in the party.

As we saw in Chapter 20, in April 1948, the House of Commons voted in favour of a Bill introduced by the left wing Labour MP for Nelson and Colne, Sidney Silverman, to suspend the death penalty for five years. This was defeated by the House of Lords. So in November 1955, Silverman tried again, introducing the Death Penalty (Abolition) Bill to the House of Commons which it passed on a free vote in February 1956 with a majority of 26. This too was rejected by the House of Lords after four days of solid debate. The Home Secretary, now Major Gwilym Lloyd George, again reprieved all those condemned whilst the matter was under discussion. Forty-nine people escaped the gallows and there were no executions between 10 August 1955 and 23 July 1957 when John Vickers was hanged (see Chapter 21).

It should be noted that opinion polls generally showed a minimum 3:1 ratio of public support for retention of capital punishment and most daily newspapers were also in favour, with the exception of *The Times*, *Guardian*, *Daily Mirror* and *News Chronicle*. However, the public attitude was often much more pro capital punishment in theory than in practice. Many would sign petitions for a reprieve in the case of a particular individual, a person with a face and a name.

The abolition of the death penalty was a major priority of the incoming Labour government of Harold Wilson in 1964 and its first Home Secretary, Sir Frank Soskice. On 28 October 1965, a Private Member's

Bill to suspend it, again sponsored by Sydney Silverman, received Royal Assent on 8 November 1965. It was supported by the government, the Home Secretary and by Lord Longford and the Lord Chancellor, Gerald Gardiner, in the House of Lords. Thus on 9 November 1965, the Murder (Abolition of Death Penalty) Act suspended the death penalty for murder in the UK for a period of five years. Treason, piracy with violence and arson in Royal Dockyards remained capital crimes. The same Act also removed the liability to capital punishment from the Army Act 1955, the Air Force Act 1955 and the Naval Discipline Act 1957 where the corresponding civil offence was murder.

The last death sentence for murder was passed on 1 November 1965 on David Stephen Chapman for a murder committed during the course of a robbery. He was automatically reprieved as were the other 16 men sentenced in late 1964 and in 1965. The House of Commons reaffirmed its decision that capital punishment for murder should be permanently abolished on 16 December 1969. In a free vote, the House voted by 343 to 185, a majority of 158, that the Murder (Abolition of Death Penalty) Act 1965 should not expire. This vote was affirmed by the House of Lords two days later and thus the death penalty for murder was finally abolished.

Two cases in 1966 were to reignite the debate over abolition and lead to a public demand for reinstatement. On 27 April 1966, Myra Hindley and Ian Brady came to trial at Chester Assizes for the infamous 'Moors Murders'. They escaped the death penalty by a couple of months as it had been suspended only four weeks before their arrest, although the murders were committed while capital punishment was still on the statute books. On 6 May 1966, they were jailed for life having been convicted of the murders of Lesley Ann Downey, aged 10, in 1964, and Edward Evans, aged 17, in 1965. Brady was also convicted of the murder of 12-year-old John Kilbride. Hindley was found guilty of being an accessory.

The second case, which shocked the nation, occurred on Friday 12 August 1966 when three career criminals – Harry Roberts, John Witney and John Duddy – brutally murdered three police officers who were trying to question them at the roadside in Braybrook Street, London. They were all convicted and given life sentences.

Since then there have been some thirteen attempts to reinstate capital punishment in Britain. All these have failed as Parliament moved further and further in favour of total abolition. The last House of Commons vote on the reintroduction of the death penalty was defeated by 403 to 159 in 1994. During Mrs Thatcher's years in office the issue was debated several times, but free votes in the House of Commons failed to get a majority. Under the provisions of the Criminal Damage Act of 1971, arson in Royal Dockyards ceased to be a capital offence being downgraded to just arson, which still carries a maximum life sentence. The death penalty remained theoretically available in Northern Ireland until the passing of the Northern Ireland (Emergency Powers) Act 1973, although there has been no execution since 1961.

Anthony Teare became the last person to be sentenced to death in the British Isles for a contract killing in the Isle of Man on 10 July 1992. The sentence was not commuted, however, because the Manx Appeal Court ordered a retrial in 1994, by which time capital punishment had been removed from the Isle of Man Criminal Code. The new sentence was therefore life in prison.

Prime Minister Tony Blair signed the Council of Europe Declaration calling for the universal abolition of the death penalty on 11 October 1997. On 20 May 1998 in a free vote during a debate on the Human Rights Bill, MPs decided by 294 to 136, a 158 majority, to adopt provisions of the European Convention on Human Rights outlawing capital punishment for murder except 'in times of war or imminent threat of war'. The Bill incorporates the European Convention on Human Rights into British law. A House of Lords amendment to the Crime and Disorder Act 1998, which came into law in July 1998, removed the death penalty for treason and piracy with violence. In October 1998, the government introduced an amendment to the Human Rights Bill that abolished the death penalty as a possible punishment for military offences under the Armed Forces Acts. There were five military wartime capital offences: serious misconduct in action; communicating with the enemy; aiding the enemy or furnishing supplies; obstructing operations or giving false air signals; mutiny or incitement to mutiny; and failure to suppress a mutiny. The last execution under military law was in 1942.

Labour Home Secretary Jack Straw signed the Sixth Protocol of the European Convention of Human Rights in Strasbourg on 27 January

1999. This states in Article 1, Abolition of the death penalty: 'The death penalty shall be abolished. No one shall be condemned to such penalty or executed.' This was ratified on 27 May 1999. On 10th December 1999, International Human Rights Day, the government ratified the Second Optional Protocol to the International Covenant on Civil and Political Rights therefore abolishing capital punishment in Britain.

Background

The press stimulated public interest in murder trials and the eventual fate of those convicted and sentenced to death. They became far less dehumanised as a result. Virtually every word of the more interesting murder trials used to be reported in the popular press in the 1940s and 50s, whereas now hardly any detail of most trials is reported. As the execution date drew near, there would be much speculation as to whether a particular prisoner would be reprieved or not and in many cases petitions for a reprieve were drawn up.

Compared to now, the post-war years were a time of relatively little serious crime and yet a surprisingly large number of murderers – 151 – were hanged in the first 10 years after the end of World War 2, including five women. There were, as stated earlier, three cases in particular that caused public concern and were of great help to the abolitionist cause. They were Timothy Evans, Derek Bentley and Ruth Ellis. The first raised serious doubts as to whether an innocent man had been hanged. Derek Bentley's execution did much to sway public opinion against capital punishment and one can only wonder what possessed the Home Secretary to take such a palpably unjust decision. One is left wondering if certain Home Office officials had a hidden agenda to end capital punishment and advised the Home Secretary against a reprieve, predicting the likely outcome but also knowing that they would remain shielded from the consequences behind the Official Secrets Act.

As the law stood in 1955, Ruth Ellis was quite correctly convicted of murder as her crime was decidedly premeditated, even if it was a 'crime of passion'. However, she was an attractive 28-year-old blonde mother of two, who through her demeanour in court and because of the violence she had suffered at the hands of Blakely attracted enormous public sympathy. Ruth Ellis had the glamour that sells newspapers, being typically described by them as a model.

Successive governments had made executions and the decisions leading to reprieve or execution matters of complete secrecy, therefore excluding the public. This has the tendency to make people wonder what the authorities have to hide and allows the press to print any sensational story, however inaccurate, about condemned prisoners and their execution. It also has the effect of focusing attention on the criminal rather than the crime. Inevitably, criminals have a 'human face' that the press exploit; these human interest stories, equally inevitably, attracted public sympathy, especially where the prisoner was young or attractive or both. Interviews with prisoners' families, who often understandably maintained that their loved ones were innocent, or even if they had done the crime did not deserve to hang for it, made good reading as people like human interest stories.

The Homicide Act 1957 tried to distinguish between different categories of murder, but probably made matters worse. In previously secret government papers released in 1995, the then prime minister, Harold Macmillan, commented to the Home Secretary, Richard Austen Butler, that the law was unworkable and would inevitably lead to abolition (see Chapter 21). It was argued by opponents of capital punishment that hanging, when carried out at the rate of 11 or so a year on average, over the first 65 years of the 20th century, served no useful purpose as a deterrent to the most serious crimes, but was rather simply an act of cruelty inflicted on a few people, often for no particularly obvious reason in the minds of the general public.

23

The reprieve system and the treatment of mentally ill criminals

The concept of the exercise of the Royal Prerogative of Mercy, i.e. reprieving people who had been sentenced to death, dates back a very long way in English law. We are all subjects of the reigning monarch and prior to 1837 only he or she ultimately had the power of life or death over us and had to personally sign the death warrant in each case. The monarch sat with the Privy Council in what were called 'Hanging Cabinets' and personally disposed of capital cases up to this time. In London, the Recorder of the Old Bailey would submit his report in person to the 'Hanging Cabinet' with his recommendations for each prisoner. Outside London, circuit judges would send in their report and recommendations after each Assize held in the county towns. Where they felt strongly that an individual should not be executed they could respite the person 'until the King's pleasure is known'. This was important as under the 1752 Act a person convicted of murder had to be executed within two days and therefore there would have been insufficient time to know what the King and Privy Council would decide.

In the 18th and early 19th centuries, with so many crimes carrying a mandatory death sentence, there had to be a means of stopping the wholesale judicial slaughter of minor criminals, if only to prevent a revolution. It has been suggested that excessive and cruel punishments were a major causal factor in the French Revolution. Murder is generally seen as the most serious crime a person can commit, but there were instances where those sentenced to hang for it were reprieved if the murder was considered to be less heinous or where there were other mitigating circumstances. For instance, 43 people were convicted of murder in Surrey between 1735 and 1804, of whom five were reprieved and one given a pardon. In the same period, 329 people were hanged for other crimes.

On 27 March 1782, the Home Office came into being, and by 1785 had a staff of just 17, including the cleaning lady. The Home Secretary, as he became known, formed part of the 'Hanging Cabinet'. In the event of a reprieve the Lord Chancellor had to be involved as he was the keeper of the Great Seal which was required where a conditional pardon was granted. The word 'reprieve' is easier to use than the phrase 'conditional pardon', but the latter is a better description of the situation. The condemned person was allowed to live on the basis that they accepted an alternative punishment – normally transportation up to the 1850s and penal servitude thereafter. In theory at least, they could refuse this offer and be hanged. Remarkably this did happen. At the Old Bailey Sessions of 27 February 1788 Martha Cutler, Sarah Cowden and Sarah Storer were condemned for various felonies and later offered pardons which all three initially refused when they were brought back to court on 22 April 1789. Four other women, Sarah Mills, Mary Burgess, Jane Tyler and Eleanor Kirvan also refused their conditional pardons at the same hearing and it took until 3 June 1789 to persuade them to finally accept. What is not clear is why the authorities were so concerned about hanging these women.

During his first term as Home Secretary from 1822 to 1827, Sir Robert Peel streamlined both the law and the reprieve process, becoming the sole adviser to King George IV on reprieves. He was the first Home Secretary to take control of reprieves from the reigning monarch and it brought him into conflict with King George who still felt that he had the power to dispense mercy. The Judgement of Death Act of July 1823 put forward by Peel allowed judges on the English and Welsh circuits to record the mandatory death sentence for felonies other than treason and murder but then immediately commute it in open court to transportation or imprisonment at their discretion.

With the last remnants of the 'Bloody Code' still in place, an amazing 11,305 death sentences were passed/recorded in the decade 1826–1835, interestingly only 154 of these being for murder. Just 514 (4.54%) were carried out. The next decade saw a sharp decline in both death sentences and executions.

The table overleaf shows the situation as we progress through the 19th century.

	1800–1834		1835–1864		1865–1899	
Sentenced to death	29,808	851.66 p/a	3014	100.47 p/a	898	25.66 p/a
Hanged for murder	523	14.9 p/a	336	57.9% of sentenced	485	54% of sentenced
Hanged for other crimes	2153	61.5 p/a	27	1.1% of sentenced	0	0
Total hanged	2676	-	363	-	485	0
Reprieved	27,132	91.03%	2651	90.54%	413	46%

You will see that after 1835 the execution rate remained fairly stable and averaged 11.2 per annum for the rest of the century. During the 19th century, the population had risen from 9 million to 24 million.

Between 1829 and 1899, 231 women were sentenced to hang in the British Isles including Ireland. Of these women, 101 were executed: 97 for murder, one for attempted murder, one for conspiracy to murder (in Ireland) and two for arson. Three women were found insane and respited to asylums. One was given a free pardon and one committed suicide. Over the period, the reprieve rate was 56.3%. Before 1868, concern was expressed at the high number of female reprieves, which was thought to be due to the dislike of hanging women in public. From 1861 to 1899, there were to be 119 women given the death sentence, of whom 28 were to be hanged (all for murder), giving a reprieve rate of 76.5%. One of the major reasons for this was that women convicted of killing their newborn babies were reprieved from 1849 onwards, and in almost all cases women who were pregnant at the time of sentence were also reprieved, with the exception of Mary Ann Cotton in 1873.

After Peel resigned from the Home Office in 1827, the King, now William IV, once again wielded the Royal Prerogative and was a great repriever until his death in 1837, after which his niece Victoria took over. Thus the decision-making power on reprieves returned to the Home Secretary, who exercised the Royal Prerogative on behalf of the 19-year-old monarch. In law any Secretary of State could perform this function if the Home Secretary was unavailable. The requirement for the monarch to sign the death warrant was also removed at the same time, and from 1837 there ceased to be a death warrant. One clause in the Central Criminal Court Act of 1837 gave judges in London the same power of reprieve as circuit judges, although they rarely used it. The ability of judges to reprieve was removed altogether by the Criminal Law Consolidation Act of 1861 and once again transferred to the Home Secretary.

The modern reprieve process

For the first 58 years of the 20th century, anyone convicted of murder was automatically sentenced to death. This situation was slightly modified by the Homicide Act of 1957 which divided murders into capital and non capital. In the 66 years in England and Wales during which the death sentence could still be passed, 1,485 people were sentenced to be hanged by civil courts for murder and 755 were executed. The remainder, effectively half of all these, were reprieved (49.2% in total). The dreaded words of the death sentence were to be pronounced on 1,340 men, and 741 of them were subsequently hanged, equating to 55.3%. In the case of women, 145 were sentenced but only 14 hanged – a reprieve rate of just over 90%.

Although the trial judge had, by law, to pass the death sentence if the jury found the prisoner guilty, he was able to make a recommendation to the Home Secretary as to whether it should be carried out. Where the judge recommended mercy, it was rarely ignored by the Home Office. In evidence to the Royal Commission on Capital Punishment (1949–1953), it was stated that there were only six occasions between 1900 and 1949 when the judge's recommendation was overruled. It was not at all unusual for the jury to add a recommendation to mercy to their guilty verdict, but this was, in reality, completely irrelevant to the final outcome.

The Criminal Appeal Act of 1907 set up the Court of Criminal Appeal which for the first time gave prisoners the chance to appeal against their conviction for murder. Previously a condemned person could only, in effect, petition the Home Secretary for mercy. This formal appeal process ran in parallel to the Home Office reprieve process outlined below. If they won their appeal, the murder conviction was quashed and they were either freed or had their conviction reduced to a lesser offence, e.g. manslaughter or, after 1957, non capital murder. However, if the appeal was dismissed they were not automatically executed and could still be reprieved. The Home Office received the case papers after the conclusion of the trial, together with the recommendation of the judge. Its officials began to prepare a report for consideration by the Permanent Secretary and the Home Secretary. It was normal for the prisoner to be examined by a panel of three Home Office psychiatrists to determine if he or she was legally sane and competent to be hanged. This psychiatric report was also sent to the Permanent Secretary and considered along with the rest of the case papers.

We can only surmise how decisions were reached in individual cases and what advice was given to the Home Secretary, as the reasons for reprieving or not reprieving a prisoner were always kept secret. Again we can only surmise as to the criteria Home Office officials used in making their decisions. It would seem that murder by poisoning or the use of a gun were seen as aggravating factors, as were loose sexual morals in the case of female prisoners. Age could be a mitigating factor, especially in the case of women. Physical injury or disability were also mitigating factors where they might lead to problems with the execution. Any sign of mental illness after sentence had been passed was usually a reason for reprieve. However, obvious mental problems could not save the likes of Christie in the face of overwhelming public opinion. If there was to be no reprieve, the Home Secretary would write 'The law must take its course' on the file and the execution would then proceed, otherwise the Home Secretary would exercise the Royal Prerogative of Mercy on behalf of the monarch. The total lack of transparency in the system was always a cause for concern and laid the Home Office open to accusations of injustice.

One can only try to imagine the emotional torture of being sentenced to death and transferred to the Condemned Cell. The light is on permanently and you are guarded round the clock by two or three warders. You are weighed regularly and will probably realise why – so that they can calculate the correct length of drop for you when the time comes. Your date with the hangman has been set, normally for a Tuesday, Wednesday or Thursday, three weeks hence. Until the governor comes to you and tells you that you have either been reprieved or not, you live in a state of constant anxiety and fear. Not knowing one's fate can be harder to cope with than actually knowing and being able to prepare oneself for it. There is little doubt that some of those sentenced to death thought that being hanged would be death by slow strangulation. That it was not was almost irrelevant, if that was how they perceived it. When prisoners were reprieved, they were often transferred to the prison hospital to recover from their emotional problems and shock before they were rehabilitated in the normal prison population.

An often overlooked fact is the stress on the warders of having to take part in the 'death watch' process. Typically a total of 8 to 10 men (or women, if the prisoner was female) would have worked eight hour shifts in the condemned cell. They had to try and occupy their prisoner and, to the extent that they were allowed to, comfort them and prevent them committing suicide. It was also their duty to record everything the prisoner said in case of a confession or partial admission of guilt or the emergence of some new evidence. Even where they may have personally strongly expected a reprieve, the guards were not allowed to inform the prisoner and had to act at all times on the basis that their charge would be hanged. Once the Home Secretary's decision was known, it was these warders who had to deal with the prisoner's emotions, particularly when they had just been told by the governor that there was to be no reprieve and that they were to be hanged on a specified day. Where there was a reprieve, it often came a day or two before the planned execution date.

Now consider the situation from the point-of-view of the members of the public who read a newspaper every day or listened to the news on the wireless, as the radio was known then. They would know of a trial for murder and hear of the guilty verdict and death sentence. And yet time and time again they would hear of a reprieve. What message did this send? A system in chaos that could not make its mind up? Or a situation in which the punishment for murder would probably not result in death? The public's perception is far more important than the actual and often well-hidden facts. If the death penalty was supposed to deter, it had to be seen to be carried out in all those instances where the crime warranted it, save in the most exceptional circumstances. Where there were genuine reasons for a reprieve, these should have been clearly stated by the Home Office so that an ordinary person could have understood them. This was not the case and the reasons for reprieving or not reprieving were never given. This is not to impugn the actions of individual civil servants in individual cases; they acted in good faith and in accordance with the guidelines set down for them, even if the system was seen as unsatisfactory.

We do know that people were hanged despite widespread public concern over their level of guilt, eg Edith Thompson and Derek Bentley. In Edith Thompson's case, it is rumoured that the Home Office believed that she had tried to murder her husband previously and this was one of the reasons that she was not reprieved. If the Home Office had such information, why was it not made public? Based upon the information in the public domain at the time, her execution seemed unjust to most people. It was hard to justify Derek Bentley's hanging by any way of looking at it. Most people have a strong and innate sense of justice. They have little sympathy for child killers and multiple murderers and typically supported the execution of the 'worst' murderers. But they equally opposed the hanging of people they saw as being less guilty. The Home Office never seemed capable of understanding public opinion and allowed executions such as Derek Bentley's on purely technical grounds, while reprieving other people for the flimsiest of reasons.

There is a huge difference between being hanged by the neck until you are dead and serving ten years in prison, which was the average for those who were reprieved between 1900 and 1964. This difference also seemed to be totally lost on the Home Office. Few of those reprieved served more than 15 years of their 'life sentences' in prison and hardly anyone served more than 20 years. Elizabeth Jones, who with her boyfriend was convicted of a very nasty robbery/murder, served just nine years of hers and that is not atypical. Christopher Craig, who was the principal in Derek Bentley's case, served ten years. Even Donald Thomas, who shot dead a police officer in London in 1948, served only 14 years. The length of time served was a particularly relevant factor where, as was often the case, the condemned person was quite young and had a great deal of potential life in front of them. The average age of all of those sentenced to death in the 20th century was 33 years. One can well understand why the families and friends of condemned prisoners drew up petitions to try and save their loved ones.

As stated earlier, 145 women were sentenced to death for murder in England and Wales in the 20th century, of whom no fewer than 131 were reprieved (90.3%). Two others were sentenced to death for espionage and both were reprieved. Interestingly Dorothy O'Grady served 14 years of her life sentence, typically more than she would have got for murder. Why were so many women sentenced to death if there was no intention of carrying out their sentences? One can, up to a point, understand the unwillingness of a male-dominated judicial system to execute women except for the most dreadful crimes. There are at least 55 instances of women who murdered their infant children being sentenced to death and then reprieved. Yet it was not until 1938, with an amendment to the Infanticide Act of 1922, that the law finally caught up with practice and public opinion and understood post-natal depression and the stigmatisation caused to a young woman of having a baby outside marriage that was prevalent at the time.

Sentenced to death, reprieved and killed again. Yes, it did happen. There are at least two cases where a man was reprieved to commit murder again after his release on parole. Christopher Simcox was convicted of his first murder on 7 July 1948, but was reprieved due to the temporary suspension of the death penalty while the Royal Commission was being set up. He was convicted of a second murder and again received the death sentence in February 1964. Again he was reprieved. Another case is that of Donald Forbes who was sentenced to death in 1958 for the murder of Allan Fisher, an Edinburgh nightwatchman, during a robbery at a fish factory. He was reprieved, but stabbed a man to death in a pub brawl in 1970, just weeks after release on licence. He was again jailed for life, but managed to escape.

As an example of the way the reprieve system worked (or did not work) here are four cases, all from the spring of 1955, under the stewardship of the same Home Secretary, Gwilym Lloyd George. Incidentally, there was no question of guilt or insanity in any of them.

A 40-year-old woman was convicted of murdering her next door neighbour, an 86-year-old, by battering her to death with a shovel after a long-running feud between the two. The case attracted virtually no publicity and it was really only her husband who made any effort to save her.

A 33-year-old army sergeant was convicted of murdering a colleague whose wife he was having an affair with at a British army base in Germany. He had killed his victim with a karate chop to the throat and tried to make the murder look like a suicide by hanging. Afterwards, he married his victim's wife.

A 28-year-old man was convicted of the murder of his girlfriend whom he had stabbed to death in a fit of jealousy. He then cut his own throat and stabbed himself but recovered from his injuries.

A 28-year-old woman shot her abusive boyfriend to death after he had refused to see her over the Easter holiday. She had recently had a miscarriage, having been punched in the stomach by him.

What happened to each of them? Were they reprieved or hanged?

Mrs Sarah Lloyd was reprieved and served just 7 years in prison.

Sgt Emmett Dunne was reprieved as Germany did not permit capital punishment, even for soldiers from a foreign country. Bear in mind that the crime was committed on a sovereign military base and therefore, at least in theory, a part of Britain. He served 11 years in prison.

Alfred John 'Jake' Wayman was reprieved on the grounds that the throat wound might open up if he was hanged and lead to an unpleasant mess, so he served 12 years of his life sentence.

Ruth Ellis was, of course, hanged.

If you can square the actual punishments to their crimes and see any proportionality in them, you are doing better than I am. And this is exactly why the reprieve system was perceived to be unjust.

Should people have been sentenced to death only where the murder(s) they had committed called for the ultimate punishment and there was every intention to follow through with execution? Sadly, English law did not allow this. Unlike America, there were no degrees of murder, although this idea had regularly been put forward. Prior to 1957, the jury were allowed three possible verdicts in a homicide case: guilty of murder, guilty of manslaughter (against tightly defined rules) or not guilty. In many instances, only the first verdict was possible. Obviously it is impossible to say in how many cases the jury would have preferred to find the defendant guilty of murder, but in the second degree, had they had the opportunity. I suspect it would have happened quite frequently, as they often made a recommendation to mercy with their guilty verdict.

A reprieve rate of perhaps 3-5% may be acceptable because there will always be special cases and exceptional circumstances in any judicial system. If it is consistently higher than that, then surely the law needed to be changed rather than just continuing to impose the death sentence, regardless of public opinion and evolving standards. I am not arguing that 95-97% of the 1,485 death sentences should have been carried out but rather that 45% of them should never have been passed in the first place. But when the law was changed in 1957 the reprieve rate dipped only slightly. It is important that the public clearly understands the penalty for specific crimes if they are expected to be deterred by this penalty. Endless reprieves undermined respect for the legal system and the administration of justice. In conclusion, it could be said that a secretive system of reprieves by the executive is no substitute for a fair and just application of the death penalty.

Insanity and the death penalty

One of the earliest recorded cases of insanity being used a defence was Rex v Arnold in 1724. Edward Arnold was tried at Kingston, Surrey, for shooting at Lord Onslow. Arnold claimed in court that the reason he had done so was because Onslow had bewitched him and had sent into his 'chamber devils and imps' that had 'invaded his bosom such that he could not sleep'. Arnold's relatives testified that he suffered from delusions. The trial judge, Mr Justice Tracy, instructed the jury that to acquit Arnold they had to decide whether the accused was totally deprived of his understanding and memory and knew 'no more than a wild beast or a brute, or an infant' what he was doing. This instruction became known as 'the wild-beast test'. Arnold was convicted and sentenced to death, but was reprieved at the urging of his victim, Lord Onslow.

Although Arnold's defence failed, juries could deliver a 'special verdict' of not guilty by reason of insanity, even if the defendant knew what he had actually done (the actus reus or guilty act) but did not know that it was wrong and therefore lacked the mens rea or guilty mind due to his insanity. The next significant development came in 1760 at the trial of Lawrence Shirley, the 4th Earl Ferrers (detailed in Chapter 9). At his trial for the murder of John Johnson in 1760, he attempted a defence of insanity. Many who knew him thought him to be insane and testified to this. The Solicitor General led the prosecution and pointed out to the court that Ferrers should be found guilty unless it could be shown that he did not possess sufficient mental capacity to understand the consequences of his action. Ferrers' fellow peers accepted this concept and he was hanged.

James Hadfield was tried for treason at the Court of King's Bench on 26 June 1800 for having shot at the king, George III, at the Theatre Royal in Drury Lane, London, on 15 May of that year. Because it was a treason trial Hadfield was allowed defence counsel in the form of the Honourable

Thomas Erskine. Owing to the gravity of the case it was heard by the Lord Chief Justice and two other senior judges and prosecuted by both the Attorney General and Solicitor General. Thomas Erskine challenged the prevailing legal definition of insanity, telling the court that a person could 'know what he was about' but be unable to resist his 'delusion'. Hadfield was examined by Dr John Monro from the Bethlem (Bedlam) Hospital who testified that Hadfield suffered from delusions, most probably brought on by serious head injuries received during the war with France in 1794. Erskine told the court that Hadfield believed that God talked to him and was told that the world was about to end. By shooting at the king, Hadfield knew that he would be executed and thus spared from committing suicide, in itself considered both a crime and a sin. The defence proved successful and Hadfield was acquitted and committed to Bethlem Hospital.

Hadfield's case led to the Criminal Lunatics Act of 1800 which provided that 'in all cases where it shall be given in evidence upon the trial of any person charged with treason, murder, or felony, that such person was insane at the time of the commission of such offence, and such person shall be acquitted, the jury shall be required to find specially whether such person was insane at the time of the commission of such offence, and to declare whether such person was acquitted by them on account of such insanity; and if they shall find that such person was insane at the time of the committing such offence, the court before whom such trial shall be had, shall order such person to be kept in strict custody, in such place and in such manner as to the court shall seem fit, until His Majesty's Pleasure shall be known.'

Britain does not have a history of assassination of its political leaders, but on 11 May 1812, just such an event occurred when John Bellingham shot and killed the prime minister, Spencer Perceval, whom he personally blamed for all his problems. He was arrested at the scene and tried four days later. His defence lawyer applied to have the trial postponed so that he could collect sufficient evidence of insanity, but this was rejected by the Lord Chief Justice, James Mansfield, and therefore Bellingham was convicted and hanged at Newgate on 18 May 1812. In his summing up Lord Mansfield told the jury: 'There is a species of insanity where people take particular fancies into their heads, who are perfectly sane and sound of mind on all other subjects, but this is not a species of insanity which can excuse any person who has committed a crime, unless it so affects his mind at the particular period when he commits the crime as to disable him from distinguishing between good and evil or to judge the consequences of his actions.'

A landmark case in 1843 that was to shape the future of the legal definition of insanity for well over a century was that of Daniel McNaughten who killed Edward Drummond, Sir Robert Peel's private secretary, on 20 January 1843. The intended victim was again the prime minister, but McNaughten mistook Drummond for the prime minister and as he left Peel's house, followed him and shot him in the back with a single round. McNaughten was arrested at the scene before he could fire again. He believed that Peel and others were watching his every move and conspiring to destroy him.

On 27 February, McNaughten came to trial at the Old Bailey before Mr Justice Tindal and evidence of the accused's insanity was placed before the jury. His father told them that his son had suffered from delusions of persecution as a teenager. McNaughten had been examined in prison whilst awaiting trial by various doctors who specialised in treating lunatics, as they were then known, and who testified to his insanity and delusional behaviour. One of these introduced the concept of monomania and felt that the delusions 'operated to the extent of depriving McNaughten of all self-control'. Mr Justice Tindal told the jury: 'The question to be determined is, whether at the time the act in question was committed, the prisoner had or had not the use of his understanding, so as to know that he was doing a wrong or wicked act.' The jury found in his favour and acquitted him – he was therefore sent to the Bethlem Hospital for the insane. The verdict caused considerable public concern, so the Lord Chancellor, Lord Lyndhurst, opened a debate on the subject of criminal responsibility in the House of Lords in March 1843 which led to the formulation of the famous McNaughten Rules. These state that: 'To establish a defence on the ground of insanity, it must clearly be proved that, at the time of the committing of the act, the party accused was labouring under such a defect of reason, from disease of the mind, as not to know the nature and quality of the act he was doing; or if he did know it, that he did not know what he was doing was wrong.'

Parliament passed the Trial of Lunatics Act on 25 August 1883, which permitted juries to find a special verdict of not guilty by reason of insanity. Queen Victoria was unhappy with this and requested that the verdict be changed to 'guilty but insane'. She had been the victim of several attacks by insane persons and therefore had a genuine personal interest in the outcome of cases. The first reading of the Criminal Lunatics Bill took place in Parliament on 19 June 1884. One of its provisions was to require the Home Secretary to order a medical examination, by two qualified medical practitioners, of any prisoner under sentence of death where there was reason to believe that the prisoner was insane. Where such evidence was found, the person was automatically reprieved and sent to Broadmoor secure mental hospital which had replaced the Bethlem Hospital. The Home Secretary could order a person accused of a felony who was certified as insane either before or after a trial to be committed to an asylum. Such persons became known as 'Secretary of State's lunatics'. This power was frequently used at the time. In 1884/5, no fewer than 938 criminal lunatics were identified, of whom 163 were sent to mental hospitals prior to trial by order of the Secretary of State.

The McNaughten Rules survived more or less intact for more than a century, but their narrow definition gave rise to increasing problems. A Committee on Insanity and Crime was set up in 1923 under the chairmanship of Lord Justice Atkin which examined the issues and reported on 1 November 1923. It recommend that a person charged with an offence should not be held responsible for his act when it was committed under an impulse which due to mental disease deprived them of any power to resist. The report pointed to the verdicts of insanity in the cases of young mothers who murdered their infant children, something that they knew to be wrong but something they were driven to do by an irresistible impulse. Under McNaughten if they could be shown to have known their action was wrong then they would have been responsible for it. Two other recommendations were that accused persons should not be found on arraignment unfit to plead except on the evidence of at least two doctors, save in very clear cases, and that provision should be made under Home Office regulations for examination of an accused person by an expert medical adviser at the request of the prosecution, the defence, or the committing magistrate.

The 1930 Select Committee on Capital Punishment and the Royal Commission on Capital Punishment that reported in 1953 also examined the issue of sanity, but in both cases their recommendations were rejected. The judiciary were unhappy with defences of partial insanity and irresistible impulses, and it was argued that such concepts would lead to 'total abandonment of criminal responsibility'. One of the most extraordinary cases of multiple murder committed by a severely mentally ill person is that of John Thomas Straffen. Twenty-one-year-old Straffen suffered from a troubled childhood and was in a mental institution from 1947 to February 1951 after assaulting a child. In August 1951, he strangled two little girls in Bath, 5-year-old Brenda Goddard and 9-year-old Cicely Batstone, but was found unfit to plead at his trial by reason of insanity and sent to Broadmoor. On 29 April 1952, he escaped and strangled 5-year-old Linda Bowyer before being recaptured the following day. He was convicted of this murder as the jury decided he was sane and sentenced to hang, but reprieved on the grounds of insanity after his appeal had been dismissed. He was never released and became Britain's longest serving prisoner, dying at Frankland prison in County Durham on 19 November 2007 at the age of 77. Strangely, he spent all of his incarceration in prisons and was never returned to a secure mental hospital, unlike Moors Murderer Ian Brady. It should be noted that inmates in Broadmoor and the other secure mental hospitals are patients rather than prisoners and can be released if in the opinion of their doctors they are sufficiently recovered.

Section 2 (1) of the Homicide Act of 1957 introduced the concept of diminished responsibility. Where this defence was successful, it reduced a charge of murder to manslaughter and permitted judges a range of sentences from life in prison, commitment to a mental hospital or even an absolute discharge. The Act stated: 'Where a person kills, or is party to the killing of another, he shall not be convicted of murder but shall be convicted of manslaughter, if he was suffering from such abnormality of mind (whether arising from a condition of arrested or retarded development of mind or any inherent causes or induced by disease or injury) as substantially impaired his mental responsibility for his acts and omissions in doing or being a party to the killing.'

24

Hangmen and women

Very few records remain of hangmen prior to 1800 outside London. Often this is because they were recruited from the ranks of the condemned themselves and reprieved on the condition of undertaking the executions of their fellow prisoners from a particular assize. Hanging in those days was hardly rocket science and anyone with a strong stomach could perform the role. Death then was something much closer to ordinary people who did not live in the sanitised world that we do and would have been quite used to the sight of death and the killing of animals for food. Generally men were ostracised by the public once they became hangmen and were not the celebrities that they became later. With the lack of a transport system it was necessary to have a hangman for each county; it was only the coming of the railways that allowed executioners to travel between counties and later throughout the country.

The name Jack Ketch became the generic name for the hangman, although the first person by that name was called John Ketch and operated at Tyburn from September 1663. It is thought that he worked for around 23 years up to 1686 when he was imprisoned before being reinstated. He, like all hangmen, had to carry out beheadings and burnings as well as hangings and it is for two horribly bungled beheadings that he is best remembered, as described in Chapter 4. Ketch was succeeded by Pasha Rose who was to be hanged at Tyburn for housebreaking and theft just four months later. Ketch returned to office and continued up to his death in November 1686. It is thought that he was succeeded by Richard Pearse of whom little is known. Even less is known of the executioner between 1686 and 1714.

John Price was appointed to the position in 1714 and held it for four years before also being hanged, on Saturday 31 May 1718, at Bunhill Fields for the murder of Elizabeth White. After the execution, Price's body was left to hang in chains at Stonebridge. William Marvell took over the office, having been a temporary replacement for Price while the latter was in prison for debt. On 24 February 1716, he beheaded Lord Derwentwater and Lord Kilmure on Tower Hill, making a rather better job than Jack Ketch had. Marvell held the job until November 1717 when he was dismissed after getting into debt, but then presumably reappointed to replace Price. He was succeeded by one Mr Banks, who was known as 'Bailiff Banks' and about whom very little else is known. Banks was succeeded by Richard Arnet around 1719. Arnet was probably responsible for the executions of Jack Shepherd and Jonathan Wild at Tyburn and carried out the burning of Catherine Hayes before dying in August 1728.

John Hooper, a turnkey at Newgate, was appointed to take over and was noted for his jokes, being dubbed the 'Laughing Hangman'. He held the post until March 1735 when he was replaced by John Thrift who reigned for nearly 18 years. Thrift had the gruesome task of hanging, drawing and quartering some of those involved in the Jacobite Rebellion between July and November 1745. Thrift succumbed to illness and died on 5 May 1752. Thomas Turlis replaced him, working for nearly 20 years until his death in April 1771 while returning home after an execution at Kingston in Surrey. His first job was to hang 12 people on Monday 4 February 1754. His most notable executions were those of Earl Ferrers and Elizabeth Brownrigg.

Edward Dennis was the official executioner for London and Middlesex from 1771 to his death in September 1786 and carried out 201 hangings at Tyburn and Newgate, plus two burnings at Newgate. Dennis hanged the Rev Dr William Dodd for forgery. On 9 December 1783, he and William Brunskill hanged nine men and one woman at the first execution outside Newgate prison. Dennis hanged 95 men and one woman between February and December of 1785, with 20 men being hanged on one day alone: Wednesday 2 February of that year. Dennis was often assisted at these marathon executions by the man who was to become his successor, William Brunskill, who went on to hang an amazing 537 people outside Newgate as principal hangman. He also executed a further 68 at Horsemonger Lane gaol in Surrey between 1800 and 1814. Brunskill carried out the last execution by burning in Britain in 1789.

Brunskill's assistant, John Langley, took over in 1814 after Brunskill suffered a stroke, hanging 37 men and 3 women, including Eliza Fenning, in his three years in office. He died in April 1817 and was succeeded in turn by his assistant, James Botting, who was known as Jemmy. Botting hanged 25 men and 2 women during his two-year tenure. In July 1820, James Foxen (also given as Foxten) assumed the position, having previously assisted Botting and hanged 206 men and 6 women over the next 11 years, including the Cato Street conspirators in 1820. Foxen was assisted by Thomas Cheshire for this high-profile execution and by an unnamed and secret person who decapitated the traitors. Foxen died on 14 February 1829. 'Old Cheese', as Cheshire was known, officiated as principal at a quadruple hanging on 24 March 1829 of three highway robbers and one man convicted of stealing in a dwelling house.

Lancashire employed its own hangman, a 'gentleman' known as Old Ned Barlow, who is reputed to have carried out around 130 hangings at Lancaster between 1782 and 1812. Edward Barlow had been condemned to death for horse theft but had his sentence commuted to 10 years' imprisonment on condition that he lived in Lancaster Castle and continued to carry out hangings and floggings. Barlow died in 1812. I have had access to the journal of the Castle's governor, John Higgin, for that period, and he records on 9 December 1812: 'Died in the castle this day Edward Barlow.' There are several sources which claim he was carrying out executions as late as 1820, but these are patently incorrect. It is unclear who succeeded Barlow, but in due course William Calcraft was to become a regular visitor to Lancaster.

Between 1802 and 1835, John (or William) Curry officiated at York hangings. He was known as 'Mutton Curry' as he had twice been convicted of sheep stealing, having had his death sentence commuted on each occasion. On the second occasion, in April 1801, he was awaiting transportation when the post of hangman became vacant and he applied for the job. He carried out around 120 executions during his 33-year reign. Curry found his job stressful and took to drinking gin to steel himself for the task. 16 January 1813 was to be Curry's busiest day with 14 men to hang. The executions were carried out in two groups, one at 11am and the other at 2pm, in what was to be York's biggest ever hanging. A 'vast concourse' of people assembled on St George's Field to see this mass 'launch into eternity'. The prisoners were Luddites who were trying to halt mechanisation of the textile industries of Yorkshire and Lancashire by violent means as this was causing widespread unemployment and destitution. Following an attempt to destroy Cartwright's textile mill at Rawfold near Brighouse in April 1812, over 100 men had been rounded up. Sixty-four were charged with a variety of offences and came before a special judicial commission at York Castle at the beginning of January 1813. Twenty-four of them were convicted and 17 sentenced to hang. The remainder were sentenced to transportation. The first of these executions was carried out on Friday 8 January when three men were executed for the murder of mill owner William Horsfall, including the Luddites' leader in Yorkshire, George Mellor, the remainder of the group being dealt with just over a week later.

On 14 April 1821, Curry was called upon to perform two executions. First he hanged highwayman Michael Shaw at York Castle and then he had to walk across town to execute William Brown for burglary at the city gaol. He was somewhat drunk by the time he got there and while waiting on the platform for the prisoner to appear, he began shaking the noose at spectators, calling out to them: 'Some of you come up and I'll try it!' When Brown appeared, Curry had to be assisted by a warder and one of the sheriff's officers. *The Times* reported on 24 April: 'The executioner, in a bungling manner and with great difficulty, being in a state of intoxication, placed the cap over the culprit's face and attempted several times to place the rope round his neck, but was unable. He missed the unfortunate man's head with the noose every time that he tried. The cap was each time removed from the malefactor's face, who stared wildly around upon the spectators.' The crowd were not amused by this and called out: 'Hang him, hang Jack Ketch.'

On 1 September 1821, Curry had to hang seven men at one time. The execution was reported by *The Yorkshire Gazette* as follows: 'On Saturday last, a few minutes before 12 o'clock, the unfortunate men were conducted from their cells to the fatal drop.' After a short time spent in prayer they were launched into eternity. None of them seemed to suffer much. However, by an unaccountable neglect of the executioner (Curry) in not keeping sufficiently clear of the drop when the bolt was pulled out, he fell into the trap along with the malefactors.'

Curry retired in 1835 and was succeeded by James Coates who was also a prisoner at York, having been sentenced to seven years' transportation for larceny at the Summer Assizes of 1835. Coates executed Charles Batty in 1836 and Thomas Williams the following year, both for attempted murder. He managed to escape from the prison around 1839 and was never heard of again. Due to the unavailability of Calcraft, who was booked for an execution at Stafford on the same day, another prisoner, Nathan Howard, took over the post in 1840 and hanged James Bradsley for the murder of his father on 11 April of that year. He went on to hang a further 14 men between then and 1853 when he bungled the hanging of murderer Henry Dobson so badly that 'when the drop fell and the rope tightened around his neck, the condemned man struggled violently' for which Howard was apparently dismissed. He was by this time old and in poor health and died six days later. There were no executions at York between April 1853 and 1856, and a new executioner had to be found to hang 28-year-old William Dove on 9 August 1856 for the murder of his wife, as Calcraft was at Dorchester that day for the execution of Elizabeth Brown. This was Thomas Askern (see later).

William Calcraft (1800–1879) from Little Baddow, near Chelmsford in Essex, was the longest serving executioner of all, working from 1829 to 1874. When he took up the job he was observed to be a respectable married man with two children who went to church on Sundays. It is not known precisely how many executions he carried out, but it is estimated at between 400 and 450, including those of at least 35 women. He was originally a shoemaker, becoming a butler in Greenwich and later a street pie seller. He sold pies at executions and was therefore able to meet the current hangman James Foxen.

Calcraft's first experience was assisting Foxen with the hangings of housebreaker Thomas Lister and highway robber George Wingfield at Lincoln on 27 March 1829. He also obtained employment flogging juvenile offenders at Newgate. Thus Calcraft was in a good position to succeed Foxen as hangman for London and Middlesex, his first job being to execute the child murderess Ester Hibner at Newgate on 13 April 1829. This was a busy year for him with no fewer than 31 hangings. He was assisted by Thomas Cheshire in some of these. Calcraft officiated at the last public hangings in England: those of Frances Kidder (the last woman) at Maidstone on 2 April 1868 and Michael Barrett outside Newgate prison on 26 May 1868. With the passing of The Capital

Punishment Within Prisons Act in 1868, Calcraft continued his trade inside prison walls, carrying out a total of 41 private hangings. He received one guinea (£1.05) a week retainer and a further guinea for each hanging at Newgate, and half a crown (12.5p) for a flogging. His earnings were greatly enhanced by executions at other prisons where he could charge higher fees, typically £10-15.

Calcraft also held the post at Surrey's Horsemonger Lane gaol and received a £5 retainer and similar fees from there. Here he hanged 24 men and 2 women between April 1829 and October 1870. He was the exclusive executioner at Maidstone prison, carrying out all 37 hangings there between 1830 and 1872. In addition to these earnings, he was also allowed to keep the clothes and personal effects of the condemned which he could sell afterwards. In the case of notorious criminals he could sell the clothes to Madame Tussauds for dressing the latest waxwork in the Chamber of Horrors. The rope which had been used at a hanging of a particularly notable criminal could also be sold for good money (up to 5 shillings or 25p an inch).

Calcraft invented the leather waist belt with wrist straps for pinioning the prisoners' arms, which must have been far less uncomfortable than the cords previously used. One of the nooses he used was on display at Lancaster Castle. It is a very short piece of ¾"-diameter rope with a loop worked into one end, with the free end of the rope passed through it and terminating in a hook with which it was attached to the chain fixed to the gallows beam. This particular noose was used for the execution of Richard Pedder on 29 August 1857. Calcraft hanged Frederick and Maria Manning at Horsemonger Lane gaol. A husband and wife being executed together was very unusual and drew the largest crowd ever recorded at a Surrey hanging. Dr Edward William Pritchard drew an even bigger crowd, estimated at around 100,000, when he was hanged at Glasgow's Jail Square on 28 July 1865 for the murders of his wife and mother-in-law.

Most of Calcraft's early work came from London and the South East, as the Midlands had George Smith and Thomas Askern operated in the North. With the rapid spread of the railway system in the mid-19th century, Calcraft was soon able to operate all over Britain and apparently loved travelling. There were 6,000 miles of railway by 1850, which meant that he could effectively and conveniently work nationwide. On 23

November 1867, Calcraft executed the Manchester Martyrs outside Salford prison, receiving the princely sum of £30 for this job. He was a regular visitor to Durham where he was to hang Britain's greatest mass murderess, Mary Ann Cotton, on 24 March 1873, probably assisted by Robert Anderson. He retired in the spring of 1874, aged 74, on a pension of 25s (£1.25) a week provided by the City of London and died on 13 December 1879 at home in Poole Street, Hoxton. The post of hangman for London and Middlesex then ceased to be a salaried position. His successors were paid a fee for each execution they carried out. It would be easy to view William Calcraft as a sadistic monster who through his use of the 'short drop' inflicted wanton cruelty on the prisoners who came his way, but in his private life he was said to be a very kind person who was fond of his children and grandchildren and his pet rabbits. One doubts that it ever occurred to him that there might be a less cruel way to hang somebody; he just kept doing what he had always done.

George Smith (1805–1874) was born in Rowley Regis in Staffordshire and was a prisoner himself at Stafford when he entered the 'trade' as an assistant to Calcraft at the double hanging of James Owen and George Thomas outside Stafford gaol on 11 April 1840. He learnt the job and was appointed by the sheriff of Staffordshire to carry out executions there, probably to save the cost of bringing Calcraft up from London. Smith's most famous solo execution was that of the 'Rugeley poisoner', Dr William Palmer, for the murder of John Parsons Cook, before a large crowd at Stafford prison on 14 June 1856. Smith was to hang a further 14 men and one woman at Stafford, two in private, the last on 13 August 1872 when he executed 34-year-old Christopher Edwards for the murder of his wife. He assisted Calcraft at the first private hanging in England. Smith was renowned for his long white coat and top hat which he wore at public hangings. His son, also George, assisted at three executions at Stafford.

Robert Anderson was a lawyer's son who had trained as a doctor but had not practised as such. He was reputed to be a man of private means who did not need the small income derived from executions and in fact gave his fee to Calcraft for the privilege of assisting him or acting as principal. 'Evans the hangman', as he was known, acted as executioner on seven occasions and as assistant on two. He carried out the treble hanging at Gloucester prison on 12 January 1874, when Mary Anne Barry, Edwin Bailey and Charles Edward Butt were executed. Anderson died in 1901.

Thomas Askern (1816–1878) was initially the hangman for Yorkshire. Askern, like all of York's hangmen up till then, was drawn from the inmate population – he was in prison for debt at the time. He also officiated at Armley prison, Leeds, from September 1864 and was responsible for four executions as well as nine at York. Askern also worked in Scotland and badly bungled the hanging of George Bryce at Edinburgh on 21 July 1864. He was to perform the last public hanging in Scotland, that of 19-year-old Robert Smith on 12 May 1868 at Dumfries for the murder of a young girl. He also hanged Priscilla Biggadyke at Lincoln in 1868, the first private female hanging. In all, he officiated at five private hangings, the last of which was that of James Dalgleish at Carlisle on 19 December 1876. Askern died in Maltby at the age of 62 on 6 December 1878.

William Marwood (1820–1883), born at Goulceby near Horncastle in Lincolnshire, was a cobbler by trade and introduced the 'long drop' method of hanging to Britain (see Chapter 14). He was duly appointed as official hangman by the sheriffs of London and Middlesex, replacing Calcraft, and received a retainer of £20 per annum plus £10 for each execution, but unlike Calcraft got no actual salary. He was still able to keep the condemned person's clothes and claim travelling expenses. His first execution at Newgate was that of Frances Stewart on 29 June 1874. The rail network was so advanced by this time that he could travel anywhere in the country with ease, thus making it possible for him to carry out the majority of executions in Britain, including Ireland. Marwood also made improvements to the noose and pinioning straps and requested improvements to the gallows, especially the removal of steps up to the platform. He found it far easier for all concerned to have the trap door level with the floor or ground.

There was a famous rhyme about Marwood at the time which went: 'If Pa killed Ma, who'd kill Pa – Marwood.' Marwood was something of a celebrity and had business cards printed: 'William Marwood Public Executioner, Horncastle, Lincolnshire', and had the words 'Marwood Crown Office' over the door of his shop. He objected to the term hangman, which he reserved for Calcraft, saying: 'He hangs them;

I execute them.' In his eleven years of service from 1874 to 1883, he hanged 181 people, including eight women, nationwide. He died of 'inflammation of the lungs' on 4 September 1883. Some of his most notable cases are described in Chapter 14. Marwood worked with George Incher on the occasions that needed two executioners, i.e. double hangings, until 1881 and then used Bartholomew Binns as an assistant until 1883 when Binns took over as 'No 1'. Marwood carried out 14 double executions, three triples and one quadruple. He worked without an assistant for most single executions, but one assumes that, if needed, the warders were able to assist him.

George Incher (also given as Meker) (1831–1897) from Dudley acted as executioner at Stafford on three occasions between 1875 and 1881: for the hangings of John Stanton, Henry Rogers and James Williams. He also assisted William Marwood at the quadruple execution of the '*Lennie* mutineers' at Newgate in May 1876.

Bartholomew Binns (c1839–1911) lived in Dewsbury in Yorkshire and was perhaps one of the least successful British hangmen, holding the job as principal only for a year, although he had assisted Marwood at executions. His first 'solo' execution was that of Henry Powell on 6 November 1883 at Wandsworth prison. He carried out 11 hangings as principal and assisted at seven. His last job was the hanging of 18-year-old Michael McLean at Walton prison on 10 March 1884. He was seen to be in a drunken state and the execution was deemed unsatisfactory. After a formal complaint about the botched execution and his drunken behaviour, Binns was removed from the Home Office List of hangmen. However, he later assisted Tommy Scott on several occasions in 1900/01 (see Chapter 15 for more details).

James Berry (1852–1913) from Heckmondwike in Yorkshire carried out 130 hangings in eight years from 1884 to 1891, including those of five women. Prior to becoming an executioner he had been a policeman in Bradford and had met Marwood and become acquainted with his methods. Like Marwood he had never assisted at an execution. He was the first British executioner to write his memoirs, *My Experiences as an Executioner*, which is still available. He was, again like Marwood, proud of his calling and both had their own waxworks in Madame Tussauds. His years in office were not without event, as noted in Chapter 15.

After Berry resigned, the Home Office maintained a list of executioners and assistants. Any form of misbehaviour or poor performance would result in the person being removed from the list. It was normal after a person successfully completed their training at Newgate or, after 1903, at Pentonville prison, for them to be added to the list and to initially work as an assistant until, in some cases, being allowed to carry out executions themselves. What is not generally known in the 20th century is that the person selected from the list received a written invitation to carry out a particular execution. They were not in any way compelled to accept it, although if they declined, their name could be removed from the list.

Thomas Henry Scott from Huddersfield acted as executioner on 17 occasions between 1892 and 1895. His last job was the hanging of Elijah Winstanley on 17 December 1895 at Walton prison. Leaving the gaol, he got into a cab with a prostitute and was robbed. He was said to be drunk at the time and was therefore removed from the list. However, he managed to continue as executioner in Ireland until 1901 when the authorities discovered that he had been sacked in England.

James Billington (1847–1901) of Farnworth near Bolton in Lancashire was the first member of what was to become a family dynasty. He ran a barber's shop and was on the official list from 1884 to 1901. Billington had a lifelong fascination with hanging and had unsuccessfully applied for Marwood's post, but managed to secure the Yorkshire hangman's position after Askern retired. He succeeded Berry as the executioner for London and Middlesex in 1892. Billington's first execution was at Armley prison in Leeds on 26 August 1884 when he hanged Joseph Laycock. This execution was judged to be successful and he went on to complete a further 150 executions, including 24 men and 3 women at Newgate prison. His final hanging was that of Patrick McKenna at Strangeways on 3 December 1901. Billington died ten days later of bronchitis and was succeeded by his two sons, William and John, who had assisted him on many occasions. Details of his more interesting cases can be found in Chapter 16.

Billington's eldest son, Thomas, (1873–1902) assisted his father and brother, William, at 20 hangings, before dying of pneumonia, aged 29. He was on the Home Office List from 1897 to 1901, but worked only as an assistant. The second of James Billington's sons, William (1875–1934), took over from his father and was assisted by his younger brother John. William was to carry out 68 executions as principal and assisted at a further 20 carrying out Newgate's last execution, that of George Woolfe on 2 May 1902. He also carried out the first hangings at Holloway prison on 3 February 1903. Assisted by Henry Pierrepoint, William carried out the first hanging at Pentonville on 30 September 1902 when they executed John MacDonald who had stabbed Henry Greaves to death. William was on the Home Office List from 1902 to 1905. John Billington (1880–1905) was also on the Home Office's approved list of executioners from 1901 to 1905 and assisted at 28 executions, carrying out 16 hangings as principal. He hanged John Thomas Kay on 16 August 1904 at Armley prison in Leeds while his brother was dealing with Samuel Holden at Winson Green prison in Birmingham on the same day.

Another and far better known dynasty of executioners was the Pierrepoint family. Between them, three members of this family executed some 830 people in eight countries over a 55-year period. The first member of it to take up the role was Henry Albert Pierrepoint (1878–1922) who was from Bradford in Yorkshire and was on the Home Office List from 1901 to 1910. Henry assisted at 30 hangings and carried out 75 executions himself in nine years. He took great pride in his work and calculated the drops most carefully. It is said that he never had a single bungled hanging. His first job was at Newgate, assisting James Billington with the execution of Marcel Fougeron on 19 November 1901. He was judged a success and between January 1902 and March 1903 he assisted at a further 15 hangings. His first lead role was to be the hanging of Richard Wigley at Shrewsbury on Tuesday 18 March 1902. Wigley had murdered his girlfriend. Henry, assisted by his brother Tom, hanged Rhoda Willis at Cardiff on 14 August 1907. Files recently released by the National Archives show that Henry Pierrepoint was sacked because he arrived for the execution of Frederick Foreman at Chelmsford in July 1910 'considerably the worse for drink' and had got into a fight with his assistant, John Ellis.

John Ellis (1874–1932) from Rochdale in Lancashire was a notably mild-mannered man who ultimately committed suicide, possibly through the stresses incurred by his job as hangman or possibly through the effects of the slump on his business as a barber. He had a particular dislike of hanging women. He was on the Home Office List from 1901 to 1923 and assisted at 46 executions, hanging a further 156 persons as principal, including several famous criminals. Notable among these was Herbert Rowse Armstrong who he hanged on 31 May 1922 at Gloucester prison for the murder by arsenic poisoning of his wife. There is now some doubt over Armstrong's guilt, new evidence having been unearthed by a present-day solicitor who acquired Armstrong's practice in Hay-on-Wye who works in his old office and even bought his house.

Dr Crippen was perhaps the most famous criminal to come Ellis' way, another being George Smith, the famous 'Brides in the Bath' murderer and a third being Sir Roger Casement. (See Chapter 17 for details of these three cases.) John Ellis carried out his final execution on 28 December 1923 when he hanged John Eastwood at Armley prison in Leeds for the murder of his wife. In March of 1924, he tendered his resignation due to poor health. Before his suicide on 20 September 1932, Ellis wrote his memoirs, *Diary of a Hangman*, which is still available.

William Willis (c1876–1939) from Accrington was on the Home Office List between 1906 and 1926 and assisted at 99 executions, helping Ellis, Henry and Tom Pierrepoint and Robert Baxter before undertaking 14 as 'No 1', including a series of six at Manchester's Strangeways prison between 1924 and 1926. While Ellis was hanging Edith Thompson, Willis was executing Frederick Edward Bywaters at Pentonville prison. Willis was sacked after he was seen to be drunk and aggressive at the hanging of Johannes Mommers at Pentonville on 27 July 1926.

Thomas William Pierrepoint (1870–1954) was on the Home Office List for 40 years from 1906. He was eight years older than his brother Henry and carried on working into his mid-seventies. Thomas assisted at 36 executions and carried out 201 civilian hangings in England and Wales. He is thought to have officiated at around 300 hangings in total. Thomas was the official executioner for Eire after the establishment of the Irish Free State and carried out 24 executions at Dublin's Mountjoy prison between 1923 and 1944. He was also appointed as executioner by the US Military and was responsible for the hangings of US servicemen at Shepton Mallet prison during World War 2, assisted by his nephew Albert. Among his better known cases are Ethel Lillie Major and nurse Dorothea Waddingham, Buck Ruxton and Charlotte Bryant (see Chapter

18). On 10 March 1931, Pierrepoint executed Alfred Arthur Rouse at Bedford prison for the murder of an unknown man. Rouse had killed the man and then put him in his (Rouse's) car and set it ablaze in an attempt to fake his own death for the insurance money.

Robert Wilson from Manchester was on the Home Office List between 1920 and 1936 and assisted at 47 executions. Robert Orridge Baxter (1877–1961) from Hertford carried out 44 executions as principal and assisted at 53 between 1915 and 1935. Assisted by William Willis and Thomas Phillips, he dealt with Jean-Pierre Vaquier at Wandsworth on 12 August 1924 for the strychnine poisoning of his lover's husband. He also hanged Frederick Guy Browne for his part in PC Gutteridge's murder at Pentonville prison. At the same moment his co-defendant, William Henry Kennedy was being hanged at Wandsworth.

Alfred Allen from Wolverhampton assisted at 14 hangings and acted as chief executioner at three more between 1932 and 1937. He was not related to Harry Allen. Thomas Mather Phillips (1899–1941) from Farnworth near Bolton in Lancashire acted as chief executioner on two occasions at Wandsworth in 1939 and 1940, having previously assisted at 51 hangings. Stanley William Cross from Fulham in London remained on the Home Office List from 1932 to 1941. He assisted at 20 executions and acted as chief executioner on four occasions. His most notable execution was the hanging of Udam Singh at Pentonville on 31 July 1940. He was also responsible for the executions of two German spies, Jose Waldeburg and Carl Meier, at Pentonville on 10 December 1940.

Albert Pierrepoint (1905–1992) came from Clayton, near Bradford in Yorkshire, and was by far the most prolific hangman of the 20th century, having executed an estimated 417 men and 17 women in his 24 years of service in this country and abroad. His tally of executions was greatly increased as a result of World War 2, working in the UK, Germany, Gibraltar and Austria, plus officiating at three British military hangings in Egypt in 1950. In England and Wales Albert assisted at 29 hangings and carried out 138 civilian executions for murder as principal, including those of the last four women to hang. Albert was to execute 14 men convicted of espionage and treason during and immediately after World War 2, including John Amery and 'Lord Haw-Haw'. Albert hanged 190 men and 10 women war criminals at Hameln prison in the British controlled sector of Germany after the war. He also hanged eight men at Karlou in Austria in 1946, and trained Austrian hangmen in the British method of hanging.

His first experience of the family 'trade' was assisting his uncle Tom in the hanging of Patrick McDermott at Mountjoy prison in Dublin on 29 December 1932. His first job in England was as second assistant (in reality, observer), again with his uncle Tom and Robert Wilson, at the execution of Jeremiah Hanbury at Winson Green prison in Birmingham on 2 February 1933. As 'No 1' his first job was that of gangster, Antonio 'Babe' Mancini, at Pentonville prison on 31 October 1941. Albert took over from his uncle as the hangman for the Irish Republic and carried out the last four executions up to 1954 when Michael Manning became the last person to be executed in Eire.

Pierrepoint resigned over a disagreement about fees in 1956. He had driven to Strangeways on a bitterly cold day in January 1956 to hang Thomas Bancroft. He arrived at the prison only for Bancroft to be reprieved later in the afternoon. He claimed the full fee of £15, but was offered just £1 in out-of-pocket expenses by the under sheriff of Lancashire. Pierrepoint appealed to his employers, the Prison Commission, who declined to get involved. The under sheriff sent him a cheque for £4 in final settlement. But to Albert this was a huge insult to his pride in his position as Britain's 'Chief Executioner' so he tendered his resignation. Albert died in a nursing home in Southport, Lancashire, on 10 July 1992 at the age of 87. His autobiography, *Executioner – Pierrepoint*, is still available.

Henry (Harry) Kirk (1893–1967) from Huntingdon worked as an assistant to Stanley Cross and Tom and Albert Pierrepoint on 47 occasions between 1941 and 1950. He had a very short career as a principal hangman. When he executed Norman Goldthorpe at Norwich on 24 November 1950 for the murder of 66-year-old Emma Howe at Yarmouth, snorting sounds were heard coming from the prisoner. This was apparently due to the hood becoming stuck in the eyelet of the noose. This would be Kirk's first and last hanging as principal.

After Albert Pierrepoint's resignation, Steve Wade and Harry Allen (see below) took over as joint 'No 1s'. Steve Wade was another man who always wanted to be an executioner, having first applied when he came out of the army at the end of World War 1 in 1918, then aged 21. His application was rejected due to his age, but he kept trying and finally made it in 1940. His first job came a year later, assisting Albert Pierrepoint with the hanging of Antonio Mancini. After the war he worked at a coach dealership in Doncaster. Having assisted both Tom and Albert Pierrepoint, he was finally allowed to be the 'No 1' at the execution of Arthur Charles at Durham on 26 March 1946. He was generally selected by the sheriff of Yorkshire for hangings at Armley prison, Leeds, from 1947 onwards. In his autobiography, Albert Pierrepoint spoke highly of Steve Wade and always found him reliable. Wade's last job, assisted by Robert Leslie Stewart, was the execution of Alec Wilkinson on 12 August 1955 at Armley jail. He resigned due to failing health in late 1955 and died in December the following year, aged 59. In all, he had carried out 29 hangings as principal and assisted at 18 others during the period 1941-1955.

Harry Bernard Allen was born on 5 November 1911 at Denaby in Yorkshire but was brought up in Ashton-under-Lyne in Lancashire. He got his first job as an assistant at Strangeways in 1940, under Tom Pierrepoint, for the hanging of Clifford Holmes. Harry and Steve Wade assisted Albert Pierrepoint at the execution of five German prisoners of war at Pentonville on 6 October 1945. Harry Allen always wore a black bow tie at executions and two of these were sold in November 2008 along with other items including his diary for £17,200. Like Albert, Harry Allen was also a publican, keeping a pub called the Rope and Anchor in Farnworth on the outskirts of Bolton. He later took over the Junction Hotel at Whitefield in Manchester.

Robert Leslie Stewart (1918–1989) was born in Edinburgh and assisted Albert Pierrepoint and Steve Wade in 20 executions between 1952 and 1959. His first recorded job was as an assistant to Albert Pierrepoint at the hanging of Alfred Bradley at Strangeways prison, Manchester, on 15 January 1952. In 1958, he was selected as principal and officiated at the execution of Vivian Frederick Teed at Swansea on 6 May. He was to hang a further five men before abolition and was on the final list of executioners issued by the Home Office in February 1964. Stewart carried out the last hanging at Glasgow's Barlinnie prison, that of 19-year-old Anthony Joseph Miller, on 22 December 1960. Miller had been convicted of the robbery murder of John Cremin in a Glasgow park. Stewart shared the distinction of carrying out one of the two last hangings in Britain. He dealt with Peter Anthony Allen at Walton prison, Liverpool.

Assistant executioners

It was normal in 20th century hangings for there to be an assistant executioner, but on at least five occasions in the early part of the century no assistant was employed. From 1892, an assistant could be employed under Home Office rules. The assistant had four roles to play. One was to assist in setting up and testing the drop, the second was to strap the prisoner's legs on the gallows and the third was to assist in taking down the body and preparing it for autopsy. Finally he had to able to take over in case the hangman fainted or became ill at the last moment.

In addition to those listed above who became executioners themselves having risen through the ranks, there were a further 21 men who were only ever assistants and never acted as principal (see below). Amongst the better known of these was Sydney Dernley (1920–1994) from Mansfield, Nottinghamshire, who assisted at 19 executions in England and Wales between 1950 and 1952, and also wrote a book called *The Hangman's Tale* detailing his experiences. Dernley's name was removed from the list in April 1954 following a conviction and six-month prison sentence for publishing obscene material.

A less well-known name is that of Royston Lawrence Rickard who assisted at 13 executions between 1953 and 1964, including those of Ruth Ellis and James Hanratty, and also at one of the two final British hangings, that of Peter Anthony Allen. The assistant at the other execution on that day, that of Gwynne Owen Evans, was Harry Robinson. The final Home Office List was issued in February 1964, comprising Robert Leslie Stewart and Harry Allen as principals, with Royston Rickard, Harry Robinson, Samuel Plant and John Underhill as assistants.

Below is a list of those who acted only as assistants in the 20th century, with dates of service and number of executions attended.

Thomas Billington 1900–1901 1
Alexander Riley 1940–1946 7
William Warbrick ....1900..............................6

Henry Critchell	1940–1948	19
Henry Pollard	1901–1906	3
Syd Dernley	1950–1952	19
William Conduit	1911	30
Harry Smith	1951–1958	15
Albert Lumb	1911–1913	2
John Broadbent	1953–1954	5
George Brown	1911–1919	11
Royston Rickard	1953–1964	13
Edward Taylor	1915–1925	20
Thomas Cunliffe	1958–1959	4
Seth Mills	1921–1923	27
Harry Robinson	1958–1964	6
Lionel Mann	1926–1930	6
Samuel Plant	1960–1964	3
Frank Rowe	1928	10
John Underhill	1960–1964	3
Herbert Morris	1939–1946	19
No assistant used		5

The post of hangman became much sought after in the mid-19th century and remained so until capital punishment was abolished. There were always large numbers of applicants, including women, writing to the Home Office. When a person applied for the job they were subjected to a police check and if this was satisfactory they would be given an interview with a local prison governor. If they passed this they had to take a medical and then would be given a week's training at Pentonville prison on all aspects of the job. A dummy was used as the condemned prisoner and the candidates would go over and over the process of calculating the drop and carrying out the execution until they were totally proficient. 'Hood, noose, pin, lever' was the maxim of the trainer at Pentonville in the 1930s, according to Albert Pierrepoint.

At the end of the training, applicants could be added to the list if they were deemed satisfactory. Merely being on the list did not automatically mean that they would be chosen by the sheriffs. Normally they would attend an execution or two as second assistant to observe the proceedings and for the governor to observe them and their reaction to the hanging. Not everyone could cope with the reality of the process. Successful candidates had to sign the Official Secrets Act and were not permitted to divulge any details of what occurred in the execution chamber, especially to the press.

The Home Office List in 1938 contained the names of seven men who were 'competent to carry out the duties'. They were apparently ordinary, stable, married men who worked in normal occupations. Reliability and stability were seen as the key requirements. Hangmen were paid a fee for each execution they carried out, these fees remaining static at £10 for the hangman and 3 guineas (£3.15) for the assistant from the 1880s to the late 1940s when the fee for the principal was increased to £15. The cost of rail travel was also reimbursed. The fees were paid half at the time and half two weeks later. It is therefore reasonable to suppose that most of those who held the post of executioner did it not for financial gain but for other, more personal, reasons.

Setting the drop correctly was a somewhat involved process in the 20th century. The length of drop was calculated from the drop table based upon the person's weight in their clothes combined with the hangman's experience and his direct observation of the prisoner. A line was painted on the noose end of the rope marking the point where the internal circumference was 18 inches (457 mm) which was deemed to be equivalent to the circumference of the neck plus the distance from the eyelet to the top of the head after the drop. The 18-inch figure allowed for the subsequent constriction of the neck. From the painted line the hangman measured along the rope and tied a piece of thread at the calculated drop distance. The rope was then attached to the 'D' shackle at the end of the chain hanging down from the beam. The chain was adjusted so that the thread mark was at the same height as the top of the prisoner's head. A sandbag of approximately the same weight as the prisoner was now attached to the noose and dropped through the trap and left hanging overnight to remove any stretch from the rope. The following morning it was removed, the trap doors reset and the rope readjusted to get the thread mark back to the correct height.

The Home Office issued the following instructions to executioners in the 1930s for the correct setting up of the drop:

> 'Obtain a rope from Execution Box B making sure that the Gutta Percha covering the splice at each end is uncracked by previous use. Find the required drop from the Official Table of Drops making allowance for age and physique. At the noose end of the rope measure thirteen inches (allowance for the neck) from the centre of the brass eye, mark this by tying round the rope a piece of pack-thread from Execution Box B. From this mark measure along the rope the exact drop required (this must be to the nearest quarter inch), mark again by a piece of pack-thread tied to the rope. Fasten the rope by pin and tackle to the chain suspended from the beams above, and, using the adjusting bracket above so adjust the rope that the mark showing the drop is exactly in accordance with the height of the condemned man. Take a piece of copper wire from Execution Box B, secure one end over the shackle on the end of the chain, and bend up the other end to coincide with the mark showing the drop. Put on the trap the sandbag, making sure it is filled with sand of an equivalent weight to the condemned man. Put the noose around the neck of the sandbag and drop the bag in the presence of the governor. The bag is left hanging until two hours before the time of execution the next morning. At this time examine the mark on the rope and copper wire to see how much the rope has stretched. Any stretch must be made good by adjusting the drop. Lift the sandbag, pull up the trap door by means of chains and pulley blocks, set the operating lever and put in the three-quarter safety pin which goes through the lever brackets to prevent the lever being accidentally moved. Coil the rope ready and tie the coil with pack-thread leaving the noose suspended at the height of the condemned man's chest. All is now ready.'

Hang-women

Ireland allowed women to be involved with executions and two were. It is reputed that in 1780 a middle-aged woman from County Kerry called Elizabeth Dolan or McDermott was sentenced to death at Roscommon for the murder of her son. The town's hangman did not turn up for the execution of Elizabeth and her 24 fellow condemned prisoners who were members of the 'White Boys', so Elizabeth told the sheriff: 'Spare me, yer Honour, spare me and I'll hang them all.' As in law he would have had to have performed the task himself if no one else could be found, the sheriff agreed. Elizabeth executed her fellow criminals and was appointed Roscommon's hang-woman and given a room of her own in the gaol. She is thought to have operated there from about 1780 until her death in 1807. Her own death sentence was commuted in 1802.

As was normal throughout the British Isles at the time, executions moved from a place outside the town to the gaol itself which was in a large square in the town. The new gallows consisted of a hinged lap board for the prisoners to stand on, set under an iron bar attached to the prison wall outside her third floor window. When the prisoner was prepared, the board was released from inside the prison by withdrawing the bolt, allowing them a short drop. Similar arrangements were used elsewhere, e.g. Kilmainham gaol in Dublin. Elizabeth became known as 'Lady Betty' and allegedly drew charcoal sketches of her victims. Her name was used by parents to frighten their misbehaving children. Perhaps the most unusual assistant executioner was Tom Kellett's. Kellett operated in Ireland circa 1829 as hangman for the North West Circuit and married a 16-year-old girl who took on the job.

25

The roles of the officials in post-1868 executions

In previous chapters the roles of the judges, Home Office and the hangmen have been discussed. Once a person had been sentenced to death they were normally returned to the prison they had been previously remanded to or later sent to a prison with the requisite facilities. The passing of a death sentence involved various officials and it is worth examining their individual roles after 1868.

Each county had a high sheriff who was appointed for a year and who had the responsibility amongst other things of carrying out death sentences ordered by the courts. It was his responsibility to select and pay the hangman and later the assistant(s) from the Home Office List. He would typically contact the chosen hangman and assistant by letter, once notified of a death sentence. The sheriff had to proceed on the basis that the sentence would be carried out, irrespective of the fact that there may be a reprieve, even at the last minute. He or the under sheriff had to be present at the execution and afterwards notify the Home Secretary that the sentence of death had been executed.

The governor of the prison had responsibility for the security of the prisoner between sentence and execution and for preventing their suicide. He would select teams of two or three warders for the 'death watch' who would guard the prisoner in three eight-hour shifts. It was the governor's painful duty to tell the person that there had not been a reprieve and thus the execution was to take place on such and such a day. He also had to be present at the hanging and not all governors found this an easy task. The governor was responsible for ensuring that the gallows was set up in an appropriate place and that the execution was carried out in an efficient and humane manner. He would ask for two or more volunteer prison officers to escort the prisoner to the gallows and support them on it. These warders received extra payment for this duty and for helping with the subsequent burial. After the hanging, the governor would send a report to the Home Office as to the conduct of the executioner and his assistant(s). This report also had to be signed by the prison doctor.

The 'death watch' officers did their best to look after the prisoner and could engage them in conversation, card games or play dominoes with them. During conversations they were expected to record in a day book anything of interest the condemned person said. The prisoner was permitted both a small amount of alcohol and tobacco. The warders would be of the same sex as the prisoner. Female staff were not expected to accompany their charges to the gallows in the 20th century, male officers being brought in for this duty, but where a woman was being hanged, a female governor or assistant governor had to be present.

The Capital Punishment (Amendment) Act of 1868 required that the prison doctor attend the hanging, examine the body of the inmate after execution to determine death had occurred and then sign a certificate to that effect. He would look after the prisoner's physical well-being up to the time of execution and could also have a say on the length of drop to be given to a particular inmate. He might prescribe them a special diet in the condemned cell and also a glass of brandy immediately before the hanging.

Certainly by the 16th century it was normal for the church to play a part in executions. It was the practice, at least from the 18th century, that when a person was sentenced to death, the judge would finish the sentence with the words: 'May the Lord have mercy upon your soul', to which the chaplain would add: 'Amen'.

Whereas the prison doctor looked after the prisoner's physical health, it was for the chaplain to look after their spiritual health and prepare them to meet their maker. Confession and repentance were seen as vitally important for their spiritual well-being in the next world, as they could still go to Heaven if they genuinely repented. The prison chaplain would spend considerable time ministering to the condemned and in earlier times try to extract a confession. Religious tracts were often sent to prisoners by well-meaning people in the 19th century.

Old drawings of 19th century executions would often show a robed chaplain reading from a prayer book. They would read the words of the burial service during the procession to the gallows and continue to pray with the prisoners until the drop fell. In the 20th century, the prisoner could request a minister of their own religion to visit them in the condemned cell and pray with them and also to be present at the execution. The priest's words were often the only ones spoken during a modern British hanging. The executioner and officials typically remained silent on the gallows and the prisoner was not invited to speak.

Up to the 1950s, the Anglican Church largely supported capital punishment and saw a role for itself in the administration of it. It was not unusual for the prisoner to take up religion in their last weeks on this earth, and it is clear that many prisoners valued the support of a priest through their ordeal, as someone who was 'on their side'. Charlotte Bryant was said to be much comforted by the ministrations of Father Barney during her period in Exeter's condemned cell in 1936. Some prisoners asked for a cross to be placed in the execution chamber where they could see it. As mentioned earlier, Styllou Christofi asked for one when she was hanged at Holloway in 1954, and this was still present the following year when Ruth Ellis was executed, along with the one she had requested.

Epilogue

Within this book I have attempted to chart the use, development and decline of capital punishment in Britain over 1500 years, together with the laws that governed its implementation. We see it being used very sparingly in early times, being abolished altogether then used increasingly in the 18th century when the death sentence was passed for every felony. Finally common sense and reason prevailed in the early 19th century and only murderers were executed from 1861, a situation that would continue into the middle of the 20th century until Britain finally abolished capital punishment.

Alongside these changes we see the evolution of execution methods from hanging, beheading and drowning, through methods that deliberately inflicted maximum pain such as burning and boiling alive, hanging with disembowelling and quartering, before returning to hanging as the universal civilian method from 1790 onwards. Executions were for the majority of the period a public spectacle enjoyed by all, before retreating behind prison walls and later into total secrecy and final oblivion.

One person who deserves special mention is the village cobbler from Essex who single-handedly introduced the concept of a humane death by hanging that came to be adopted in Britain, its colonies and by other countries throughout the world. This man was William Marwood. One wonders whether he could have realised the significance of his work at the time. As we passed into the 20th century, his methods were continuously refined until execution by hanging became arguably the least cruel form of capital punishment.

It was to take the abolitionists over 150 years to finally abolish the death penalty in Britain, slicing away, bit by bit in the face of an intransigent system. Perhaps it was the intransigence of the system that finally allowed them to succeed. I have never personally been in favour of mandatory sentencing policies that do not distinguish between degrees of guilt, and yet this was in effect what we always had despite repeated suggestions of introducing degrees of murder with proportionate punishments as in the USA. These sentencing policies, combined with poor administration of capital punishment by the Home Office, led to obvious injustice and fuelled the abolitionist cause.

So in 1964 capital punishment came to an end, despite the views of the majority. Writing now, 45 years later, I am amazed that the death penalty is still such a live issue. There is a majority in favour of the death penalty and it is supported by young people, as witness the number of pro-death penalty groups on the social networking site Facebook and visitors to my website seeking information for school projects. Yet these are people who have never known a British execution.

Why is this? Why is the phrase 'Broken Britain' in common usage now? We have seen a steady and continuing rise in homicides (the government refuses to break down the figures into murder and non-murder) over the last 45 years. Not only has the murder rate risen, but as a crime, it has changed in character. At the beginning of the 20th century it was largely a domestic crime where friction in relationships built up and finally exploded into violence, as divorce was difficult to obtain and was an emotionally and financially scarring process. Murder is now seen as an almost random crime that anyone can be the victim of. Since it has become effectively impossible to own a firearm legally in Britain, the knife and broken bottle have replaced the gun as the weapons of choice. Stabbings are commonplace as is the beating and kicking to death of anyone who dares to reprimand or get in the way of people who are often high on drink or drugs.

Against this backdrop it is hardly surprising that many people would like the death penalty reinstated and to see what they deem to be justice done. However, living as we do under a European Union version of democracy there is no chance of this happening.

English and Welsh Executions

1900–1931

Name	Age	Date	Place	Victim(s)
1900				
Louisa Masset (f)	33	9 January	Newgate	Manfred Louis Masset (son)
Ada Chard-Williams (f)	24	6 March	Newgate	Selina Ellen Jones
Henry Grove	26	22 May	Newgate	Henry Smith
Alfred Highfield	22	17 July	Newgate	Edith Margaret Poole (girlfriend)
William Irwin	61	14 August	Newgate	Catherine Amelia Irwin (wife)
Charles Backhouse	23	16 August	Leeds	PC John William Kew
Thomas Mellor	29	16 August	Leeds	Ada & Annie Beecroft (daughters)
William Lacey	29	21 August	Cardiff	Pauline Lacey (wife)
Charles Blewitt	33	28 August	Leeds	Mary Ann Blewitt (wife)
John Charles Parr	19	2 October	Newgate	Sarah Willett (girlfriend)
William Burrett	35	3 October	Chelmsford	Ada Gubb Burrett (wife)
Joseph Holden	57	4 December	Manchester	John Dawes (grandson)
John Bowes	50	12 December	Durham	Isabella Bowes (wife)
James Bergin	26	27 December	Liverpool	Margaret Morrison (girlfriend)
Total: 14 (12 + 2)				
1901				
Samson Salmon	32	19 February	Newgate	Lucy Smith (cousin)
George Parker (Hill)	23	19 March	Wandsworth	William Pearson
Herbert Bennett	22	21 March	Norwich	Mary Jane Bennett (wife)
Joseph Shufflebotham	38	2 April	Stafford	Elizabeth Shufflebotham (wife)
Valeri Giovanni	31	9 July	Bodmin	Victor Baileff
Charles Watkins	54	30 July	Maidstone	Frederick Hamilton
Ernest Wickham	30	13 August	Wandsworth	Amy Eugenie Russell (girlfriend)
John Joyce	36	20 August	Birmingham	John Nugent
Marcel Fougeron	23	19 November	Newgate	Hermann Francis Jung
Patrick McKenna	53	3 December	Manchester	Anna McKenna (wife)
John Miller &	67	7 December	Newcastle	John Ferguson
John Robert Miller	31			

John Thompson	38	10 December	Durham	Maggie Ann Lieutand (girlfriend)
Alexander Claydon	43	13 December	Northampton	Louisa Claydon (wife)
John Harrison	31	24 December	Liverpool	Alice Ann Wright (girlfriend)

Total: 15

1902

Harold Amos Apted	20	18 March	Maidstone	Frances Eliza O'Rourke
Richard Wigley	34	18 March	Shrewsbury	Mary Ellen Bowen (girlfriend)
Arthur Richardson	30	25 March	Hull	Sarah Hebden (aunt)
Charles Robert Earl	56	29 April	Wandsworth	Margaret Pamphilon
George Woolfe	21	6 May	Newgate (last)	Charlotte Cheeseman (girlfriend)
Thomas Marsland	21	20 May	Liverpool	Elizabeth Marsland (wife)
Samuel Middleton	46	15 July	Worcester	Hannah Middleton (wife)
William Churcher	35	22 July	Winchester	Sophia Jane Hepworth (girlfriend)
John Bedford	41	30 July	Derby	Nancy Price (girlfriend)
William Lane	47	12 August	Stafford	Elizabeth Dyson (girlfriend)
George Hibbs	40	13 August	Wandsworth	Miriam Jane Tye
John MacDonald	24	30 September	Pentonville	Henry Groves
Henry Williams	31	11 November	Pentonville	Margaret Anne Andrew (daughter)
Henry McWiggins	30	2 December	Manchester	Esther Elizabeth Bedford (girlfriend)
William Chambers	47	4 December	Bedford	Emily Chambers (wife), Mary Oakley (mother-in-law)
Thomas Barrow	49	9 December	Pentonville	Emily Coates (step-daughter/girlfriend)
Jeremiah Callaghan	42	12 December	Usk	Hannah Shea (girlfriend)
Samuel Walton	31	16 December	Durham	Isabella Walton (wife), Nora Walton (daughter), Mrs Young (mother-in-law)
Thomas Nicholson	24	16 December	Durham	Mary Ina Stewart
William Brown	42	16 December	Wandsworth	Elizabeth Brown (wife)
William Bolton	44	23 December	Hull	Jane Elizabeth Allen (girlfriend)

George Place	28	30 December	Warwick	Eliza Chetwynd, Eliza Chetwynd, (mother & daughter) unnamed child by Eliza

Total: 22

1903

Amelia Sach & Annie Walters (f)	29 54	3 February	Holloway (first at Holloway)	Male baby called Galley (baby farmers)
William Hughes	42	17 February	Ruthin	Jane Hannah Hughes (wife)
Edgar Owen	44	3 March	Wandsworth	John William Darby, Beatrice Darby & Ethel Darby
Samuel Henry Smith	45	10 March	Lincoln	Lucy Margaret Lingard (girlfriend)
George Chapman	37	7 April	Wandsworth	Isabella Mary Spink, Elizabeth Taylor, Maud Eliza Marsh (girlfriends)
William Hudson	26	12 May	Manchester	Harry Short
Gustav Rau & Willem Schmidt		2 June	Liverpool	Alexander MacLeod, Julius Herrson, Patrick Durran, Fred Abrahamson, Captain Alexander Shaw, Gustav Johansen, Alexander Bravo
JCharles Howell	30	7 July	Chelmsford	Maud Luen (girlfriend)
Samuel Dougal	57	14 July	Chelmsford	Camille Cecile Holland (girlfriend)
Thomas Porter & Thomas Preston	29 24	21 July	Leicester	PC William Ariel Wilkinson
Leonard Pachett	26	28 July	Lincoln	Sarah Ann Pachett (wife)
William Tuffen	23	11 August	Wandsworth	Caroline Tuffen (wife)
Charles Slowe	28	10 November	Pentonville	Martha Jane Hardwick
Edward Palmer	24	17 November	Devizes	Esther Swinford (ex-girlfriend)
Bernard White	21	1 December	Chelmsford	Maud Garrett (ex-girlfriend)
Charles Whittaker	43	2 December	Manchester	Eliza Range (girlfriend)
James Duffy	46	8 December	Durham	Ellen Newman (girlfriend)
William Haywood	61	15 December	Hereford	Jane Haywood (wife)
William Brown & Thomas Cowdrey	27 36	16 December	Winchester	Esther Atkins

Charles Ashton	19	22 December	Hull	Annie Marshall
John Gallagher &	30	29 December	Leeds	William Swann
Emily Swann (f)	42			(Emily's husband)
Henry Bertram Starr	31	29 December	Liverpool	Mary Hannah Starr (wife)
Total: 27 (24 + 3)				
1904				
Sidney George Smith	23	9 March	Gloucester	Alice Woodman (girlfriend)
James Clarkson	19	29 March	Leeds	Elizabeth Mary
Lynas Henry Jones	50	29 March	Stafford	Mary Elizabeth Gilbert (girlfriend)
Charles Samuel Dyer	25	5 April	Birmingham	Martha Eliza Simpson (girlfriend)
William Kirwan	39	31 May	Liverpool	Mary Pike (sister-in-law)
Ping Lun	43	31 May	Liverpool	John Go Hing
John Sullivan	40	12 July	Pentonville	Dennis Lowthian
Samuel Rowledge	37	13 July	Northampton	Alice Foster (girlfriend)
George Breeze	21	2 August	Durham	Margaret Jane Chisholm (girlfriend)
John Thomas Kay	52	16 August	Leeds	Jane Hirst (girlfriend)
Samuel Holden	43	16 August	Birmingham	Susan Humphries (girlfriend)
Joseph Potter &	35	13 December	Pentonville	Matilda Emily Farmer
Charles Wade	22			
Edmund Hall	49	20 December	Leeds	John Dalby (father-in-law)
Eric Lange	30	21 December	Cardiff	John Emlyn Jones
Arthur Jeffries	44	29 December	Leeds	Samuel Barker
Total: 16				
1905				
Edward Harrison	62	28 February	Wandsworth	Elizabeth Jane Rickus (daughter)
John Hutchinson	29	29 March	Nottingham	Albert Matthews
Alfred Bridgeman	22	26 April	Pentonville	Catherina Balhard
Alfred Stratton &	22	23 May	Wandsworth	Thomas Farrow,
Albert Ernest Stratton	20			Ann Farrow
Alfred John Heal	22	20 June	Wandsworth	Ellen Maria Goodspeed (girlfriend)
Ferat Ben Ali	19	1 August	Maidstone	Hadjou Idder

William Hancocks	35	9 August	Knutsford	Mary Elizabeth Hancocks (daughter)
Arthur Devereux		15 August	Pentonville	Beatrice Devereux (wife), Laurence, Rowland Devereux, Evelyn Lancelot Devereux (sons)
Thomas Tattersall	31	15 August	Leeds	Rebecca Tattersall (wife)
George Butler	50	7 November	Pentonville	Mary Allen (girlfriend)
William Yarnold	48	5 December	Worcester	Annie Yarnold (wife)
Henry Perkins	40	6 December	Newcastle	Patrick Durkin
Samuel Curtis	60	20 December	Maidstone	Alice Clover (girlfriend)
Frederick Edge	23	27 December	Stafford	Francis Walter Evans
George Smith	50	28 December	Leeds	Martha Smith (wife)
John Silk	30	29 December	Derby	Mary Fallon (mother)
Total: 17				

1906

Jack Griffiths	19	27 February	Manchester	Catherine Garrity (ex-girlfriend)
Harold Walters	39	10 April	Wakefield	Sarah Ann McConnell (girlfriend)
Edward Glynn	26	7 August	Nottingham	Jane Gamble (ex-girlfriend)
Thomas Mouncer	25	9 August	Wakefield	Elizabeth Baldwin (girlfriend)
Frederick Reynolds	23	13 November	Wandsworth	Sophie Lovell (ex-girlfriend)
Edward Hartigan	58	27 November	Knutsford	Catherine Hartigan (wife)
Richard Buckham	20	4 December	Chelmsford	Albert Watson, Emma Watson
Walter Marsh	39	27 December	Derby	Eliza Marsh (wife)
Total: 8				

1907

John Davis	53	1 January	Warwick	Jane Harrison (girlfriend)
Joseph Jones	60	26 March	Stafford	Edmund Clarke (son-in-law)
Edwin James Moore	33	2 April	Warwick	Fanny Adelaide Moore (mother)
William Slack	47	16 July	Derby	Lucy Wilson
Charles Patterson	37	7 August	Liverpool	Lillian Jane Charlton (girlfriend)

Richard Brinkley	53	13 August	Wandsworth	Richard Beck, Elizabeth Beck
Rhoda Willis (f)	44	14 August	Cardiff	Female child (surname Treasure)
William Austin	31	5 November	Reading	Unity Annie Butler
William Duddles	47	20 November	Lincoln	Catherine Gear
George Stills	30	13 December	Cardiff	Rachel Hannah Stills (mother)

Total: 10 (9 + 1)

1908

Joseph Noble	48	24 March	Durham	John Patterson
Robert Lawman	35	24 March	Durham	Amelia Bell Wood (girlfriend)
John Ramsbottom	34	12 May	Manchester	James MacCraw (brother-in-law)
Fred Ballington	41	28 July	Manchester	Ellen Ann Ballington (wife)
Thomas Siddle	29	4 August	Hull	Gertrude Siddle (wife)
Matthew Dodds	44	5 August	Durham	Mary Jane Dodds (wife)
James Phipps	21	12 November	Knutsford	Elizabeth Warburton
James Nicholls	35	2 December	Norwich	Susan Wilson
John Ellwood	44	3 December	Leeds	Thomas Wilkinson
William Bauldry	41	8 December	Maidstone	Margaret Bauldry (wife)
Harry Taylor Parker	32	15 December	Warwick	Thomas Tompkins
Patrick Collins	24	30 December	Cardiff	Annie Dorothy Lawrence (ex-girlfriend)

Total: 12

1909

John Esmond Murphy	21	6 January	Pentonville	Frederick Schlitte
Jeremiah O'Connor	52	23 February	Durham	Mary Donnelly
Ernest Hutchinson	24	2 March	Wakefield	Hannah Maria Whiteley (girlfriend)
Thomas Mead	33	12 March	Leeds	Clara Howell (girlfriend)
Edmund Elliott	19	30 March	Exeter	Clara Jane Hannaford (ex-girlfriend)
See Lee	38	30 March	Liverpool	Yun Yap
Joseph Edwin Jones	39	13 April	Stafford	Charlotte Jones (wife)

William Joseph Foy	25	8 May	Swansea	Mary Ann Rees (girlfriend)
Morris Reuben & Marks Reuben	23 22	20 May	Pentonville	William Sproull
John Edmunds	24	3 July	Usk	Cecilia Harris
Walter Davis	37	9 July	Wakefield	Hester Harriet Richards (girlfriend)
William Hampton	23	20 July	Bodmin	Emily Tredrea (girlfriend)
Mark Shawcross	30	3 August	Manchester	Emily Ramsbottom (girlfriend)
Julius Wammer	43	10 August	Wandsworth	Cissie Archer
Madar Lal Dhingra	25	31 August	Pentonville	Sir William Hutt Curzon-Wylie, Dr Cawas Lalcaca
John Freeman	46	7 December	Hull	Florence Lily Freeman (sister-in-law)
Abel Atherton	29	8 December	Durham	Elizabeth Ann Patrick
Samuel Atherley	30	14 December	Nottingham	Matilda Lambert, John Lambert, Annie Lambert, Samuel Lambert

Total: 19

1910

William Murphy	49	15 February	Carnarvon	Gwen Ellen Jones (girlfriend)
Joseph Wren	23	22 February	Manchester	John Collins
George Perry	27	1 March	Pentonville	Annie Covell (girlfriend)
Thomas Clements	62	24 March	Usk	Charles Thomas, Mary Thomas
Thomas Jesshope	32	25 May	Wandsworth	John Healey
James Hancock	55	14 June	Cambridge	Alfred Doggett
Thomas Craig	24	12 July	Durham	Thomas William Henderson
Frederick Foreman	45	14 July	Chelmsford	Elizabeth Ely (girlfriend)
John Raper Coulson	32	9 August	Leeds	Jane Ellen Coulson (wife), Thomas Coulson (son)
John Dickman	45	9 August	Newcastle	John Innes Nisbet
Thomas Rawcliffe	31	15 November	Lancaster	Louisa Ann Rawcliffe (wife)

Henry Thompson	54	22 November	Liverpool	Mary Thompson (wife)
Hawley Harvey Crippen	48	23 November	Pentonville	Cora Turner (Belle Elmore) (wife)
William Broome	26	24 November	Reading	Isabella Wilson
Andrew Noah Woolf	58	21 December	Pentonville	Andrew Simon
Henry Ison	45	29 December	Leeds	Mary Jenkin (girlfriend)
Total: 16				

1911

George Newton	19	31 January	Chelmsford	Ada Roker (girlfriend)
Thomas Seymour	65	9 May	Liverpool	Mary Seymour (wife)
Michael Collins	26	24 May	Pentonville	Elizabeth Anne Kempster (girlfriend)
Arthur Garrod	49	20 June	Ipswich	Sarah Chilvers (girlfriend)
William Palmer	50	19 July	Leicester	Ann Harris
Francisco Godhino	40	17 October	Pentonville	Alice Emily
Brewster Edward Hill	41	17 October	Pentonville	Mary Jane Hill (wife)
Frederick Thomas	38	15 November	Wandsworth	Harriett Ann Eckhardt (girlfriend)
Michael Fagan	27	6 December	Liverpool	Lucy Kennedy
Walter Martyn	22	12 December	Manchester	Edith Griffiths (girlfriend)
John Tarkenter	41	12 December	Manchester	Rosetta Tarkenter (wife)
Henry Phillips	44	14 December	Swansea	Margaret Phillips (wife)
Joseph Fletcher	40	15 December	Liverpool	Caroline Fletcher(wife)
George Parker	26	19 December	Maidstone	Mary Elizabeth Speller (girlfriend)
Charles Coleman	36	21 December	St Albans	Rose Anna Gurney
George Loake	64	28 December	Stafford	Elizabeth Loake (wife)
Total: 16				

1912

Myer Abramovitch	28	6 March	Pentonville	Solomon Milstein, Annie Milstein
John Williams	38	19 March	Knutsford	Hilda Williams (wife)
Henry Seddon	40	18 April	Pentonville	Eliza Mary Barrow
Arthur Birkett	22	23 July	Manchester	Alice Beetham (ex-girlfriend)
Sargent Philp	33	1 October	Wandsworth	Rose Philp (wife)
Robert Galloway	27	5 November	Norwich	Minnie Morris (girlfriend)

Gilbert Smith	35	26 November	Gloucester	Rosabella Smith (wife)
William Beal	20	10 December	Chelmsford	Clara Ellizabeth Carter (girlfriend)
Alfred Lawrence	32	18 December	Maidstone	Emily Violet Hubbard (girlfriend)
William Wallace	27	20 December	Wakefield	Mary May Galbraith (wife)

Total: 10

1913

Albert Rumens	44	7 January	Lewes	Mabel Ann Maryan
George Mackay	29	29 January	Lewes	Arthur Walls
Edward Hopwood	45	29 January	Pentonville	Florence Silles (girlfriend)
Eric Sedgewick	29	4 February	Reading	Annie Wentworth Davis (girlfriend)
George Cunliffe	28	25 February	Exeter	Kate (Kitty) Butler (girlfriend)
Edward Palmer	23	19 March	Bristol	Ada Louisa James (girlfriend)
Walter Sykes	24	23 April	Wakefield	Amy Collinson, Frances Alice Nicholson
William Burton	29	24 June	Dorchester	Winifred Mary Mitchell (girlfriend)
Henry Longden	52	8 July	Pentonville	Alice Catlow More (girlfriend)
Thomas Fletcher	28	9 July	Worcester	Lillian Wharton (girlfriend)
John Vickers Amos	35	22 July	Newcastle	Andrew Barton, George Mussles, Sarah Grice
Frank Greening	34	13 August	Birmingham	Elizabeth Ellen Hearne (girlfriend)
James Ryder	47	13 August	Manchester	Ann Elizabeth Ryder (wife)
Hugh McLaren	29	14 August	Cardiff	Julian Biros
Fred Seekings	39	4 November	Cambridge	Martha Jane Beeby (girlfriend)
Augustus Penny	30	26 November	Winchester	Matilda Penny (mother)
Frederick Robertson	26	27 November	Pentonville	Nellie Robertson, Beatrice Robertson (daughters), Frederick Robinson (son)

Ernest Kelly	20	17 December	Manchester	Daniel Wright Bardsley
George Law	34	31 December	Wakefield	Annie Cotterill
Total: 19				

1914

George Ball	22	26 February	Liverpool	Christina Catherine Bradfield
Josiah Davies	58	10 March	Stafford	Martha Hodgkins
James Honeyands	21	12 March	Exeter	Amelia Bradfield
Robert Upton	50	24 March	Durham	Charles Gribben
Edgar Bindon	19	25 March	Cardiff	Maud Mulholland (girlfriend)
Joseph Spooner	42	14 May	Liverpool	Elizabeth Alice Spooner (daughter)
Walter White	22	16 June	Winchester	Frances Priscilla Hunter (girlfriend)
Herbert Brooker	32	28 July	Lewes	Ada Stone (girlfriend)
Percy Clifford	32	11 August	Lewes	Maud Clifford (wife)
Charles Frembd	71	4 November	Chelmsford	Louisa Frembd (wife)
John Eayres	59	10 November	Northampton	Sarah Ann Eayres (wife)
Henry Quartley	55	10 November	Shepton Mallet	Henry Pugsley
Arnold Warren	32	12 November	Leicester	James Warren (son)
George Anderson	59	23 December	St Albans	Harriett Ann Whybrow (step-daughter)
Total: 14				

1915

Walter Marriott	24	10 August	Wakefield	Nellie Marriott (wife)
Frank Steele	28	11 August	Durham	Nora Barrett (girlfriend)
George Joseph Smith	43	13 August	Maidstone	Beatrice Mundy, Margaret Lofty, Alice Burnham ("Brides in the Bath" murders)
George Marshall	45	17 August	Wandsworth	Alice Anderson (girlfriend)
William Reeve	42	16 November	Bedford	Harriett Reeve (wife)
John Thornley	26	1 December	Liverpool	Frances Johnson (girlfriend)
Young Hill	28	1 December	Liverpool	James Crawford
Harry Thompson	55	22 December	Wakefield	Alice Kaye (girlfriend)
John McCartney	40	29 December	Wakefield	Charlotte Kent (bigamous wife)
Total: 9				

1916

Lee Kun	27	1 January	Pentonville	Clara Thomas (ex-girlfriend)
Frederick Holmes	44	8 March	Manchester	Sarah Woodall (girlfriend)
Reginald Haslam	25	29 March	Manchester	Isabella Conway (girlfriend)
William Butler	39	16 August	Birmingham	Florence Beatrice Butler
Daniel Sullivan	38	6 September	Swansea	Catherine Sullivan (wife)
Frederick Brooks	28	12 December	Exeter	Alice Clara Gregory
James Hargreaves	54	19 December	Manchester	Caroline McGhee (girlfriend)
Joseph Deans	44	20 December	Durham	Catherine Convery (girlfriend)

Total: 8

1917

Thomas Clinton	28	21 March	Manchester	Henry Lynch
John Thompson	43	27 March	Leeds	Lily Tindale
Leo O'Donnell	26	29 March	Winchester	William F. Watterton
Alec Bakerlis	24	10 April	Cardiff	Winifred Ellen Fortt (girlfriend)
William Robinson	26	17 April	Pentonville	Alfred Williams
Robert Gadsby	65	18 April	Leeds	Julia Ann Johnson (girlfriend)
William Hodgson	34	16 August	Liverpool	Margaret Alderson Hodgson, Margaret Hodgson (wife & daughter)
William Cavanagh	29	18 December	Newcastle	Henry Arthur Hollyer
Thomas Cox	59	19 December	Shrewsbury	Elizabeth Cox (wife)

Total: 9

1918

Arthur Stamrowsky	26	12 February	Wandsworth	Edward Tighe
Joseph Jones	26	21 February	Wandsworth	Oliver Gilbert Imlay
Louis Voisin	42	2 March	Pentonville	Emilienne Gerard
Verney Hasser	30	5 March	Shepton Mallet	Joseph Harold Durkin
Louis Van Der Kerkhove	32	9 April	Birmingham	Clemence Verelst (girlfriend)
William Rooney	51	17 December	Manchester	Mary Ellen Rooney (sister-in-law)
John Walsh	35	17 December	Leeds	Ruth Elizabeth Moore (girlfriend)

Total: 7

1919

George Cardwell & Percy Barrett	22 20	6 January	Leeds	Rhoda Walker
Benjamin Benson	41	7 January	Leeds	Annie Mayne (girlfriend)
Joseph Rose	25	19 February	Oxford	Sarah Rose & Isabell Rose
Henry Beckett	36	10 July	Pentonville	Walter Cornish, Alice Cornish, Alice Cornish, Marie Cornish
John Crossland	34	22 July	Liverpool	Ellen Crossland (wife)
Thomas Foster	46	31 July	Pentonville	Minnie Foster (wife)
Henry Gaskin	27	8 August	Birmingham	Elizabeth Gaskin (wife)
Frank Warren	41	7 October	Pentonville	Lucy Nightingale
Ernest Scott	28	26 November	Newcastle	Rebecca Jane Quinn (girlfriend)
Ambrose Quinn	28	26 November	Newcastle	Elizabeth Ann Quinn (wife)
Djang Djing Sung	33	3 December	Worcester	Zee Ming Wu

Total: 12

1920

Lewis Massey	29	6 January	Leeds	Margaret Hird (wife)
Hyman Perdovitch	39	6 January	Manchester	Soloman Franks
David Caplan	42	6 January	Manchester	Freda Caplan, Herman Caplan, Maurice Caplan (wife/sons)
William Wright	39	10 March	Lincoln	Annie Coulbeck (girlfriend)
William Hall	66	23 March	Durham	Mary Ann Dixon (girlfriend)
Frederick Rothwell Holt	32	13 April	Manchester	Kathleen Breaks (girlfriend)
Thomas Caler	23	14 April	Cardiff	Gladys Ibrahim, Aysha Ibrahim
Miles McHugh	32	16 April	Leeds	Edith Annie Swainston (girlfriend)
Thomas Wilson	45	6 May	Leeds	Annie Maria Wilson (wife)
Herbert Salisbury	35	11 May	Liverpool	Alice Pearson (girlfriend)
William Waddington	35	11 May	Liverpool	Ivy Woolfenden
Frederick Storey	42	16 June	Ipswich	Sarah Jane Howard (girlfriend)
William Aldred	54	22 June	Manchester	Ida Prescott

Arthur Goslett	44	27 July	Pentonville	Evelyn Goslett (wife)
James Ellor	35	11 August	Liverpool	Ada Ellor (wife)
James Riley	50	30 November	Durham	Mary Riley (wife)
Cyril Saunders	21	30 November	Exeter	Dorothy May Saunders (cousin)
Marks Goodmacher	47	30 December	Pentonville	Fanny Zetoun (daughter)
Edwin Sowerby	28	30 December	Leeds	Jane Darwell ex-girlfriend)
Samuel Westwood	26	30 December	Birmingham	Lydia Westwood (wife)
Charles Colclough	45	31 December	Manchester	George Henry Shenton
Total: 21				
1921				
George Lever	51	7 January	Maidstone	Harriet Lever (wife)
Jack Field & William Gray	19 29	4 February	Wandsworth	Irene Violet Munro
George Bailey	22	2 March	Oxford	Kate Lilian Bailey (wife)
Frederick Quarmby	47	6 May	Manchester	Christine Smith (girlfriend)
Thomas Wilson	43	24 May	Manchester	Olive Jackson
Lester Hamilton	25	16 August	Cardiff	Doris Appleton (girlfriend)
Edward O'Connor	43	22 December	Birmingham	Thomas O'Connor (son)
Total: 8				
1922				
James Williamson	37	21 March	Durham	Mary Williamson (wife)
William Sullivan	41	23 March	Usk	Margaret Thomas
Edward Ernest Black	36	24 March	Exeter	Annie Black (wife)
Percy Atkin	29	7 April	Nottingham	Maud Atkin (wife)
Frederick Keeling	54	11 April	Pentonville	Emily Agnes Dewberry
Edmund Tonbridge	38	18 April	Pentonville (girlfriend)	Margaret Evans
Hiram Thompson	52	30 May	Manchester	Ellen Thompson (wife)
Herbert Armstrong	53	31 May	Gloucester	Katharine Mary Armstrong (wife)
Henry Julius Jacoby	18	7 June	Pentonville	Alice White
Joseph O'Sullivan & Reginald Dunne	25 24	10 August	Wandsworth	Field Marshall Sir Henry Wilson
Elijah Pountney	48	11 August	Birmingham	Alice Gertrude Pountney (wife)
Thomas Henry	36	19 August	Winchester	Irene May Wilkins Allaway

William Yeldham	23	5 September	Pentonville	George Stanley Grimshaw
George Robinson	27	13 December	Lincoln	Frances Florence Pacey (girlfriend)
Frank Fowler	35	13 December	Lincoln	Ivy Dora Prentice
William Rider	40	19 December	Birmingham	Rosilla Patience Barton (bigamous wife)

Total: 17

1923

George Edisbury	44	3 January	Manchester	Winifred Drinkwater
Lee Doon	27	5 January	Leeds	Sing Lee
Edith Thompson (f)	30	9 January	Holloway	Percy Thompson
& Frederick Bywaters	21		Pentonville	(her husband)
George Perry	50	28 March	Manchester	Emma Perry (sister-in-law)
Daniel Cassidy	60	3 April	Durham	Bernard Quinn (son-in-law)
Bernard Pomroy	25	5 April	Pentonville	Alice May Cheshire (girlfriend)
Frederick Wood	29	10 April	Liverpool	Margaret Gilchrist White
Rowland Duck	25	4 July	Pentonville	Nellie Pearce
William Griffiths	57	24 July	Shrewsbury	Catherine Hughes (mother)
Hassen Mohamed	33	8 August	Durham	Jane Nagi (Brown) (girlfriend)
Albert Burrows	57	8 August	Nottingham	Hannah Calladine, Albert Edward Calladine (Burrows), Elsie Calladine (Large), Thomas Johnson Wood
Frederick Jesse	26	1 November	Wandsworth	Mabel Jennings Edmunds (aunt)
John Eastwood	39	28 December	Leeds	John Joseph Clarke

Total: 14 (13 + 1)

1924

Matthew Nunn	24	2 January	Durham	Minetta Mary Kelly (girlfriend)
Francis Booker	28	8 April	Manchester	Percy Sharpe
William Wardell	47	18 June	Leeds	Elizabeth Reaney
Abraham Goldenberg	22	30 July	Winchester	William Edward Hall
Jean Vaquier	45	12 August	Wandsworth	Alfred George Poynter Jones
John Horner	23	13 August	Manchester	Norman Widdowson Pinchin

Patrick Mahon	34	3 September	Wandsworth	Emily Kaye (girlfriend)
Fred Southgate	52	27 November	Ipswich	Elizabeth Southgate (wife)
William Smith	26	9 December	Hull	Elizabeth Bousfield
Arthur Simms	25	17 December	Nottingham	Rosa Armstrong (sister-in-law)

Total: 10

1925

William Bignell	32	24 February	Shepton Mallet	Margaret Legg (girlfriend)
William Bressington	21	31 March	Bristol	Gilbert Caleb Amos
George Barton	59	2 April	Pentonville	Mary May Palfrey (girlfriend)
Henry Graham	42	15 April	Durham	Margaret Ann Graham (wife)
Thomas Shelton	25	15 April	Durham	Ruth Surtees Rodgers (girlfriend)
John Thorne	24	22 April	Wandsworth	Elsie Emily Cameron (girlfriend)
Patrick Power	41	26 May	Manchester	Sarah Ann Sykes
Hubert Dalton	39	10 June	Hull	Francis Ward
James Winstanley	29	5 August	Liverpool	Edith Horrocks-Wilkinson (girlfriend)
James Makin	25	11 August	Manchester	Sarah Elizabeth Clutton
Arthur Bishop	18	14 August	Pentonville	Francis Edward Rix
William Cronin	54	14 August	Pentonville	Alice Garnett (girlfriend)
Alfred Bostock	25	3 September	Leeds	Elizabeth M. Sherratt (girlfriend)
Wilfred Fowler	23	3 September	Leeds	William F. Plommer
Lawrence Fowler	25	4 September	Leeds	
Herbert Whiteman	27	12 November	Norwich	Clara Squires, Alice Squires
Samuel Johnson	29	15 December	Manchester	Beatrice Martin (girlfriend)

Total: 17

1926

John Fisher	58	5 January	Birmingham	Ada Taylor (girlfriend)
Lorraine Lax (m)	28	7 January	Leeds	Elizabeth Lax (wife)
Herbert Burrows	23	17 February	Gloucester	Ernest George Elton Laight,Doris Sabrina Laight, Robert Laight
John Lincoln	23	2 March	Shepton Mallet	Edward Charles Ingram Richards

George Thomas	26	9 March	Cardiff	Marie Thomas (girlfriend)
Henry Thompson	36	9 March	Maidstone	Rose Smith (girlfriend)
William Thorpe	45	16 March	Manchester	Frances Clark (ex-girlfriend)
Lock Ah Tam	54	23 March	Liverpool	Catherine Ah Tam, Doris Ah Tam, Cecilia Ah Tam (wife & daughters)
Ewen Stitchell	25	24 March	Pentonville	Polly Edith Walker
George Sharples	20	13 April	Birmingham	Milly Crabtree
Louie Calvert (f)	33	24 June	Manchester	Lily Waterhouse
Johannes Mommers	43	27 July	Pentonville	Augusta Pionbini
James Smith	23	10 August	Durham	Catherine Smith (wife)
Charles Finden	22	12 August	Winchester	John Richard Thompson
Hashankhan Samander	36	2 November	Pentonville	Khannar Jung Baz
James Leah	60	16 November	Liverpool	Louise Leah (daughter)
Charles Houghton	45	3 December	Gloucester	Eleanor Woodhouse, Martha Woodhouse

Total: 17 (16 + 1)

1927

William Jones	22	5 January	Leeds	Winifred Jones (wife)
James Stratton	26	29 March	Pentonville	Madge Dorothy Maggs (ex-girlfriend)
William Knighton	22	27 April	Nottingham	Ada Knighton (mother)
Fred Fuller &	35	3 August	Wandsworth	James Staunton
James Murphy	29			
John Robinson	36	12 August	Pentonville	Minnie Alice Bonati
Arthur Harnett	28	2 September	Leeds	Isabella Moore
William Robertson	32	6 December	Liverpool	Evelyn Mary Jennings (girlfriend)

Total: 8

1928

Frederick Fielding	24	3 January	Manchester	Eleanor Pilkington (girlfriend)
Bertram Kirby	47	4 January	Lincoln	Minnie Eleanor Kirby (wife)
John Thomas Dunn	52	6 January	Durham	Ada Elizabeth Dunn (wife)
Sidney Goulter	25	6 January	Wandsworth	Constance Gertrude Oliver

Samuel Case	24	7 January	Leeds	Mary Alice Mottram (girlfriend)
Edward Rowlands &	40	27 January	Cardiff	David (Dai) Lewis
Daniel Driscoll	34			
James Power	32	31 January	Birmingham	Olive Gordon Turner
James Gillon	30	31 January	Wandsworth	Annie Gillon (sister)
George Hayward	32	10 April	Nottingham	Amy Collinson
Frederick Lock	39	12 April	Wandsworth	Florence Alice Kitching (girlfriend)
Frederick Browne	47	31 May	Pentonville	PC George William Gutteridge
William Kennedy	36	31 May	Wandsworth	
Frederick Stewart	28	6 June	Pentonville	Alfred Charles Bertram Webb
Walter Brooks	48	28 June	Manchester	Beatrice Brooks (wife), Alfred Moore
Albert Absalom	28	25 July	Liverpool	Mary Alice Reed (girlfriend)
William Maynard	36	27 July	Exeter	Richard Francis Roadley
Norman Elliott	23	10 August	Durham	William Byland Abbey
William Benson	25	20 November	Wandsworth	Charlotte Alice Harber (girlfriend)
Chung Yi Miao	28	6 December	Manchester	Wai Sheung Sui (wife)
Trevor Edwards	21	11 December	Swansea	Elsie Cook (girlfriend)
Total: 21				

1929

Charles Conlin	22	4 January	Durham	Thomas Kirby, Emily Kirby (grandparents)
Frank Hollington	25	20 February	Pentonville	Annie Elizabeth Hatton (girlfriend)
William John Holmyard	24	27 February	Pentonville	William Holmyard (grandfather)
Joseph Clarke	21	12 March	Liverpool	Alice Fontaine
George Cartledge	27	4 April	Manchester	Ellen Cartledge (wife)
James Johnson	43	7 August	Durham	Mary Annie Johnson (wife)
Arthur Raveney	24	14 August	Leeds	Leslie Godfrey White
John Maguire	43	26 November	Liverpool	Ellen Maguire (wife)
Total: 8				

1930

Sidney Harry Fox	31	8 April	Maidstone	Rosalie Fox (mother)
William Podmore	29	22 April	Winchester	Vivian Messiter
Albert Marjeram	23	11 June	Wandsworth	Edith May Parker
Total: 3				

1931

Victor Betts	21	3 January	Birmingham	William Thomas Andrews
Frederick Gill	26	4 February	Leeds	Oliver Preston
Alfred Rouse	36	10 March	Bedford	Unknown man
Francis Land	39	16 April	Manchester	Sarah Ellen Johnson (girlfriend)
Alex Anastassiou	23	3 June	Pentonville	Evelyn Victoria Holt (girlfriend)
William Shelley & Oliver Newman	57 61	5 August	Pentonville	Herbert William Ayres
William Corbett	32	12 August	Cardiff	Ethel Louisa Corbett (wife)
Henry Seymour	39	10 December	Oxford	Annie Louisa Kempson
Solomon Stein	21	15 December	Manchester	Annie Riley
Total: 10				

13 men were executed for treason/spying during World War 1;
11 of them were shot by military firing squads at the Tower of London, the other two being hanged at London's Pentonville and Wandsworth prisons

Carl Hans Lody:	6 November 1914 (Shot)
Carl Muller:	23 June 1915 (Shot)
Robert Rosenthal:	15 July 1915 (Hanged at Wandsworth)
Haicke Janssan & Willem Roos:	30 July 1915 (Shot)
Ernest Melin:	10 September 1915 (Shot)
Augusto Roggen:	17 September 1915 (Shot)
Fernando Buschman:	19 October 1915 (Shot)
George Breeckow:	26 October 1915 (Shot)
Irving Guy Ries:	27 October 1915 (Shot)
Albert Meyer:	27 November 1915 (Shot)
Ludovico Zender:	11 April 1916 (Shot)
Roger Casement:	3 August 1916 (Treason) (Hanged at Pentonville)

English and Welsh Executions 1932–1964

1932

Name	Age	Date	Place	Victim(s)
George Rice	32	3 February	Manchester	Constance Inman
William Goddard	25	23 February	Pentonville	Charles William Lambert
George Pople	22	9 March	Oxford	Mabel Elizabeth Mathews
George Michael	49	27 April	Hull	Theresa Mary Hempstock (girlfriend)
John Roberts	23	28 April	Leeds	Alfred Gill
Thomas Riley	36	28 April	Leeds	Elizabeth Castle (girlfriend)
Maurice Freedman	36	4 May	Pentonville (girlfriend)	Annette Friedson
Charles Cowle	19	18 May	Manchester	Naomi Annie Farnworth
Ernest Hutchinson	43	23 November	Oxford	Gwendoline Annie Warren (girlfriend)

Total: 9

1933

Name	Age	Date	Place	Victim(s)
Jeremiah Hanbury	49	2 February	Birmingham	Jessie Payne (girlfriend)
Jack Puttnam	31	8 June	Pentonville	Elizabeth Mary Standley (aunt)
Richard Hetherington	36	20 June	Liverpool	Joseph Nixon, Mary Ann Nixon
Frederick Morse	34	25 July	Bristol	Doris (Dorothy) Winifred Brewer (niece)
Varnavas Antorka	31	10 August	Pentonville	Boleslar Pankorski
Robert James Kirby	26	11 October	Pentonville	Grace Ivy Newing (girlfriend)
Ernest Parker	25	6 December	Durham	Lily Parker (Scott) (sister)
William Burtoft	47	19 December	Manchester	Frances Levin
Stanley Hobday	21	29 December	Birmingham	Charles William Fox

Total: 9

1934

Name	Age	Date	Place	Victim(s)
Roy Gregory	28	3 January	Hull	Dorothy Margaret Addinall (step-daughter)
Ernest Brown	35	6 February	Leeds	Frederick Ellison Morton
Louis Hamilton	25	6 April	Leeds	Maud Hamilton (wife)

Reginald Hinks	32	3 May	Bristol	James Pullen (father-in-law)
Albert Probert &	26	4 May	Wandsworth	Joseph Bedford
Frederick Parker	31			
Harry Tuffney	36	9 October	Pentonville	Edith Kate Longshaw (girlfriend)
John Stockwell	19	14 November	Pentonville	Dudley Henry Hoard
Ethel Lillie Major (f)	42	19 December	Hull	Arthur Major (husband)
Total: 9 (8 + 1)				

1935

Fred Rushworth	29	1 January	Leeds	(daughter)
David Blake	24	7 February	Leeds	Emily Yeomans
Charles Lake	37	13 March	Pentonville	George Hamblin
Leonard Brigstock	33	2 April	Wandsworth	Hubert Sidney Deggan
Percy Anderson	21	16 April	Wandsworth	Edith Constance Drew-Bear (girlfriend)
John Bainbridge	24	9 May	Durham	Edward Frederick Herdman
John Harris Bridge	25	30 May	Manchester	Amelia Nuttall (girlfriend)
Arthur Franklin	44	25 June	Gloucester	Bessie Gladys Nott (girlfriend)
Walter Worthington	57	10 July	Bedford	Sybil Emily Worthington (wife)
George Hague	23	16 July	Durham	Amanda Sharp (girlfriend)
Raymond Bousquet	30	29 October	Wandsworth	Hilda Meek (girlfriend)
Allan Grierson	27	30 October	Pentonville	Louise Berthe Gann
Total: 12				

1936

Dorothea Waddingham (f)	36	16 April	Birmingham	Louisa Baguley, Ada Baguley
Buck Ruxton	36	12 May	Manchester	Isabella Ruxton (wife), Mary Rogerson (servant)
Frederick Field	32	30 June	Wandsworth	Beatrice Vilna Sutton
George Bryant	38	14 July	Wandsworth	Ellen Whiting (girlfriend)
Charlotte Bryant (f)	33	15 July	Exeter	Frederick Bryant (husband)
Wallace Jenden	57	5 August	Wandsworth	Alice Whye (girlfriend)
Christopher Jackson	24	16 December	Durham	Harriet Linney (aunt)
Total: 7 (5 + 2)				

1937

Max Mayer Haslam	23	4 February	Manchester	Ruth Clarkson
Andrew Bagley	62	10 February	Leeds	Irene Hart
Philip Davis	30	27 July	Exeter	Wilhelmina Davis (wife), Monica Rowe (niece)
Horace Brunt	32	12 August	Manchester	Kate Elizabeth Collier
Leslie Stone	24	13 August	Pentonville	Ruby Anne Keen (ex-girlfriend)
Frederick Murphy	53	17 August	Pentonville	Rosina Field
John Rodgers	22	18 November	Pentonville	Lilian Maud Chamberlain
Ernest John Moss	28	7 December	Exeter	Kitty Bennett (girlfriend)
Frederick Nodder	44	30 December	Lincoln	Mona Tinsley

Total: 9

1938

Walter Smith	33	8 March	Norwich	Albert Baker
Charles Caldwell	49	20 April	Manchester	Eliza Caldwell (wife)
Robert Hoolhouse	21	26 May	Durham	Margaret Jane Dobson
Jan Mohamed	30	8 June	Liverpool	Aminul Hag
Alfred Richards	38	12 July	Wandsworth	Kathleen Richards (wife)
William Graves	38	19 July	Wandsworth	Tony Ruffle (son)
William Parker	25	26 July	Durham	Jane Parker (wife)
George Brain	27	1 November	Wandsworth	Rose Muriel Atkins

Total: 8

1939

John Daymond	19	8 February	Durham	James Percival
Harry Armstrong	38	21 March	Wandsworth	Peggy Pentecost (girlfriend)
William Butler	29	29 March	Wandsworth	Ernest Key
Ralph Smith	40	7 June	Gloucester	Beatrice Baxter - (ex-girlfriend)
Leonard Hucker	30	10 October	Wandsworth	Mary Moncrieff (Fullick)
Stanley Boon &	27	25 October	Wandsworth	Mabel Bundy
Arthur Smith	26	26 October		

Total: 7

1940

Peter Barnes &	32	7 February	Birmingham	Elsie Ansell, Gwilym Rowland, John Arnott, James Clay, Rex Gentle
James Richards	29			
Ernest Hamerton	25	27 March	Wandsworth	Elsie Ellington (girlfriend)
William Cowell	38	24 April	Wandsworth	Anne Cook

Vincent Ostler & William Appleby	24 27	11 July	Durham	William Shiell
Udam Singh	37	31 July	Pentonville	Sir Michael O'Dwyer
George Roberts	29	8 August	Cardiff	Arthur Allen
John Wright	41	10 September	Durham	Alice Wright (wife)
Stanley Cole	23	31 October	Wandsworth	Doris Girl
William Cooper	24	26 November	Bedford	John Harrison
Edward Scollen	42	24 December	Durham	Beatrice Scollen (wife)
Total: 12				

1941

Clifford Holmes	24	11 February	Manchester	Irene Holmes (wife)
Henry White	39	6 March	Durham	Emily Wardle (girlfriend)
Samuel Morgan	28	9 April	Liverpool	Mary Hagan
David Jennings	21	24 July	Dorchester	Albert Farley
Edward Anderson	19	31 July	Durham	William Anderson
John Smith	32	4 September	Manchester	Margaret Knight (ex-girlfriend)
Eli Richards	45	19 September	Birmingham	Jane Turner
Antonio Mancini	39	31 October	Pentonville	Harry Distleman
Lionel Watson	30	12 November	Pentonville	Phyllis Crocker, Eileen Crocker (wife/daughter)
John Ernest Smith	21	3 December	Wandsworth	Christina Dicksee (girlfriend)
Thomas Thorpe	61	23 December	Leicester	Nellie Thorpe (wife)
Total: 11				

1942

Arthur Peach	23	30 January	Birmingham	Kitty Lyon
Harold Trevor	62	11 March	Wandsworth	Theodora Greenhill
David Williams	33	25 March	Liverpool	Elizabeth Smith (girlfriend)
Cyril Johnson	20	15 April	Wandsworth	Maggie Small
Frederick Austin	28	30 April	Bristol	Lillian Austin (wife)
Harold Hill	26	1 May	Oxford	Doreen Hearne, Kathleen Trundell
Douglas Edmondson	28	24 June	Liverpool	Imeldred Osliff (girlfriend)
Gordon Cummins	28	25 June	Wandsworth	Evelyn Hamilton, Evelyn Oatley, Margaret Lowe, Doris Jouannet
Arthur Anderson	52	21 July	Wandsworth	Pauline Barker (ex-girlfriend)

George Silverosa &	22	10 September	Pentonville	Leonard Moules
Samuel Dashwood	23			
Harold Merry	40	10 September	Birmingham	Joyce Dixon (girlfriend)
Patrick Kingston	38	6 October	Wandsworth	Sheila Wilson
William Collins	21	28 October	Durham	Margaret Rice
Herbert Bounds	42	6 November	Wandsworth	Elizabeth Bounds (wife)
Total: 15				

1943

Harry Dobkin	49	27 January	Wandsworth	Rachel Dobkin (wife)
Ronald Roberts	28	10 February	Liverpool	Nellie Pearson
William Turner	19	24 March	Pentonville	Ann Wade
Dudley Rayner	26	31 March	Wandsworth	Josephine Rayner (wife)
Gordon Trenoweth	33	6 April	Exeter	Albert Bateman
August Sangret	30	29 April	Wandsworth	Joan Wolfe (girlfriend)
Charles Raymond	23	10 July	Wandsworth	Marguerite Burge
William Quayle	52	3 August	Birmingham	Vera Clarke
Gerald Roe	41	3 August	Pentonville	Elsie Roe (wife)
Trevor Elvin	21	10 September	Leeds	Violet Wakefield (girlfriend)
Charles Gauthier	25	24 September	Wandsworth	Annette Pepper (girlfriend)
Terence Casey	22	19 November	Wandsworth	Bridget Mitton
Charles Koopman	23	15 December	Pentonville	Gladys Brewer, Shirley Brewer
John Dorgan	47	22 December	Wandsworth	Florence Dorgan (wife)
Thomas James	26	29 December	Liverpool	Gwendoline Sweeney
Total: 15				

1944

Christos Georghiou	37	2 February	Pentonville	Savvas Demetriades
Mervin McEwen	35	3 February	Leeds	Mark Turner
Ernest Digby	34	16 March	Bristol	Dawn Digby (daughter)
Sidney Delasalle	39	13 April	Durham	Ronald Murphy
Ernest Kemp	21	6 June	Wandsworth	Iris Deeley
John Davidson	19	12 July	Liverpool	Gladys Appleton
James Galbraith	26	26 July	Manchester	James Percey
William Meffen	52	8 August	Leicester	Winifred Stanley - (step-daughter)
William Cowle	31	8 August	Leicester	Nora Payne (ex-girlfriend)
Total: 9				

1945

Horace Gordon	28	9 January	Wandsworth	Dorothy Hillman
Andrew Brown	26	30 January	Wandsworth	Amelia Knowles
Arthur Thompson	34	31 January	Leeds	Jane Coulton
Karl Hulten	22	8 March	Pentonville	George Heath
Arthur Heys	37	13 March	Norwich	Winifred Evans
Howard Grossley	37	5 September	Cardiff	Lily Griffiths (girlfriend)
Thomas Richardson	27	7 September	Leeds	David Dewar
Joachim Palme-Goltz,	20	6 October	Pentonville	Sergeant Major Wolfgang Rosterg
Kurt Zuchlsdorff,	20			
Heintz Brueling,	22			
Erich Koenig &	20			
Josep Mertins	21			
Ronald Mauri	32	31 October	Wandsworth	Vera Guest (girlfriend)
Armin Kuehne &	21	16 November	Pentonville	Gerhardt Rettig
Emil Schmittendorf	31			
John Riley Young	40	21 December	Pentonville	Frederick Lucas, Cissie Lucas
James McNicol	30	21 December	Pentonville	Sgt Donald Kirkaldie
Robert Blaine	24	29 December	Wandsworth	John Ritchie

Total: 18

1946

William Batty	27	8 January	Leeds	Samuel Gray
Michal Niescior	29	31 January	Wandsworth	Charles Elphick
Charles Prescott	23	5 March	Durham	Sarah Young
Arthur Clegg	42	19 March	Wandsworth	Jill Clegg (granddaughter)
Arthur Charles	34	26 March	Durham	John Duplessis
Marion Grondkowski (m)	32	2 April	Wandsworth	Rueben Martirosoff
Henryk Malinowski	24			
Harold Berry	30	9 April	Manchester	Bernard Phillips
Martin Coffey	24	24 April	Manchester	Henry Dutton
Leonard Holmes	32	28 May	Lincoln	Peggy Holmes (wife)
Thomas Hendren	31	17 July	Liverpool	Ella Staunton (girlfriend)
Walter Clayton	22	7 August	Liverpool	Joyce Jacques (girlfriend)
Sydney John Smith	24	6 September	Wandsworth	John Whatman
David Mason	39	6 September	Wandsworth	Dorothy Mason (wife)
Neville Heath	28	16 October	Pentonville	Margery Gardner (girlfriend), Doreen Marshall
Arthur Boyce	45	1 November	Pentonville	Elizabeth McLindon (girlfriend)

Frank Freiyer	26	13 November	Wandsworth	Joyce Brierley (girlfriend)
Arthur Rushton	31	19 November	Liverpool	Catherine Cooper (girlfriend)
John Mathieson	23	10 December	Pentonville	Mona Vanderstay
Total: 19				
1947				
Stanley Sheminant	28	3 January	Liverpool	Harry Berrisford
Albert Sabin	21	30 January	Leeds	Neil MacLeod
Walter Rowland	39	27 February	Manchester	Olive Balchin
Harold Hagger (Sidney Sinclair)	45	18 March	Wandsworth	Dagmar Petrzywalkski
Frederick Reynolds	39	26 March	Pentonville	Beatrice Greenberg (girlfriend)
David Williams	26	15 April	Wandsworth	Margaret Williams (wife)
Eric Briggs	40	20 June	Leeds	Gertrude Briggs (wife)
William Smedley	38	14 August	Leeds	Edith Simmonite
John Gartside	24	21 August	Leeds	Percy Baker, Alice Baker
Charles Jenkins &	21	19 September	Pentonville	Alec de Antiquis
Christopher Geraghty	23			
Eugeniusz Jurkiewicz	34	30 December	Bristol	Emily Bowers
Total: 12				
1948				
George Whelpton	31	7 January	Leeds	Alison Parkin (girlfriend), Joyce & Maurice Parkin
Evan Hadyn Evans	22	3 February	Cardiff	Rachel Allen
Walter John Cross	21	19 February	Pentonville	Percy Bushby
Stanley Clark	34	18 November	Norwich	Florence Bentley (girlfriend)
Peter Griffiths	22	19 November	Liverpool	June Devaney
George Russell	45	2 December	Oxford	Minnie Lee
Clifford Wills	31	9 December	Cardiff	Sillvinea Parry (girlfriend)
Arthur Osborne	28	30 December	Leeds	Ernest Westwood
Total: 8				
1949				
Margaret "Bill" Allen (f)	42	12 January	Manchester	Nancy Chadwick
George Semini	24	27 January	Liverpool	Joseph Gibbons
Kenneth Strickson	21	22 March	Lincoln	Irene Phillips
James Farrell	19	29 March	Birmingham	Joan Marney
Harry Lewis	21	21 April	Pentonville	Harry Michaelson
Dennis Neville	22	2 June	Leeds	Marian Poskitt

Bernard Cooper	40	21 June	Pentonville	Mary Cooper (wife)
Sydney Chamberlain	31	28 July	Winchester	Doreen Messenger (girlfriend)
Rex Harvey Jones	21	4 August	Swansea	Beatrice Watts
Robert Mackintosh	21	4 August	Swansea	Beryl Beechey
John George Haigh	40	10 August	Wandsworth	William Donald McSwann, William McSwann, Amy McSwann, Archibald Henderson, Rosalie Henderson, Olive Durand-Deacon
William Davies	30	16 August	Wandsworth	Lucy Wilson (girlfriend)
William Jones	31	28 September	Pentonville	Waltraut Lehman
John Wilson	26	13 December	Durham	Lucy Nightingale
Benjamin Roberts	23			Lillian Vickers
Ernest Couzins	49	30 December	Wandsworth	Victor Elias
Total: 16 (15 + 1)				
1950				
Daniel Raven	23	6 January	Pentonville	Leopold Goodman, Esther Goodman (in-laws)
James Rivett	21	8 March	Norwich	Christine Cuddon (girlfriend)
Timothy John Evans	25	9 March	Pentonville	Beryl Evans, Geraldine Evans (wife/daughter)
George Kelly	27	28 March	Liverpool	Leonard Thomas, John Bernard Catterall
Piotr Maksimowski	33	29 March	Birmingham	Dilys Campbell (girlfriend)
Walter Sharpe	20	30 March	Leeds	Abraham Levine
Albert Jenkins	38	19 April	Swansea	William Llewellyn
Zbigniew Gower &	23	7 July	Winchester	Robert Taylor
Roman Redel	23			
George Brown	23	11 July	Durham	Mary Longhurst (girlfriend)
Ronald Atwell	24	13 July	Bristol	Lily Palmer
John Walker	48	13 July	Durham	Francis Wilson
Albert Price	32	16 August	Wandsworth	Doris (wife), Jennifer & Maureen (daughters)
Patrick Turnage	31	14 November	Durham	Julia Beesley
Norman Goldthorpe	40	24 November	Norwich	Emma Howe
James Corbitt	37	28 November	Manchester	Eliza Wood (girlfriend)
Edward Woodfield	49	14 December	Bristol	Ethel Worth
Nicholas Crosby	22	19 December	Manchester	Ruth Massey
Total: 18				

1951

Frank Griffin	40	4 January	Shrewsbury	Jane Edge
Nenad Kovacevic	29	26 January	Manchester	Radomir Djorovic
William Watkins	49	3 April	Birmingham	(unnamed son)
Edward Smith &	33	25 April	Wandsworth	Frederick Gosling
Joseph Brown	33			
James Virrels	56	26 April	Wandsworth	Alice Roberts
James Inglis	29	8 May	Manchester	Alice Morgan
William Shaughnessy	48	9 May	Winchester	Marie & Joyce Shaughnessy (wife/daughter)
John Dand	32	12 June	Manchester	Walter Wyld
Jack Wright	31	3 July	Manchester	Mona Mather
Dennis Moore	22	19 July	Norwich	Eileen Cullen (girlfriend)
Alfred Reynolds	25	19 July	Norwich	Ellen Ludkin (girlfriend)
John O'Connor	29	24 October	Pentonville	Eugenie le Maire
Herbert Mills	19	11 December	Lincoln	Mabel Tattershaw

Total: 14

1952

Horace Carter	31	1 January	Birmingham	Sheila Attwood
Alfred Bradley	24	15 January	Manchester	George Camp
Alfred Moore	36	6 February	Leeds	Duncan A. Fraser, Arthur Jagger
Herbert Harris	23	26 February	Manchester	Eileen Harris (wife)
Tahir Ali	39	21 March	Durham	Evelyn McDonald (girlfriend)
Edward Devlin &	22	25 April	Liverpool	Alice Rimmer
Alfred Burns	21			
Ajit Singh	27	7 May	Cardiff	Joan Thomas (girlfriend)
Backary Manneh	25	27 May	Pentonville	Joseph Aaku
Harry Huxley	43	8 July	Shrewsbury	Ada Royce (girlfriend)
Thomas Eames	31	15 July	Bristol	Muriel Bent (girlfriend)
Frank Burgess	21	22 July	Wandsworth	Johanna Hallahan
Oliver George Butler	24	12 August	Oxford	Rose Meadows (girlfriend)
Mahmood Mattan	28	3 September	Cardiff	Lily Volpert (later found innocent)
John Howard Godar	31	5 September	Pentonville	Maureen Cox (girlfriend)
Dennis Muldowney	41	30 September	Pentonville	Countess Krystyna Skarbek
Raymond Cull	25	30 September	Pentonville	Jean Cull (wife)
Peter Johnson	24	9 October	Pentonville	Charles Mead
Donald Neil Simon	32	23 October	Shrewsbury	Eunice Simon (wife), Victor Brades

Eric Norcliffe	30	12 December	Lincoln	Kathleen Norcliffe (wife)
John Livesey	23	17 December	Wandsworth	Stephanie Small mother-in-law)
Leslie Green	29	23 December	Birmingham	Alice Wiltshaw
Herbert Appleby	21	24 December	Durham	John Thomas
Total: 23				

1953				
John James Alcott	22	2 January	Wandsworth	Geoffrey Dean
Derek Bentley	19	28 January	Wandsworth	PC Sidney Miles
Miles Giffard	27	24 February	Bristol	Charles & Elizabeth Giffard (parents)
John Todd	20	19 May	Liverpool	George Walker
John Christie	55	15 July	Pentonville	Ruth Fuerst, Muriel Eady, Beryl Evans, Ethel Christie (wife), Kathleen Maloney, Rita Nelson, Hectorina MacLennan
Philip Henry	25	30 July	Leeds	Flora Gilligan
Louisa Merrifield (f)	46	18 September	Manchester	Sarah Ricketts
John Greenway	27	20 October	Bristol	Beatrice Court
John Reynolds	31	17 November	Leicester	Janet Warner
Stanislaw Juras	43	17 December	Manchester	Irene Wagner
John Wilkinson	24	18 December	Wandsworth	Miriam Gray
Alfred Whiteway	22	22 December	Wandsworth	Barbara Songhurst, Christine Reed
George Newland	21	23 December	Pentonville	Henry Tandy
Total: 13 (12 + 1)				

1954				
Robert Moore	26	5 January	Leeds	Edward Watson
Czeslaw Kowalewski	32	8 January	Manchester	Doris Douglas (girlfriend)
Desmond Hooper	27	26 January	Shrewsbury	Betty Smith
Wilhelm Lubina	42	27 January	Leeds	Charlotte Ball
James Doohan	24	14 April	Wandsworth	Herbert Ketley
Albert George Hall	46	22 April	Leeds	Mary Hackett
Thomas Harries	25	28 April	Swansea	John Harries, Phoebe Harries (uncle/aunt)
Kenneth Gilbert & Ian Arthur Grant	22 24	17 June	Pentonville	George Smart
Milton Taylor	23	22 June	Liverpool	Marie Bradshaw (girlfriend)
William Hepper	62	11 August	Wandsworth	Margaret Spevick

Harold Fowler	21	12 August	Lincoln	Kenneth Mulligan
Edward Reid	24	1 September	Leeds	Arthur White
Rupert Wells	53	1 September	Wandsworth	Nellie Officer (girlfriend)
Styllou Christofi (f)	53	15 December	Holloway	Hella Christofi (daughter-in-law)

Total: 15 (14 + 1)

1955

William Salt	43	29 March	Liverpool	Dennis Shenton
Sydney Clarke	33	14 April	Wandsworth	Rose Fairhurst
Winston Shaw	39	4 May	Leeds	Jean Tate (ex-girlfriend)
James Robinson	27	24 May	Lincoln	Mary Dodsley
Richard Gowler	43	21 June	Liverpool	Mary Boothroyd
Kenneth Roberts	24	12 July	Lincoln	Mary Roberts
Ruth Ellis (f)	28	13 July	Holloway	David Blakely (boyfriend)
Frederick Cross	33	26 July	Birmingham	Donald Lainton
Norman Green	25	27 July	Liverpool	William Harmer, Norman Yates
Corbett Roberts	46	2 August	Birmingham	Doris Roberts (wife)
Ernest Harding	42	9 August	Birmingham	Evelyn Higgins
Alec Wilkinson	22	12 August	Leeds	Clara Farrell (mother-in-law)

Total: 12 (11 + 1)

1956

There were no executions

1957

The Homicide Act of 1957 applies from here on

John Vickers	22	23 July	Durham	Jane Duckett
Dennis Howard	24	4 December	Birmingham	David Keasey

Total: 2

1958

Vivian Teed	24	6 May	Swansea	William Williams
Matthew Kavanagh	32	12 August	Birmingham	Isaiah Dixon
Frank Stokes	44	3 September	Durham	Linda Ash
Brian Chandler	20	17 December	Durham	Martha Dodd

Total: 4

1959

Ernest Jones	39	10 February	Leeds	Richard Turner
Joseph Chrimes	30	28 April	Pentonville	Norah Summerfield
Ronald Marwood	25	8 May	Pentonville	Raymond Summers
Michael Tatum	24	14 May	Winchester	Charles Barrett
Bernard Walden	35	14 August	Leeds	Joyce Moran, Neil Saxton
Guenther Podola	30	5 November	Wandsworth	DS Raymond William Purdy

Total: 6

1960

John Constantine	23	1 September	Lincoln	Lily Perry
Norman Harris &	23	10 November	Pentonville	Allan Jee
Francis Forsyth	18			

Total: 3

1961

Wasyl Gnypiuk	34	27 January	Lincoln	Louise Surgey
George Riley	21	9 February	Shrewsbury	Adeline Smith
Jack Day	31	29 March	Bedford	Keith Arthur
Victor John Terry	20	25 May	Wandsworth	John Pull
Zsiga Pankotia	31	29 June	Leeds	Eli Myers
Edwin Bush	21	6 July	Pentonville	Elsie Batten
Henryk Niemasz	49	8 September	Wandsworth	Alice Buxton (girlfriend), Hubert Buxton

Total: 7

1962

James Hanratty	25	4 April	Bedford	Michael Gregsten
Oswald Grey	20	20 November	Birmingham	Thomas Bates
James Smith	26	28 November	Manchester	Sarah Cross

Total: 3

1963

Russell Pascoe &	24	17 December	Bristol	William Garfield Rowe
Dennis Whitty	22		Winchester	

Total: 2

1964

Peter Anthony Allen	22	13 August	Liverpool	John Alan West
& Gwynne	24	Manchester		
Owen Evans				
(real name John Robson Walby)				

Total: 2

Spies and traitors

16 men were executed for spying during or after World War 2;
1 of them was shot by military firing squad at the Tower of London, the remainder being hanged at Pentonville (6) and Wandsworth (9);
a further 3 men were hanged for treason after the war

Name	Age	Date	Place
Jose Waldeburg &	25	10 Dec 1940	Pentonville
Carl Meier	24		
Charles Kieboom	26	17 Dec 1940	Pentonville
George Armstrong	39	9 July 1941	Wandsworth
Werner Henrich Walti	34	6 Aug 1941	Wandsworth
& Karl Drucke	25		
Josef Jakobs	43	14 Aug 1941	Tower of London (Shot)
Karel Richter	29	10 Dec 1941	Wandsworth
Alphonse Timmerman	28	7 July 1942	Wandsworth
& Jose Estella Key	34		
Duncan Scott-Ford	21	3 Nov 1942	Wandsworth
Johannes Dronkers	46	31 Dec 1942	Wandsworth
Franciscus Winter	40	26 Jan 1943	Wandsworth
Oswald John Job	58	16 Mar 1944	Pentonville
Pierre Neukermans	28	23 June 1944	Pentonville
Joseph Van Hove	27	12 July 1944	Pentonville
John Amery	33	19 Dec 1945	Wandsworth
William Joyce			
("Lord Haw-Haw")	39	3 January 1946	Wandsworth
Theodore Schurch	27	4 January 1946	Pentonville

Total: 19 (16 + 3)

US Servicemen

18 American servicemen were executed at Shepton Mallet During World War 2, under US Military jurisdiction

Name	Age	Date	Crime (method)
David Cobb (Hanged)	21	12 Mar 1943	Murder of Robert Cobnor
Harold A. Smith (Hanged)		25 Jun 1943	Murder of Henry Jenkins
Lee A. Davis (Hanged)		14 Dec 1943	Murder of Cynthia Lay
John Waters (Hanged)	39	10 Feb 1944	Murder of Doris Staples
J. C. Leatherberry (Hanged)		16 Mar 1944	Murder of Henry Hailstone
Wiley Harris (Hanged)		26 May 1944	Murder of Harry Coogan
Alex Miranda (Shot)	20	30 May 1944	Murder of Thomas Evison
Eliga Brinson & Willie Smith (Hanged)		11 Aug 1944	Rape of Dorothy Holmes
Madison Thomas (Hanged)		12 Oct1944	Rape of Beatrice Reynolds
Benjamin Pyegate (Shot)		28 Nov 1944	Murder of James Alexander
Ernest Clarke & Augustine Guerra (Hanged)		8 Jan 1945	Murder of Elizabeth Green
Robert Pearson & Parson Jones (Hanged)		17 Mar 1945	Rape of Joyce Brown
William Harrison (Hanged)		7 Apr 1945	Murder of Patricia Wylie
George Smith (Hanged)		8 May 1945	Murder of Eric Teichman
Aniceto Martinez (Hanged)		15 Jun 1945	Rape of Agnes Cope
Total: 18			

Northern Ireland executions in the 20th century (16 in total)

Name	Date	Place	Victim(s)
William Woods	11/01/1901	Belfast	Bridget McGivern
Joseph Moran	05/01/1904	Londonderry	Rose Ann McCann
Joseph Fee	22/12/1904	Armagh	John Flanagan
John Berryman	20/08/1908	Londonderry	William Berryman, Jean Berryman
Richard Justin	19/08/1909	Belfast	Annie Thompson
Simon McGeown	17/08/1922	Belfast	Margaret (Maggie) Fullerton
William Rooney	08/02/1923	Londonderry	Lily Johnston
Michael Pratley	08/05/1924	Belfast	Nelson Leech
William Smiley	08/08/1928	Belfast	Margaret Macauley, Sarah Macauley
Samuel Cushnan	08/04/1930	Belfast	James McCann
Thomas Dornan	31/07/1931	Belfast	Isabella Aitken, Margaret Aitken

Eddie Cullens	13/01/1932	Belfast	Achmet Musa
Harold Courtney	07/04/1933	Belfast	Minnie Reid
Thomas Joseph Williams	02/09/1942	Belfast	Patrick Murphy
Samuel McLaughlin	25/07/1961	Belfast	Nellie (Maggie) McLaughlin
Robert McGladdery	20/12/1961	Belfast	Pearl Gamble

Scottish executions in the 20th century (34 in total)

Name	Date	Prison	Victim(s)
Patrick Leggett	12/11/1902	Duke St. Glasgow	Sarah Jane Leggett
Thomas Gunning	26/07/1904	Duke St. Glasgow	Agnes Allen
Pasha Liffey	14/11/1905	Duke St. Glasgow	Mary Jane Welsh
Joseph Hume	05/03/1908	Inverness	John Barclay Smith
Edward Johnstone	19/08/1908	Perth	Jane Wallace (Withers)
Alexander Edmundstone	16/07/1909	Perth	Michael Swinton Brown
Patrick Higgins	02/10/1913	Calton Edinburgh	William Higgins, John Higgins
Thomas McGuiness	16/05/1917	Duke St. Glasgow	Alexander Imlach
James Adams	11/11/1919	Duke St. Glasgow	Mary Doyle (Kane)
Albert James Fraser	26/05/1920	Duke St.	Henry Senior
James Rollins	26/05/1920	Duke St.	Henry Senior
William Harkness	21/02/1922	Duke St.	Elizabeth Benjamin
John Henry Savage	11/06/1923	Calton Edinburgh	Wilhemina Nicholson (Grierson)
Susan Newell	10/10/1923	Duke St. Glasgow	John Johnston
Philip Murray	30/10/1923	Calton Edinburgh	William Ronald Cree
John Keen	24/09/1925	Duke St. Glasgow	Noorh Mohammed
James McKay	24/01/1928	Duke St. Glasgow	Agnes Arbuckle
George Reynolds	03/08/1928	Duke St. Glasgow	Thomas Lee
Allen Wales	13/08/1928	Saughton Edinburgh	Isabella Wales

John Lyon	08/02/1946	Barlinnie Glasgow	John Brady
Patrick Carraher	06/04/1946	Barlinnie Glasgow	John Gordon
John Caldwell	10/08/1946	Barlinnie Glasgow	James Straiton
Stanislaw Miszka	06/02/1948	Perth	Catherine McIntyre
Christopher Harris	30/10/1950	Barlinnie Glasgow	Martin Dunleavy
James Robertson	16/12/1950	Barlinnie Glasgow	Catherine McCluskey
Robert Dobie Smith	15/09/1951	Saughton Edinburgh	William Gibson
James Smith	12/04/1952	Barlinnie Glasgow	Martin Joseph Malone
Patrick Gallagher Deveney	29/05/1952	Barlinnie Glasgow	Jeannie Deveney
George Francis Shaw	26/01/1953	Barlinnie Glasgow	Michael Connolly (Conly)
John Lynch	23/04/1954	Saughton E/burgh	Lesley Jean Nisbet (Sinclair), Margaret Curran (Johnson)
George Alexander Robertson	23/06/1954	Saughton E/burgh	Elizabeth Robertson, George Alexander Robertson
Peter Manuel	11/07/1958	Barlinnie Glasgow	Marion Hunter McDonald Watt, Vivienne Isabella Reid Watt, Margaret Hunter Brown, Isabelle Wallace Cooke, Peter James Smart, Doris Smart, Michael Smart
Anthony Miller	22/12/1960	Barlinnie Glasgow	John Cremin
Henry John Burnett	15/08/1963	Aberdeen	Thomas Guyan

Index